Projects for Microsoft® Excel 97

Microsoft® Certified Blue Ribbon Edition

Yvonne Johnson

Philip A. Koneman
Colorado Christian University

Pamela R. Toliver

An imprint of Addison Wesley Longman, Inc.

Reading, Massachusetts • Menlo Park, California • New York • Harlow, England
Don Mills, Ontario • Sydney • Mexico City • Madrid • Amsterdam

Acquisitions Editor: Anita Devine
Editorial Assistant: Holly Rioux
Senior Marketing Manager: Tom Ziolkowski
Senior Marketing Coordinator: Deanna Storey
Production Supervision: Patty Mahtani and Diane Freed
Copyediting: Krista Hansing, Barb Terry, and Robin Drake
Technical Editing: Pauline Johnson and Emily Kim
Proofreader: Holly McLean-Aldis
Indexer: Irv Hershman
Composition and Art: Gillian Hall, The Aardvark Group
Cover Illustration: © Frederic Joos/SIS
Cover Designer: Anthony Saizon
Design Supervisor: Regina Hagen
Manufacturing: Sheila Spinney

Microsoft, Word, Excel, Access, and PowerPoint are registered trademarks of Microsoft Corporation.

Copyright © 1999 by Addison Wesley Longman, Inc.

All rights reserved. No part of this publication may be reproduced, stored in a retrieval system, or transmitted, in any form or by any means, electronic, mechanical, photocopying, recording, or otherwise, without the prior written permission of the publisher. Printed in the United States of America.

0-201-43862-3

Ordering from the SELECT System
For more information on ordering and pricing policies for the SELECT Lab Series and supplements, please contact your Addison Wesley Longman sales representative or fax 1-800-284-8292 or email: exam@awl.com. Questions? Email: is@awl.com

Addison-Wesley Publishing Company
One Jacob Way
Reading, MA 01867
http://hepg@awl.com/select

1 2 3 4 5 6 7 8 9 10-DOW-01009998

Preface

Microsoft Certified

Welcome to the *Microsoft® Certified Blue Ribbon Edition of Select: Projects for Excel 97*. This project-based visual text is approved courseware for the Microsoft® Office User Specialist program. After completing the projects in this book, students will be prepared to take the Proficient level exams for Excel 97. Successful completion of this exam gives students marketable skills that they can use for summer jobs or after they graduate. The *Microsoft® Certified Blue Ribbon Edition of Select: Projects for Excel 97* allows students to explore the essentials of the software application and learn the basic skills that are the foundation for business and academic success. Step-by-step exercises and full-color illustrations show students what to do, how to do it, and the exact result of their action.

QWIZ Assessment Software is a task-based test that simulates the Office 97 environment and tests students on measurable skills using the features of Office 97.

The Select Lab Series

Greater access to ideas and information is changing the way people work and learn. With Microsoft Office 97 software applications, you have greater integration capabilities and access to Internet resources than ever before. The *Select Lab Series* manuals help you take advantage of these valuable resources, with special assignments devoted to the Internet.

Dozens of proven and class-tested lab manuals are available within the *Select Lab Series*, from the latest operating systems and browsers to the most popular applications software for word processing, spreadsheets, databases, presentation graphics, and integrated packages to HTML and programming. The *Select Lab Series* also offers individually bound texts for each *Office 97* application. Knowing that you have specific needs for your lab course, we offer the quick and affordable TechSuite program. For your lab course, you can choose the combination of software lab manuals in *Brief*, *Standard*, or *Plus* Editions that best suits your classroom needs. Your choice of lab manuals will be sent to the bookstore, in a TechSuite box, allowing students to purchase all books in one convenient package at a significant discount.

In addition, your school may qualify for full Office 97 upgrades or licenses. Your Addison Wesley Longman representative will be happy to work with you and your bookstore manager to provide the most current menu of application software in addition to *Select Lab Series* offerings. Your

EX-iii

representative will also outline the ordering process, and provide pricing, ISBNs, and delivery information. Call 1-800-447-2226 or visit our Web site at http://hepg.awl.com and click on ordering information.

Organization

Before launching into the application, the *Microsoft® Certified Select: Projects for Excel 97 Blue Ribbon Edition* familiarizes students with the operating system and Internet functionality with an Overview of Windows 95, Windows 95 Active Desktop, and Windows 98. Students learn the basics of starting Windows 95, using a mouse, using the basic features of Windows 95, and organizing files. Your computer may also be set up with Windows 95 Active Desktop or Windows 98—we have included a new section that shows what the different desktops may look like, what makes them similar, and what differentiates them.

Spreadsheets using Excel 97 is covered in depth in six projects that teach beginning to intermediate skills. It begins with an Overview that introduces the basic concepts of the application and provides hands-on instructions to put students to work using the applications immediately. As they work through the projects, students learn problem-solving techniques that provide practical, relevant, real-life business scenarios.

Approach

The *Microsoft® Certified Select: Projects for Excel 97 Blue Ribbon Edition* uses a document-centered approach to learning that focuses on *The Willows*; a running case study that helps students understand how the applications are used in a business setting. Each project begins with a list of measurable **Objectives**, a realistic case scenario called **The Challenge**, a well-defined plan called **The Solution**, and an illustration of the final product. **The Setup** enables students to verify that the settings on the computer match those needed for the project.

The project is arranged in carefully divided, highly visual objective-based tasks that foster confidence and self-reliance. Each project closes with a wrap-up of the project called **The Conclusion**, followed by summary questions, exercises, and assignments geared to reinforcing the information taught throughout the project.

Preface EX-V

PROJECT 1
Creating a Workbook

In order to use Excel 97 effectively, you must know how to create, save, and print workbooks. In this project, you will enter text and numbers and calculate the numbers with formulas and functions to create a simple worksheet. (This might sound like a lot, but I promise you won't have to use all 16,777,216 cells!)

The Introduction sets up the real-world scenario that serves as the environment for learning.

Objectives

After completing this project, you will be able to:

- Create a new workbook
- Move around in a worksheet and a workbook
- Name worksheets
- Enter data
- Enter simple formulas and functions
- Save a workbook
- Preview and print a worksheet
- Close a worksheet

Clearly defined and measurable **objectives** give students direction and focus they need to learn new material.

The Challenge

Mr. Gilmore, manager of The Grande Hotel, wants a down-and-dirty worksheet to compare the January receipts to the February receipts for both restaurants in the hotel (the Atrium Café and the Willow Top Restaurant). Since the worksheet is just for him, you won't have to worry about formatting right now.

The **Challenge** introduces the goal of the project, the document, spreadsheet, database, or presentation to be created.

EX-16

EX-100

You need to delete some information, add some information, make some adjustments in the columns and rows, and add a header and footer.

The Solution

You will begin your edits by deleting one of the worksheets, inserting a new worksheet, and rearranging worksheets. Then you will adjust the width of columns and the height of rows as needed. Next, you will insert and delete columns, rows, and cells, and, finally, you will add the headers and footers. Figure 4.1 shows the first worksheet in the workbook.

To obtain the files you need for this project, download them from the Addison Wesley Longman web site (http://hepg.awl.com/select) or obtain them from your instructor.

The **Solution** describes the plan for completing the project, which consists of tasks leading to the final product.

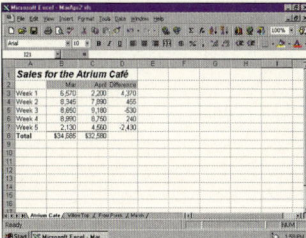
Figure 4.1

An illustration shows the outcome of the project.

The Setup

So that your screen will match the illustrations and the tasks in this project will function as described, make sure that the Excel settings listed in Table 4.1 are selected on your computer. Because these are the default settings for the toolbars and view, you may not need to make any changes to your setup.

Table 4.1: Excel Settings

Location	Make these settings:
View, Toolbars	Deselect all toolbars except Standard and Formatting.
View	Use the Normal view and display the Formula Bar and Status Bar.

The **Setup** tells the students exactly which settings should be chosen to match those in the illustrations.

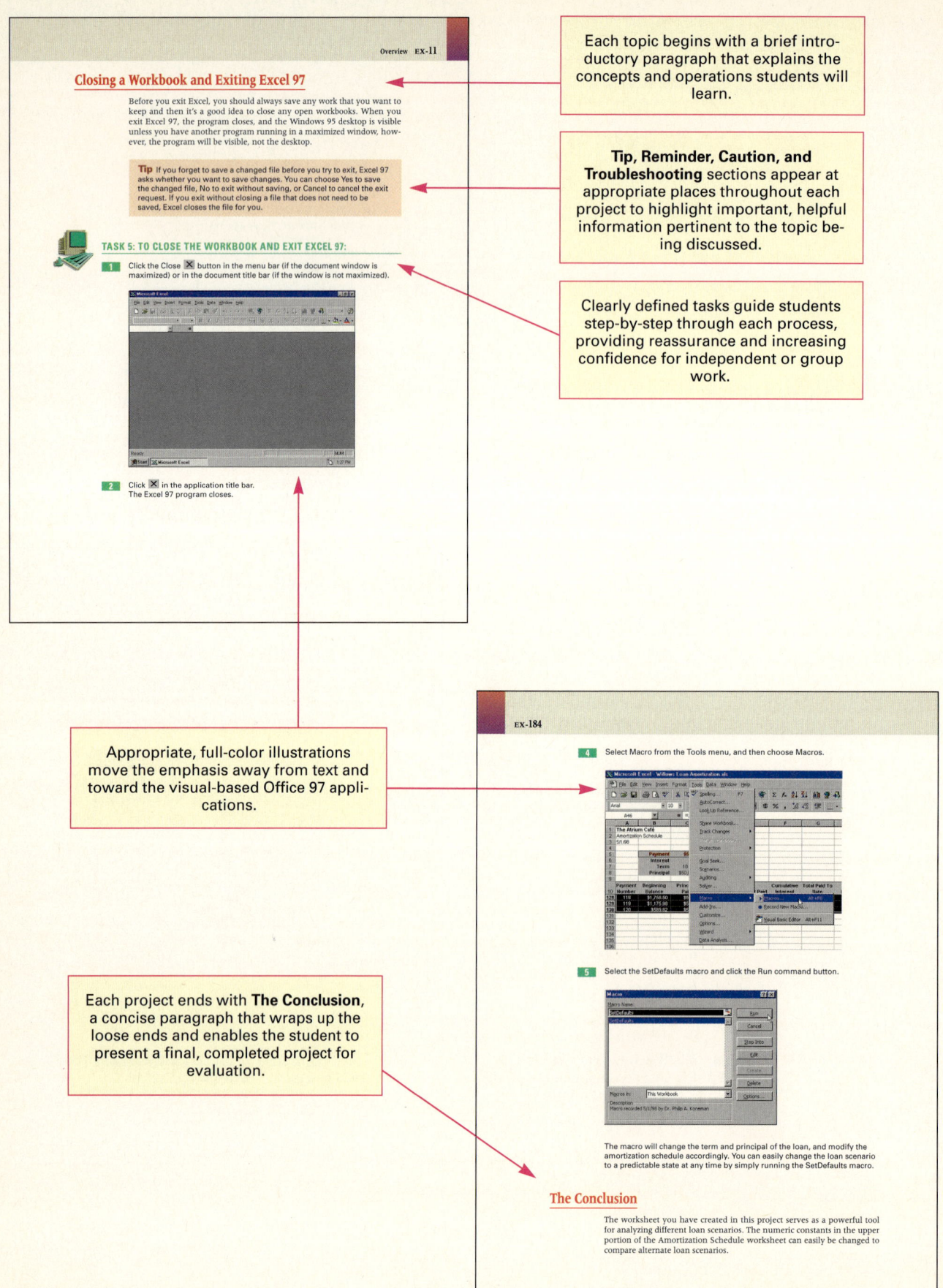

Preface EX-vii

> A **Summary** in bulleted-list format further reinforces the Objectives and the material presented in the project.

> **Key terms** are boldface and italicized throughout each project, and then listed for handy review in the summary section at the end of the project.

> **Study questions** (Multiple Choice, Short Answer, and For Discussion) bring the content of the project into focus again and allow for independent or group review of the material learned.

Summary and Exercises

Summary
- You can format text with bold, italic, underline, different fonts and font sizes, and so on.
- Data in a cell can be left, right, or center aligned.
- Excel provides many formats for displaying numbers.
- You can apply a border to any side of a cell.
- You can apply a background color to a cell.
- You can apply a color to text.
- The Page Break view shows where page breaks are located.
- You can rearrange page breaks in the Page Break view.
- An AutoFormat can be applied to a worksheet or a range.

Key Terms and Operations

Key Terms	Operations
border	add a border
fill	add fill
page break	align cells
Page Break view	AutoFormat
pattern	change a page break
shading	format dates
	format numbers
	format text
	view a page break

Study Questions

Multiple Choice

1. If you type text in cell A1 and you want to center the text across cells A1 through A5,
   a. merge the cells and click the Center button.
   b. select A1:A5 and click the Center button.
   c. select A1:A5 and choose Format, Cells, Alignment, Center, and click OK.
   d. merge the cells, and choose Format, Align, Center.

2. You can apply an AutoFormat
   a. to a cell.
   b. only to a complete worksheet.
   c. to a single range.
   d. to noncontiguous ranges.

3. To make text bold,
   a. click in the cell, type the text, click the Bold button, and press Enter.
   b. select the cell and click the Bold button.
   c. select the cell and choose Format, Bold.
   d. All of the above.

EX-94

EX-188

For Discussion

1. What is the FV function? How does the data it returns differ from the PV function?
2. What is a macro? How is a macro recorded and applied?
3. How can worksheets, such as the amortization schedule you created in this project, be protected from changes?
4. What arguments are required by the PMT function? Is the order in which these appear in a formula significant?

Review Exercises

1. Protecting cells in a workbook
In many settings, portions of a worksheet should be protected to prohibit users from inadvertently making destructive changes to the workbook. By unlocking the cells to which users need access and protecting the worksheet, this objective can easily be achieved. Open the *Willows Loan Amortization* workbook and do the following:

1. Select the following nonadjacent ranges: C6:C8 and A13:H370.
2. Select Cells from the Format menu.
3. Click the Protection tab.
4. Deselect the Locked check box in the Format Cells dialog box.
5. Click the OK button.
6. Select Protection from the Tools menu.
7. Select Protect Sheet from the cascading menu.
8. Do not enter a protection password in the Protect Sheet dialog box.
9. Click OK.
10. Save the updated workbook as *Protected Loan Analysis.xls*.

2. Creating a worksheet to predict the future value of an investment
The FV function is similar to the PV function, except that it returns the future value of an investment, assuming a constant interest rate. Create the workbook shown below as follows:

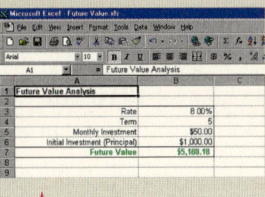

Project 6: Using Financial Functions EX-189

1. Launch Excel if isn't already running.
2. Create a new workbook.
3. Save the workbook as *Future value.xls*.
4. Enter the text and numeric constants shown in the figure on the previous page into the worksheet.
5. Type **=FV(B3/12,B4*12,-B5,-B6,1)** as the formula in cell B7. Look up FV in the Excel Help System for information about the arguments.

Assignments

1. Creating macros to enable and disable protection for a worksheet
Open the *Protected loan analysis.xls* workbook. Create two macros: one that sets the protection for the worksheet, and one that removes the worksheet protection. Save the workbook as *Protected Loan Y-N.xls*.

2. Repaying a loan early
Visit Microsoft's New Spreadsheet Solutions site, which contains spreadsheet solutions created by Village Software. (http://www.microsoft.com/excel/freestuff/templates/villagesoftware/). Download the Loan Manager file self-extracting file (*Loan.exe*), and install the *Loan.xlt* template to your floppy diskette. Open the *Loan.xlt* file, and enter the loan data from this project. Make three additional payments of $100.00 each. Save the workbook as *Prepaid.xls*.

> **Review Exercises** present hands-on tasks for building on the skills acquired in the project.

> **Assignments** invoke critical thinking and integration of project skills.

Other Features

In addition to the document-centered, visual approach of each project, this book contains the following features:

- An **Overview** of Windows 95 and the software application to help students feel comfortable and confident in the working environment.
- A **Function Reference Guide** for each application. Functions are arranged alphabetically rather than by menu.
- **Keycaps** and **toolbar button icons** within each step so students can quickly perform the required action.
- A comprehensive, well-organized end-of-the-project **Summary** and **Exercises** section for reviewing, integrating, and applying new skills.
- Illustrations or descriptions of the results of each step so students know they're on the right track throughout the project.

Student Supplements

QWIZ Assessment Software is a network-based skills assessment-testing program that measures student proficiency with Windows 95, Word 97, Excel 97, Access 97, and PowerPoint 97. Professors select the tasks to be tested and get student results immediately. The test is taken in a simulated software environment. On-screen instructions require students to perform tasks just as though they were using the actual application. The program automatically records responses, assesses student accuracy and reports the resulting score both in a printout or disk file as well as to the instructor's gradebook. The students receive immediate feedback from the program, including learning why a particular task was scored as incorrect and what part of the lab manual to review.

Instructor Supplements

On the Web: Instructors get extra support for this text from supplemental materials that can be downloaded from our password-protected Web site at http://hepg.awl.com/select/instructor. These materials include:

- Screen shots corresponding to key figures in the book that can be used for classroom presentation. Screen-by-screen steps in a project can be displayed in class or reviewed by students in the computer lab.
- The entire Instructor's Manual in Microsoft Word format
- Computerized Test Bank files. With these, you can create printed tests by viewing and editing test bank questions, make multiple versions of tests, easily search for and rearrange questions, and add or modify the questions. In addition, you can administer tests on a network, as well as convert your tests to HTML to post to the Web for students to use for practice. Self-assessment quizzes for the Internet are available also.

- Project Outlines
- Solution files
- Text updates

Student data files are available at http://hepg.awl.com/select

Contact your Addison Wesley Longman sales representative for your ID and password for the Instructor's site.

Printed Materials: The printed Instructor's Manual includes a Test Bank and Transparency Masters for each project in the student text. The Test Bank contains two separate tests with answers, and consists of multiple choice, true/false, and fill-in questions that refer to pages in the student text. Transparency Masters illustrate key concepts and screen captures from the text.

In addition, the printed Instructor's Manual includes expanded student objectives, answers to study questions, and additional assessment techniques.

Acknowledgments

When a *team* combines their knowledge and skills to produce a work designed to meet the needs of students and professors across the country, they take on an unenviable challenge.

To **Anita Devine** for the steady editorial focus needed to make the *Microsoft Certified Blue Ribbon Edition* happen.

To **Phil Koneman**, Series Consulting Editor, your suggestions and comments were invaluable.

Thanks to **Emily Kim** and **Pauline Johnson** who were more than just technical editors, but who also made sure things worked the way we said they would. To those in production, especially to **Gillian Hall**, **Diane Freed**, and **Pat Mahtani**, your efforts have paid off in a highly user-friendly book!

To **Tom Ziolkowski** and **Deanna Storey**, thanks for your strong marketing insights for this book.

Many people helped form the cornerstone of the original work, and we would like to thank **Barb Terry**, **Robin Drake**, **Chuck Hutchinson**, **Martha Johnson**, **Robin Edwards**, and **Deborah Minyard**.

And, finally, thanks to everyone at Addison Wesley Longman who has followed this project from start to finish.

P. T.
Y. J.

Acknowledgments

Addison-Wesley Publishing Company would like to thank the following reviewers for their valuable contributions to the *SELECT Lab Series*.

James Agnew
Northern Virginia Community College

Joseph Aieta
Babson College

Dr. Muzaffar Ali
Bellarmine College

Tom Ashby
Oklahoma CC

Bob Barber
Lane CC

Robert Caruso
Santa Rosa Junior College

Robert Chi
California State Long Beach

Jill Davis
State University of New York at Stony Brook

Fredia Dillard
Samford University

Peter Drexel
Plymouth State College

David Egle
University of Texas, Pan American

Linda Ericksen
Lane Community College

Jonathan Frank
Suffolk University

Patrick Gilbert
University of Hawaii

Maureen Greenbaum
Union County College

Sally Ann Hanson
Mercer County CC

Sunil Hazari
East Carolina University

Gloria Henderson
Victor Valley College

Bruce Herniter
University of Hartford

Rick Homkes
Purdue University

Lisa Jackson
Henderson CC

Martha Johnson
(technical reviewer)
Delta State University

Cynthia Kachik
Santa Fe CC

Bennett Kramer
Massasoit CC

Charles Lake
Faulkner State Junior College

Ron Leake
Johnson County CC

Randy Marak
Hill College

Charles Mattox, Jr.
St. Mary's University

Jim McCullough
Porter and Chester Institute

Gail Miles
Lenoir-Rhyne College

Steve Moore
University of South Florida

Anthony Nowakowski
Buffalo State College

Gloria Oman
Portland State University

John Passafiume
Clemson University

Leonard Presby
William Paterson College

Louis Pryor
Garland County CC

Michael Reilly
University of Denver

Dick Ricketts
Lane CC

Dennis Santomauro
Kean College of New Jersey

Pamela Schmidt
Oakton CC

Gary Schubert
Alderson-Broaddus College

T. Michael Smith
Austin CC

Cynthia Thompson
Carl Sandburg College

Marion Tucker
Northern Oklahoma College

JoAnn Weatherwax
Saddleback College

David Whitney
San Francisco State University

James Wood
Tri-County Technical College

Minnie Yen
University of Alaska Anchorage

Allen Zilbert
Long Island University

Contents

Overview of Windows 95   WIN-1

Objectives   WIN-1
Launching Windows 95   WIN-2
Identifying the Desktop Elements   WIN-2
Using a Mouse   WIN-3
Using the Basic Features of Windows 95   WIN-4
   Using the Start Menu   WIN-4
   Using Windows   WIN-5
   Using Menu Bars and Toolbars   WIN-7
   Using Dialog Boxes   WIN-8
Getting Help   WIN-10
Exiting Windows 95   WIN-16

Windows 95 Active Desktop and Windows 98 Preview   WIN98-1

Objectives   WIN98-1
Identifying Elements of the Windows 95
     Active Desktop   WIN98-3
     Displaying the Internet Explorer Channel
       Bar   WIN98-4
     Displaying the Active Desktop Wallpaper
       WIN98-5
   Using Desktop ToolTips   WIN98-6
   Launching Programs   WIN98-7
   Customizing the Windows 95 Active
     Desktop   WIN98-10
     Sizing and Repositioning the Taskbar
       WIN98-10
     Displaying Additional Toolbars on the
       Taskbar   WIN98-11
     Customizing Taskbar Toolbars
       WIN98-11
   Editing the Start Menu   WIN98-13
     Creating Shortcuts from the Start Menu
       WIN98-13
     Adding Items to the Start Menu
       WIN98-14
   Restoring the Desktop   WIN98-15
Conclusion   WIN98-16

Overview   2

Objectives   2
   Identifying the Excel 97 Features   2
   Launching Excel 97   3
   Identifying Excel 97 Screen Elements   4
     Working with Toolbars   6
   Getting Help   8
     Using the Office Assistant   8

     Getting Help from the World
       Wide Web   10
   Closing a Workbook and Exiting
     Excel 97   11
Summary and Exercises   12
Summary   12
Key Terms and Operations   12
   Key Terms   12
   Operations   12
Study Questions   13
   Multiple Choice   13
   Short Answer   14
   For Discussion   14
Review Exercises   14
   1. Starting Excel and Exploring the Workbook   14
   2. Getting Help on the Web   15
   3. Displaying and Docking Toolbars and Getting
      Help from the Office Assistant   15
Assignments   15
   1. Getting Online Help   15
   2. Using the Web Toolbar   15

Project 1 Creating a Workbook   16

Objectives   16
The Challenge   16
The Solution   17
The Setup   17
   Creating a New Workbook   18
   Moving Around in a Worksheet and
     a Workbook   18
   Naming Worksheets   22
   Entering Data   24
     Entering Text   24
     Entering Data on
       Multiple Worksheets   25
     Entering Numbers   30
   Entering Simple Formulas
     and Functions   31
   Saving a Workbook   36
   Previewing and Printing a Worksheet   38
   Closing a Workbook   40
The Conclusion   40
Summary and Exercises   41
Summary   41
Key Terms and Operations   41
   Key Terms   41
   Operations   41
Study Questions   41
   Multiple Choice   41

EX-xi

Short Answer   42
For Discussion   43
Review Exercises   43
   1. Creating an Expense Account   43
   2. Calculating Savings   44
   3. Creating a Sales Analysis Worksheet   45
Assignments   46
   1. Creating a Timesheet   46
   2. Creating a Worksheet that Compares Menu Prices   46

Project 2 Editing a Workbook   47

Objectives   47
The Challenge   47
The Solution   47
The Setup   48
   Opening a Workbook   49
   Finding Data   50
   Editing Data   52
   Working with Data   55
      Selecting Cells   55
      Copying Data   58
      Deleting Data   61
      Moving Data   63
   Adding Comments   65
   Checking Spelling   69
Conclusion   70
Summary and Exercises   71
Summary   71
Key Terms and Operations   71
   Key Terms   71
   Operations   71
Study Questions   71
   Multiple Choice   71
   Short Answer   72
   For Discussion   73
Review Exercises   73
   1. Revising the Restaurant Sales Worksheet   73
   2. Revising a Time Sheet   73
   3. Moving and Copying Data in a Worksheet   74
Assignments   74
   1. Creating and Revising a Budget   74
   2. Tracking the American Stock Exchange   74

Project 3 Enhancing the Appearance of a Workbook   75

Objectives   75
The Challenge   76
The Solution   76
The Setup   76
   Formatting Text   77
   Changing Cell Alignment   78
   Formatting Numbers   81
   Formatting Dates   84
   Formatting Numbers as Text   86
   Adding Borders and Fill   88
   Viewing and Changing a Page Break   91
   Using AutoFormat   92
The Conclusion   93
Summary and Exercises   94
Summary   94
Key Terms and Operations   94
   Key Terms   94
   Operations   94
Study Questions   94
   Multiple Choice   94
   Short Answer   95
   For Discussion   96
Review Exercises   96
   1. Enhancing the Restaurant Sales Worksheet   96
   2. Creating a Concert List   97
   3. Enhancing the Container Corporation Sales Worksheet   97
Assignments   97
   1. Reformatting the Income.xls File   98
   2. Using AutoFormat   98

Project 4 Editing the Structure of a Worksheet and a Workbook   99

Objectives   99
The Challenge   99
The Solution   100
The Setup   100
   Inserting, Deleting, and Arranging Worksheets   101
   Changing the Size of Columns and Rows   104
      Using AutoFit   106
      Adjusting Row Height   107
   Inserting Columns, Rows, and Cells   109
   Deleting Columns, Rows, and Cells   112
   Creating Headers and Footers   114
      Creating a Custom Header and Footer   117
The Conclusion   119
Summary and Exercises   120
Summary   120
Key Terms and Operations   120
   Key Terms   120
   Operations   120
Study Questions   120
   Multiple Choice   120
   Short Answer   121
   For Discussion   122

Review Exercises   122
   1. Editing the MarApr2 Workbook   122
   2. Creating a Sales Workbook for the Sandwich Shops and Snack Bars   123
   3. Editing and Enhancing the Container Corporation Sales Worksheet   123
Assignments   124
   1. Creating a Banquet Workbook   124
   2. Creating a Shopping List   124

Project 5 Creating a More Complex Workbook   125

Objectives   125
The Challenge   125
The Solution   126
The Setup   126
   Copying Data from Another Workbook   126
   Sorting Data   129
   Entering Formulas with Relative References   130
   Using Headings in Formulas   133
   Entering Formulas with Absolute References   133
      Pointing to Enter Absolute References   135
      Using Headings with Absolute References   136
   Creating and Modifying a Chart   136
      Moving and Sizing a Chart   139
      Changing Chart Data   140
      Formatting Chart Elements   143
      Changing the Chart Type   145
      Changing the Chart Options   146
      Creating a Pie Chart   147
The Conclusion   152
Summary and Exercises   153
Summary   153
Key Terms and Operations   153
   Key Terms   153
   Operations   153
Study Questions   153
   Multiple Choice   153
   Short Answer   155
   For Discussion   155
Review Exercises   155
   1. Revising the Gift Inventory and Sales Workbook   155
   2. Creating a New Items Workbook   156
   3. Sorting Data and Creating a Sales Charting Worksheet   156

Assignments   157
   1. Creating a Chart of Expenditures   157
   2. Completing a Vacation Package Workbook   157

Project 6 Using Financial Functions   158

Objectives   159
The Challenge   159
The Solution   159
The Setup   160
   Defining the Structure of the Amortization Schedule   161
   Entering Numeric Constants   164
   Calculating the Loan Payment   166
   Calculating the Beginning Balance Using the PV Function   169
   Calculating the Principal Paid in Each Payment   170
   Calculating the Interest Paid in Each Payment   172
   Constructing Formulas to Calculate the Cumulative Principal, Cumulative Interest, Total Payments, and Ending Balance   173
   Using the Fill Handle to Complete the Amortization Schedule   174
   Freezing Worksheet Panes to Assist in Viewing Large Worksheets   177
   Changing the Loan Scenario   179
   Creating Excel Macros   181
   Running a Macro   182
The Conclusion   183
Summary and Exercises   184
Summary   184
Key Terms and Operations   184
   Key Terms   184
   Operations   184
Study Questions   185
   Multiple Choice   185
   Short Answer   186
   For Discussion   187
Review Exercises   187
   1. Protecting Cells in a Workbook   187
   2. Creating a Worksheet to Predict the Future Value of an Investment   187
Assignments   188
   1. Creating Macros to Enable and Disable Protection for a Worksheet   188
   2. Repaying a Loan Early   188

More Excel 97   189

Modifying Workbooks   189
- Rotating and Indenting Text   189
- Revise Formulas   189

Print Workbooks   189
- Printing the Screen and Ranges   189

Creating and Applying Ranges   190
- Creating and Naming Ranges   190

Using Draw   190
- Creating and Modifying Lines and Objects   190
- Creating and Modifying 3D Shapes   190

Using Charts   191
- Previewing and Printing Charts   191

Saving Spreadsheets as HTML   191
- Saving Spreadsheets as HTML Documents   191

Formatting Worksheets   192
- Applying Outlines   192

Function Reference Guide   Guide-1

Glossary   Gloss-1

Index   Index-1

Overview of Windows 95

Overview of Windows 95

Microsoft Windows 95 is an *operating system,* a special kind of computer program that performs three major functions. First, an operating system controls the actual *hardware* of the computer (the screen, the keyboard, the disk drives, and so on). Second, an operating system enables other software programs such as word processing or spreadsheet *applications* to run. Finally, an operating system determines how the user operates the computer and its programs or applications.

As an operating system, Windows 95 and all other programs written to run under it provide *graphics* (or pictures) called *icons* to carry out commands and run programs. For this reason, Windows 95 is referred to as a *Graphical User Interface* or GUI (pronounced *gooey*). You can use the keyboard or a device called a *mouse* to activate the icons.

This overview explains the basics of Windows 95 so that you can begin using your computer quickly and easily.

Objectives

After completing this project, you will be able to:

- ▶ Launch Windows 95
- ▶ Identify the desktop elements
- ▶ Use a mouse
- ▶ Use the basic features of Windows 95
- ▶ Organize your computer
- ▶ Work with multiple programs
- ▶ Get help
- ▶ Exit Windows 95

Launching Windows 95

Because Windows 95 is an operating system, it launches immediately when you turn on the computer. Depending on the way your computer is set up, you may have to type your user name and password to log on — to get permission to begin using the program. After Windows 95 launches, the working environment, called the *desktop,* displays on the screen.

Identifying the Desktop Elements

Figure W.1 shows the Windows 95 desktop with several icons that represent the hardware and the software installed on the computer. *My Computer* enables you to organize your work. The *Recycle Bin* is a temporary storage area for files deleted from the hard disk. At the bottom of the desktop is the *Taskbar* for starting programs, accessing various areas of Windows 95, and switching among programs.

Figure W.1

> **Note** The desktop can be customized, so the desktop on the computer you're using will not look exactly like the one shown in the illustrations in this overview.

Using a Mouse

A pointing device is almost an indispensable tool for using Windows 95. Although you can use the keyboard to navigate and make selections, using a mouse is often more convenient and efficient.

When you move the mouse on your desk, a pointer moves on the screen. When the pointer is on the object you want to use, you can take one of the actions described in Table W.1 to give Windows 95 an instruction.

Table W.1 Mouse Actions

Action	Description
Point	Slide the mouse across a smooth surface (preferably a mouse pad) until the pointer on the screen is on the object.
Click	Press and release the left mouse button once.
Drag	Press and hold down the left mouse button while you move the mouse, and then release the mouse button to complete the action.
Right-click	Press and release the right mouse button once. Right-clicking usually displays a shortcut menu.
Double-click	Press and release the left mouse button twice in rapid succession.

TASK 1: TO PRACTICE USING THE MOUSE:

1. Point to the My Computer icon, press and hold down the left mouse button, and then drag the mouse across the desk.
   The icon moves.
2. Drag the My Computer icon back to its original location.
3. Right-click the icon.

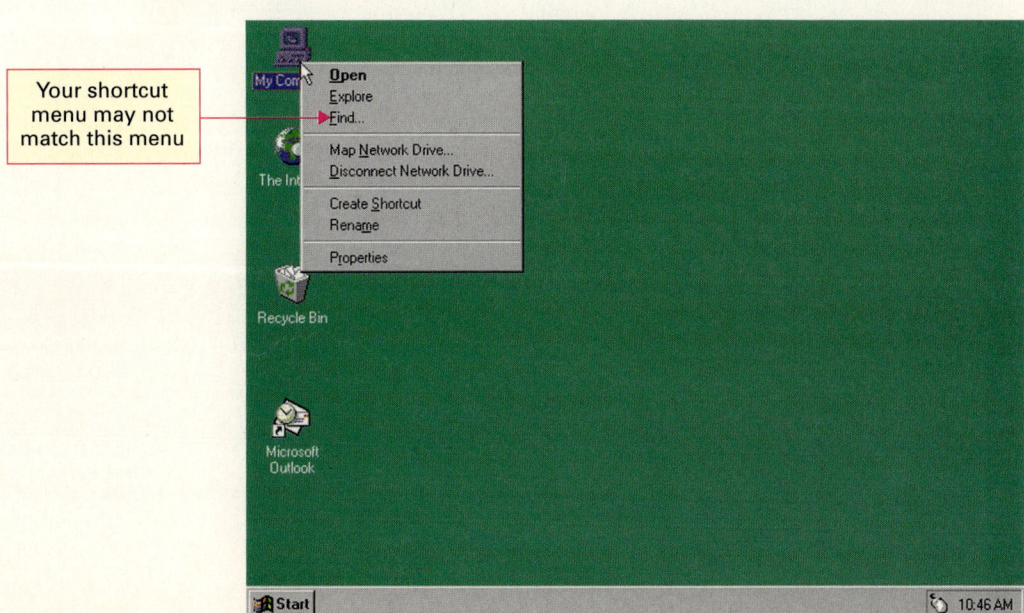

Your shortcut menu may not match this menu

4 Click a blank space on the screen.
The shortcut menu closes.

5 Double-click the My Computer icon.

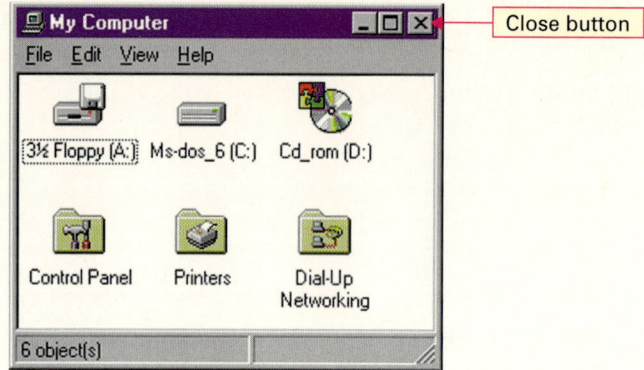

6 Click the Close ❌ button to close the My Computer window.

Using the Basic Features of Windows 95

The basic features of Windows 95 are menus, windows, menu bars, dialog boxes, and toolbars. These features are used in all programs that are written to run under Windows 95.

Using the Start Menu

Menus contain the commands you use to perform tasks. In Windows 95, you can use the Start menu shown in Figure W.2 to start programs and to access other Windows options.

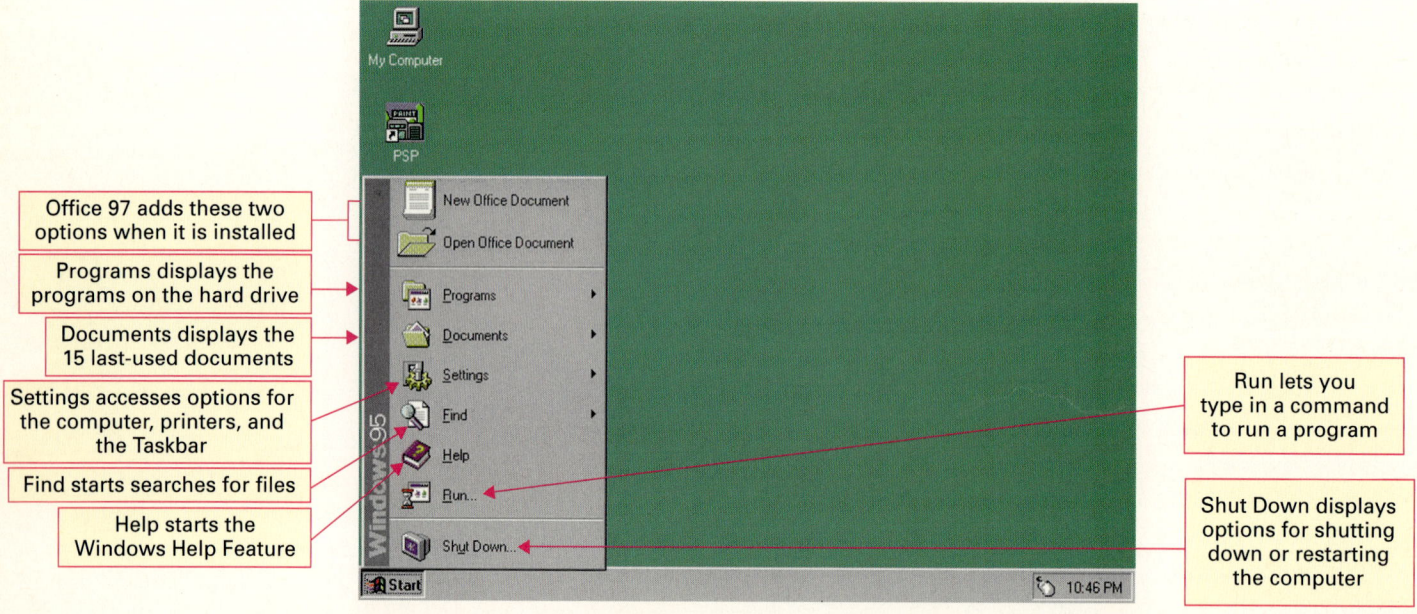

Figure W.2

Overview WIN-5

TASK 2: TO USE THE START MENU TO LAUNCH A PROGRAM:

1 Click the Start button.
The triangles beside several of the menu options indicate that the options will display another menu.

2 Point to Programs and click the Windows Explorer icon on the cascading menu.
The Exploring window opens (see Figure W.3). You can use this feature of Windows 95 to manage files.

Using Windows

Clicking on the Windows Explorer icon opened a *window,* a Windows 95 feature that you saw earlier when you opened the My Computer window. Figure W.3 shows the common elements that most windows contain.

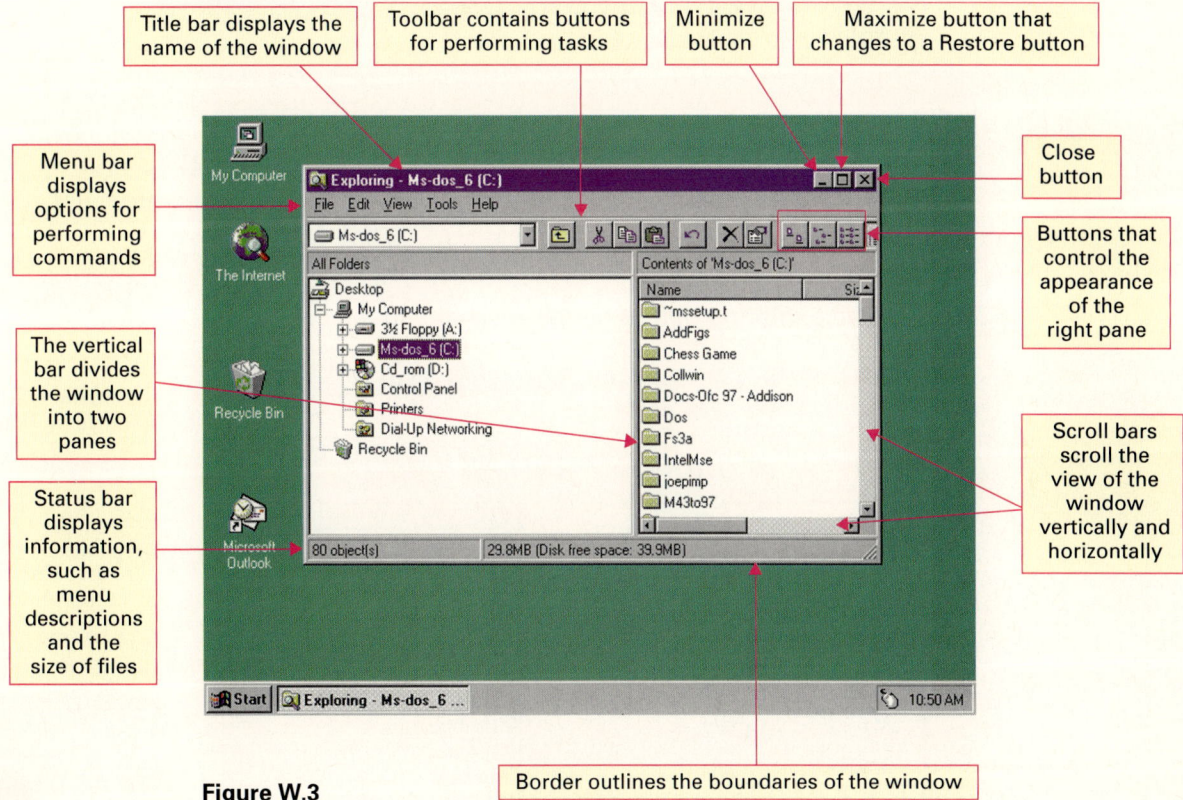

Figure W.3

TASK 3: TO WORK WITH A WINDOW:

1 Click the Maximize button if it is displayed. If it is not displayed, click the Restore button, and then click the Maximize button.
The Maximize button changes to a Restore button.

2 Click the Minimize button.

WIN-6

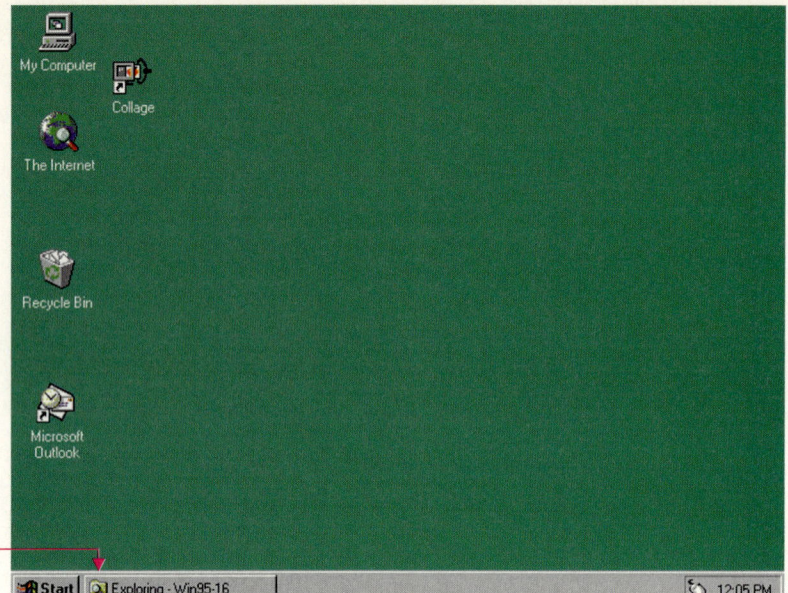

Exploring window button

Warning When you minimize a window, the program in the window is still running and therefore using computer memory. To exit a program that is running in a window, you must click the Close button, not the Minimize button.

3   Click the Exploring button on the Taskbar and then click 🗗.

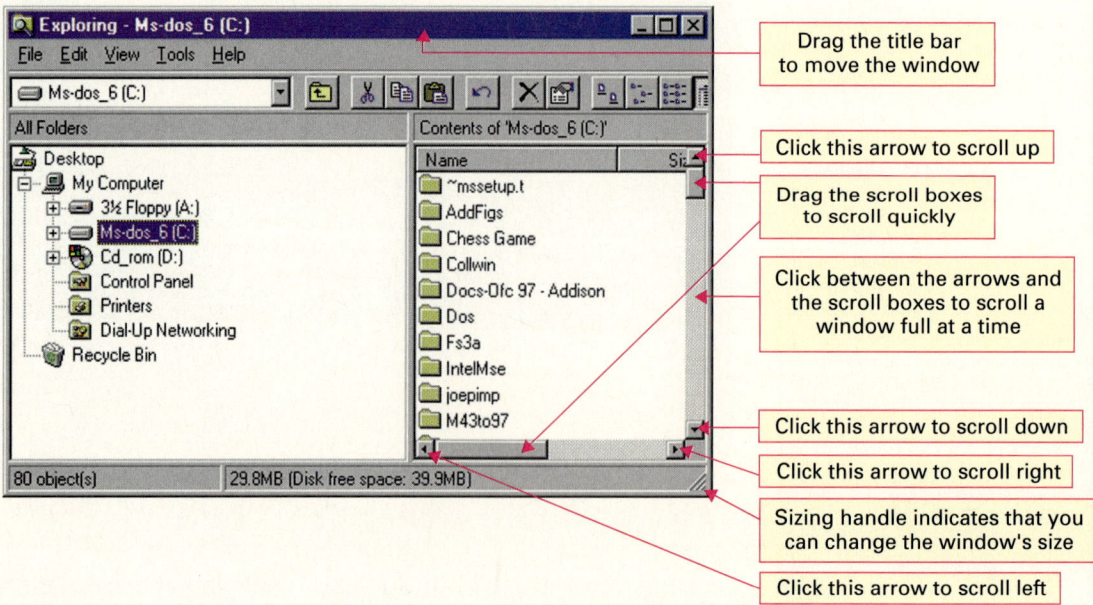

Drag the title bar to move the window

Click this arrow to scroll up

Drag the scroll boxes to scroll quickly

Click between the arrows and the scroll boxes to scroll a window full at a time

Click this arrow to scroll down

Click this arrow to scroll right

Sizing handle indicates that you can change the window's size

Click this arrow to scroll left

4   Point to the border of the Exploring window until the pointer changes to a double-headed black arrow, and then drag the border to make the window wider. (Be sure that all the buttons in the toolbar are visible.)

5   Practice scrolling.

6   When you are comfortable with your scrolling expertise, click 🗖.

Using Menu Bars and Toolbars

Menu bars and toolbars are generally located at the top of a window. You can select a menu option in a menu bar by clicking the option or by pressing ALT and then typing the underlined letter for the option. When you select an option, a drop-down menu appears. Figure W.4 shows a menu with many of the elements common to menus.

> **Note** Because you can select menu commands in two ways, the steps with instructions to select a menu command will use the word choose instead of dictating the method of selection.

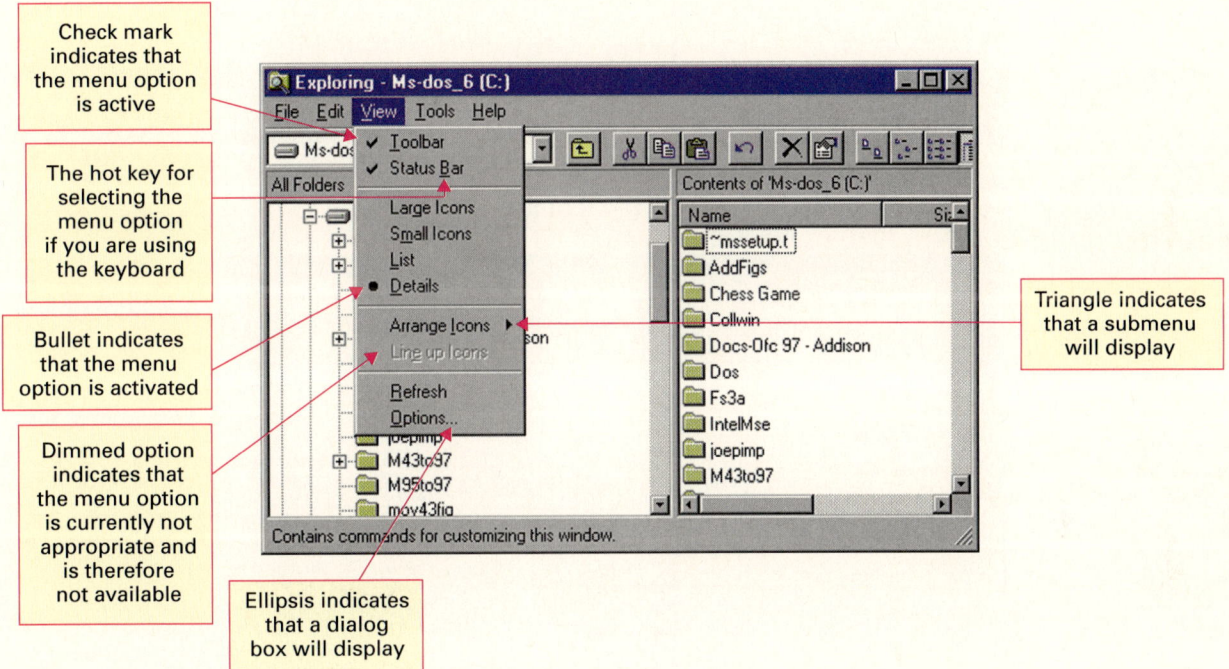

Check mark indicates that the menu option is active

The hot key for selecting the menu option if you are using the keyboard

Bullet indicates that the menu option is activated

Dimmed option indicates that the menu option is currently not appropriate and is therefore not available

Ellipsis indicates that a dialog box will display

Triangle indicates that a submenu will display

Figure W.4

Toolbars contain buttons that perform many of the same commands found on menus. To use a toolbar button, click the button; Windows 95 takes an immediate action, depending on the button's function.

> **Tip** If you don't know what a button on the toolbar does, point to the button; a ToolTip, a brief description of the button, appears near the button.

TASK 4: TO USE MENUS AND TOOLBARS:

1 Choose View in the Exploring window.
The View menu shown in Figure W.4 displays.

2 Choose Large Icons.

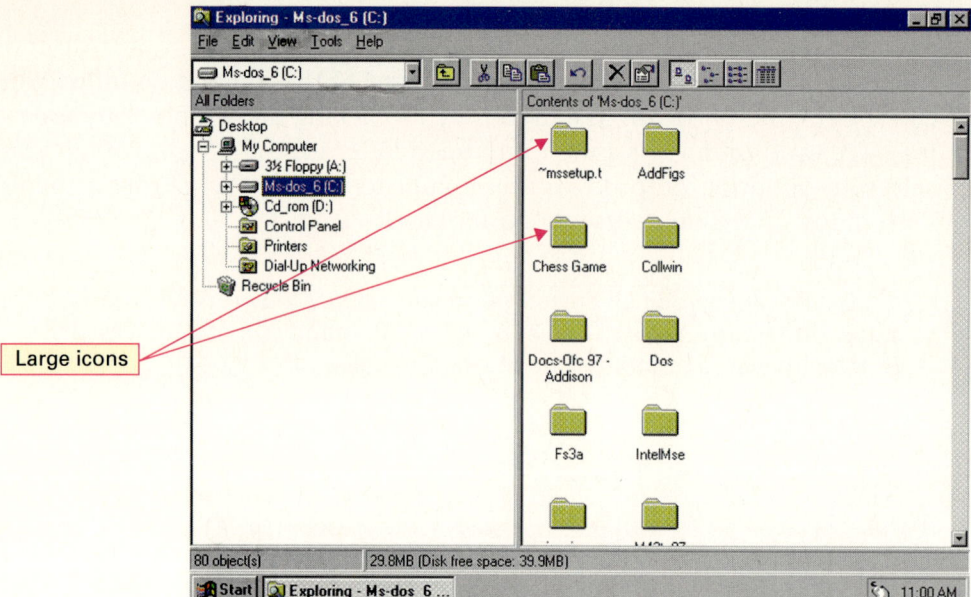

3 Click the Details button on the toolbar.

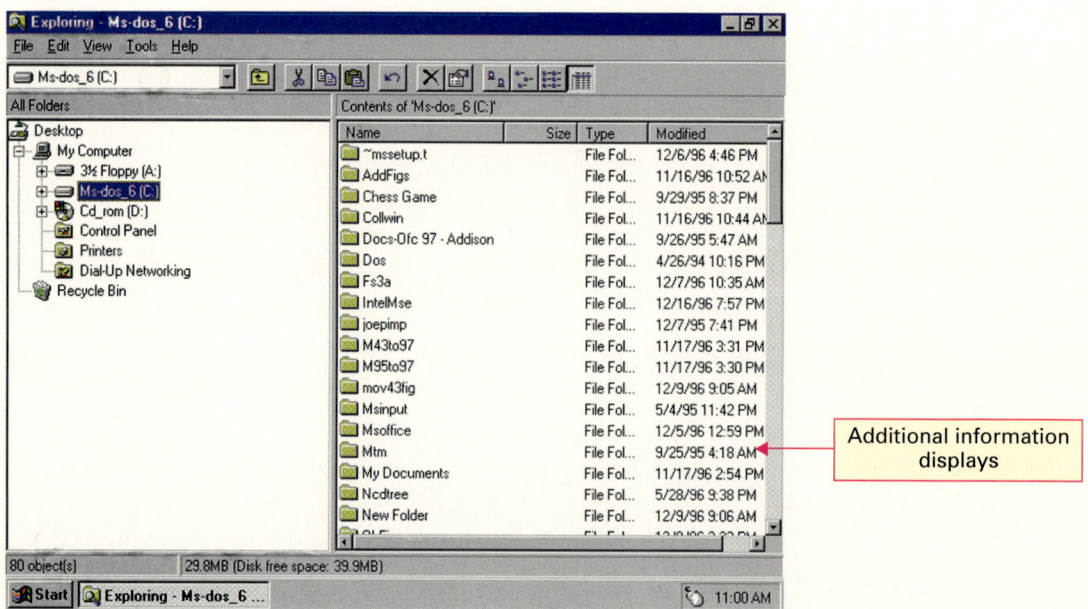

Using Dialog Boxes

When many options are available for a single task, Windows 95 conveniently groups the options in one place, called a ***dialog box.*** Some functions have so many options that Windows 95 divides them further into groups and places them on separate pages in the dialog box. Figures W.5 and W.6 show dialog boxes with different types of options. Throughout the remainder of this project, you practice using dialog boxes.

Overview **WIN-9**

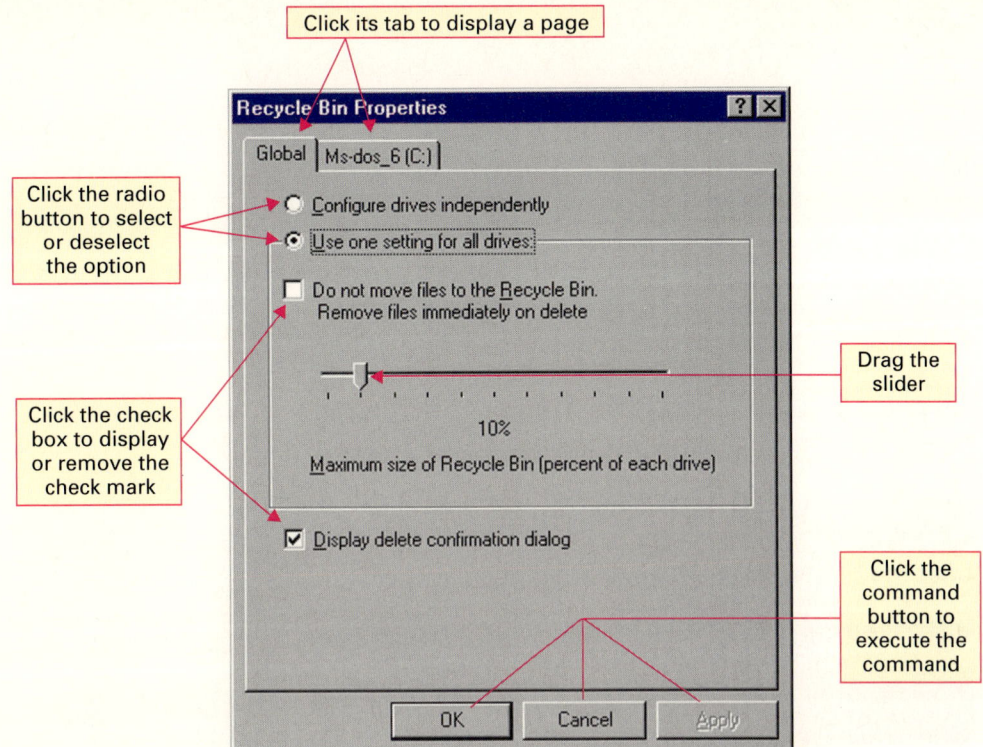

Figure W.5

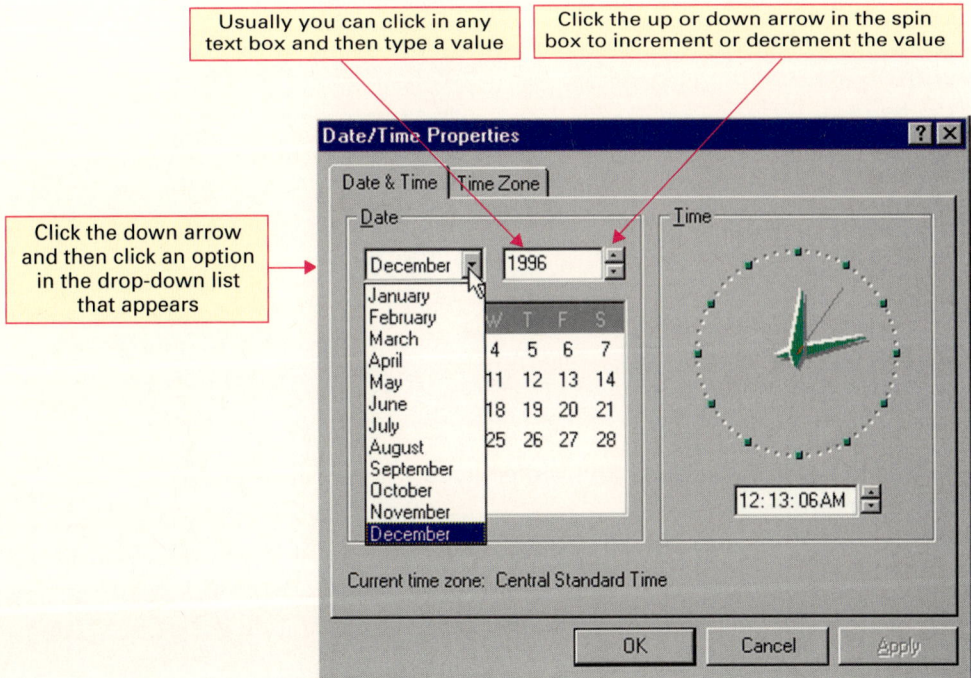

Figure W.6

Getting Help

Windows 95 provides you with three methods of accessing help information: You can look up information in a table of contents; you can search for information in an index; or you can find a specific word or phrase in a database maintained by the Find feature.

Additionally, Windows 95 provides **context-sensitive help,** called **What's This?** for the topic you are working on. This type of help is generally found in dialog boxes.

After you learn to use Help in Windows 95, you can use help in any Windows program because all programs use the same help format.

TASK 12: TO USE HELP CONTENTS, INDEX, AND FIND:

1 Click the Start button on the Taskbar and click Help.

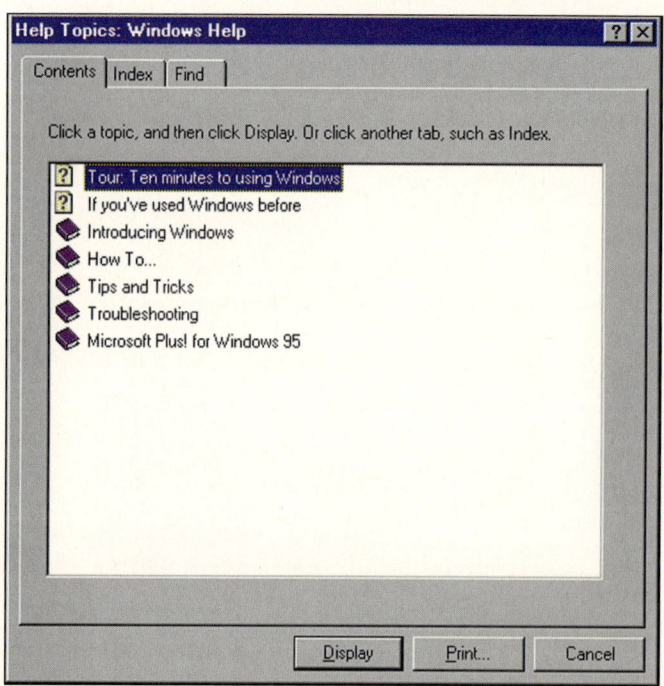

2 Click the Contents tab if a different page is displayed. The Contents page displays.

3 Double-click Tips and Tricks.

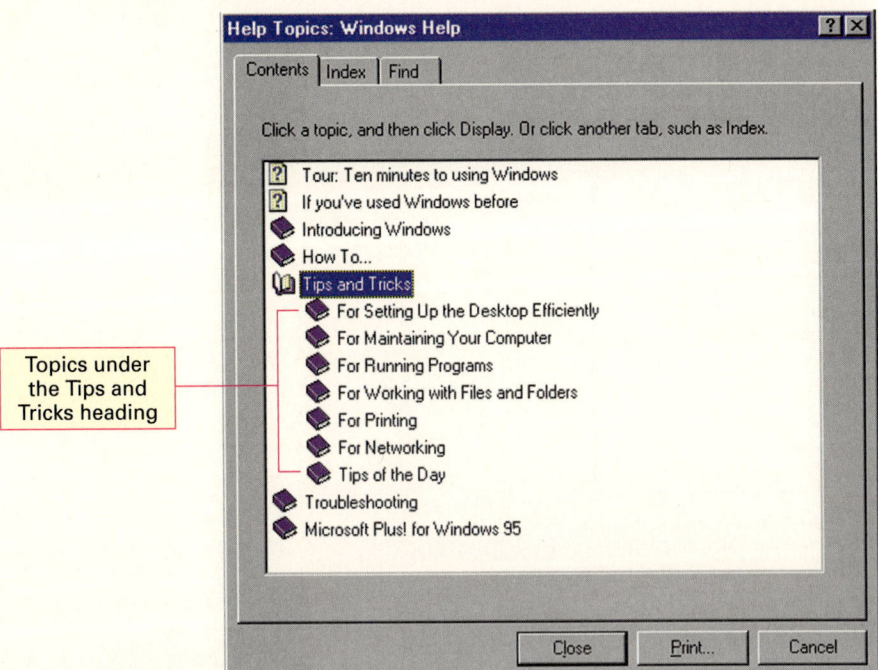

Topics under the Tips and Tricks heading

4 Double-click Tips of the Day.

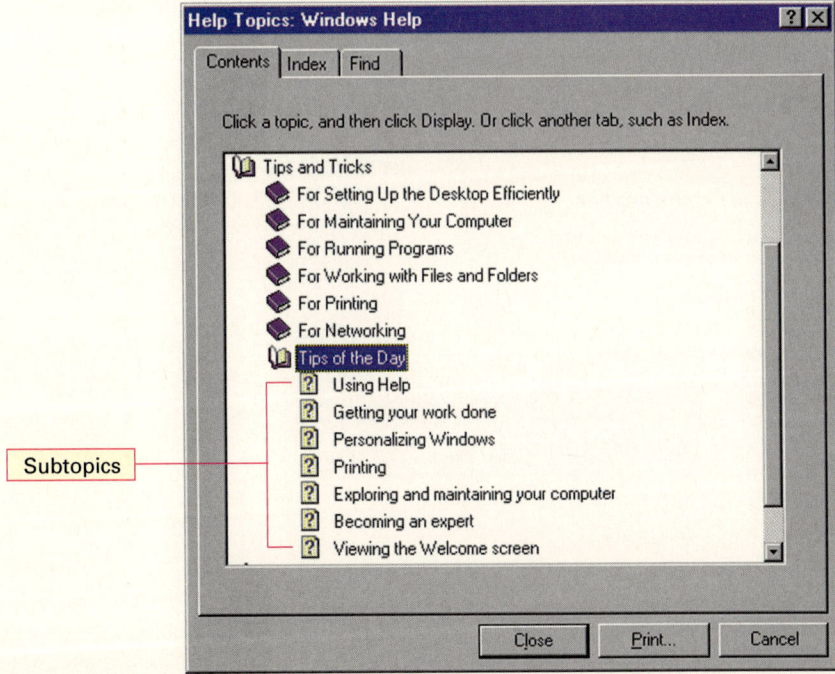

Subtopics

5 Double-click Using Help.

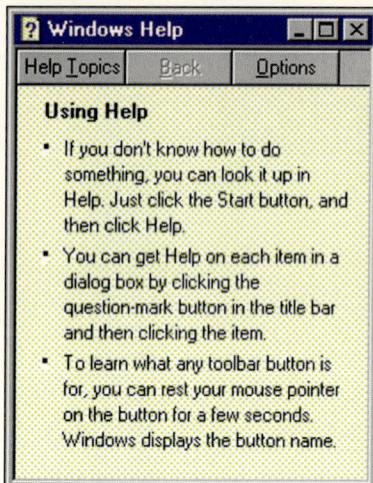

6 Read the information, click the Help Topics button, and then click the Index tab.

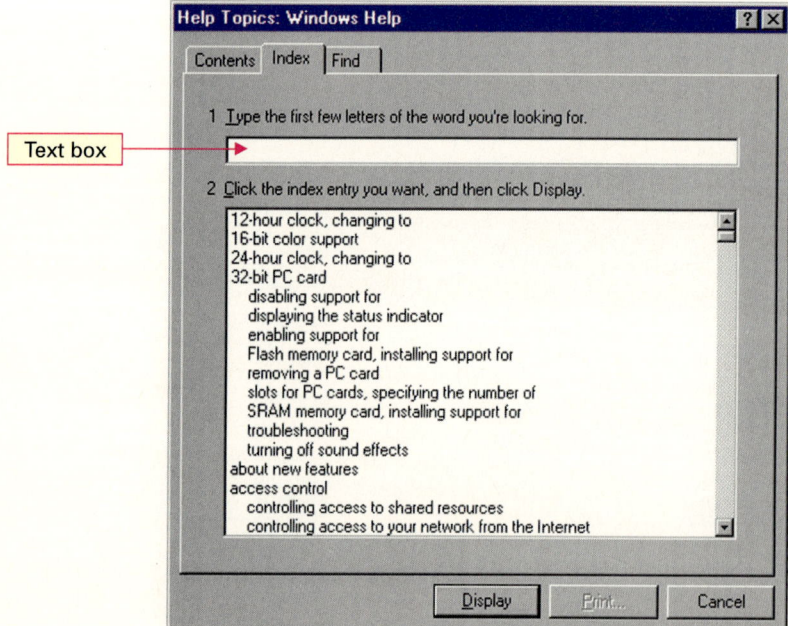

7 Type **shortcut** in the textbox.

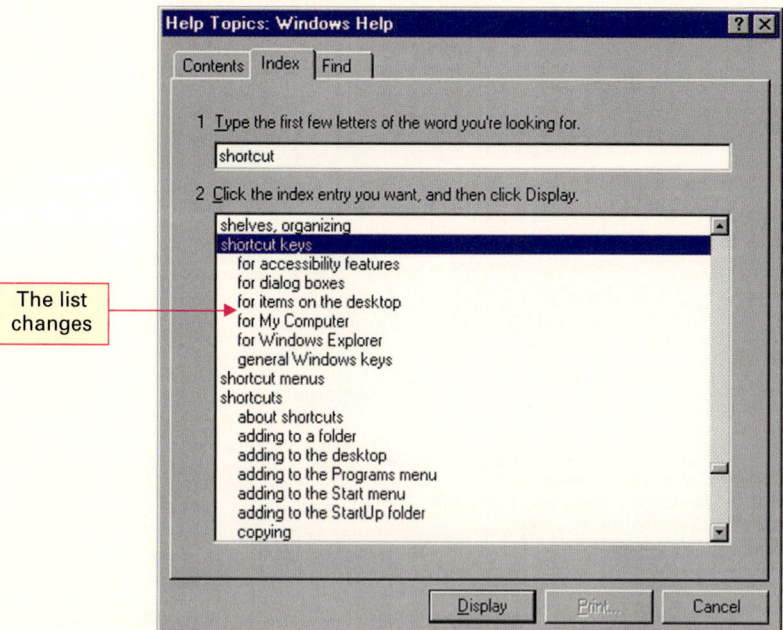

The list changes

8 Double-click "shortcut menus" in the list.

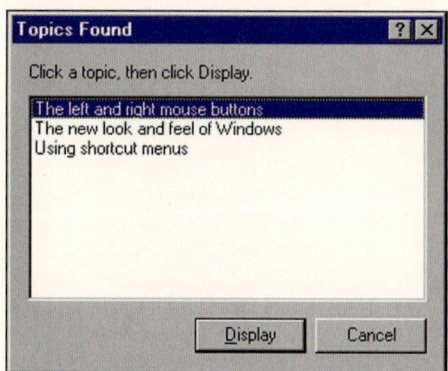

9 Double-click "Using shortcut menus."

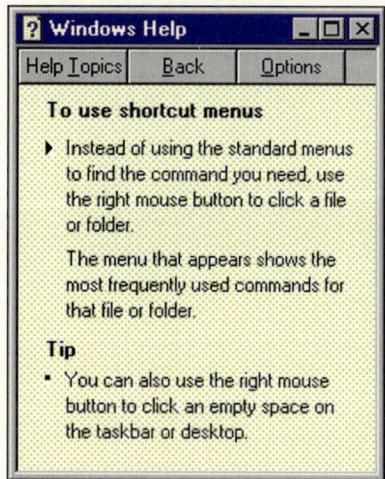

WIN-14

10 Read the information, click the Help Topics button, and then click the Find tab.

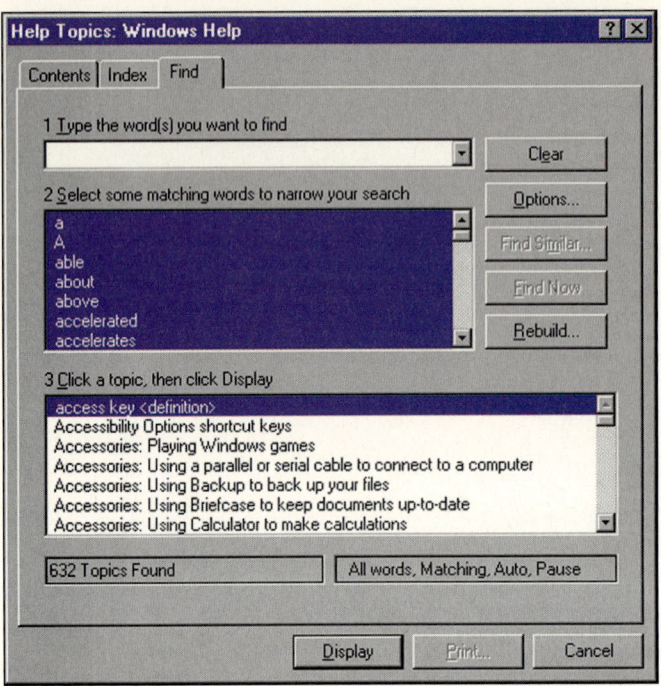

11 Click the What's This 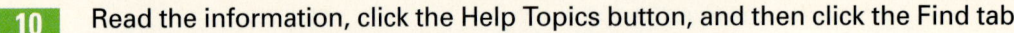 button in the Help Topics title bar. A question mark is attached to the mouse pointer.

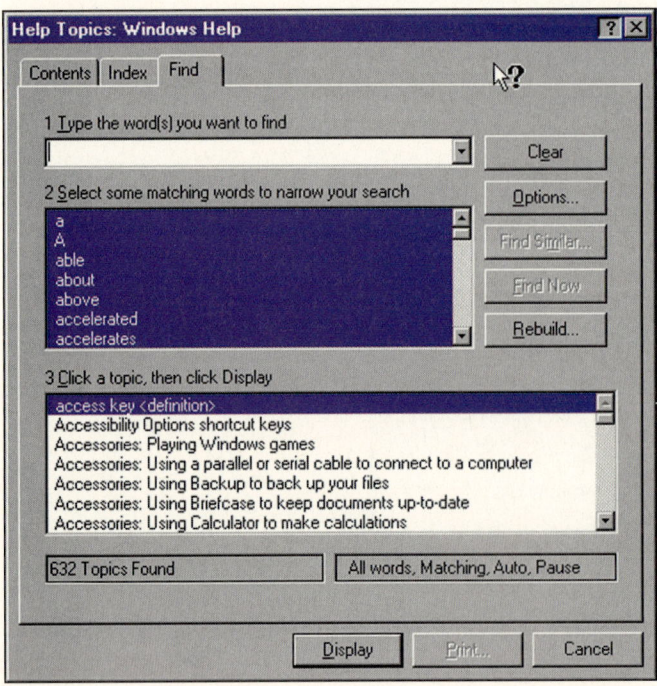

Overview **WIN-15**

12 Click the Options button.

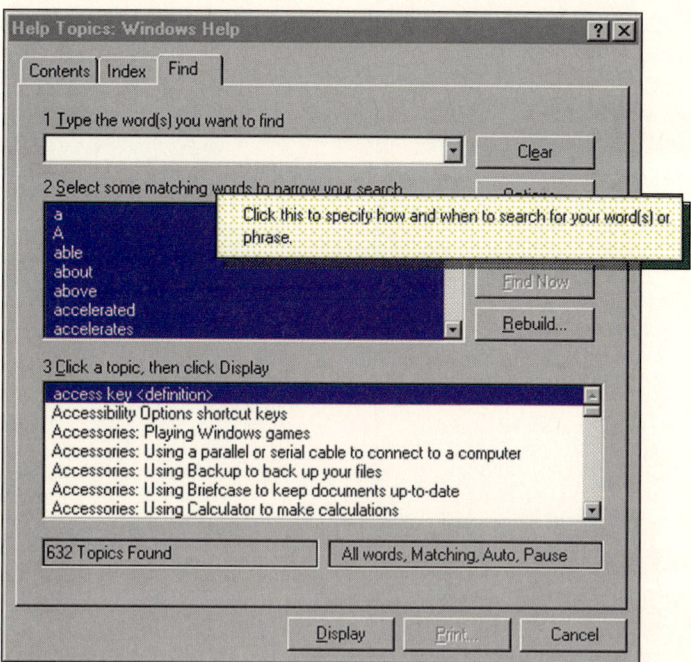

13 Read the pop-up message and then click it. The message closes.

14 Type **printing help.** (If the list at the bottom of the screen doesn't change, click the Find Now button.)

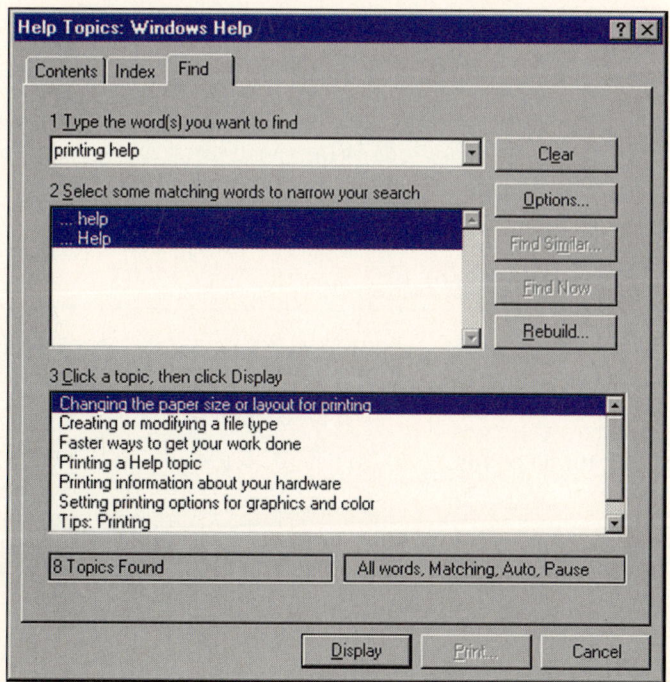

15 If necessary, scroll to "Printing a Help topic" in the list that displays and then double-click it.

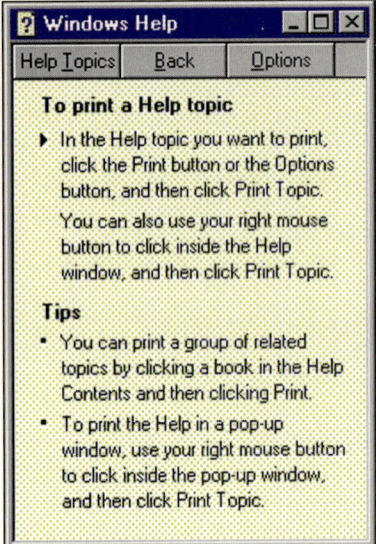

16 Click .
The Help dialog box closes.

> **Tip** You can print any help article by right-clicking anywhere in the article and choosing Print Topic.

Exiting Windows 95

When you are ready to turn off the computer, you must exit Windows 95 first. You should never turn off the computer without following the proper exit procedure because Windows 95 has to do some utility tasks before it shuts down. Unlike most of us, Windows 95 likes to put everything away when it's finished. When you shut down improperly, you can cause serious problems in Windows 95.

TASK 13: TO EXIT WINDOWS 95:

1 Click the Start button and then click Shut Down.

2 Click Shut down the computer? and then click Yes.

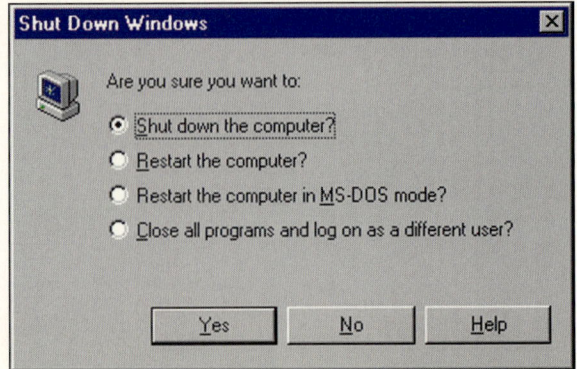

3 When the message "It's now safe to turn off your computer" appears, turn off the computer.

Windows 95 Active Desktop and Windows 98 Preview

Active Desktop and Windows 98 Preview

If you are running Windows 95 and your desktop looks significantly different from the desktop pictures found in the Overview of Windows 95, you may have Internet Explorer 4.0 installed with the Active Desktop. The Active Desktop contains features such as Taskbar toolbars, Internet Explorer Channel bar, and a Web-designed desktop background—features also available in Windows 98.

Other Windows 98 features—such as memory managers and file allocation tables—operate behind the scenes to improve the efficiency of your computer. Like Windows 95, Windows 98 is an operating system. Windows 98, however, operates with increased memory management capabilities. As a result, unless your computer is an older computer running less than 166 MHz, you should notice smoother transition when you move between programs, increased speed when performing basic tasks, and fewer program errors.

Many of the basic Windows 95 features, such as toolbars, are updated with a new look in Windows 98 because of the Active Desktop enhancement and the integration of Internet Explorer 4.0. Other features—such as the title bar and the minimize, maximize, and close buttons—remain unchanged. You will find that both Windows 98 and the Windows 95 Active Desktop are intimately integrated with the Internet and the World Wide Web. With the Active Desktop features, these "worlds" are literally just a click away.

This Active Desktop overview provides a preview of what to expect with Windows 98. You'll find that, in most cases, the procedures for using Windows 95 Active Desktop/Windows 98 features are identical to the procedures for using Windows 95 features.

Objectives

After completing this project, you will be able to:

- ▶ **Identify elements of the Windows 95 Active Desktop**
- ▶ **Use desktop ToolTips**
- ▶ **Launch programs**
- ▶ **Customize the Windows 95 Active Desktop**

WIN98-2

➤ **Edit the Start menu**
➤ **Restore the desktop to its original format**

Identifying Elements of the Windows 95 Active Desktop

Both Windows 95 and Windows 98 start automatically each time you power up your computer. The appearance of the Active Desktop is controlled by options you choose when you install Internet Explorer 4.0. When you install Windows 98 the Active Desktop is installed, and the Web Channels bar displays automatically on your computer. You can choose to view your desktop as a Web page and to view the Internet Explorer Channel bar to provide easy access to pre-defined Web sites. These features are identified in the Active Desktop displayed in Figure A.1. If these features were not selected when you installed Internet Explorer 4.0 or Windows 98 on your computer, you can display the features from the Active Desktop.

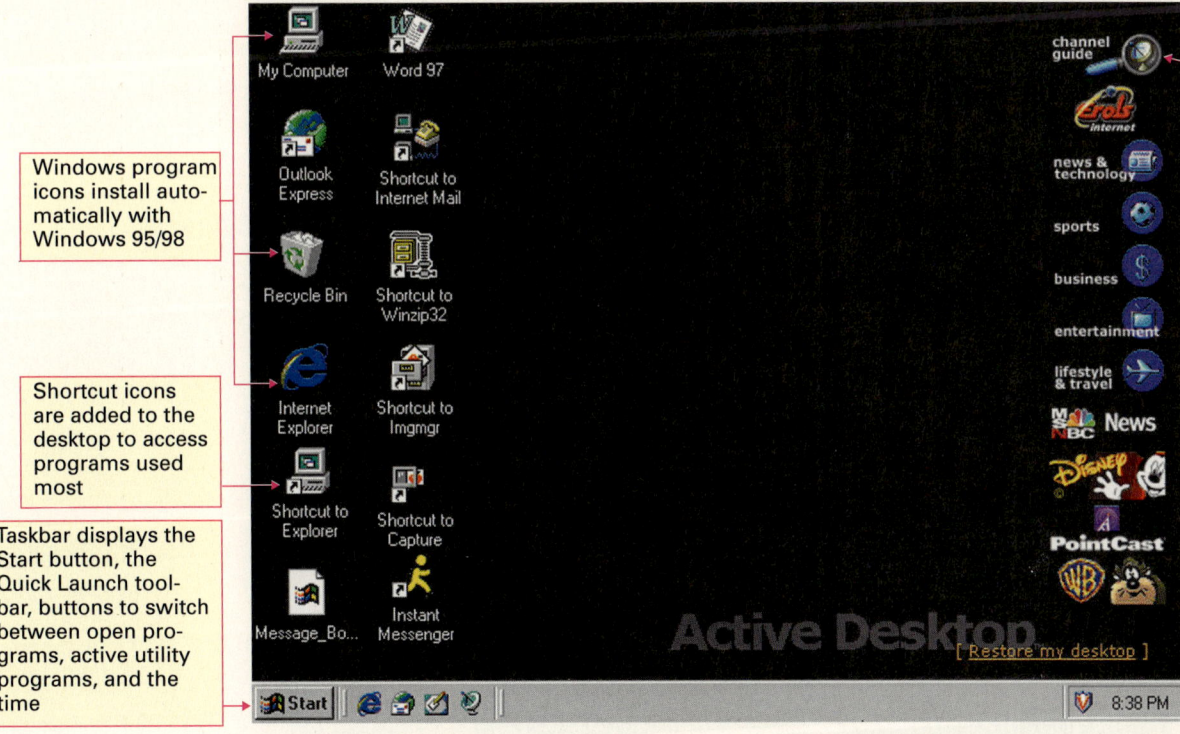

Figure A.1

> **Note** Because the desktop can be customized, your desktop may not appear exactly as the one shown in the illustrations in this preview — even if you choose to display the Internet Explorer Channel bar and the desktop as a Web page.

Displaying the Internet Explorer Channel Bar

The Internet Explorer Channel bar appears in its own window when it is active. As a result, you can close the window by clicking the Close button that appears when you position the mouse pointer near the top edge of the Channel Guide button at the top of the Channel bar. Then use these procedures to restore the Internet Explorer Channel bar.

TASK 1: TO DISPLAY THE INTERNET EXPLORER CHANNEL BAR AFTER INSTALLATION:

1 Right-click a blank area of the Active Desktop and choose Active Desktop, as shown in the following figure.

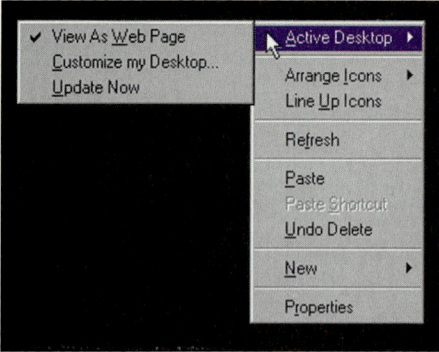

2 Choose Customize my Desktop.
The Display Properties dialog box opens.

3 Click the Web page tab, if necessary, as illustrated in the following figure.

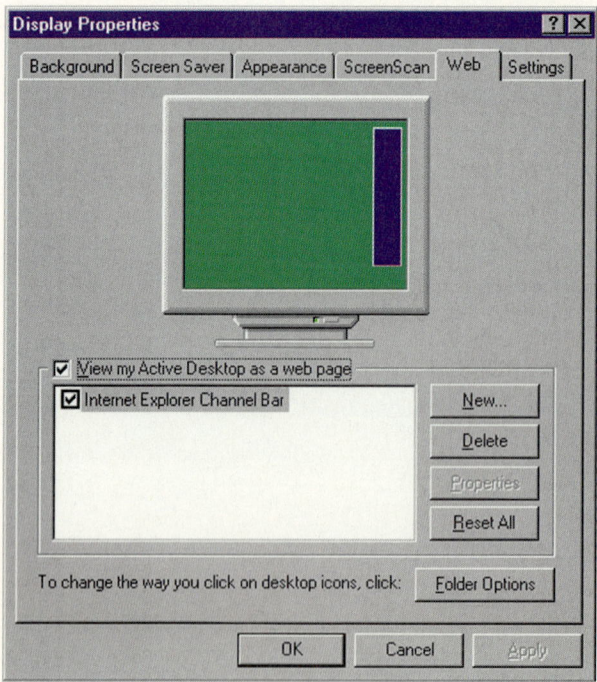

4 Check the View my Active Desktop as a web page check box, if necessary.

5. Check the Internet Explorer Channel Bar check box.
The Internet Explorer Channel bar shape appears in the preview monitor.

6. Choose Apply and then choose OK.

Displaying the Active Desktop Wallpaper

The default Active Desktop Web wallpaper displays a pre-formatted background. If your desktop is formatted with a different background, you can change the wallpaper to the Active Desktop Web wallpaper.

TASK 2: TO DISPLAY THE ACTIVE DESKTOP WALLPAPER AFTER INSTALLATION:

1. Right-click on a blank area on the Active Desktop and choose Properties.
The Display Properties dialog box opens.

2. Click the Background page tab, if necessary, to display the options shown in the following figure.

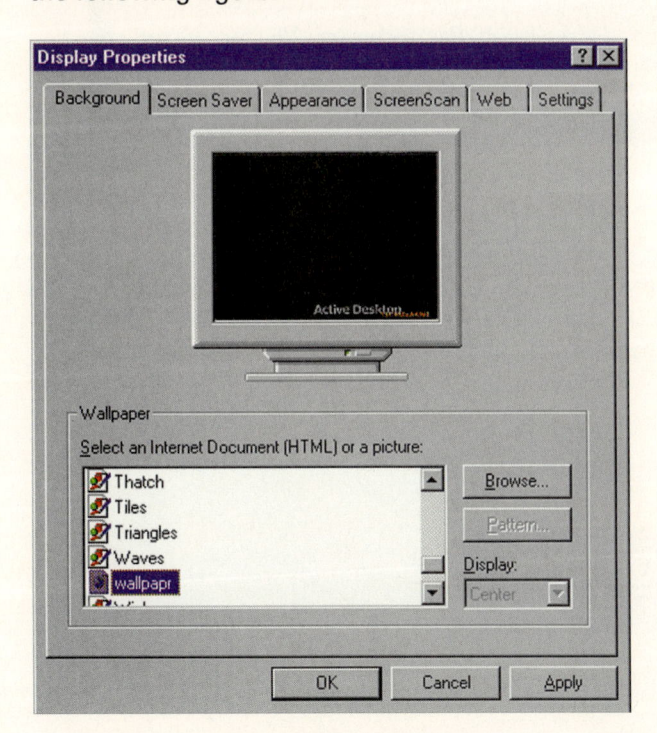

3. Select wallpapr from the Wallpaper list.
The preview monitor displays the Active Desktop Web wallpaper.

> **Note** The list of background designs varies depending on programs previously installed on your computer. If wallpapr is unavailable, select the background identified by your instructor.

4. Choose Apply and then choose OK.
The desktop is reformatted.

Using Desktop ToolTips

Other features that have been enhanced by the Active Desktop and Windows 98 include desktop ToolTips and shortcut menus. With the Active Desktop, simply pointing to an icon or desktop feature identifies the feature and, in some instances, displays explanatory information about the feature.

TASK 3: TO DISPLAY DESKTOP TOOLTIPS:

1 Click on a blank area of the Desktop to make it active. The Desktop must be active before ToolTips appear.

2 Position the mouse pointer on the selected icon, as shown in the following figure.

The ToolTip explains how to use the My Computer program.

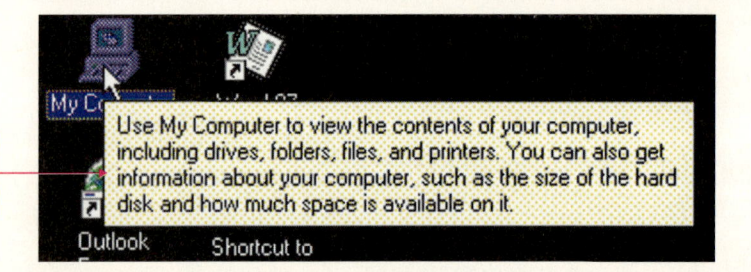

Note The ToolTip appears different, depending on how the Active Desktop is installed on your computer. If it is installed using Internet Explorer 4.0 with Windows 95, it displays as shown in the figure. If the Active Desktop is installed with Windows 98, the information provided by the ToolTip will be different.

3 Point to the Start button.

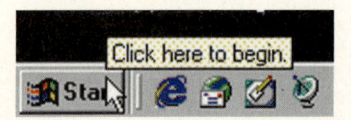

4 Point to a button on the Internet Explorer Channel bar, as shown here.

5 Point to the Time at the right end of the Taskbar, as shown in this figure.

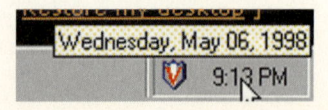

6 Point to an icon on the Quick Launch toolbar, as shown here.

Launching Programs

The same basic techniques used to launch programs in Windows 95 can be used to launch programs from the Active Desktop and Windows 98 Start menu and desktop shortcuts. The Active Desktop, however, enables you to use the Quick Launch toolbar located on the Taskbar to launch programs. In addition, you can change the setup of your desktop so that all program icons, shortcuts, and filenames act as hyperlinks. Clicking a filename, program icon, shortcut, or folder that is formatted as a hyperlink automatically opens the item. You'll also find that when Start menus contain more items than will fit on a cascading menu, the cascading menu displays an arrow at the top and/or bottom to indicate the presence of additional items.

TASK 4: TO LAUNCH PROGRAMS FROM THE ACTIVE DESKTOP:

1 Click the Outlook Express button on the Quick Launch toolbar, to launch the program shown here.

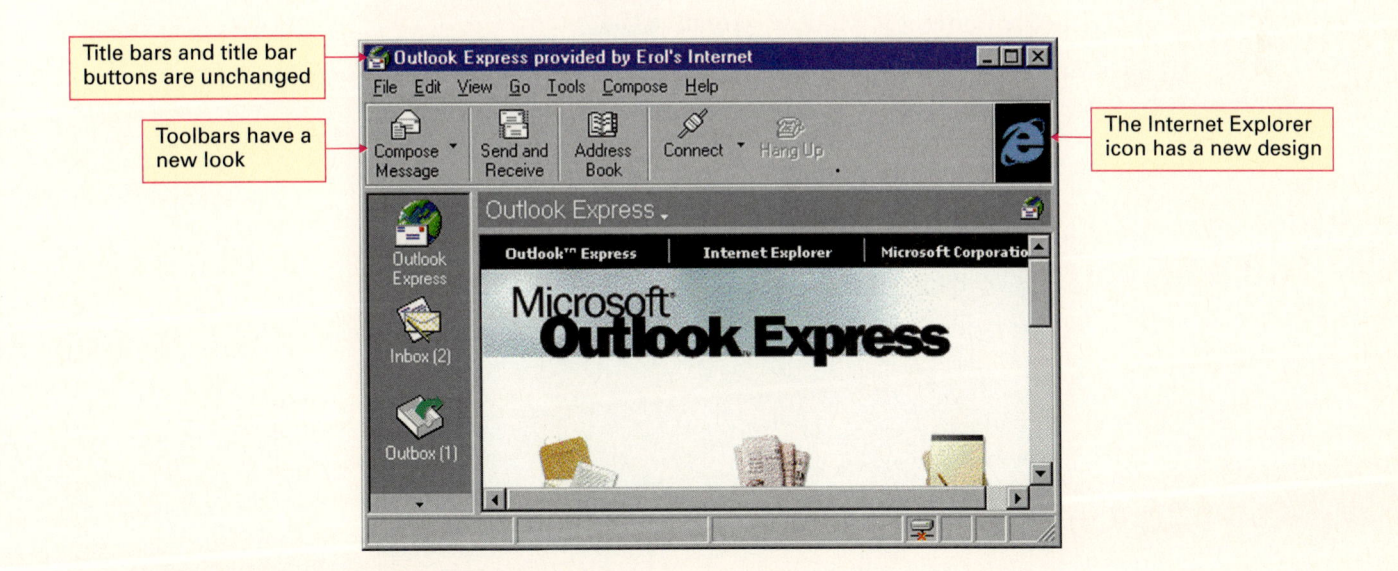

Title bars and title bar buttons are unchanged

Toolbars have a new look

The Internet Explorer icon has a new design

WIN98-8

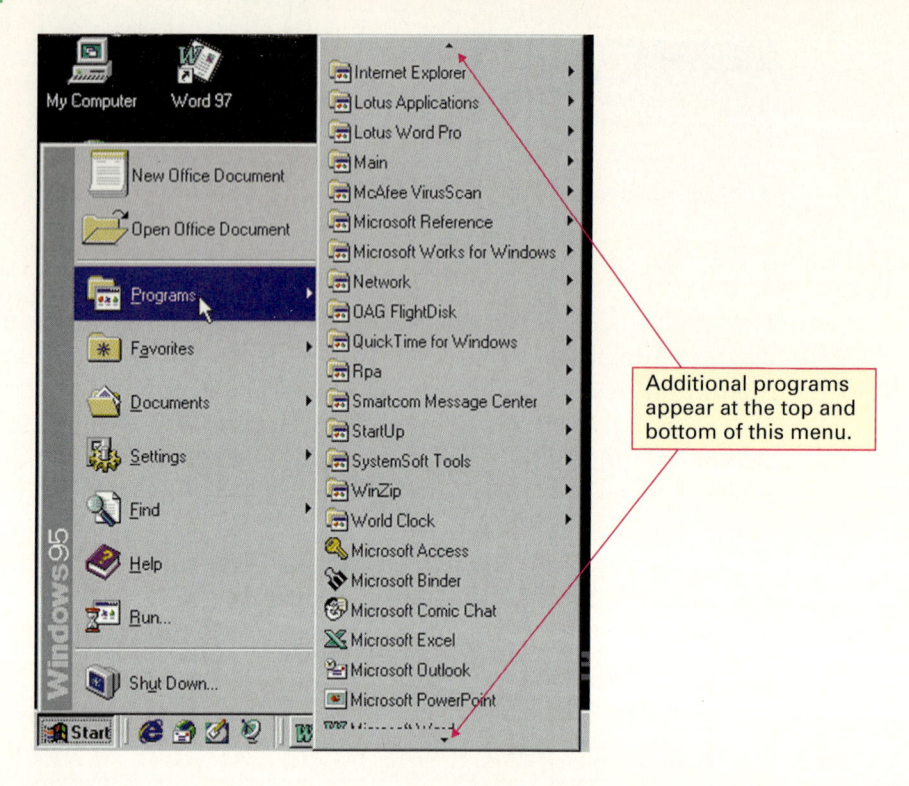

2 Choose Start, Programs, to display the Programs list shown here.

Additional programs appear at the top and bottom of this menu.

3 Click the arrow at the top or bottom of the cascading menu. Additional menu items scroll onscreen.

4 Double-click My Computer.
The My Computer window opens.

5 Maximize the window and click once on the hard disk drive for your computer, as shown in the next figure.

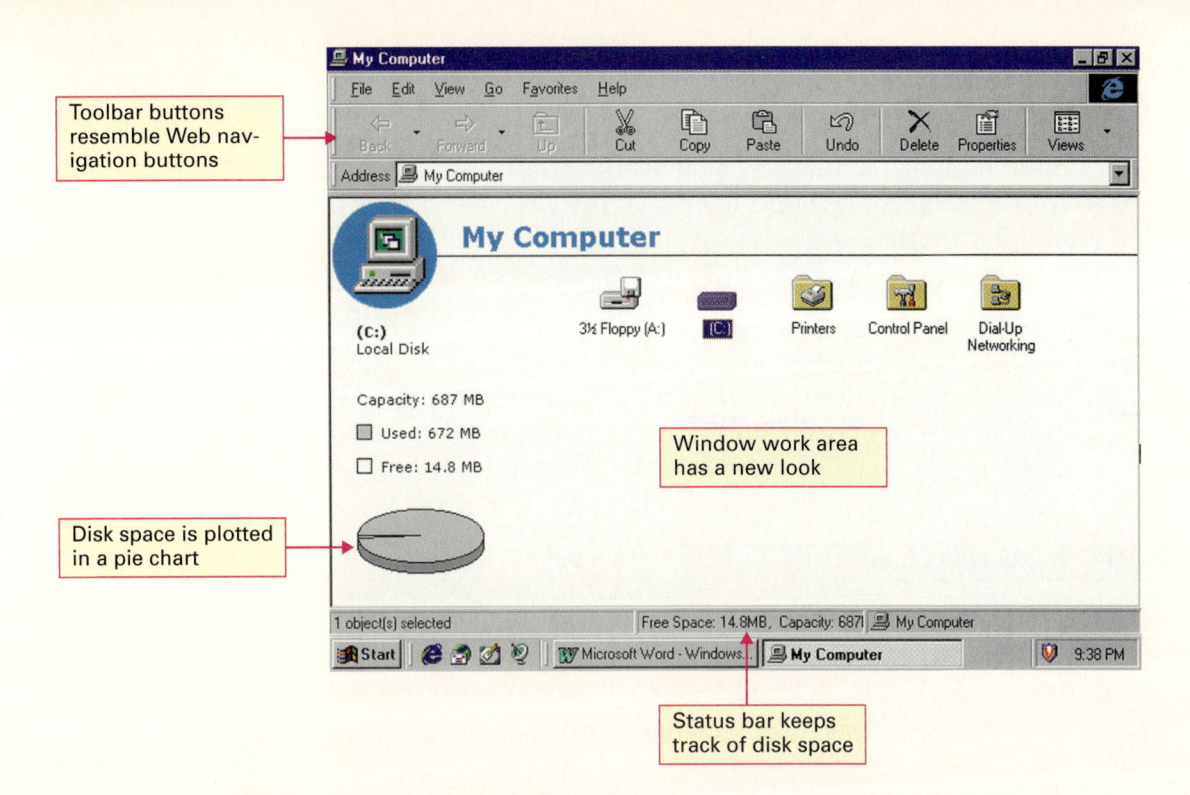

Toolbar buttons resemble Web navigation buttons

Window work area has a new look

Disk space is plotted in a pie chart

Status bar keeps track of disk space

6 Choose View, Folder Options to display the dialog box shown here.

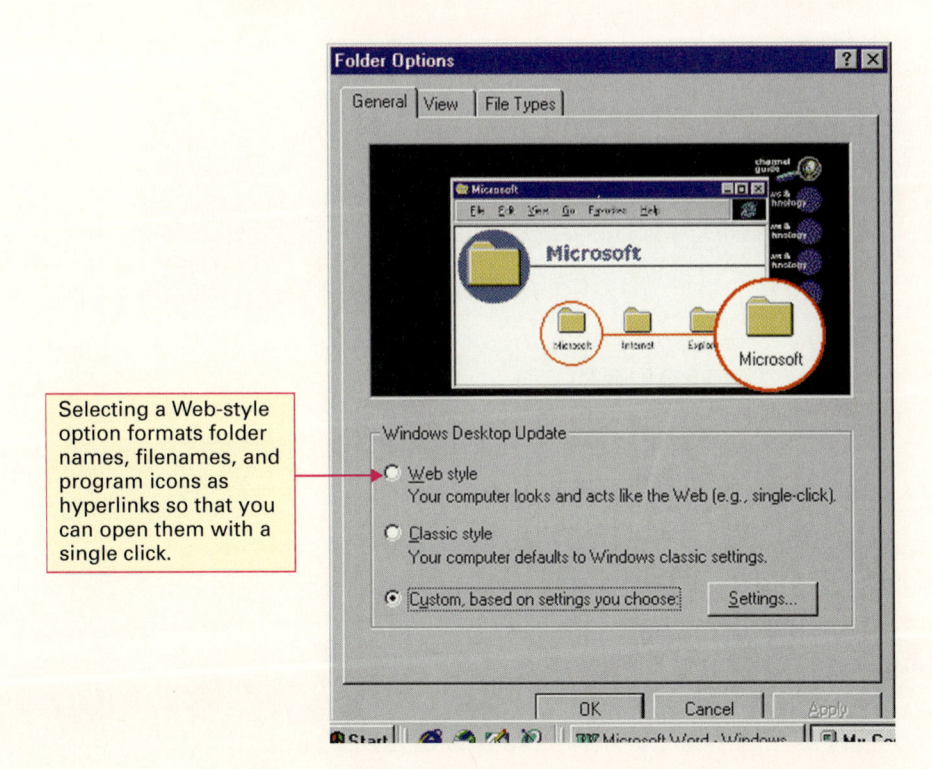

Selecting a Web-style option formats folder names, filenames, and program icons as hyperlinks so that you can open them with a single click.

7 Choose Cancel and close the My Computer window.

Customizing the Windows 95 Active Desktop

Windows 95 Active Desktop enables you to customize the Windows 95 environment for the way you work. You've already explored changing the Desktop background to the Web-style wallpaper. Now you'll move and size the Taskbar.

Sizing and Repositioning the Taskbar

The default position for the Taskbar is at the bottom of the desktop. The Taskbar can be expanded to provide more space for the features displayed and moved to a new location on the desktop.

TASK 5: TO MOVE AND SIZE THE TASKBAR:

1. Position the mouse pointer on the border between the desktop and the Taskbar.
   The mouse pointer appears as a two-headed vertical arrow.

2. Drag the border toward the top of the desktop, as shown in this figure.

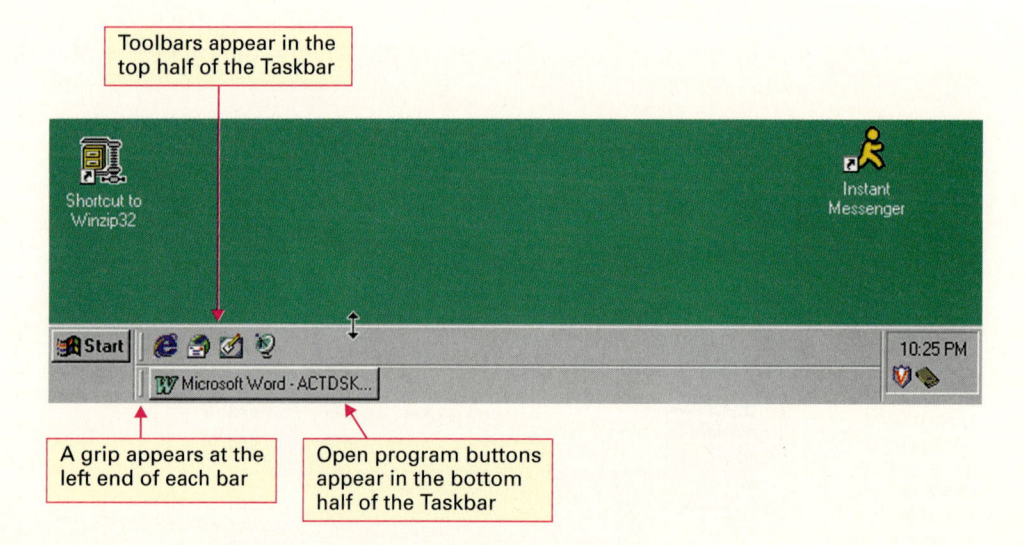

   Toolbars appear in the top half of the Taskbar

   A grip appears at the left end of each bar

   Open program buttons appear in the bottom half of the Taskbar

3. Drag the border of the Taskbar to its original size.

4. Position the mouse pointer on a blank area of the Taskbar.
   The mouse pointer should be a white arrow.

5. Click and drag the Taskbar to the top of the desktop, and drop it.
   The Taskbar appears at the top of the desktop.

6. Drag the Taskbar to the right or left side of the desktop, and drop it.
   The Taskbar appears as a vertical bar down the side of the desktop.

7. Return the Taskbar to its original position.

Active Desktop **WIN98-11**

Displaying Additional Toolbars on the Taskbar

The Active Desktop provides four toolbars that you can display on the Taskbar. The Quick Launch toolbar is displayed by default. You can also display the Address, Links, and Web toolbars.

TASK 6: TO DISPLAY ADDITIONAL TOOLBARS:

1 Point to a blank area of the Taskbar, and right-click.
The Taskbar shortcut menu opens.

2 Choose Toolbars, as shown in this figure.

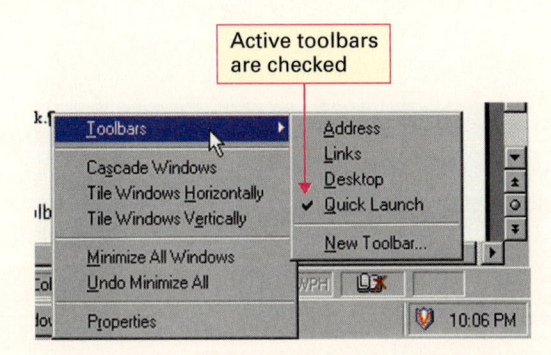

Active toolbars are checked

3 Choose Desktop, illustrated in this figure.

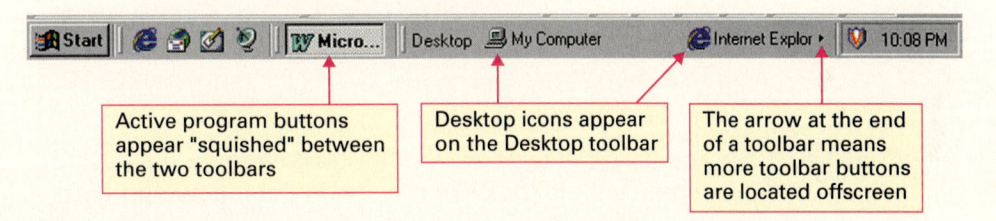

Active program buttons appear "squished" between the two toolbars

Desktop icons appear on the Desktop toolbar

The arrow at the end of a toolbar means more toolbar buttons are located offscreen

4 Right-click a blank area of the Taskbar, choose Toolbars, and choose Desktop to remove the toolbar.
The Desktop toolbar is removed from the Taskbar, and the Taskbar program buttons are restored.

Customizing Taskbar Toolbars

Each of the toolbars displayed on the Taskbar can be customized to contain the tools you use most. To remove tools from the toolbars, drag the button from the toolbar. To add a tool, drag a program item or feature onto the toolbar.

TASK 7: TO CUSTOMIZE THE QUICK LAUNCH TOOLBAR:

1 Click the Show Desktop button on the Quick Launch Toolbar.
All open programs minimize and the Active Desktop is visible.

2 Click and drag the Launch Internet Explorer Browser button from the Quick Launch Toolbar onto the desktop, and drop it.
The program button appears as a shortcut on the desktop, and the button no longer appears on the toolbar.

3 Select the Launch Internet Explorer Browser shortcut icon on the desktop, and drag and drop it in its original position on the Quick Launch toolbar.
The toolbar button appears on the toolbar, and the shortcut remains on the desktop.

4 Click the shortcut icon on the desktop, and press DEL.
The Confirm File Deletion dialog box opens.

5 Choose Yes to confirm the deletion.

Floating and Restoring Toolbars

Toolbars take up valuable space on the Taskbar. When you have more programs active than will comfortably fit on the Taskbar, you can drag a toolbar to the desktop so that program buttons have more space.

TASK 8: TO MOVE AND RESTORE A TASKBAR TOOLBAR:

1 Position the mouse pointer on the Quick Launch toolbar grip.

> **Note** The mouse pointer appears as a horizontal mouse shape when you point to the grip.

2 Click and drag the toolbar from the Taskbar onto the desktop.
Your screen should look like the one in the following figure.

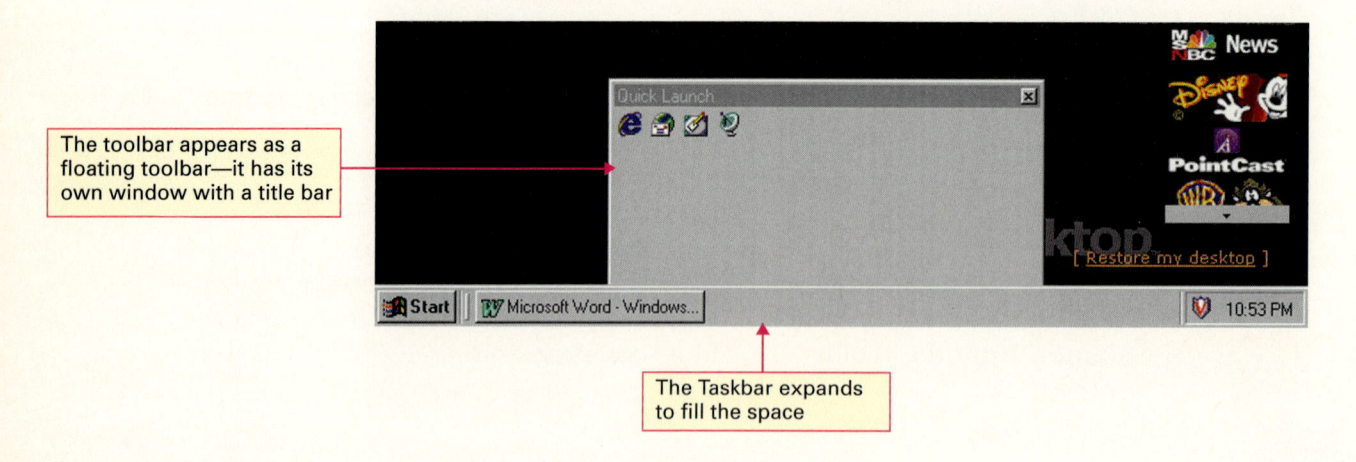

The toolbar appears as a floating toolbar—it has its own window with a title bar

The Taskbar expands to fill the space

3 Click and drag the Quick Launch title bar until the mouse pointer crosses the border of the Taskbar, as shown in this figure.

The toolbar stretches across the desktop just above the Taskbar after the mouse pointer crosses the Taskbar border—the toolbar will hop onto the Taskbar when you release the mouse button.

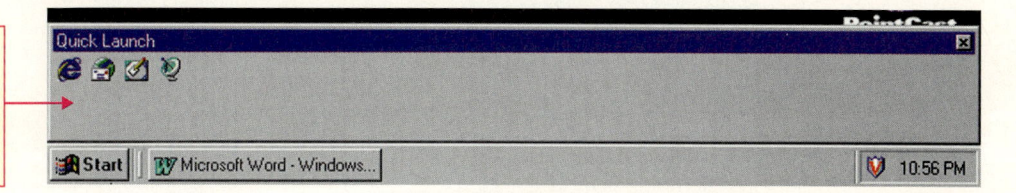

4 Release the mouse button.
The Quick Launch toolbar appears at the right side of the Taskbar.

5 Drag the grip beside the Start button to the right end of the Taskbar.
When the Taskbar grip is dragged past the Quick Launch toolbar, the toolbar assumes its original position.

6 Drag the toolbar and Taskbar grips until the Taskbar returns to normal.

Editing the Start Menu

The Active Desktop makes customizing the Start menu quick and easy. You can remove items from the Start menu to the desktop, or you can drag items from dialog boxes, the desktop, and folders and then place them on the Start menu.

Creating Shortcuts from the Start Menu

Dragging an item from the Start menu removes the item from the menu. To leave items on the Start menu and create shortcuts for the item on the desktop, you generally want to copy the Start menu item as you drag it to the desktop. You can drag Start menu items to the desktop or to an open dialog box or folder.

TASK 9: TO CREATE SHORTCUTS FROM THE START MENU:

1 Choose Start, Programs.
The Programs cascading menu opens.

2 Press and hold CTRL, then click and drag the Windows Explorer icon and title to the desktop.

WIN98-14

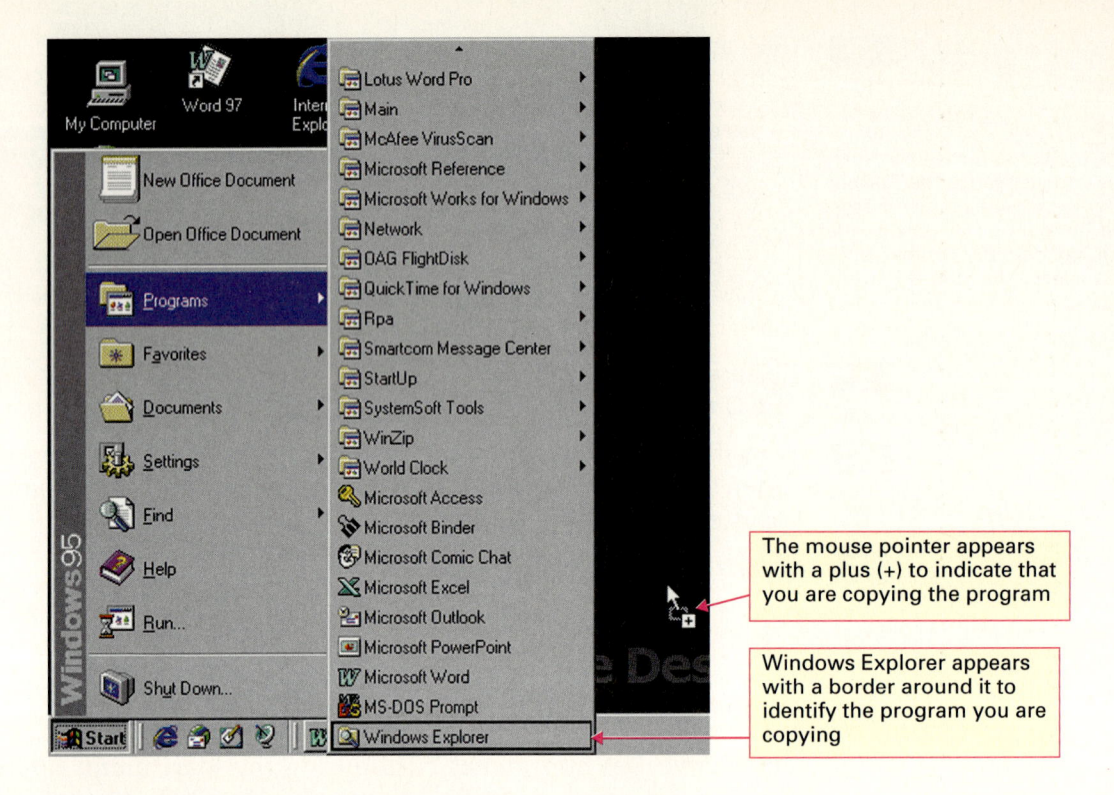

> The mouse pointer appears with a plus (+) to indicate that you are copying the program

> Windows Explorer appears with a border around it to identify the program you are copying

3 Drop the program on the desktop.
A Windows Explorer shortcut appears on the desktop.

4 Choose Start, Programs to ensure that the Windows Explorer icon remains on the menu.

Adding Items to the Start Menu

Adding items to the Start menu is as easy as copying shortcuts from the menu. Simply drag the item to the Start button and position the item on the menu in the desired position. It is important to keep the mouse button depressed from the time you start dragging the icon until it is properly positioned. You can also use the techniques presented here to reorganize items on the Start menu.

TASK 10: TO ADD ITEMS TO THE START MENU:

1 Drag the Windows Explorer Shortcut icon to the Start button.
The Start menu opens.

> **Troubleshooting** Do not release the mouse button until the item is properly positioned.

2 Drag the icon to the top of the Start menu, as shown in this figure.

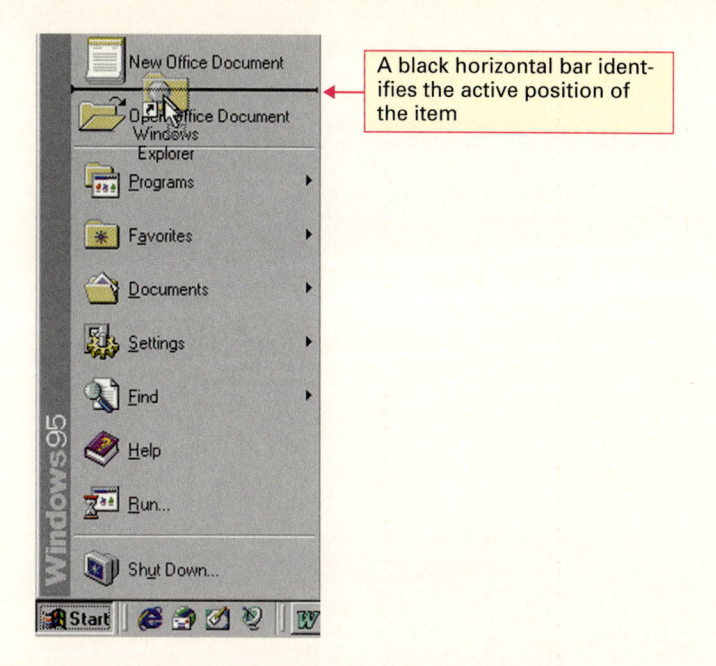

Active Desktop WIN98-15

A black horizontal bar identifies the active position of the item

3 Release the mouse button when the item is appropriately positioned.

4 Choose Start and drag the Windows Explorer from the top of the menu to the desktop.

5 Select the Windows Explorer shortcut on the desktop, and press DEL.

Restoring the Desktop

Tasks in this preview have most likely left your desktop in a bit of a mess. You can restore the desktop to its original format using the desktop itself.

TASK 11: RESTORING THE DESKTOP:

1 Point to the Restore my desktop hyperlink on the Active Desktop, as shown in this figure.

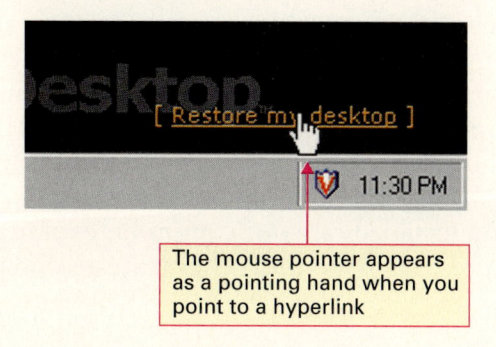

The mouse pointer appears as a pointing hand when you point to a hyperlink

2 Click the hyperlink, to display the dialog box shown here.

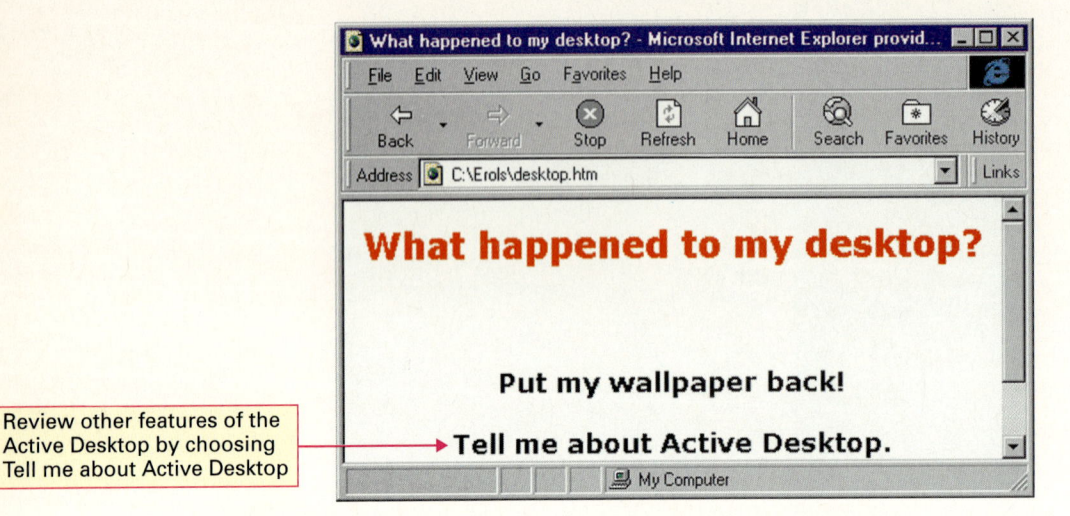

Review other features of the Active Desktop by choosing Tell me about Active Desktop

3 Choose Put my wallpaper back.
The dialog box shown in this figure appears.

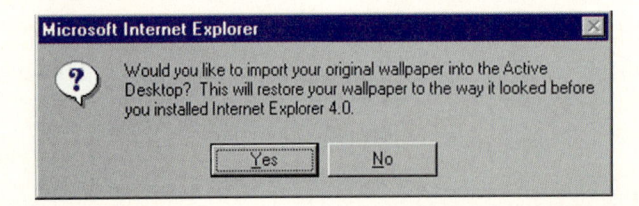

4 Choose Yes.
The original wallpaper forms the desktop background.

5 Close all open programs, if necessary, and shut down Windows 95.

Conclusion

While Windows 95 Active Desktop offers the capabilities you've worked with in this Project, Windows 98 Active Desktop enables users to add new and different objects to the Desktop. For example, with Windows 98 Active Desktop, you can add Java programs such as stock market tickers to the Desktop. In addition, you can subscribe to Web services and newsgroups and add shortcuts to these features to your Desktop. When Windows 98 is available and installed on your computer, explore Windows 98 and look for these features. Then identify other features and benefits Windows 98 has available.

Spreadsheets
Using Microsoft Excel 97

Overview

Excel is a tool you can use for organizing, calculating, and displaying numerical data. You might use Excel to record your checking account transactions, plan a budget, prepare a bid, control inventory, track sales, or create an expense report. Before you can become proficient with Excel 97, however, you need to get acquainted with the program and learn how to perform some of the most basic functions. Then you will be ready to start working on the projects in this part of the book.

Objectives

After completing this project, you will be able to:

- ➤ **Identify Excel 97 Features**
- ➤ **Launch Excel 97**
- ➤ **Identify Excel 97 Screen Elements**
- ➤ **Get help**
- ➤ **Close a workbook**
- ➤ **Exit Excel 97**

Identifying Excel 97 Features

Excel 97 is the electronic equivalent of one of those green (or buff color) columnar pads that bookkeepers and accountants use. Excel calls the area in which you work a *worksheet* — other programs call this a spreadsheet. An Excel worksheet has 256 *columns* and 65,536 *rows*, for a whopping total of 16,777,216 cells. Is that big or what?

> **Note** A *cell* is the intersection of a column and a row.

Overview EX-3

An Excel worksheet is actually a page in a *workbook* file. By default, a new workbook file has three worksheets, but you can add additional worksheets if you need them — as many as your computer memory allows.

You can do more than store numbers with Excel 97; you can use it to perform calculations, recalculate formulas when numbers are changed, analyze data, and create charts and maps from the data that you enter. Many of the same text features available in a word processing program are also available in Excel. For example, you can check the spelling of words, use text styles, add headers and footers, and insert graphics and other objects. Figure 0.1 shows a worksheet with numbers, calculations, text formatted with styles, a graphic, and a chart.

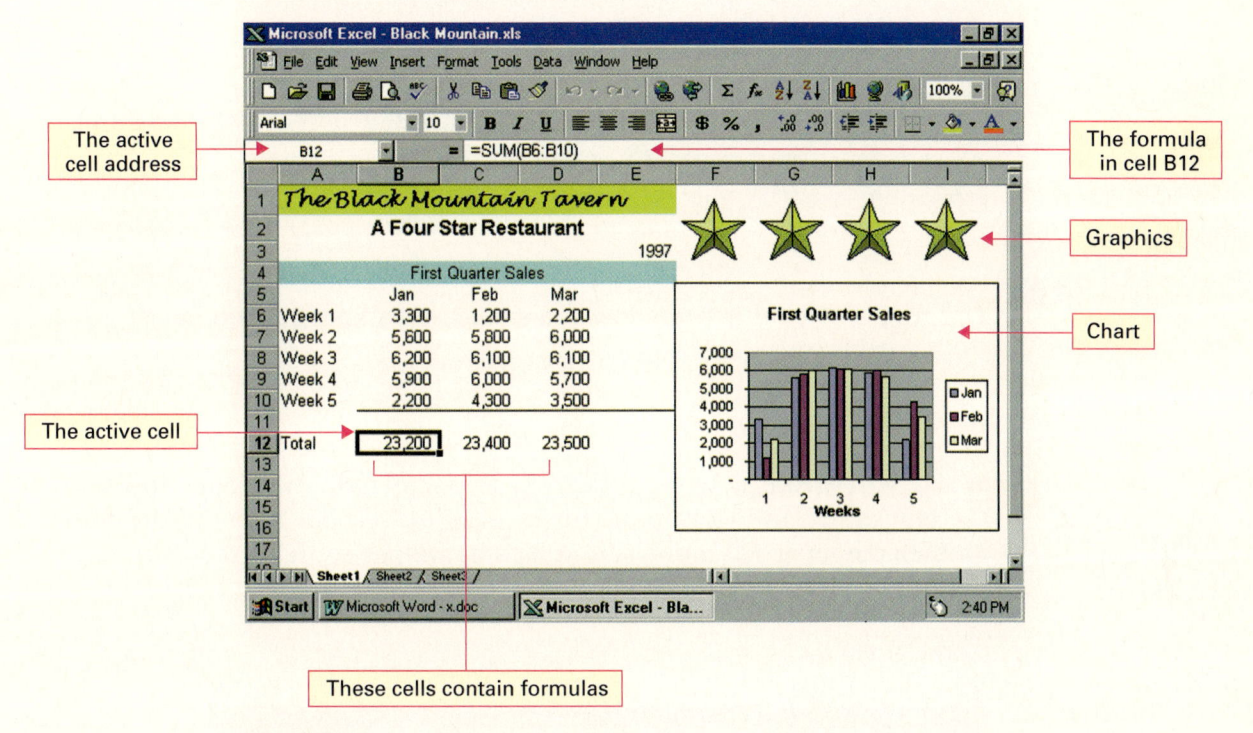

Figure O.1

Launching Excel 97

When you start your computer, you may have to log on to a network or perform some other steps before Windows 95 starts. After the Windows 95 desktop displays on the screen, you're ready to launch Excel 97.

TASK 1: TO LAUNCH EXCEL 97:

1. Click the Start **Start** button and point to Programs.

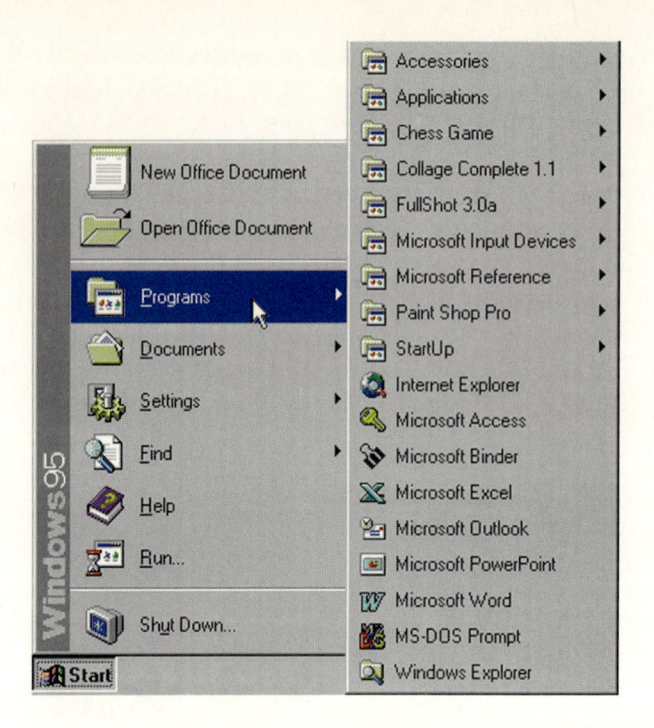

2   Point to Microsoft Excel and click.
The program opens in a window and creates a workbook called *Book1*.

Identifying Excel 97 Screen Elements

When you create a new workbook, the screen should look similar to the one shown in Figure O.2. The Excel 97 screen has many of the common elements of a Windows 95 screen as well as some elements that are unique to the Excel 97 program.

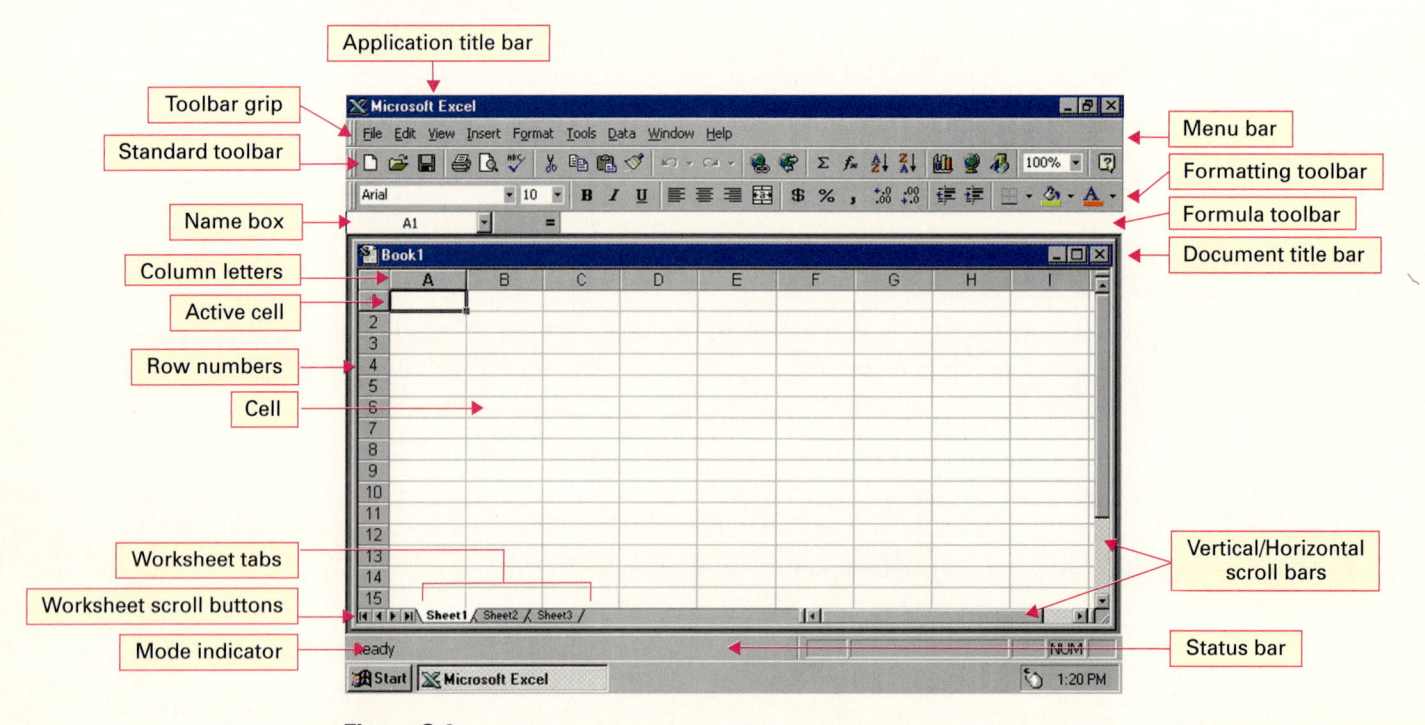

Figure O.2

> **Note** The screen displays two Close buttons. The button in the Application title bar closes Excel 97; the button in the document title bar closes the current workbook. If the document window is maximized, the Close button for the document appears in the menu bar.

Table 0.1 lists the elements of the Excel 97 screen.

Table O.1 Elements of the Excel 97 Screen

Element	Description
Application title bar	Displays the name of the application and the Minimize, Maximize/Restore, and Close buttons. If the document window is maximized, the name of the workbook also displays in the application title bar.
Document title bar	Displays the name of the workbook file and the Minimize, Maximize/Restore, and Close buttons. If the window is maximized, there is no document title bar and the document buttons display in the menu bar.
Menu bar	Contains menu options. To use the menu, click an option to display a drop-down menu, and then click a command on the drop-down menu to perform the command, view another menu, or view a dialog box.
Standard toolbar	Contains buttons for accomplishing commands. To use the toolbar, click the button for the command you want to perform.
Formatting toolbar	Contains buttons and controls for formatting. To use the toolbar, click the button for the command you want to perform or click a drop-down list arrow to make a selection.
Name box	Displays the address of the active cell.
Formula bar	Displays the cell address and the contents of the active cell. Also used to enter and edit formulas.
Active cell	Marks the cell where data will be entered with a black border.
Scroll bars	Vertical and horizontal Scroll bars scroll the screen vertically and horizontally.
Worksheet tabs	Display the names of worksheets in the current workbook. Clicking a tab displays the worksheet.
Worksheet scroll buttons	Scroll the worksheet tabs (if you have too many worksheets to display all the tabs).
Status bar	Displays information about the current workbook. The Mode indicator displays on the far left side of the status bar. The right side of the status bar displays "NUM" if the Num Lock Key is on and "CAPS" if the Cap Lock key is on.
Row numbers	Indicate the numbers associated with the rows.
Column letters	Indicate the letters associated with the columns.
Cell	The intersection of a column and a row, referred to with an address that combines the column letter(s) with the row number, such as A1, AA223, and so on.
Mode	Displays on the left side of the status bar and shows a word that describes the current working condition of the workbook. For example, the word *"Ready"* means that the worksheet is ready to receive data or execute a command. Other modes include ***Edit***, ***Enter***, ***Point***, ***Error***, and ***Wait***.

> **Note** Although you can turn off the display of certain screen elements (toolbars, the Formula bar, and the Status bar), generally all the screen elements are displayed in Excel 97 because they are used so often.

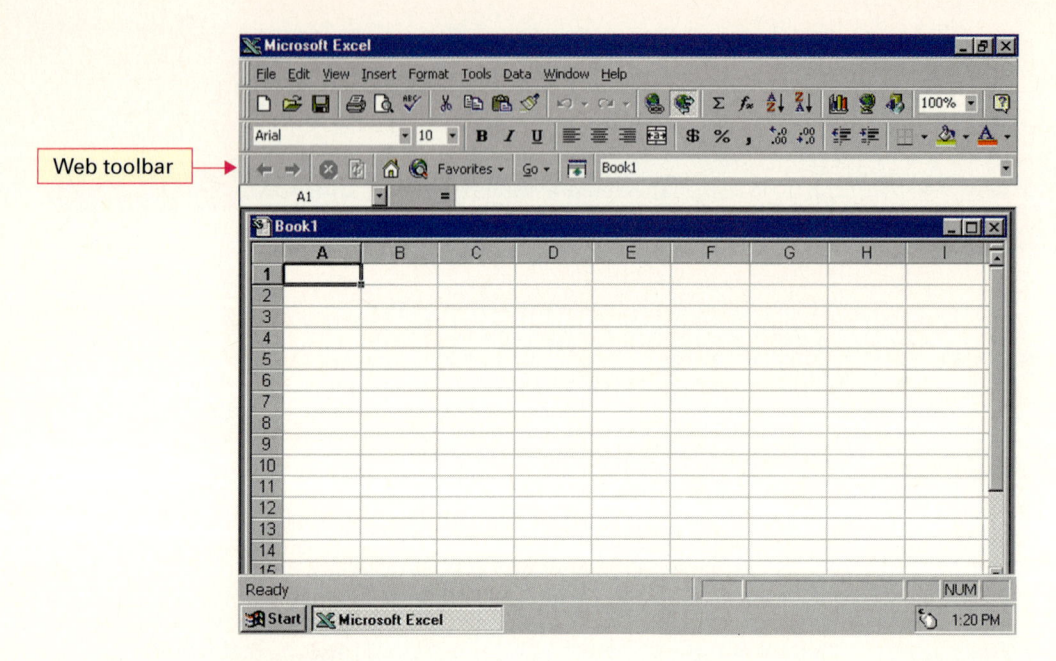

Web toolbar →

Figure O.3

Working with Toolbars

Toolbars contain buttons that perform functions. Usually the tools grouped together on a toolbar perform tasks that are all related. For example, the buttons on the Chart toolbar all perform tasks related to creating and modifying charts.

The Standard toolbar and the Formatting toolbar are the default toolbars, the ones that Excel 97 automatically displays. You can display or hide as many toolbars as desired. You also can move toolbars to different locations on the screen. When a toolbar is displayed, Excel places it where it was last located.

If you use the Internet frequently, you may want to display the **Web toolbar** by clicking the Web Toolbar button in the Standard toolbar. With the Web toolbar displayed, your screen should look like Figure O.3. To hide the Web toolbar, click the Web Toolbar button again.

Overview   EX-7

TASK 2: TO WORK WITH TOOLBARS:

1 Choose View, Toolbars.

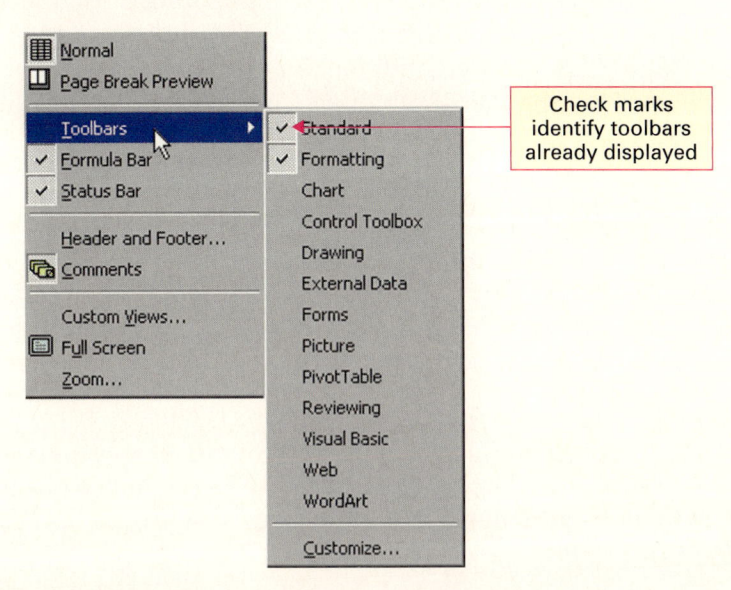

Check marks identify toolbars already displayed

2 Choose Chart.

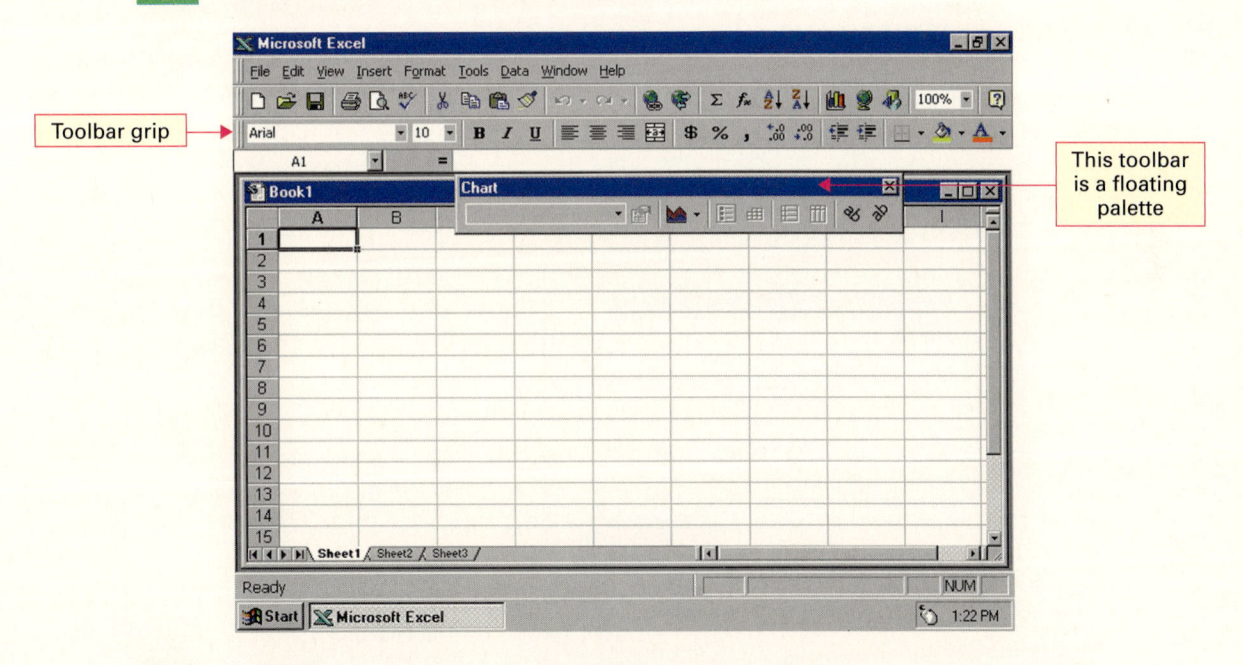

Toolbar grip

This toolbar is a floating palette

3 Point to the title bar of the Chart toolbar and drag the toolbar to a new location. If the toolbar doesn't appear as a palette, drag the toolbar by grabbing the grip.
The toolbar moves.

4 Choose View, Toolbars, Chart.
The toolbar no longer displays.

Getting Help

Excel 97 provides several ways to get help. You can use the standard help dialog box that contains the Contents, Index, and Find pages and the What's This Help feature. Additionally, you can use the Office Assistant and Microsoft on the Web, both of which are help features unique to Office 97.

Using the Office Assistant

The Office Assistant offers help on the task you are performing, often referred to as *context-sensitive help*. If the Office Assistant doesn't display the help you want, you can type a question to obtain the desired help.

> **Note** Sometimes the Office Assistant offers unsolicited help. When this happens, you can choose to read the help or just close the Office Assistant. Unfortunately, there is no way for a user to deactivate the Office Assistant.

TASK 3: TO USE THE OFFICE ASSISTANT:

1. Click the Office Assistant button if you don't see the Office Assistant.

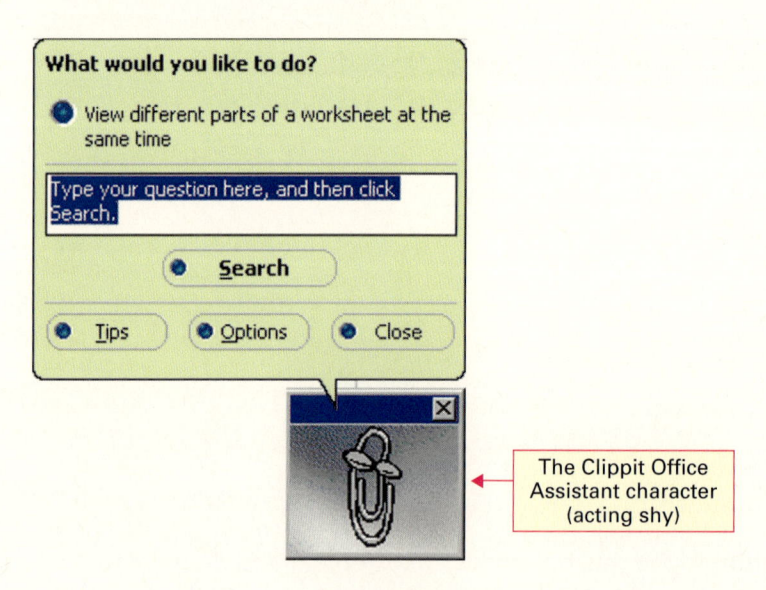

The Clippit Office Assistant character (acting shy)

Overview **EX-9**

2 Type **How do you enter a formula?**

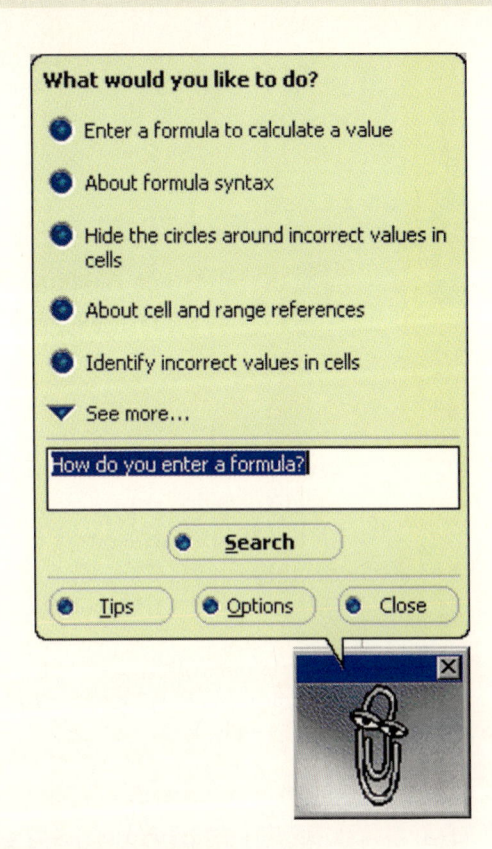

> **What would you like to do?**
> - Enter a formula to calculate a value
> - About formula syntax
> - Hide the circles around incorrect values in cells
> - About cell and range references
> - Identify incorrect values in cells
> - ▼ See more...
>
> How do you enter a formula?
>
> - **Search**
> - Tips
> - Options
> - Close

3 Click Search and then click About formula syntax.

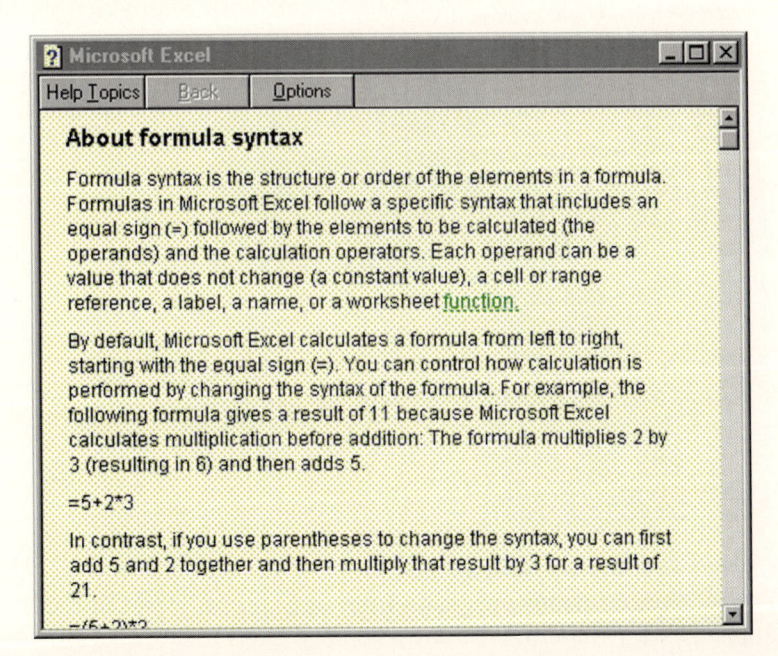

> **Microsoft Excel**
> Help Topics | Back | Options
>
> **About formula syntax**
>
> Formula syntax is the structure or order of the elements in a formula. Formulas in Microsoft Excel follow a specific syntax that includes an equal sign (=) followed by the elements to be calculated (the operands) and the calculation operators. Each operand can be a value that does not change (a constant value), a cell or range reference, a label, a name, or a worksheet function.
>
> By default, Microsoft Excel calculates a formula from left to right, starting with the equal sign (=). You can control how calculation is performed by changing the syntax of the formula. For example, the following formula gives a result of 11 because Microsoft Excel calculates multiplication before addition: The formula multiplies 2 by 3 (resulting in 6) and then adds 5.
>
> =5+2*3
>
> In contrast, if you use parentheses to change the syntax, you can first add 5 and 2 together and then multiply that result by 3 for a result of 21.

4 Read the Help dialog box and then click ☒ on the Help title bar.
The Help dialog box closes, but the Office Assistant window remains open.

5 Click the Office Assistant character in the Office Assistant window.
The Office Assistant asks what you want to do.

EX-10

> **Note** The default Office Assistant is a paper clip named Clippit. Other assistants include Shakespeare, a robot, and a cat — to name a few.

6 Click Close.
The "bubble" closes.

7 Click ❌ on the Office Assistant title bar.
The Office Assistant window closes.

Getting Help from the World Wide Web

Microsoft maintains several sites on the Web that have useful information, user support, product news, and free programs and files that you can download. If your system is connected to the Internet, you can access this type of help easily. The Microsoft sites are open to all users.

> **Note** When Microsoft is beta testing a program, the company maintains "closed sites" open only to beta testers with a valid password.

TASK 4: TO READ ANSWERS TO FREQUENTLY ASKED QUESTIONS:

1 Choose Help, Microsoft on the Web.

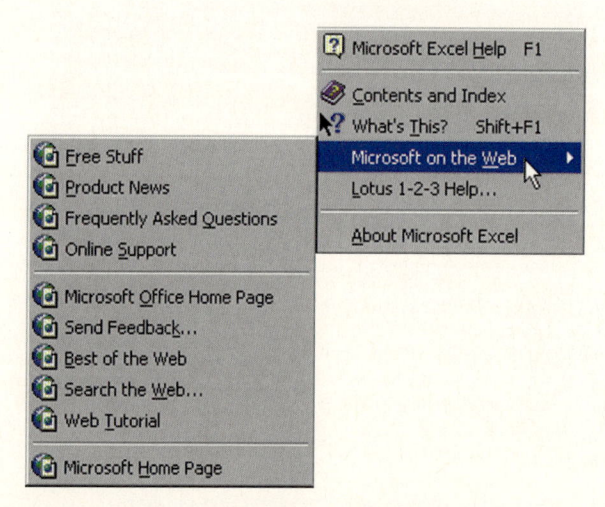

2 Choose Frequently Asked Questions.
The Internet browser program Internet Explorer starts and connects to the appropriate Web site. (You may be prompted to connect to the Internet.)

3 When you finish browsing the Web, click ❌ in the browser window. (I know you're tempted to start browsing around, but you can do that later.)

Closing a Workbook and Exiting Excel 97

Before you exit Excel, you should always save any work that you want to keep and then it's a good idea to close any open workbooks. When you exit Excel 97, the program closes, and the Windows desktop is visible unless you have another program running in a maximized window. In that case, the program will be visible, not the desktop.

> **Tip** If you forget to save a changed file before you try to exit, Excel 97 asks whether you want to save changes. You can choose Yes to save the changed file, No to exit without saving, or Cancel to cancel the exit request. If you exit without closing a file that does not need to be saved, Excel closes the file for you automatically.

TASK 5: TO CLOSE THE WORKBOOK AND EXIT EXCEL 97:

1 Click the Close ✖ button in the menu bar (if the document window is maximized) or in the document title bar (if the window is not maximized).

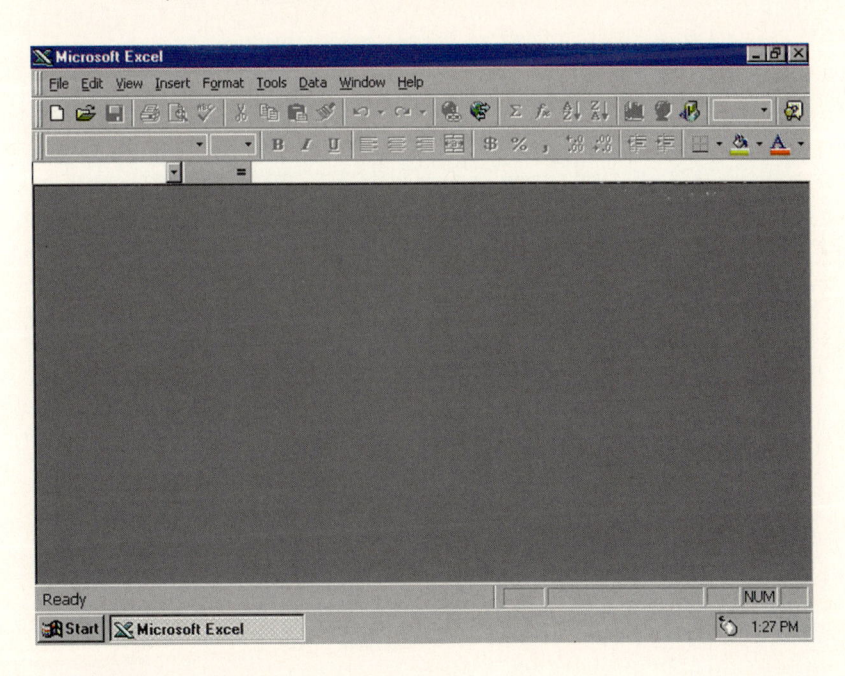

2 Click ✖ in the application title bar.
The Excel 97 program closes.

Summary and Exercises

Summary

- Excel 97 is a full-featured spreadsheet program that's easy to use.
- An Excel workbook includes three worksheets by default.
- Worksheets enable you to store numbers, perform calculations and recalculations, analyze data, and create charts and maps.
- Many features found in Word are also available in Excel 97.
- Excel 97 provides a variety of Help features.
- Excel 97 warns you if you try to exit the program without saving your work.

Key Terms and Operations

Key Terms
active cell
cell
column
column indicators
Edit mode
Enter mode
Error mode
Formatting toolbar
formula bar
menu bar
mode indicator
Office Assistant
Point mode
Ready mode
row
row indicators
scroll bars
Standard toolbar
status bar
title bar
toolbar
Wait mode
Web toolbar
What's This?
workbook
worksheet
worksheet scroll buttons
worksheet tab

Operations
exit Excel 97
get help from the Web
start Excel 97
use Office Assistant

Study Questions

Multiple Choice

1. Another name for a columnar worksheet is a
    a. workbook.
    b. spreadsheet. ✓
    c. cell.
    d. booksheet.

2. The intersection of a column and a row is
    a. a worksheet tab.
    b. a cell. ✓
    c. an active cell.
    d. an indicator.

3. The number of worksheets in a workbook is limited
    a. by default. ✓
    b. to three.
    c. by memory.
    d. to 256.

4. The size of an Excel worksheet is
    a. 128 columns by 9,999 rows.
    b. 65,536 columns by 256 rows.
    c. over 256 million cells.
    d. 256 columns by 65,536 rows. ✓

5. The name of a worksheet displays
    a. in the column letters.
    b. on the worksheet tab. ✓
    c. in the row number.
    d. in the status bar.

6. Which of the following applications would most likely be created in Excel?
    a. a letter
    b. a budget ✓
    c. a memo
    d. a meeting report

7. The standard Windows 95 help features used in Excel include all of the following except
    a. What's This?
    b. Contents. ✓
    c. Index.
    d. Office Assistant.

8. Before exiting Excel 97, you should
    a. save all files and then close all files.
    b. close all files, saving only those that you want to keep. ✓
    c. close all files without saving because Excel saves them automatically.
    d. close the Office Assistant.

9. Which of the following statements are false?
   a. The Office Assistant gives context-sensitive help and unsolicited help.
   b. The Office Assistant is an animated character.
   c. The Office Assistant can be deactivated.
   d. The Office Assistant displays help in a bubble.

10. Which of the following are false statements?
    a. The formula bar displays the cell address and the cell contents of the active cell.
    b. The formula bar is a floating palette.
    c. The formula bar is used for typing formulas.
    d. The formula bar can be hidden.

Short Answer

1. How do you start Excel?
2. What is a cell address? Give examples.
3. How are columns and rows identified?
4. How do you display the Web toolbar?
5. Why are screen elements not usually hidden in Excel?
6. Name some of the things that Excel can do.
7. Name some of the word processing features that are found in Excel.
8. Name and describe the different help features in Excel.
9. Name some of the mode indicators in Excel.
10. How many cells are in a worksheet?

For Discussion

1. Name some tasks that you could perform in Excel for your own personal use.
2. Discuss the advantages of using a program like Excel over keeping columnar records manually.
3. Name examples of situations that would benefit from having multiple worksheets in the same file.
4. Discuss the value of a chart in a worksheet.

Review Exercises

1. Starting Excel and exploring the workbook

In this exercise, you will start Excel 97 and move around in the workbook.

1. Start Excel 97.
2. Turn on the Web toolbar if it isn't displayed.
3. What text is displayed in the status bar?
4. What text is displayed in the Name box?

5. Click the tab that says Sheet2.

6. Is there any change in the status bar and in the Name box?

7. Turn the Web toolbar on if necessary and then turn it off.

2. Getting help on the Web
In this exercise, you will explore the help feature on the World Wide Web.

1. Choose Help, Microsoft on the Web.

2. Choose Product News.

3. Print the initial Web page that displays.

4. Disconnect from the Internet and exit Internet Explorer.

3. Displaying and docking toolbars and getting help from the Office Assistant

1. Launch Excel 97, if necessary.

2. Display the Control Toolbox toolbar.

3. Float the Excel 97 menu bar.

4. Display the Office Assistant and move the Office Assistant to a different location on-screen.

5. Ask the Office Assistant how to change the name of a worksheet.

6. Select a topic from among those the Office Assistant identifies about renaming a worksheet and print a copy of the topic.

7. Dock the menu bar at its original position by dragging its title bar.

8. Close the Control Toolbox toolbar and the Office Assistant.

9. Exit Excel without saving the worksheet.

Assignments

1. Getting online help
Start Excel 97 and use the Office Assistant to find and open a help topic about the Text Import Wizard. Choose Options and print the topic. When finished, close the Help dialog box.

2. Using the Web toolbar
Start Excel 97 and display the Web toolbar in the new workbook if it isn't already displayed. Go to this address: http://www.dominis.com/Zines/ and explore the site. Give a brief description of what you find. When finished, close Internet Explorer, disconnect from the Internet, and exit Excel 97.

PROJECT 1

Creating a Workbook

In order to use Excel 97 effectively, you must know how to create, save, and print workbooks. In this project, you will enter text and numbers and calculate the numbers with formulas and functions to create a simple worksheet. (This might sound like a lot, but I promise you won't have to use all 16,777,216 cells!)

Objectives

After completing this project, you will be able to:

- ➤ Create a new workbook
- ➤ Move around in a worksheet and a workbook
- ➤ Name worksheets
- ➤ Enter data
- ➤ Enter simple formulas and functions
- ➤ Save a workbook
- ➤ Preview and print a worksheet
- ➤ Close a worksheet

The Challenge

Mr. Gilmore, manager of The Grande Hotel, wants a down-and-dirty worksheet to compare the January receipts to the February receipts for both restaurants in the hotel (the Atrium Café and the Willow Top Restaurant). Since the worksheet is just for him, you won't have to worry about formatting right now.

The Solution

You will create a workbook with a page for the Atrium Café and a page for the Willow Top Restaurant as shown in Figure 1.1. (For now, don't worry about aligning headings such as Jan and Feb. You'll learn this in a later project.)

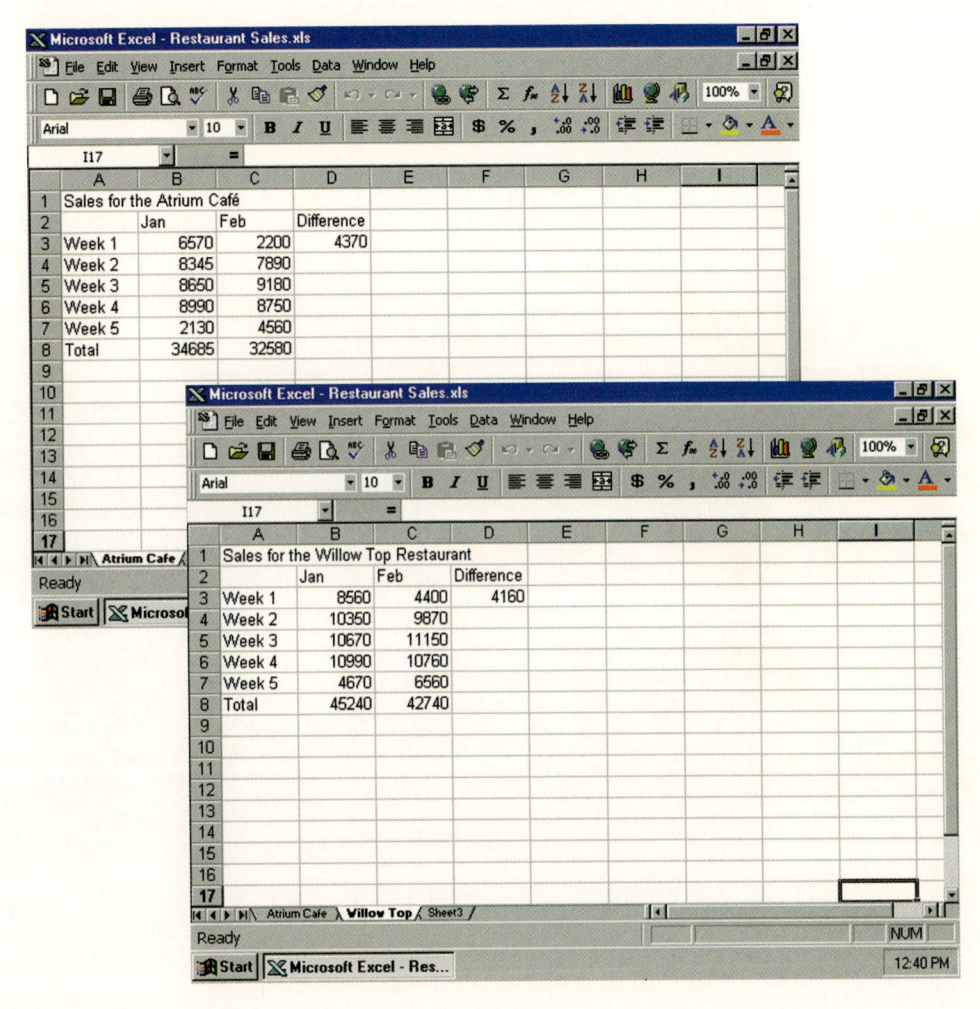

Figure 1.1

The Setup

So that your screen will match the illustrations in this chapter and to ensure that all the tasks in this project will function as described, you should set up Excel as described in Table 1.1. Because these are the default settings for the toolbars and view, you may not need to make any changes to your setup.

EX-18

Table 1.1   Excel Settings

Location	Make these settings:
View, Toolbars	Deselect all toolbars except the Standard and Formatting.
View	Use the Normal view and display the Formula Bar and the Status Bar.

Creating a New Workbook

When you launch Excel 97, a new blank workbook named Book1 automatically opens for you, and you can begin to enter data.

TASK 1: TO CREATE A NEW WORKBOOK:

1 Click the Start [Start] button and point to Programs.

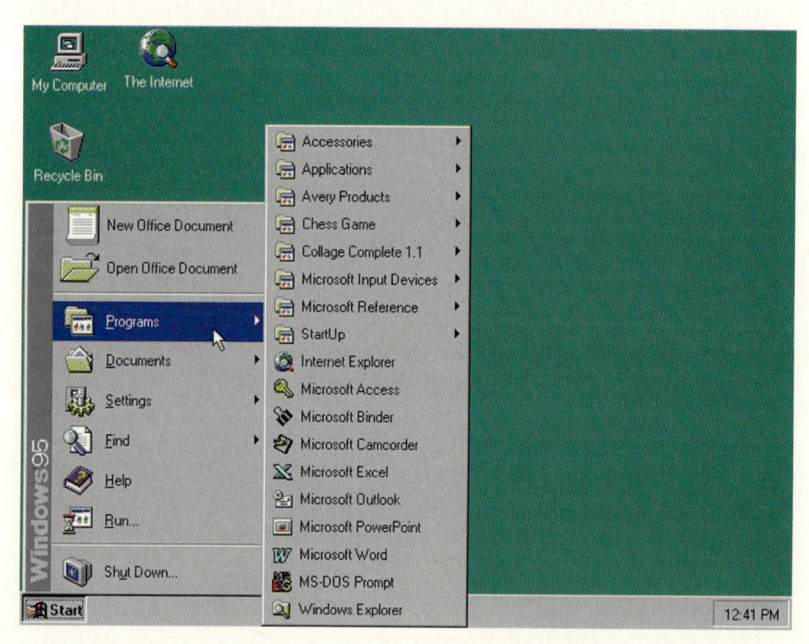

2 Choose Microsoft Excel.
The program launches and creates a workbook called Book1.

> **Note** If Excel is already started and you don't see a workbook on the screen, click the New button on the standard toolbar, and Excel will create one for you.

Moving Around in a Worksheet and a Workbook

To enter data in a worksheet like the one shown on the next page in Figure 1.2, you must move to the desired cell. The *active cell* is outlined with a black border. You make a cell the active cell by clicking in the cell or by moving to the cell with keystrokes. Table 1.2 lists the navigational keystrokes used to move to the desired cell.

Project 1: Creating a Workbook EX-**19**

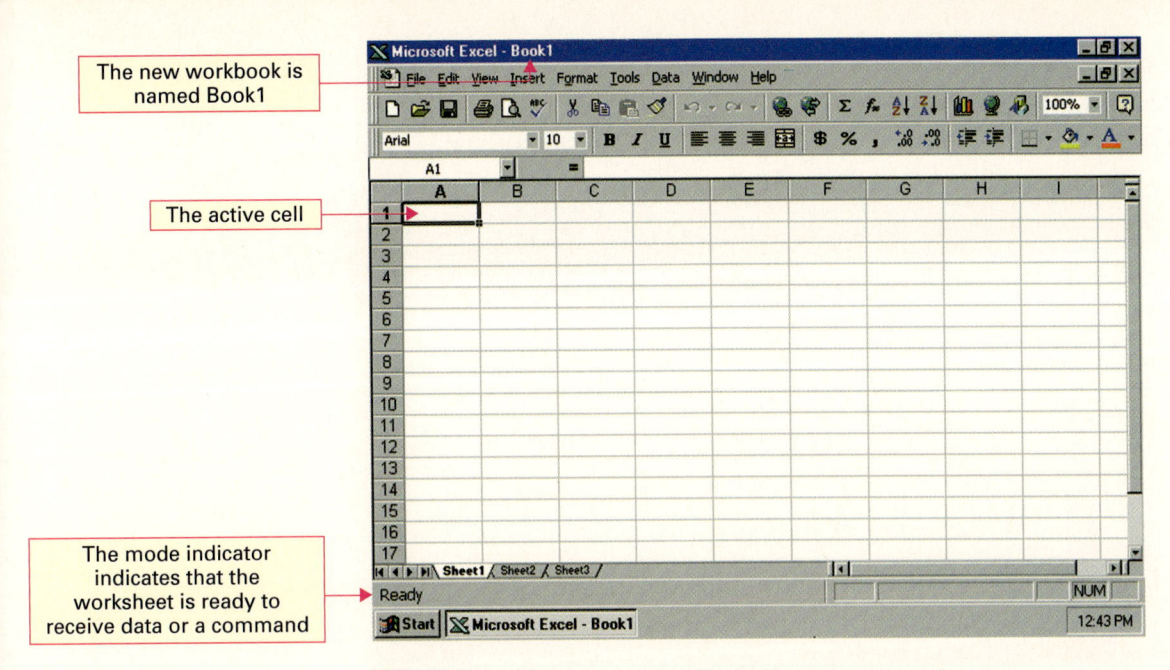

- The new workbook is named Book1
- The active cell
- The mode indicator indicates that the worksheet is ready to receive data or a command

Figure 1.2

> **Note** If you want to click in a cell you can't see on the screen, use the vertical or horizontal scroll bar to scroll the worksheet until you see the cell.

Table 1.2 Navigational Keystrokes

Target Location	Keystroke
Cell to the right of the active cell	→ or TAB
Cell to the left of the active cell	← or SHIFT+TAB
Cell below the active cell	↓ or ENTER
Cell above the active cell	↑ or SHIFT+ENTER
Upper-left corner of the worksheet	CTRL+HOME
Lower-right corner of the active area of the worksheet	CTRL+END
Down one screen	PGDN
Up one screen	PGUP
Right one screen	ALT+PGDN
Left one screen	ALT+PGUP

To display a different worksheet, click the worksheet tab. If you can't see the tab for the worksheet that you want to display, click the appropriate scroll button (the arrows just to the left of the worksheet tabs) to display the tab.

EX-20

TASK 2: TO MOVE AROUND IN A WORKSHEET AND A WORKBOOK:

1 Press PGDN.

Cell A18 becomes the active cell

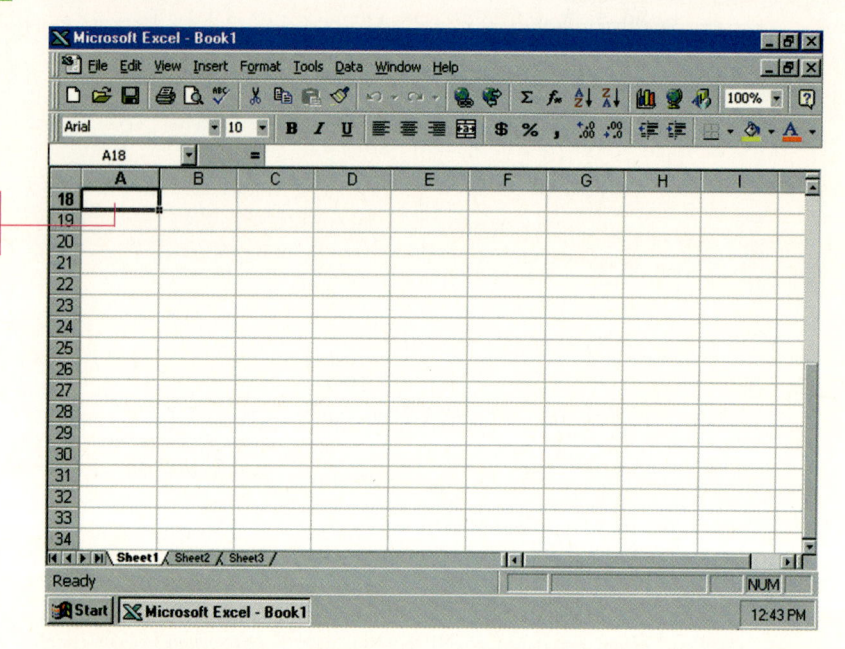

Note The monitor's size and resolution determine the number of columns and rows displayed on a screen. When you press PGDN, PGUP, ALT+PGDN, or ALT+PGUP, the active cell may be different from those shown in the illustrations.

2 Press → five times.

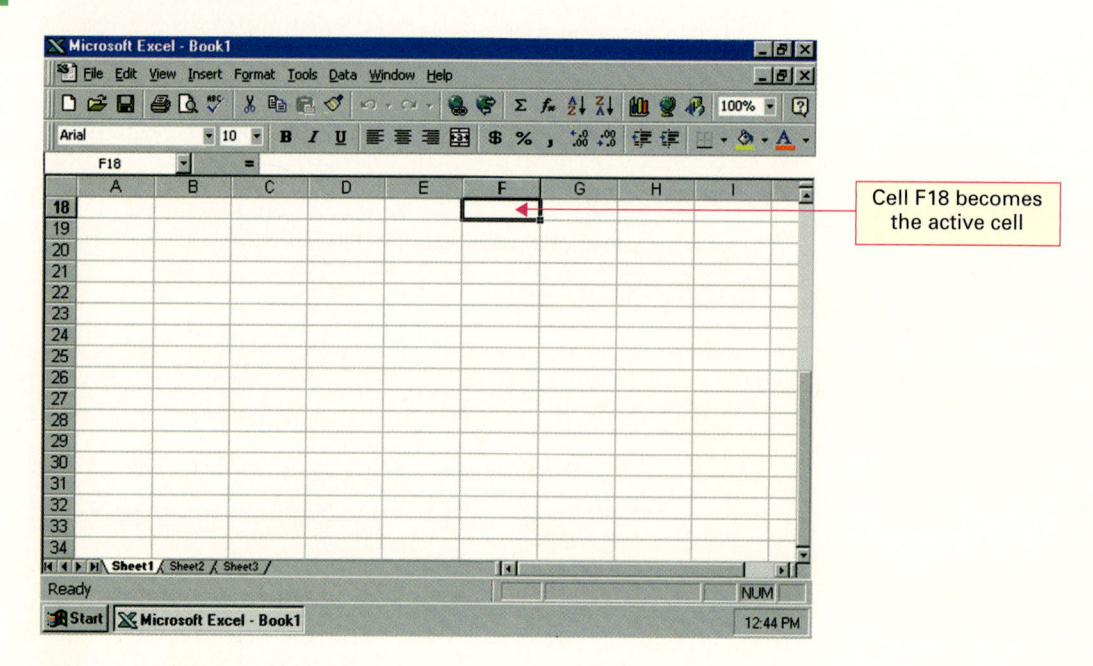

Cell F18 becomes the active cell

3 Type **88** and press ENTER.
The number displays in cell F18, and cell F19 becomes the active cell.

> **Note** Instead of pressing the ENTER key to enter data in a cell, you can press any one of the arrow keys (↑, ↓, ←, or →) or any key that moves the cell pointer, such as the PGUP key or the PGDN key. When you enter data across a row, it's more efficient to use the → key than to use the ENTER key.

4 Press CTRL+HOME.
Cell A1 becomes the active cell.

5 Drag the box in the vertical scroll bar until you see Row 4 in the ScrollTip box.

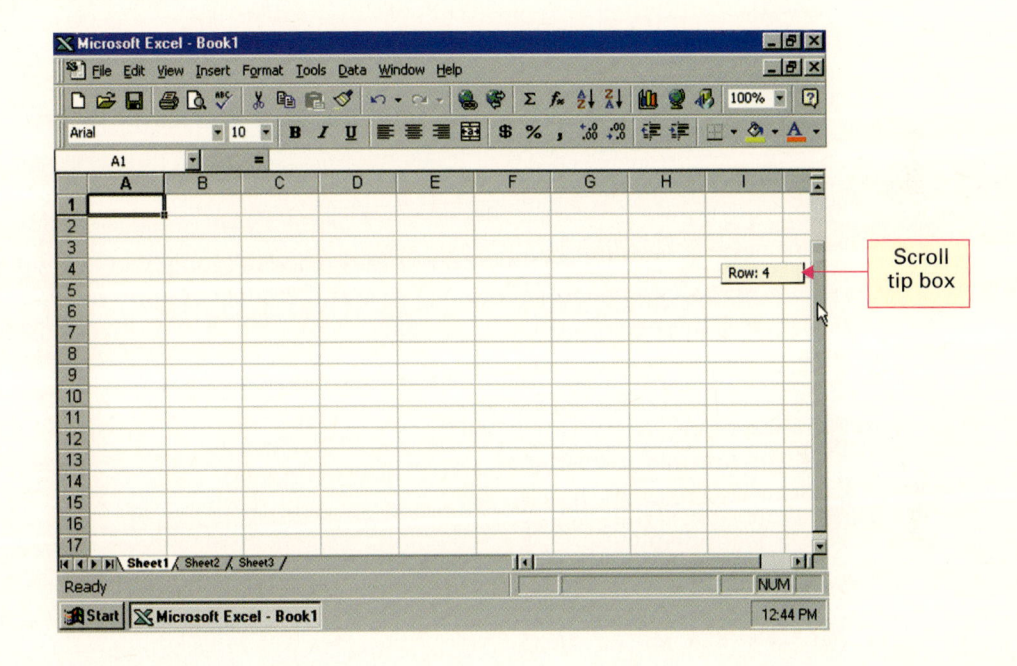

Scroll tip box

6 Click in cell D5.
Cell D5 becomes the active cell.

EX-22

7 Press CTRL+END.

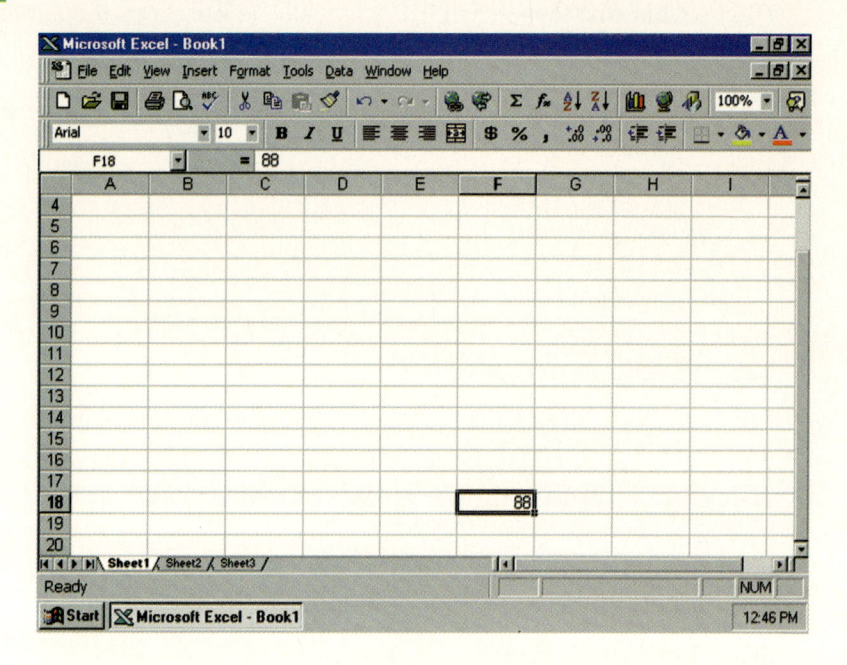

Note The lower right corner of the active worksheet is always the cell at the intersection of the last row and the last column used, and it doesn't necessarily contain data.

8 Press DEL.
The number is deleted.

9 Click the Sheet2 tab.
Sheet2 displays.

Naming Worksheets

The three worksheets created by default in a new workbook are named Sheet1, Sheet2, and Sheet3. Not very imaginative or meaningful names, are they? You can give the worksheets better names to help you identify the content of the worksheet.

TASK 3: TO NAME A WORKSHEET:

1 Point to the Sheet1 tab and right-click.

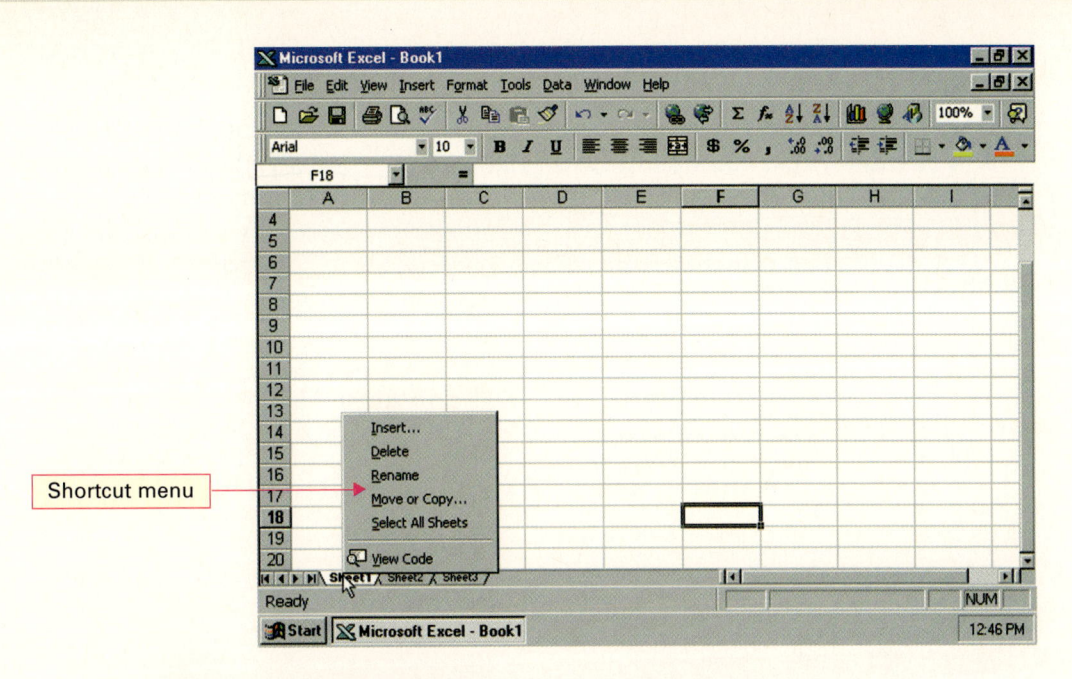

Project 1: Creating a Workbook   EX-23

Shortcut menu (screenshot of Microsoft Excel - Book1 with shortcut menu showing: Insert..., Delete, Rename, Move or Copy..., Select All Sheets, View Code)

2 Choose Rename.
The current name on the tab is highlighted.

3 Type **Atrium Cafe** and press ENTER.

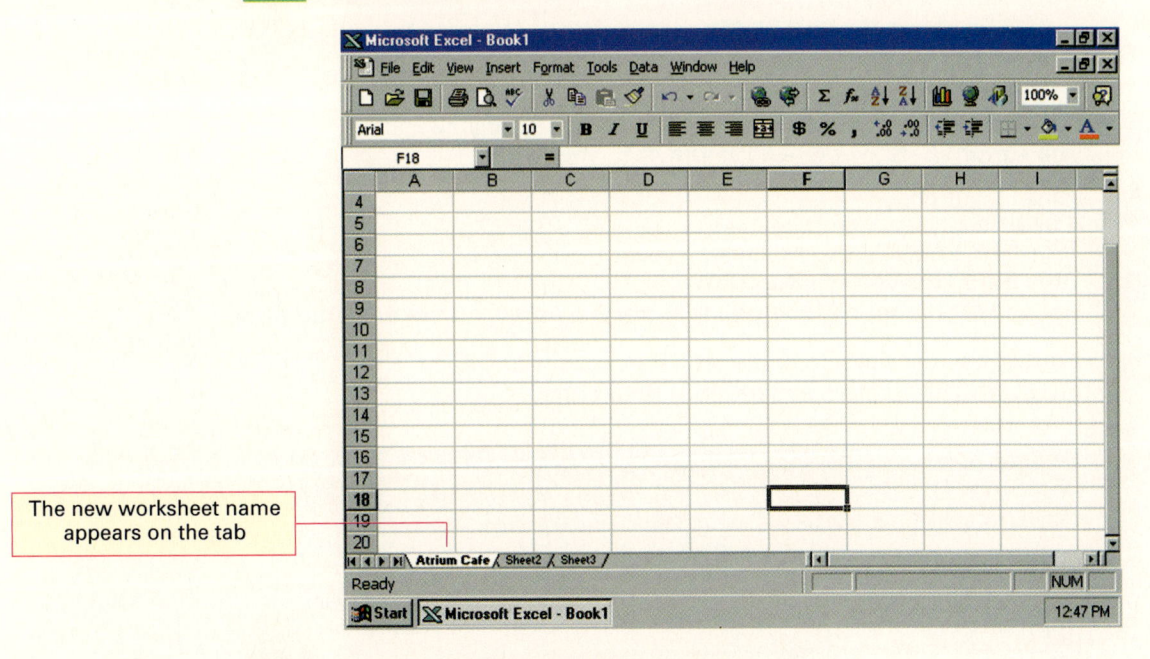

The new worksheet name appears on the tab (screenshot showing Atrium Cafe tab)

4 Point to the Sheet2 tab and right-click.
The shortcut menu displays.

5 Choose Rename.
The current name on the tab is highlighted.

6 Type **Willow Top** and press ENTER.
The name displays on the tab.

Entering Data

Excel 97 recognizes several different types of data—text, dates, numbers, and formulas. Text can include any characters on the keyboard as well as special characters such as the symbols for the British pound or the Japanese Yen. Dates can be entered with numbers separated with a slash or a dash. Numbers can include only these characters:

1 2 3 4 5 6 7 8 9 0 + − ( ) , / $ % . E

> **Tip** To enter a fraction instead of a date, precede the fraction with a zero. For example, to enter the fraction one-half, type 0 1/2 instead of 1/2 which Excel interprets as a date.

Entering Text

When you enter text in a cell, if the cell isn't wide enough to hold the text, the text will spill over into the next cell (if it's empty).

> **Tip** Any time you enter data that doesn't fit in a cell, you can widen the column and the data will display, or you can wrap the text in the cell.

TASK 4: TO ENTER DATA IN THE WORKSHEET:

1 Click the Atrium Cafe tab.
The Atrium Cafe worksheet displays.

2 Click in cell A1.
Cell A1 becomes the active cell.

3 Type **Sales for the Atrium Cafe**.
Notice that the mode changes to **Enter** because you are entering data.

4 Press (ENTER). Notice that Excel adds an accent to the "e" in "cafe" after you press the (ENTER) key to accept your data entry.

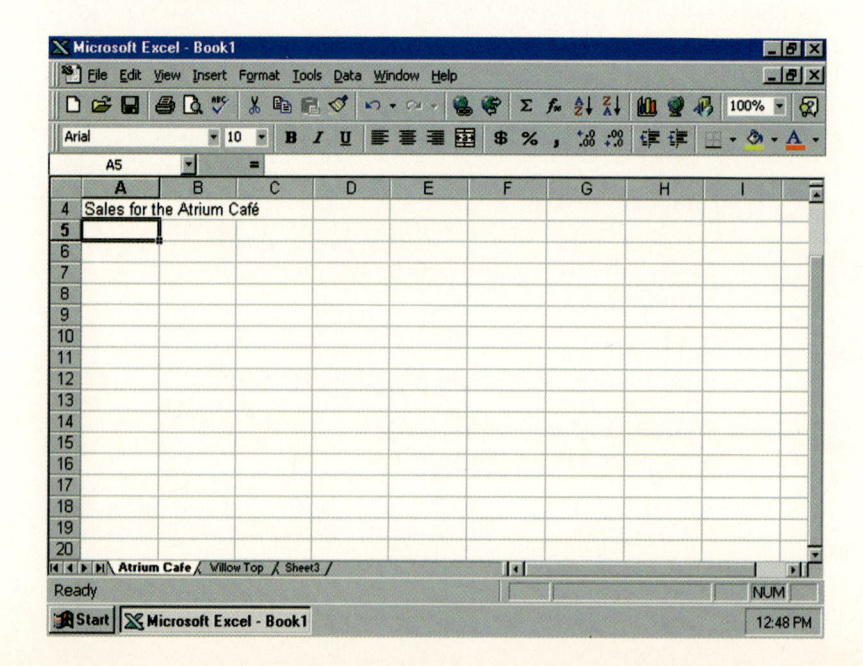

Project 1: Creating a Workbook EX-25

> **Tip** If you make a mistake while typing, simply press the Backspace key and retype the text before you press ENTER. If you change your mind about entering the data in the current cell, press ESC instead of pressing ENTER.

5 Click the Willow Top tab.
The Willow Top worksheet displays.

6 Click in cell A1 if necessary.
Cell A1 becomes the active cell.

7 Type **Sales for the Willow Top Restaurant** and press ENTER.

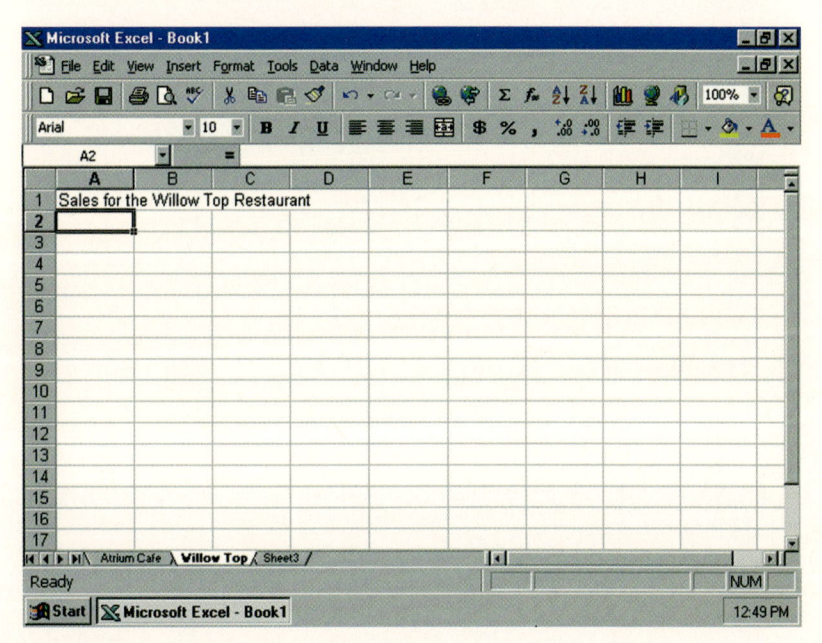

Entering Data on Multiple Worksheets

Sometimes the worksheets that you create have the same data entered several times. If the repetitive data that you are entering is text, the **Auto-Complete** feature of Excel 97 may complete the entry for you if the repetitive text appears in the same column. If the automatic completion isn't appropriate, just continue typing the text that you want.

If you are creating multiple worksheets in a workbook, you may want to use the same data for the column and row headings. To save time, you can enter the data that is the same on all worksheets at the same time.

TASK 5: TO ENTER THE SAME DATA ON MULTIPLE WORKSHEETS AT THE SAME TIME:

1 Press CTRL and click the Atrium Cafe tab.
Both the Atrium Cafe worksheet and the Willow Top worksheet are selected.

2 Click in cell B2 and type **Jan**.

EX-26

> **Note** The Group indicator displays in the title bar when multiple worksheets are selected.

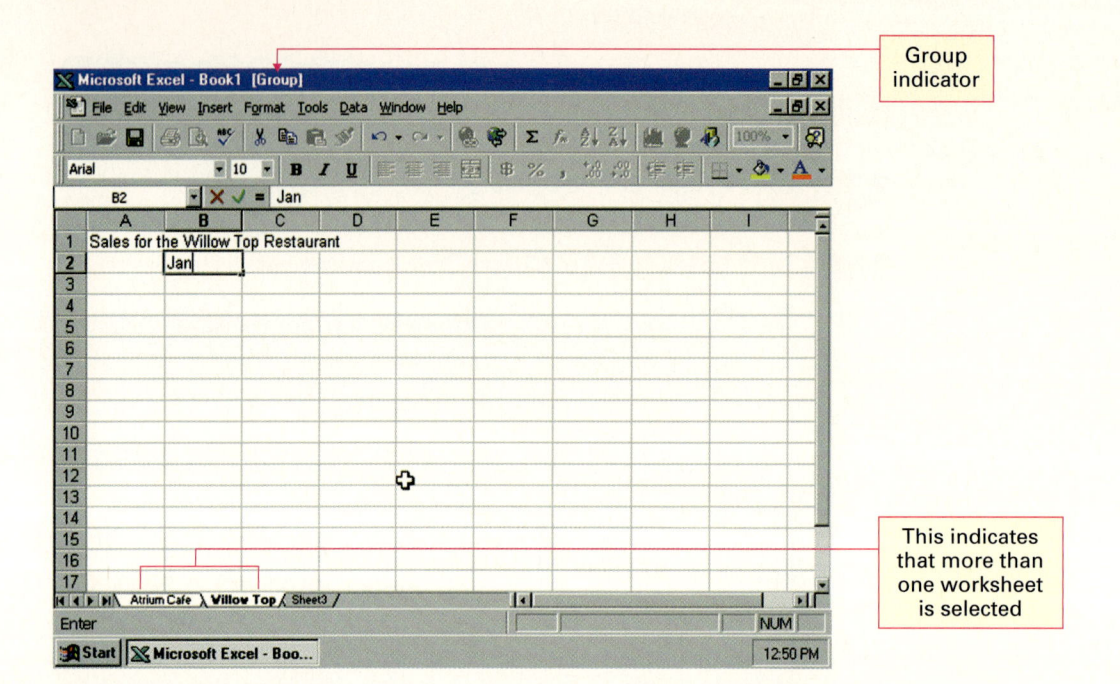

Group indicator

This indicates that more than one worksheet is selected

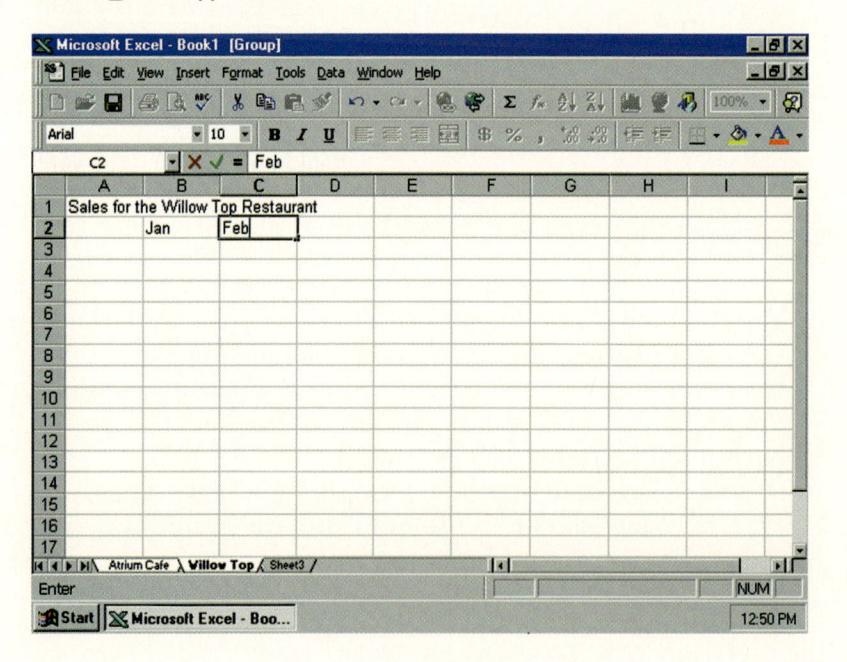

3 Press → and type **Feb**.

Project 1: Creating a Workbook EX-27

4 Press → and type **Difference**.

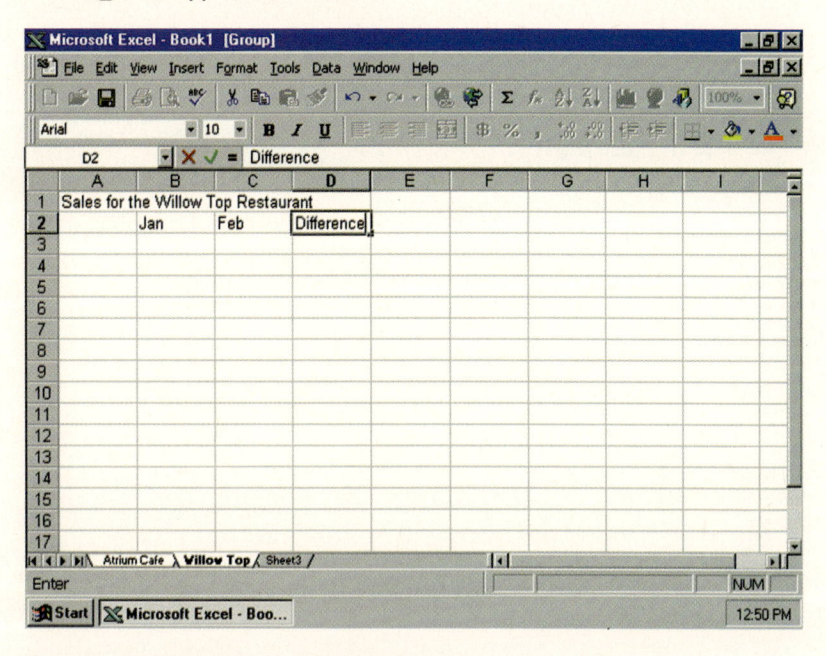

5 Click in cell A3 and type **Week 1**.

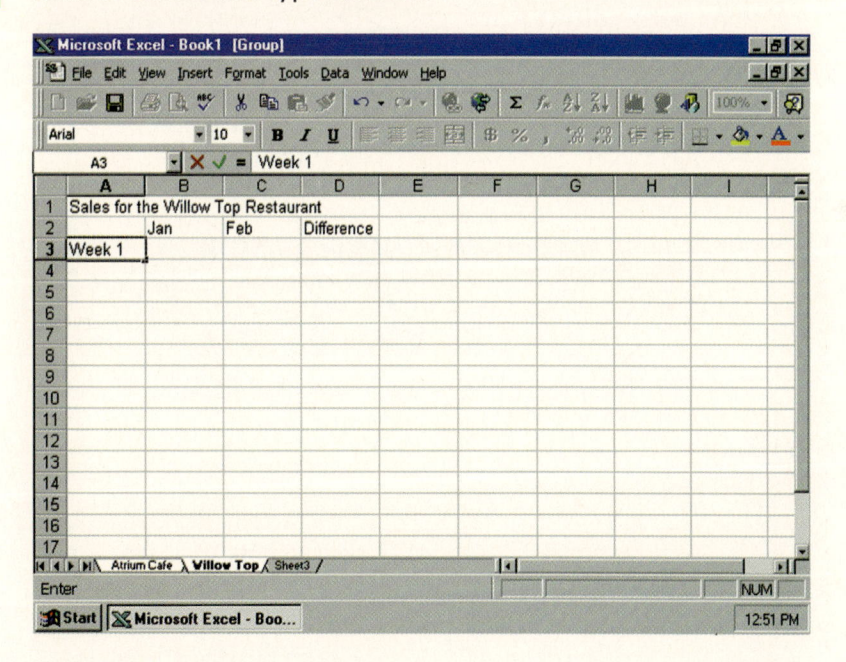

6 Press (ENTER) and type **Week**.
The AutoComplete feature completes the entry as Week 1.

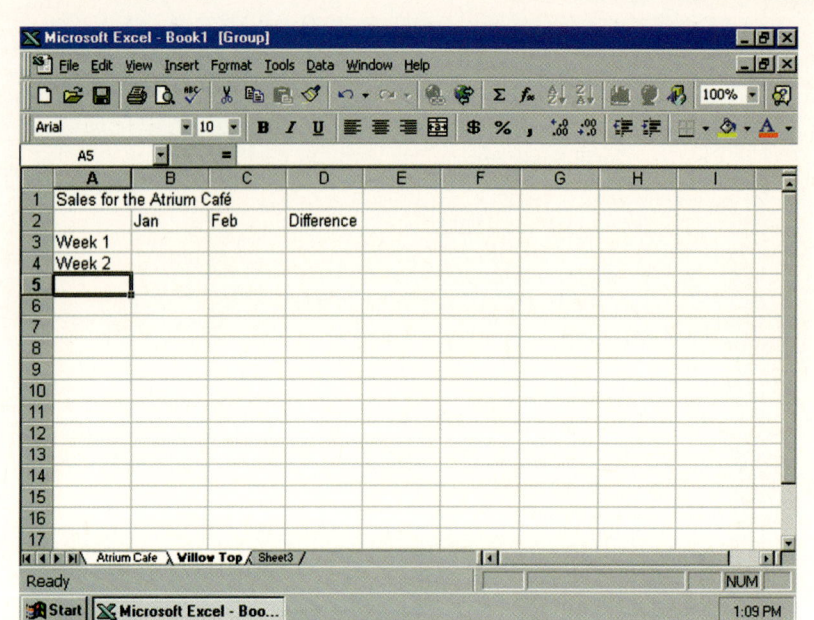

7 Continue typing so that the entry is "Week 2" and then press ENTER.

8 Click in cell A4.
Cell A4 becomes the active cell.

9 Point to the handle in the lower right corner of the cell.

> **Note** The pointer appears as a plus when you point to the handle.

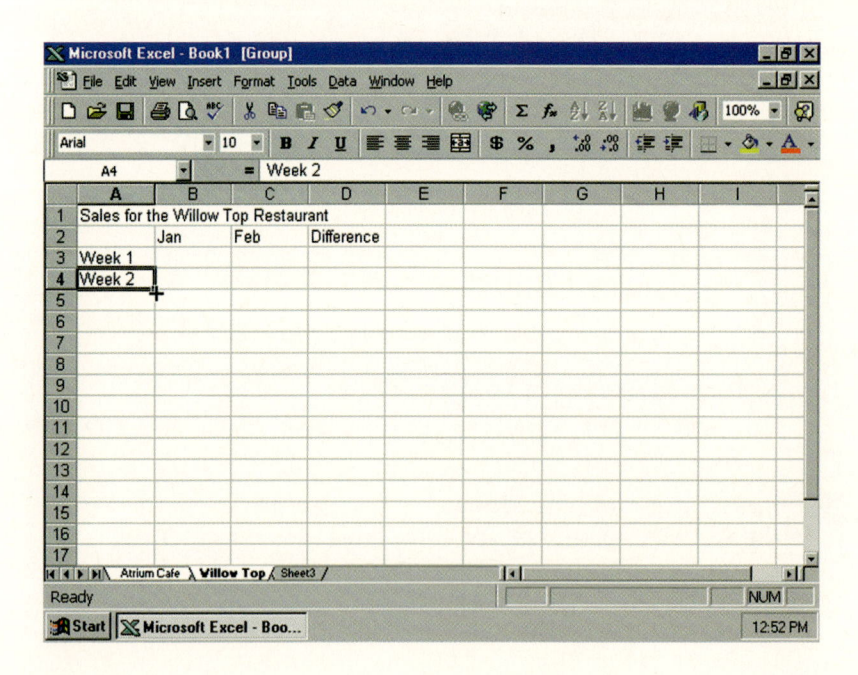

Project 1: Creating a Workbook   EX-29

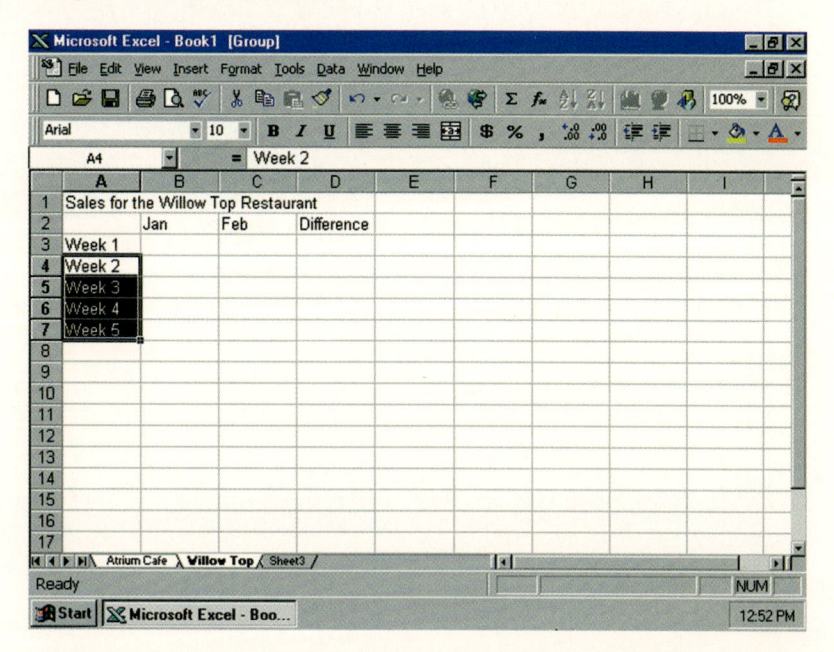

10 Drag the handle to cell A7.

Tip You can use the dragging technique to enter almost any type of series (except the World Series, of course).

11 Click in cell A8, type **Total** and press (ENTER).

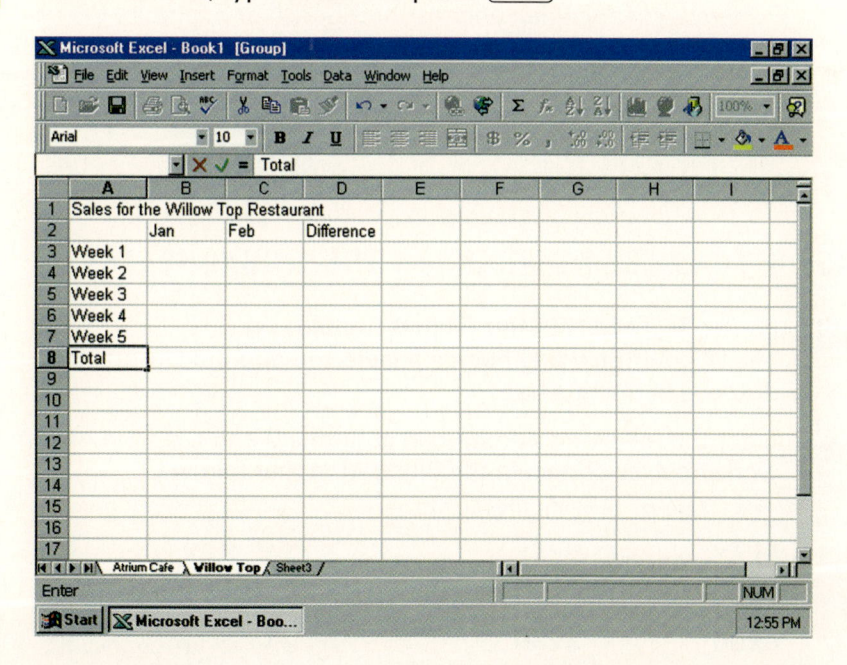

12 Click the Atrium Cafe tab to verify that the information appears on both worksheets.

EX-30

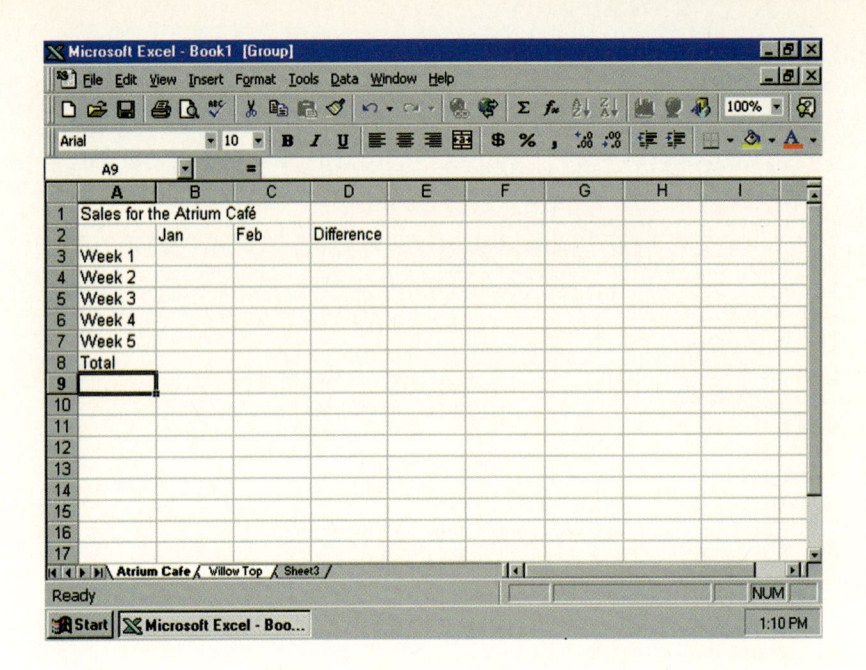

[Screenshot of Microsoft Excel - Book1 [Group] showing worksheet with "Sales for the Atrium Café" in A1, "Jan" in B2, "Feb" in C2, "Difference" in D2, and "Week 1" through "Week 5" and "Total" in A3:A8. Sheet tabs show Atrium Cafe, Willow Top, Sheet3.]

Entering Numbers

If you enter a number that doesn't fit in a cell, Excel 97 either converts the number to *scientific notation* or displays pound signs (#) in the cell. If you enter a date that doesn't fit in a cell, Excel 97 displays pound signs.

> **Note** Scientific notation is a number format used for very large numbers and very small decimal numbers. For example, the scientific notation for 1,000,000,000 is 1E+09 which means 1 times 10 to the ninth power. Perhaps our government should consider using scientific notation to express the national debt; maybe it wouldn't look so bad.

TASK 6: TO ENTER NUMBERS IN THE WORKSHEETS:

1. Press CTRL and click the Willow Top tab.
   The Willow Top worksheet is deselected and the Group indicator no longer displays in the title bar.

2. Enter the following numbers in columns B and C on the Atrium Cafe worksheet, as shown in the illustration that follows.

COLUMN B	COLUMN C
6570	2200
8345	7890
8650	9180
8990	8750
2130	4560

Project 1: Creating a Workbook EX-31

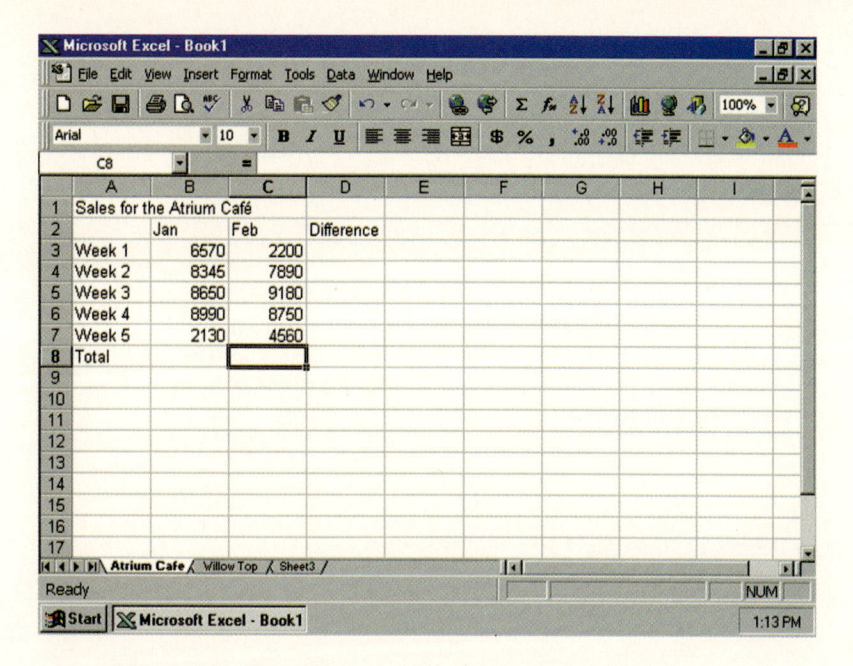

[Screenshot of Microsoft Excel - Book1 showing the Atrium Cafe worksheet:]

	A	B	C	D
1	Sales for the Atrium Café			
2		Jan	Feb	Difference
3	Week 1	6570	2200	
4	Week 2	8345	7890	
5	Week 3	8650	9180	
6	Week 4	8990	8750	
7	Week 5	2130	4560	
8	Total			

3 Click the Willow Top tab.
The Willow Top worksheet displays.

4 Enter the following numbers in columns B and C on the Willow Top worksheet:

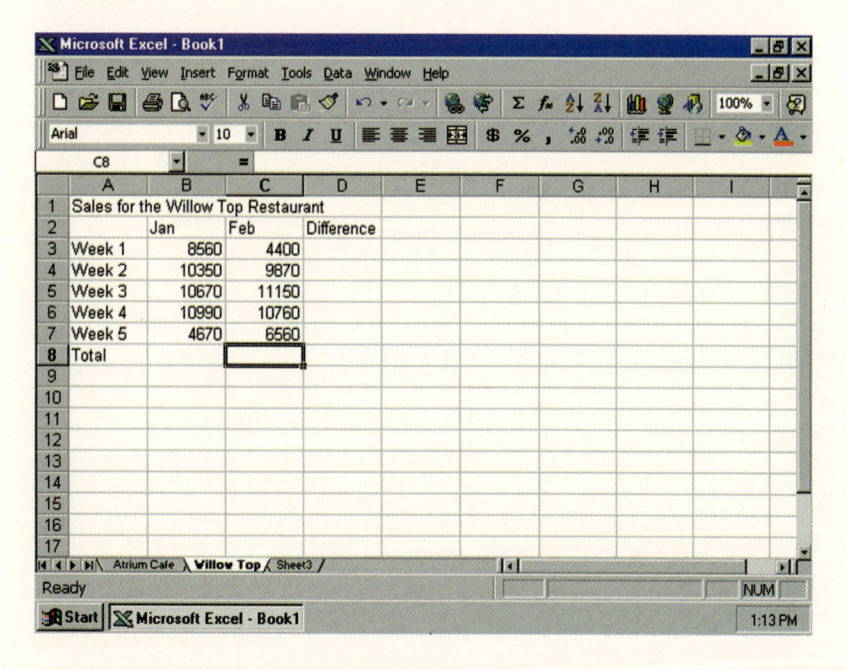

[Screenshot of Microsoft Excel - Book1 showing the Willow Top worksheet:]

	A	B	C	D
1	Sales for the Willow Top Restaurant			
2		Jan	Feb	Difference
3	Week 1	8560	4400	
4	Week 2	10350	9870	
5	Week 3	10670	11150	
6	Week 4	10990	10760	
7	Week 5	4670	6560	
8	Total			

Entering Simple Formulas and Functions

Formulas and *functions* are mathematical statements that perform calculations. Formulas are made up and entered by the user to perform the specific calculation needed. Functions are formulas that are included in Excel 97. They perform calculations that are commonly used such as calculating a sum or an average. Functions require specific information, called *arguments*, to perform the calculations. Formulas and functions must start with the equal sign (=), and they can contain cell addresses, numbers, and *arithmetic operators*. Table 1.3 describes the arithmetic operators and gives examples. Table 1.4 lists some of the commonly used functions.

> **Tip** Some formulas and functions refer to a block of cells, called a *range*. The address of a range includes the first and last cells in the range separated by a colon. For example, the address of the range from cell A1 through cell B10 is A1:B10.

Table 1.3 Arithmetic Operators

Operator	Meaning	Example	Result (if A1 = 20 and A2 = 2)
+	Addition	=A1+A2	22
−	Subtraction	=A1−A2	18
*	Multiplication	=A1*10	200
/	Division	=A1/A2	10
%	Percent	=A1%	.2
^	Exponentiation	=A1^A2	400

Table 1.4 Commonly Used Functions

Function	Meaning	Example	Result (if A1 = 1, A2 = 2 and A3 = 3)
=SUM(*argument*)	Calculates the sum of the cells in the argument	=SUM(A1:A3)	6
=AVERAGE(*argument*)	Calculates the average of the cells in the argument	=AVERAGE(A1:A3)	2
=MAX(*argument*)	Finds the largest value in the cells in the argument	=MAX(A1:A3)	3
=MIN(*argument*)	Finds the smallest value of the cells in the argument	=MIN(A1:A3)	1
=COUNT(*argument*)	Counts the number of cells in the argument that have a numeric value	=COUNT(A1:A3)	3

Project 1: Creating a Workbook EX-33

TASK 7: TO ENTER FORMULAS AND FUNCTIONS:

1 Press CTRL and click the Atrium Cafe tab.
Both worksheets are selected, and the data you enter will display on both worksheets. Notice that the Group indicator displays in the title bar.

2 Click in cell D3 and click the equal sign in the formula bar. (If the Office Assistant opens, choose No, don't provide help now.)

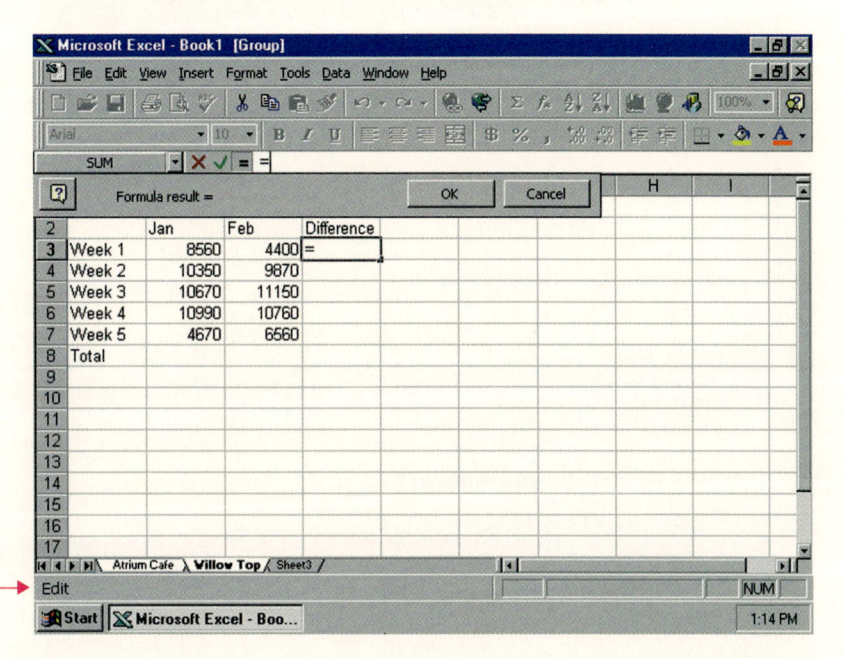

The mode changes to Edit because the data is being entered in the formula bar

3 Click in cell B3.
The mode changes to **Point** because you are pointing to cells to build the formula.

4 Type a minus sign (−).

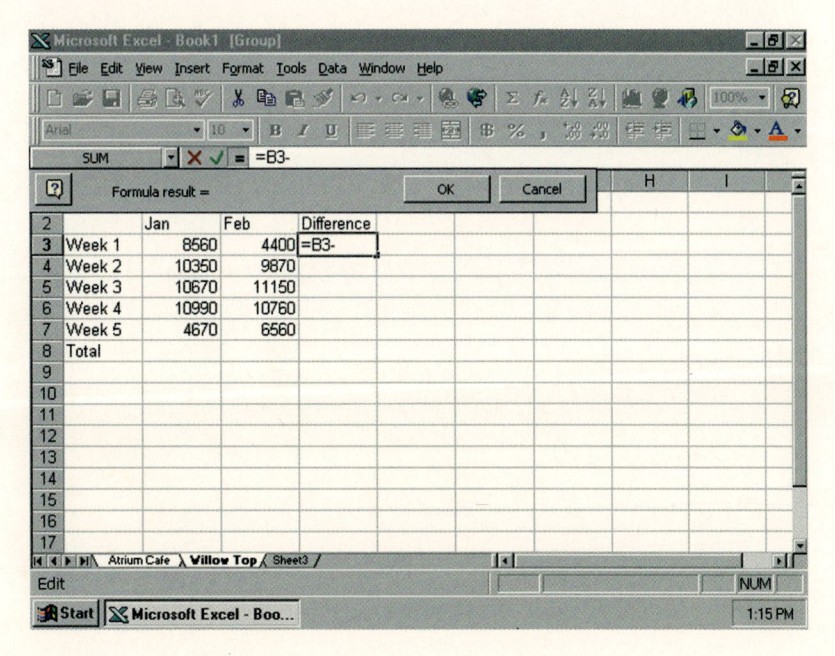

EX-34

5 Click in cell C3 and then click the Enter ✓ button in the formula bar.

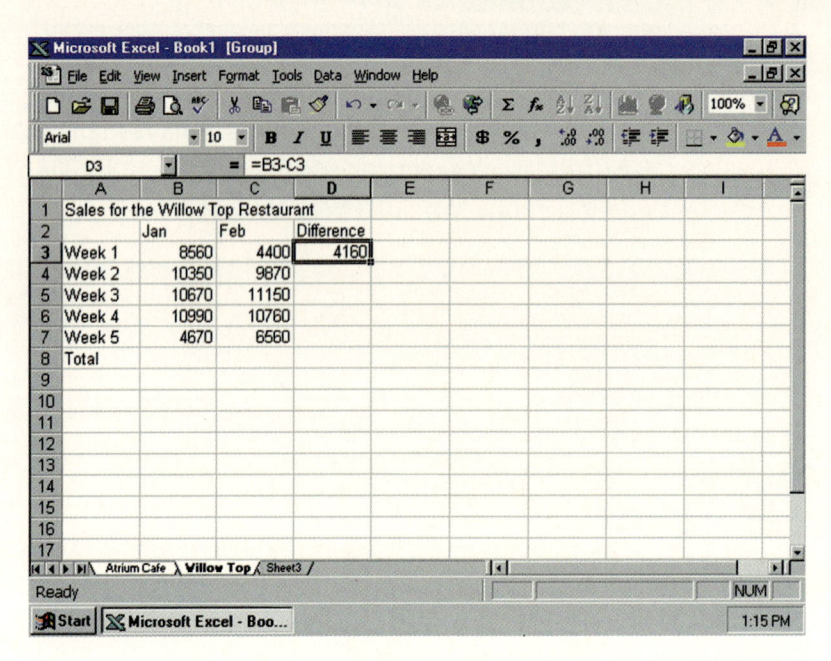

6 Click in cell B8 and type **=sum(**

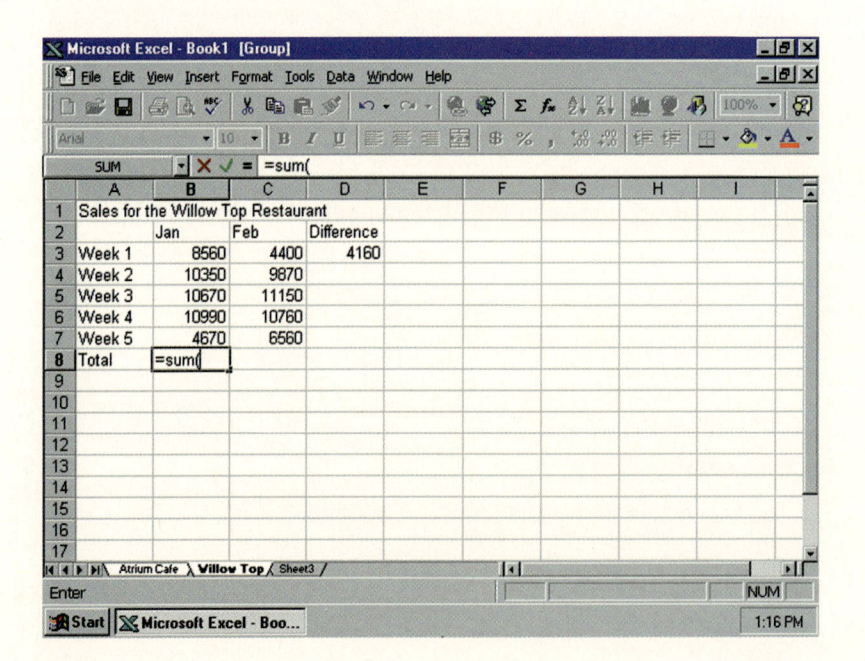

Project 1: Creating a Workbook   EX-35

7 Drag the cursor from cell B3 through cell B7.

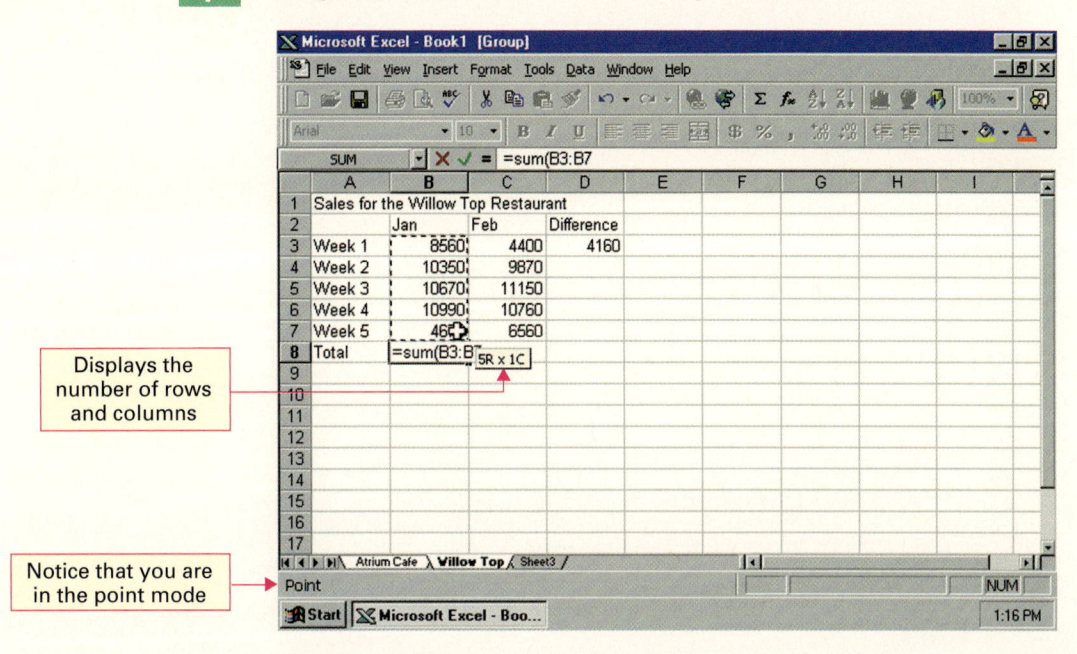

Displays the number of rows and columns

Notice that you are in the point mode

8 Press ENTER.

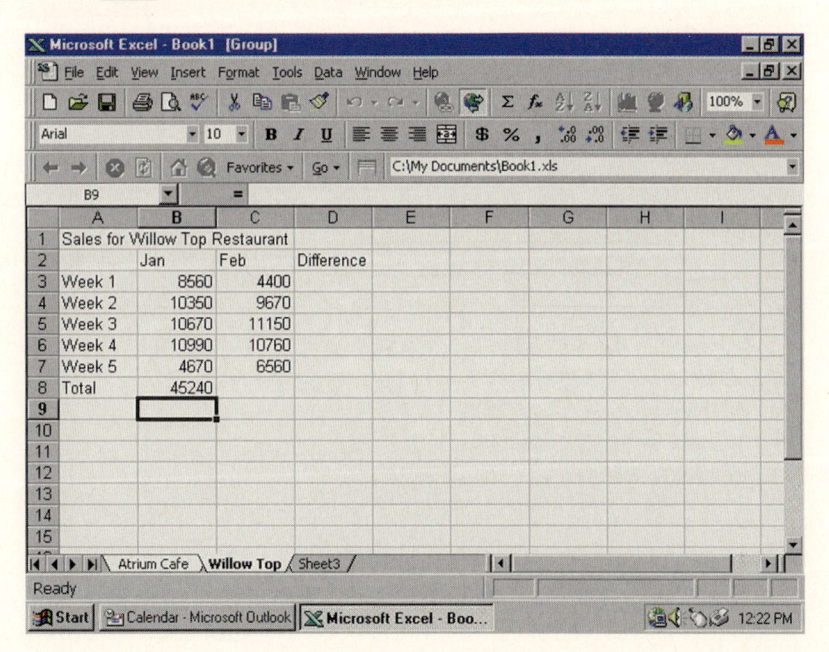

9 Click in cell C8 and click the AutoSum Σ button on the Standard toolbar.

EX-36

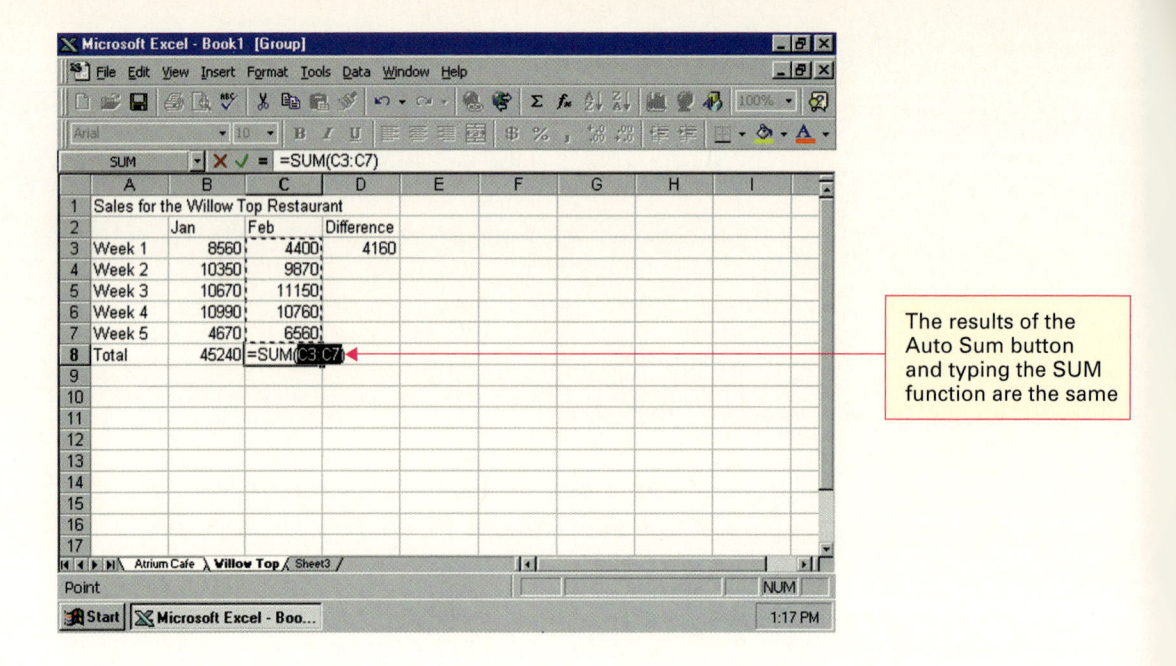

[Screenshot of Microsoft Excel - Book1 [Group] showing the Willow Top worksheet with Sales data. Cell C8 shows =SUM(C3:C7) being entered. Callout: "The results of the Auto Sum button and typing the SUM function are the same"]

10 Press ENTER.
The numbers in column C are totaled.

> **Note** If you change a number in a cell, Excel 97 automatically recalculates all formulas or functions that might be affected.

> **Key Concept** When a formula has more than one operation, Excel 97 follows an *order of precedence* to determine the sequence in which each operation should be performed. The order is as follows: exponentiation first, then multiplication or division (from left to right), and finally addition or subtraction (from left to right). If the formula has parentheses, the operation(s) in the parentheses are performed first. You can use the phrase "Please excuse my dear Aunt Sally" to remember "p" for parentheses, "e" for exponent, "m" for multiplication, "d" for division, "a" for addition, and "s" for subtraction.

Saving a Workbook

If you want to keep the data that you have entered in a workbook, you must save the file. When saving the file, you specify a name for the document and a location where it will be stored.

> **Tip** Because Excel 97 a 32-bit program, the name of a workbook can be a *long filename.* Long filenames (including the full path of the file) can use up to 255 characters. Although you can use as many spaces and periods in the filename as you want, you can't use ? or : or *. Older versions of Excel prior to Excel 7.0 do NOT use long filenames and will convert a long filename to eight characters (plus the extension).

Project 1: Creating a Workbook   EX-37

TASK 8: TO SAVE A WORKBOOK:

1 Click the Atrium Cafe tab if it isn't the displayed worksheet.
The Atrium Cafe worksheet displays.

2 Press CTRL and click the Willow Top tab.
The Willow Top worksheet is deselected.

> **Tip** When you are ready to save and close a workbook and you have more than one worksheet selected, you might want to deselect all but one worksheet by pressing CTRL and clicking the tabs you want to deselect. If you don't deselect worksheets, the next time you open the workbook, the worksheets will still be selected and any changes you make will be made on all worksheets if you don't notice the Group indicator.

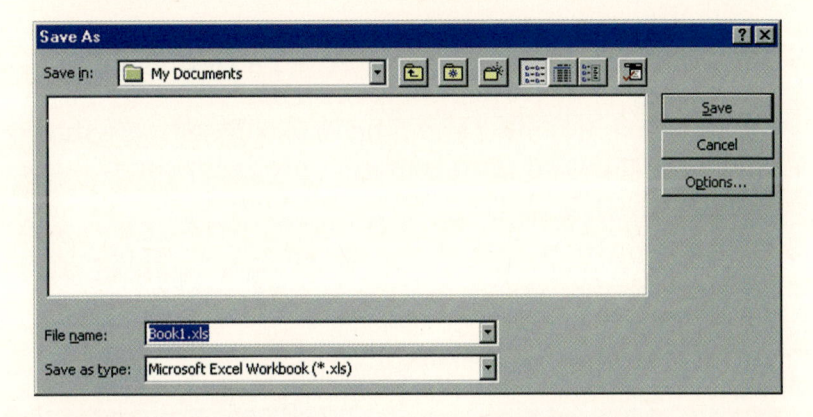

3 Click the Save button.

4 Type **Restaurant Sales** in the File Name text box.
Excel 97 adds the default extension xls to the filename when the file is saved.

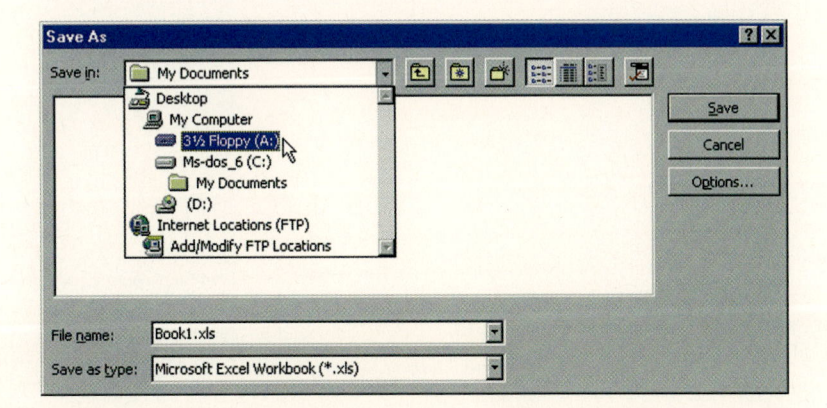

5 Click the down arrow in the Save In text box and choose drive A: (or the drive and folder designated by your professor or lab assistant).

6 Click Save.
The dialog box closes, the file is saved on the disk, and the title bar displays the name of the file.

Tip After saving a file for the first time, you should save the document periodically as you continue to work on it in case your system goes down for some reason. After a file has a name, you can save the file again simply by clicking the Save button.

Note To save a file in a different location or with a different name, choose File, Save As.

Previewing and Printing a Worksheet

Before you print a file, you should preview it to see if it looks like what you expect. (You don't want any surprises.) The *Print Preview* shows the full page of the current worksheet and allows you to zoom in on the worksheet so you can actually read the data, if necessary.

You can print a worksheet in the Print Preview mode or in Normal view. Clicking the Print button prints one copy of the complete workbook. If you want to print only part of the workbook or more than one copy, you should use the Print command from the File menu because it allows you to make selections from the Print dialog box.

TASK 9: TO PREVIEW AND PRINT A WORKSHEET:

1. Click the Print Preview button on the Standard toolbar.

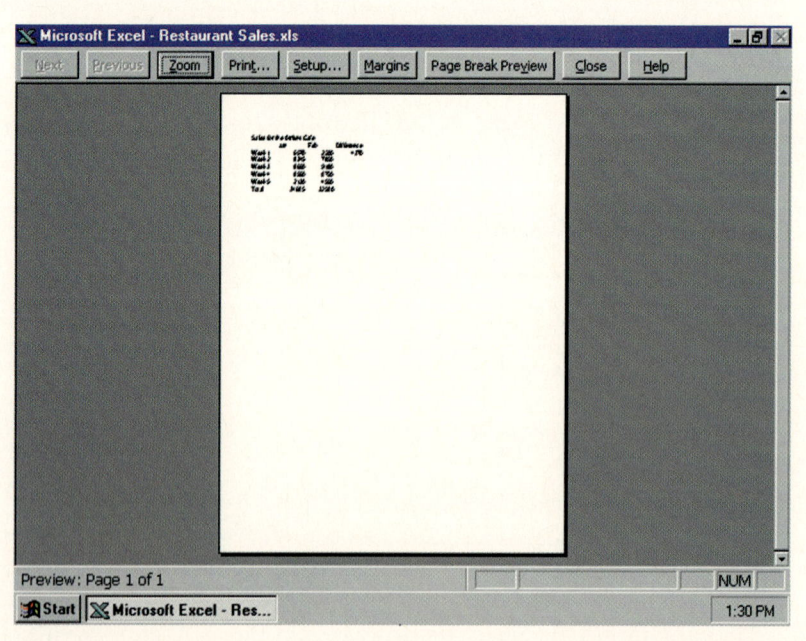

2. Click the pointer, now shaped like a magnifying glass, at the top of the worksheet.

Project 1: Creating a Workbook   EX-39

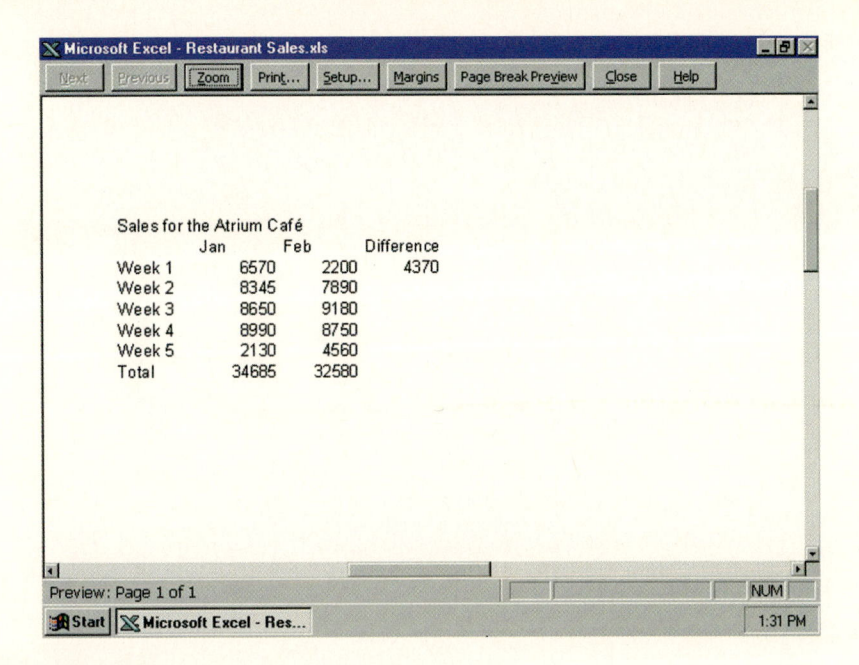

3 Click again.
The full page displays again.

4 Click Close in the Print Preview toolbar.
The Print Preview mode closes and the worksheet screen displays.

5 Ensure that the computer you are using is attached to a printer and that the printer is online.

6 Choose File from the menu bar.

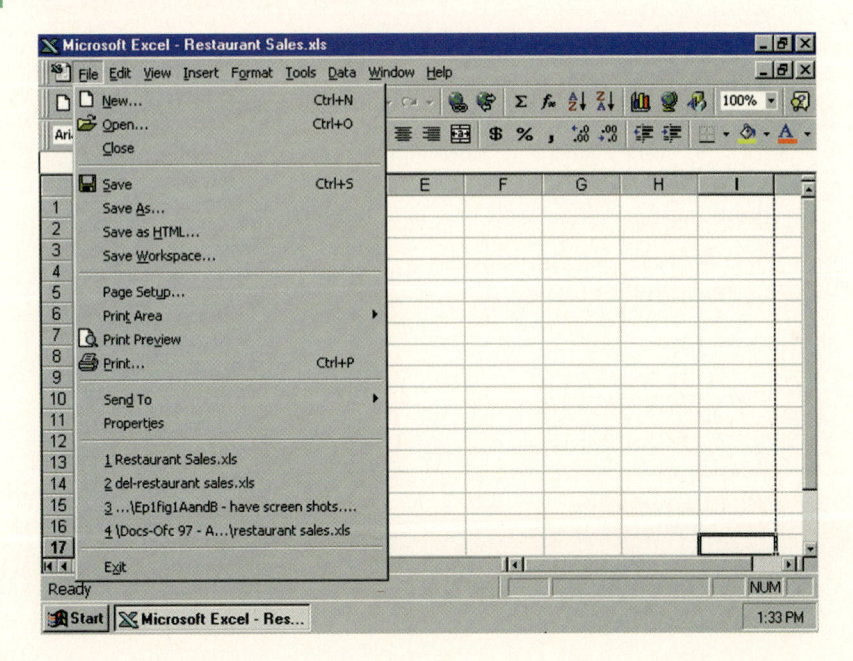

EX-40

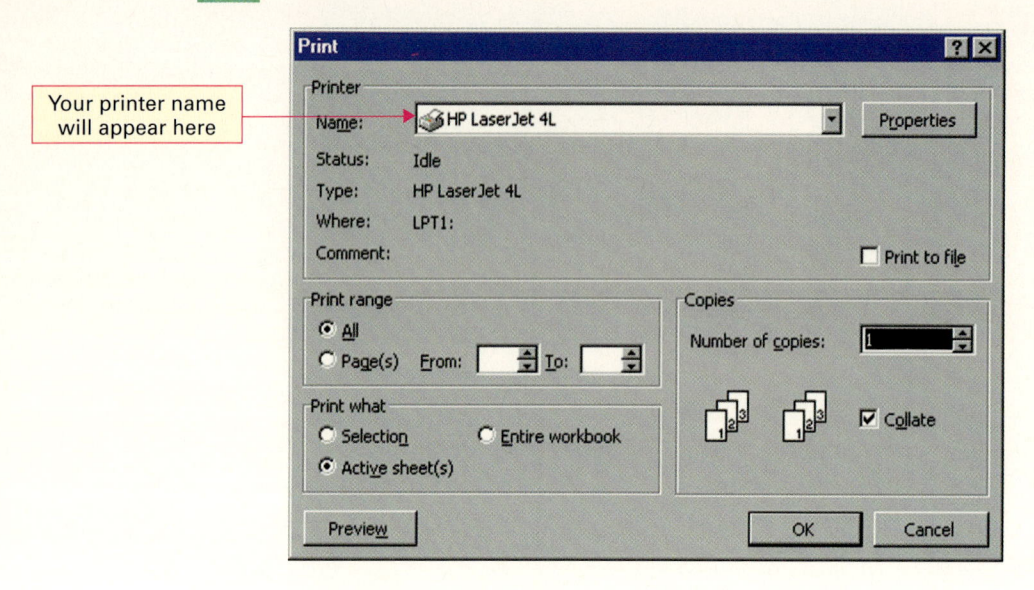

7 Choose Print.

> Your printer name will appear here

8 Click OK.
The workbook prints.

Closing a Workbook

When you are finished with a workbook, you can close it. If you have made changes that you want to keep, you should save the workbook before closing it. If you forget to save a workbook before closing, Excel 97 asks if you want to save changes.

TASK 11: TO SAVE AND CLOSE A FILE:

1 Click 🖫.
The worksheet is saved.

2 Click ✖ on the Menu bar.
The file closes.

The Conclusion

You can exit Excel 97 now by clicking ✖ on the application title bar, or you can work on the Review Exercises and Assignments.

Summary and Exercises

Summary

- When you launch Excel 97 a workbook named Book1 is created automatically.
- To enter data in a worksheet, the cell pointer must be positioned in the desired cell.
- By default, a new workbook has three worksheets.
- Excel 97 recognizes several different types of data: text, dates, numbers, and formulas.
- Formulas and functions are mathematical statements that perform calculations.
- Files can be saved with long filenames.
- Before you print a worksheet, you can preview it to see if it looks acceptable.
- When you close a file, if you haven't saved changes to the file, Excel 97 asks if you want to save the changes.

Key Terms and Operations

Key Terms
active cell
arithmetic operators
AutoComplete
Edit mode
Enter mode
formula
function
order of precedence
Point mode
Print Preview mode
range
scientific notation

Operations
close a workbook
create a workbook
enter data
enter formulas and functions
move in a workbook
name a workbook
name a worksheet
preview a worksheet
print a worksheet
save a workbook

Study Questions

Multiple Choice

1. Using the order of precedence, solve the formula 5−2*(8+2). What is the answer?
   a. 26
   b. −15
   c. −9
   d. 30

2. To move to the cell below the active cell, press
   a. ENTER.
   b. PGDN.
   c. TAB.
   d. CTRL+↓.

3. Which of the following is a range address?
   a. D1;D10
   b. D1,D10
   c. D1 D10
   d. D1:D10

4. Which of the following cannot be included in numeric data?
   a. 1
   b. 2
   c. E
   d. =

5. Which of the following is an example of scientific notation?
   a. 1.5E+11
   b. 1^10
   c. 7.8!
   d. $A$2

6. If A1 is 10, A2 is 15, and A3 is 20, what is the result of =SUM(A1:A2)?
   a. 10
   b. 15
   c. 25
   d. 45

7. If A1 is 10, A2 is 15, and A3 is 20, what is the result of =AVERAGE(A1:A3)?
   a. 10
   b. 15
   c. 25
   d. 45

8. If A1 is 10, A2 is 15, A3 is 20, and A4 says "Total," what is the result of =COUNT(A1:A4)?
   a. 3
   b. 15
   c. 45
   d. 4

9. The Preview mode shows
   a. all pages of a workbook.
   b. the current page of the workbook.
   c. the formulas.
   d. the formulas and functions.

10. When you press CTRL+END, what cell becomes the active cell?
    a. IV65536
    b. The last cell in the current column.
    c. The cell in the lower right corner.
    d. The cell in the lower right corner of the active area of the worksheet.

Short Answer

1. What happens when you change a number in a cell that is included in a formula?

2. What should you do before you close a workbook?

3. How do you rename a worksheet?

4. What is the order of precedence?

5. What displays in a cell if you enter 1/10?

6. How can you make 1/10 display as a fraction in a cell?

7. Write the formula to add the numbers from cell A1 through cell A5.

8. Write the function to add the numbers from cell A1 through cell A5.

9. How do you enter the same data on more than one worksheet?

10. What function finds the smallest value?

For Discussion

1. Describe a situation in which you would use several worksheets in the same workbook.

2. The cell displays #######. What caused the problem and how can you solve it?

3. Discuss the reasons you might rename worksheets in a workbook.

4. What is a range and how is it addressed?

Review Exercises

1. Creating an expense account

Your good friend Karl Klaus, the head chef at the 4-star restaurant in *The Grande Hotel*, has asked you to create an expense report for him because he can't type. In this exercise, you will create a worksheet that lists the expenses Karl had on a recent trip for the hotel.

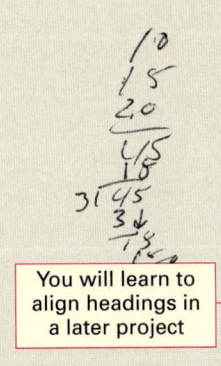

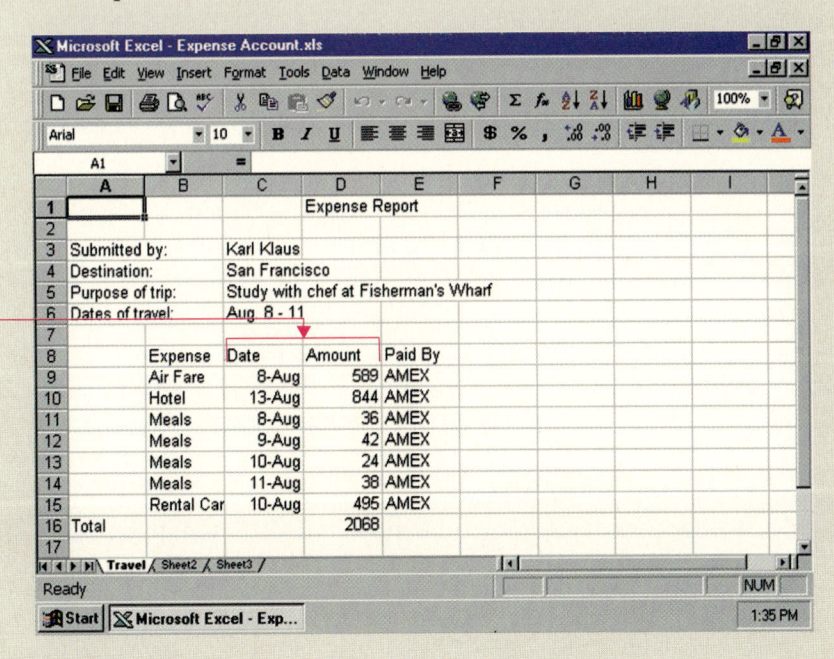

Figure 1.3

1. Create a new workbook.

2. Rename Sheet1 to Travel.

3. Enter the data shown in Figure 1.3 except for Row 16.

> **Note** The format for dates might be different on your computer.

4. Use the AutoSum button to calculate the total expenses.

5. Save the workbook as *Expense Account.xls*.

2. Calculating savings

In this exercise, you will use a worksheet to calculate the amount of money you will have in twenty years, based on different variables such as the amount you can save each year and the rate of interest you earn.

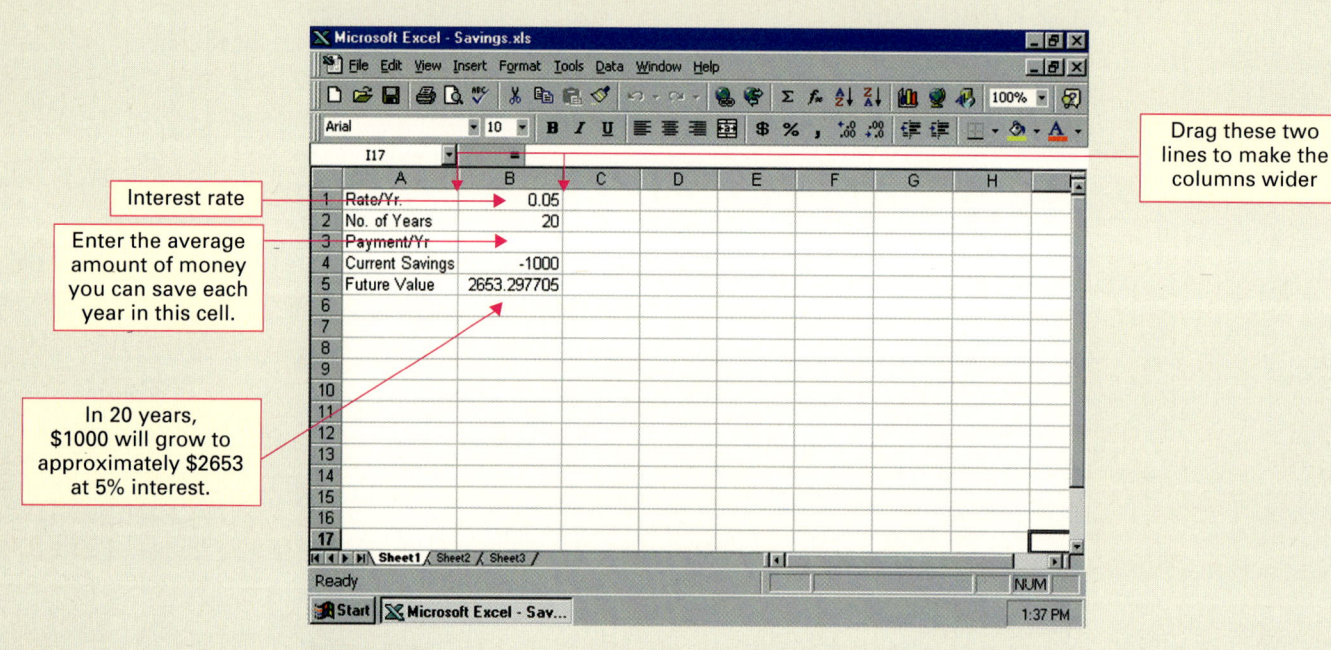

Figure 1.4

1. Go to this address on the Web:
   http://www.finaid.org/finaid/calculators/finaid_calc.html.

2. Select the Savings Plan Designer.

3. If you currently have $1000 in savings and you can get 5 percent interest, how much will you have to save each month to have $200,000 in 20 years?

4. Create a new worksheet and enter the data for A1, A2, A3, A4, A5, B1, B2, and B4 as shown in Figure 1.4. Be sure to enter the data in the same cells shown in the figure.

> **Note** The values for current savings is a negative number due to the use of debits and credits in standard accounting procedures.

5. In cell B5, type this function: =FV(B1,B2,B3,B4,1).

6. In cell B3, enter the number that is 12 times the answer you got in step 3. Precede the number with a minus sign. The answer in cell B5 should be approximately 200,000.

7. Change the Payment/Yr amount to −2000 and change the Rate/Yr to .15.

8. Save the worksheet as *Savings.xls*.

3. Creating a sales analysis worksheet

1. Launch Excel 97, if necessary, or create a new blank workbook.

2. Create the worksheet displayed in Figure 1.5.

> **Tip** The product description of rows 5–7 contains the word cardboard.

	A	B	C	D	E
1	Multi-Size Container Corporation				
2	Sales Analysis				
3					
4	Product #	Product	Actual	Expected	Actual-Expected
5	3-453	3" Cardboa	145300	156900	
6	3-455	5" Cardboa	132900	186700	
7	3-457	7" Cardboa	865330	163300	
8	5-852	2" Glass	655900	567000	
9	5-854	4" Glass	754980	641500	
10					

Figure 1.5

3. Name the worksheet *<Current year> Sales*, substituting the current year as indicated.

4. Save the workbook using the filename *Container Corporation Sales xxx* (where *xxx* represents your initials).

5. Add a formula to Column E that calculates the difference between the actual sales and the amount expected.

6. Add a formula to Row 10 that calculates the total actual sales, the total expected sales, and the total difference.

7. Save the changes to the workbook and print a copy of the worksheet.

8. Close the workbook and exit Excel.

Assignments

1. Creating a timesheet
Create a workbook with a worksheet for each of your classes. List the dates and the number of hours that you spend for each class (including class time, lab time, and homework) in a week. Total the number of hours. Save the worksheets and workbook, using an appropriate filename.

2. Creating a worksheet that compares menu prices
Go to http://www.metrodine.com and follow links to find restaurant menus that list entrees and prices. Search for "menu." Create a worksheet that lists the entrees and prices for at least two restaurants. Use the MIN and MAX functions to show the lowest and highest priced entree for each restaurant. Save the worksheets and workbook, using an appropriate filename.

PROJECT 2

Editing a Workbook

Moving a title to a different location, deleting last week's totals, copying this month's totals to the summary worksheet, adding comments to a cell, checking the spelling — an Excel user's work is never done! In this project, you will edit a workbook and modify the data using some basic editing tasks.

Objectives

After completing this project, you will be able to:

- ▶ Open a workbook
- ▶ Find data
- ▶ Edit data
- ▶ Work with data
- ▶ Add comments
- ▶ Check spelling

The Challenge

Mr. Gilmore was impressed at how quickly you created his "down-and-dirty" worksheet, but he wants a few changes made to it. Specifically, he wants you to add some comments and create a new worksheet that includes the January sales figures from both restaurants.

The Solution

To make the changes Mr. Gilmore wants, you will open the Restaurant Sales workbook, revise some of the data, move and copy some of the cells, add comments, and check the spelling. The finished workbook will look like Figure 2.1.

EX-**48**

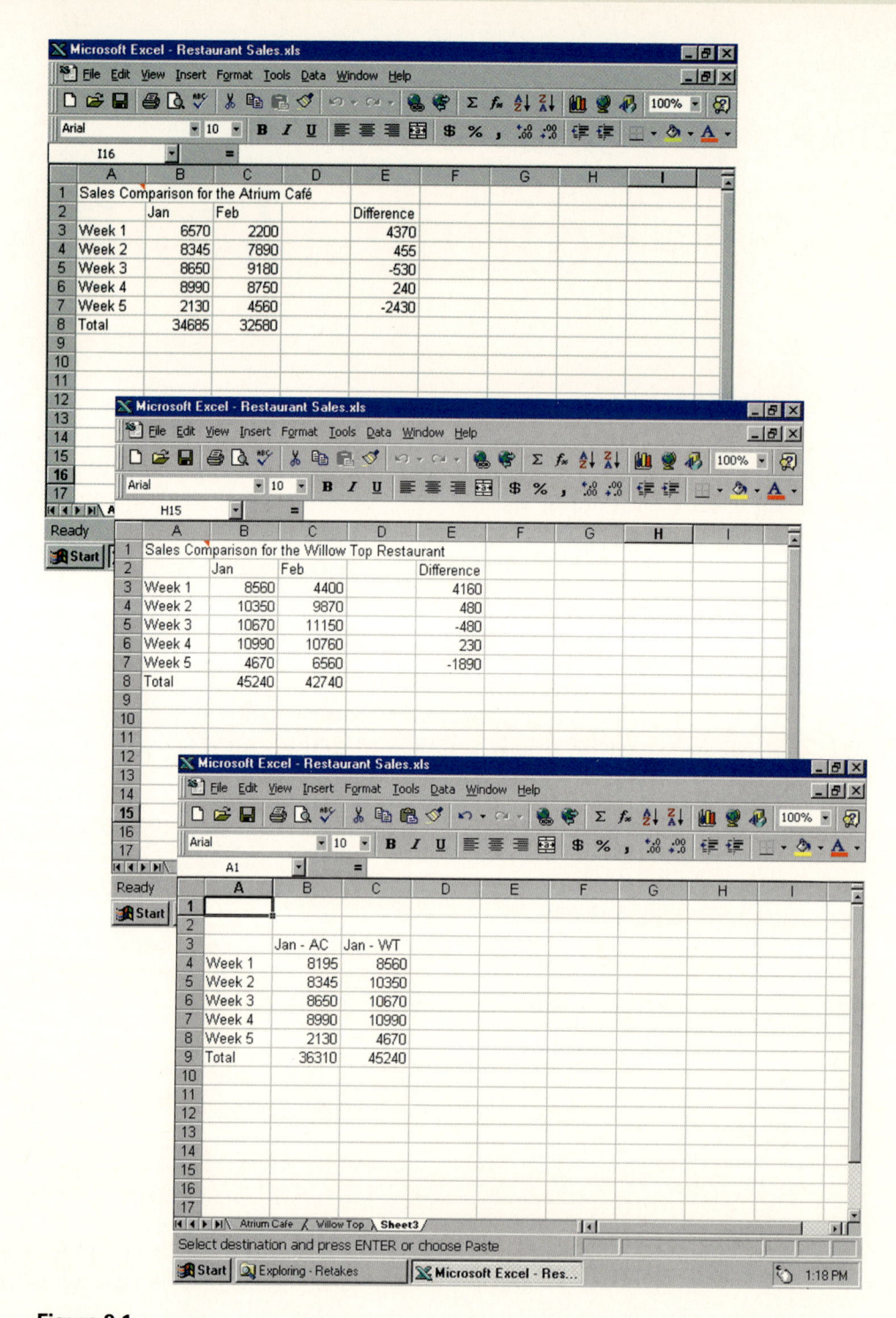

Figure 2.1

The Setup

So that your screen will match the illustrations in this chapter and to ensure that all the tasks in this project will function as described, you should set up Excel as described in Table 2.1. Because these are the default settings for the toolbars and view, you may not need to make any changes to your setup.

Project 2: Editing a Workbook   EX-49

Table 2.1   Excel Settings

Location	Make these settings:
View, Toolbars	Deselect all toolbars except Standard and Formatting
View	Use Normal and display the Formula Bar and the Status Bar.

Opening a Workbook

When you want to view or revise a workbook that you have saved, you must open the workbook first. The worksheet and cell that were active when you last saved and closed the workbook are active when you open the workbook.

> **Tip** If the workbook is one that you have opened recently, you may see it listed at the bottom of the File menu. To open the file, simply select it from the menu.

TASK 1: TO OPEN A WORKBOOK:

1. Click the Open button.

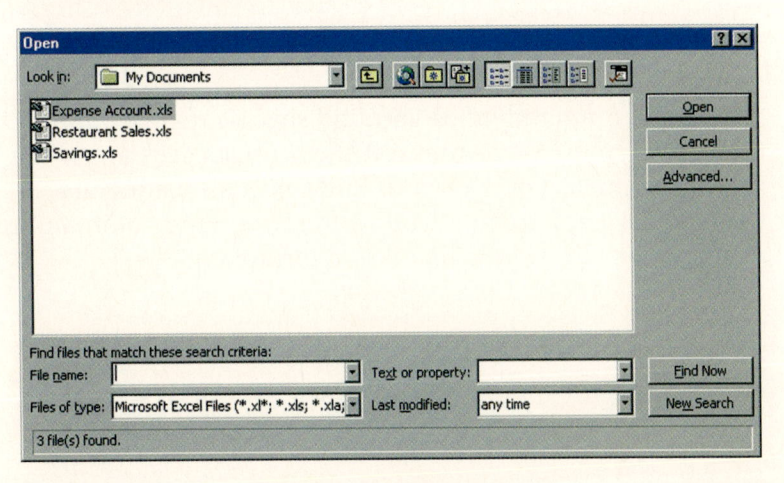

2. Click on the arrow in the Look in text box to display the drop down list if the desired folder does not display automatically.

3. Select the correct path and folder.
   The folder name appears in the Look in text box.

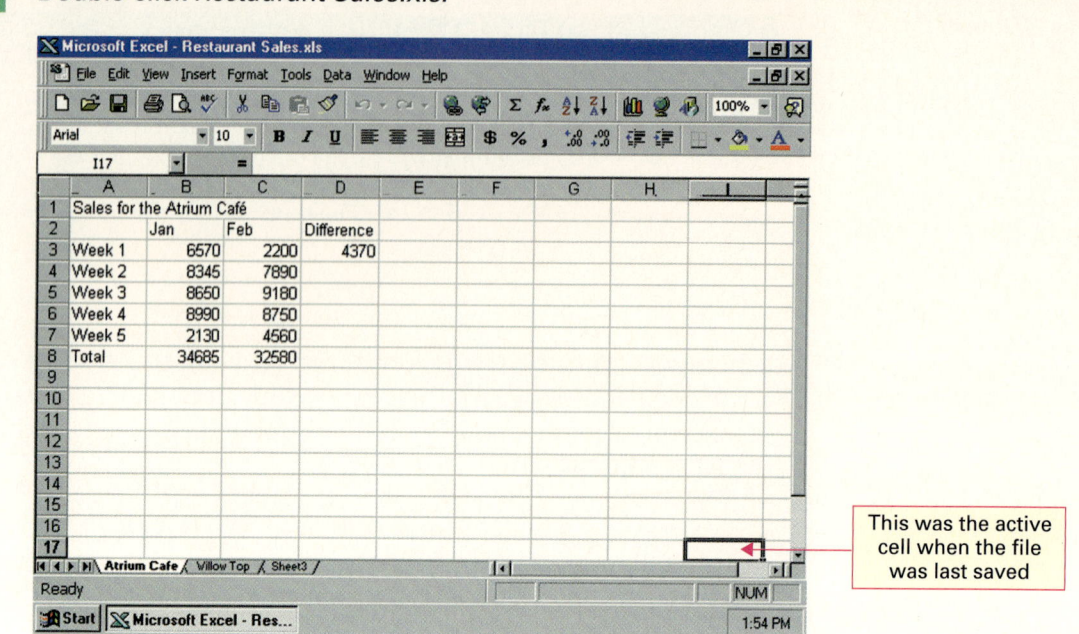

4 Double-click *Restaurant Sales.xls*.

This was the active cell when the file was last saved

When you open a workbook, it opens to the location where you were when you last saved and closed it.

5 Click the Atrium Cafe tab if necessary.
The Atrium Cafe worksheet displays.

Finding Data

The Find command helps you find specific text or values in a worksheet. The command is very useful if the worksheet is large, but it also can be useful in small worksheets to find text and values that aren't shown on the screen. For example, you can use the Find command to find a word, number, or cell address that is in a formula.

TASK 2: TO FIND DATA:

1. Press CTRL+HOME.
2. Choose Edit.

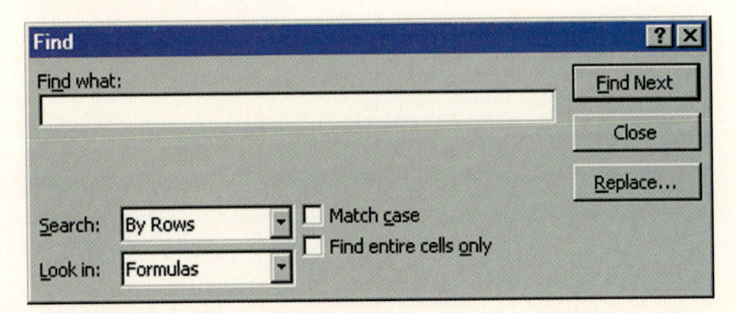

3. Choose Find.

4. Type **Sum** in the Find what text box and ensure that Formulas is selected in the Look in text box.

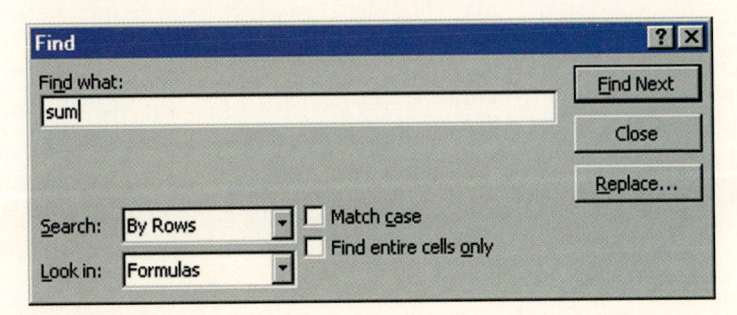

5. Click Find Next.
   Cell B8 becomes the active cell.

6 Click Find Next.
Cell C8 becomes the active cell.

7 Click Find Next.
Cell B8 becomes the active cell again even though the next worksheet has a SUM function.

> **Tip** The Find command searches only the current worksheet.

8 Click Close.
The Find dialog box closes.

Editing Data

If you want to change the data that is entered in a cell, just click in the cell and type the new data. If the data is lengthy, it is more efficient to edit the existing data unless the new data is completely different. If the cell that you edit is used in a formula or function, Excel 97 recalculates automatically to update the worksheet.

TASK 3: TO EDIT DATA IN A CELL:

1 Click in cell A1 in the Atrium Cafe worksheet.
Cell A1 becomes the active cell.

2 Click in the formula bar before the "f" in "for."

The insertion point should be here

3 Type **Comparison** and then press SPACE BAR.

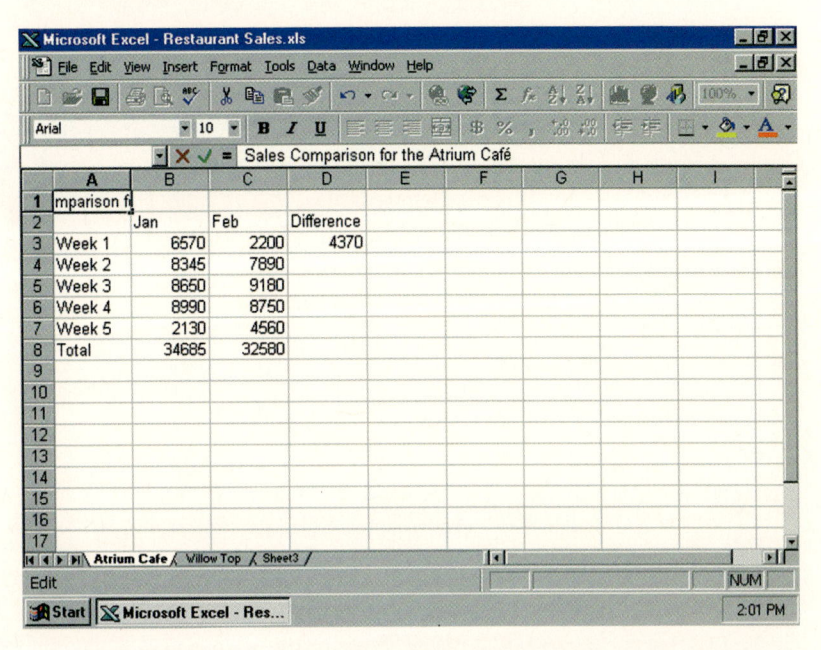

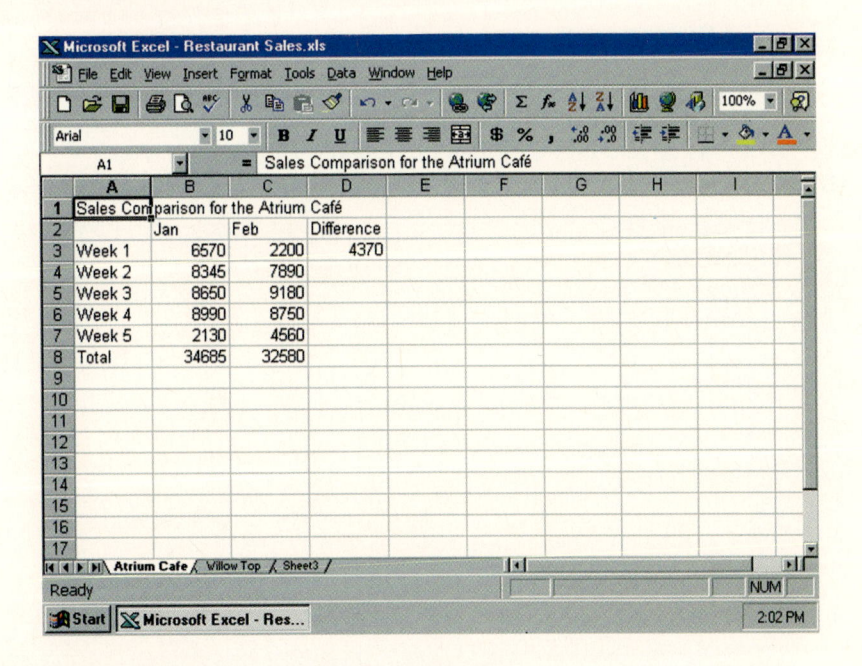

4 Press ENTER.

5 Click the Willow Top tab.
The Willow Top worksheet displays.

6 Click in cell A1.
Cell A1 becomes the active cell.

EX-54

7 Click in the formula bar before the "f" in "for."

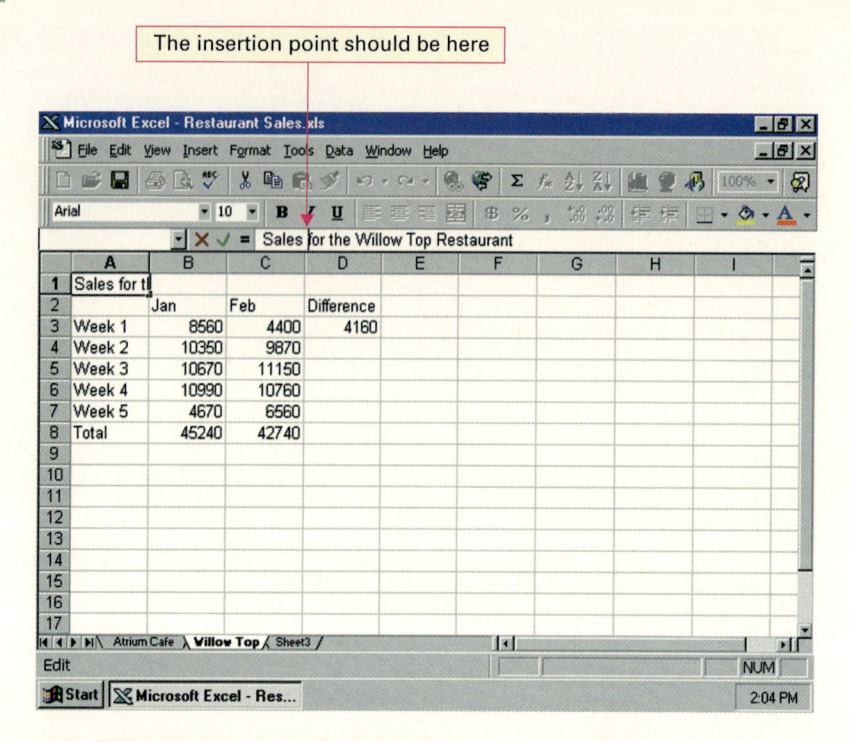

The insertion point should be here

8 Type **Comparison**, press (SPACE BAR), and press (ENTER).

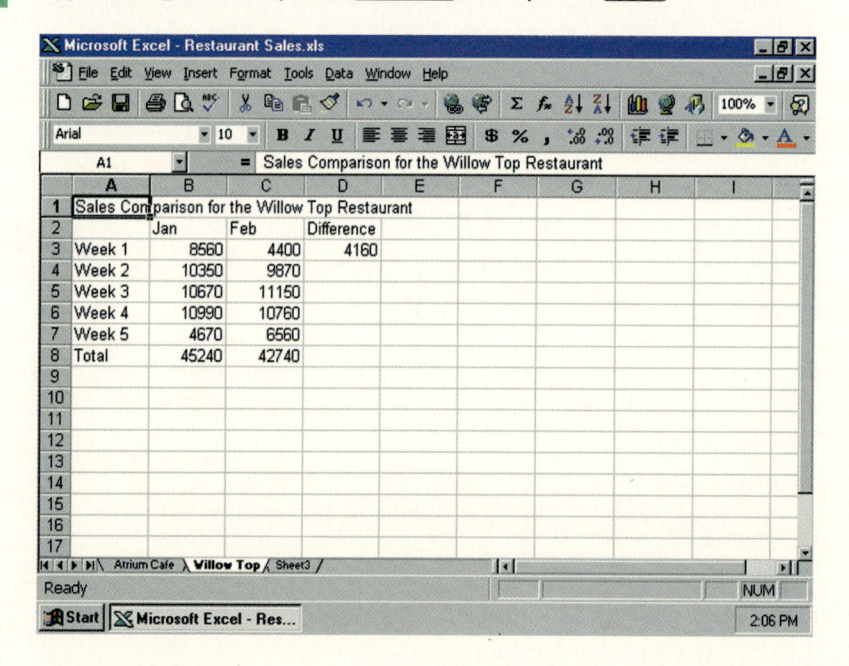

9 Click in cell B3.
Cell B3 becomes the active cell.

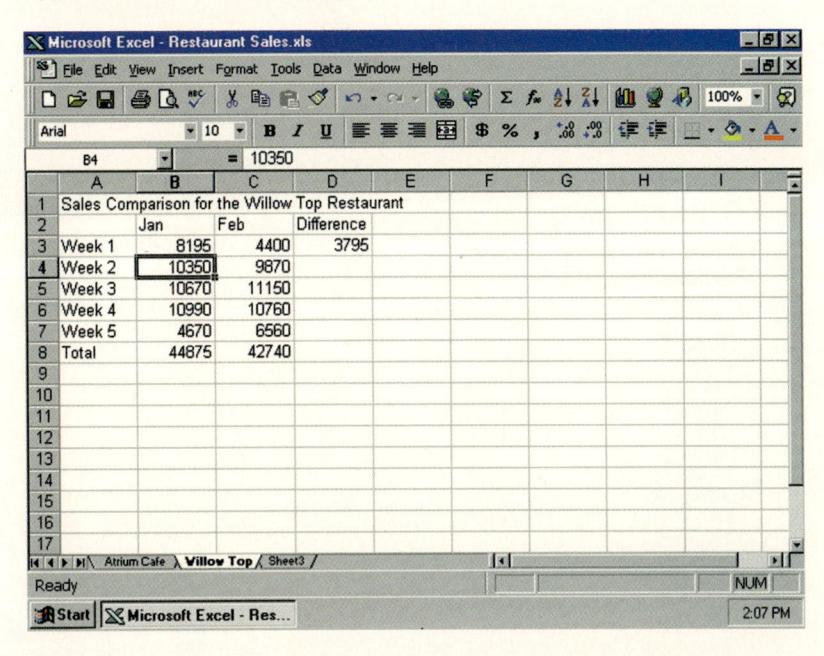

10 Type **8195** and press ENTER.

Working with Data

After you have entered data in a worksheet, you may find that you need to make some changes. You may have to copy, delete, or move the data. All of these types of revisions require selecting cells.

Selecting Cells

When you select cells, they are highlighted. In most cases, the easiest way to select cells is to drag the mouse pointer over the cells, but Table 2.2 describes other ways of selecting cells that are appropriate in many situations.

Table 2.2   Selection Methods

Selection	Method
Entire column	Click the column letter at the top of the column.
Entire row	Click the row number at the left of the row.
Entire worksheet	Click the blank button above the row numbers and to the left of the column letters.
Adjacent columns	Drag the pointer through the column letters.
Adjacent rows	Drag the pointer through the row numbers.
Non-adjacent ranges	Select the first range (the range can be an entire column or row) and then press CTRL while you select additional ranges.

EX-56

TASK 4: TO SELECT RANGES:

1 Click the column letter above column A.

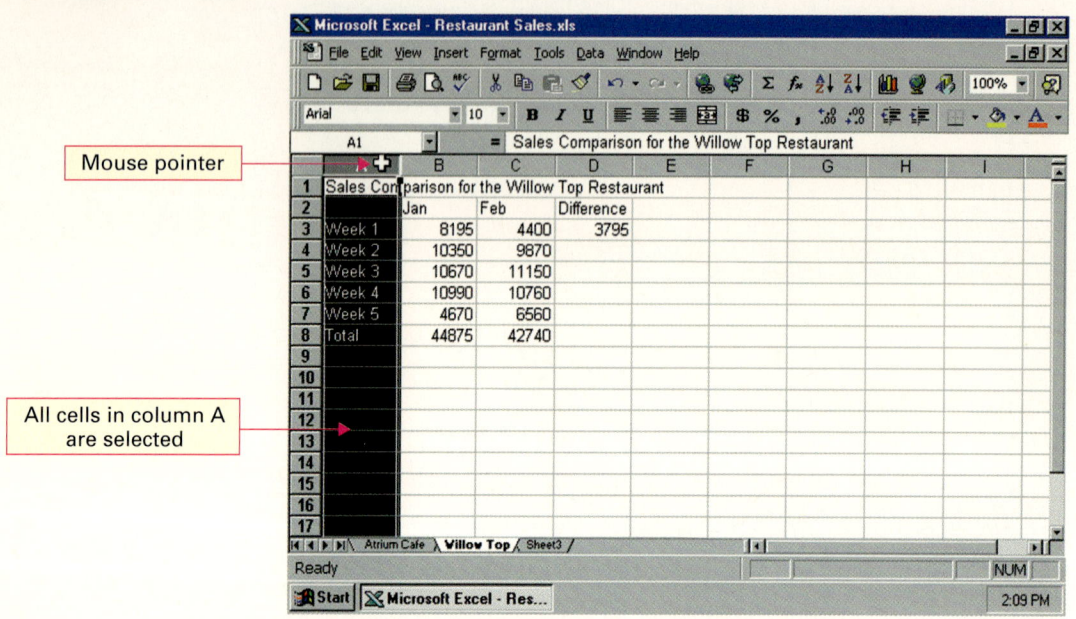

Mouse pointer

All cells in column A are selected

2 Drag the pointer through row numbers 3 and 4.

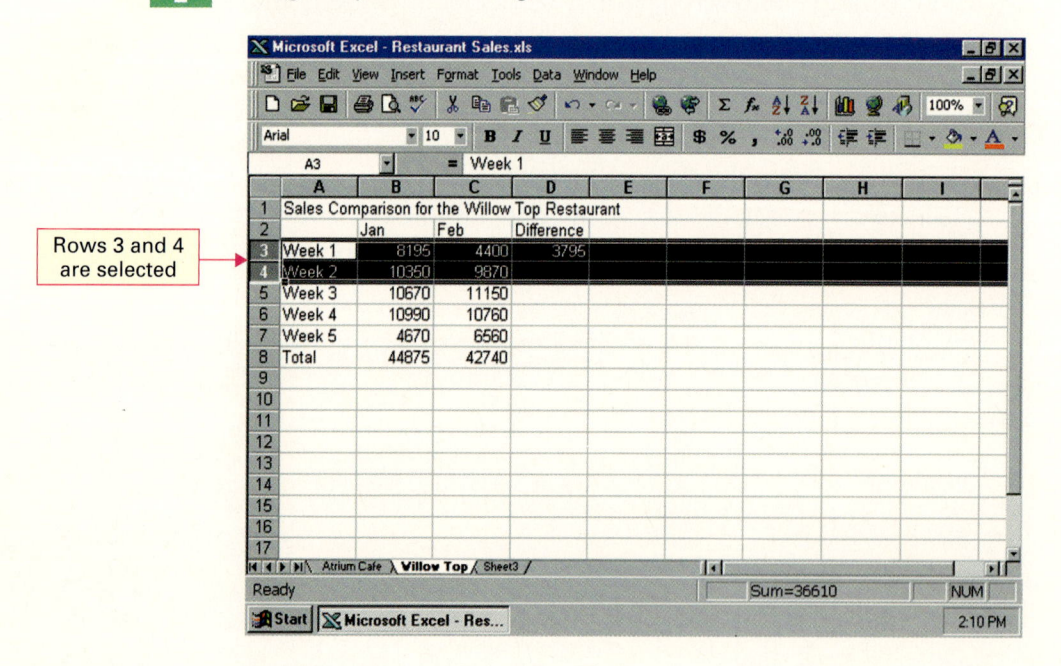

Rows 3 and 4 are selected

Project 2: Editing a Workbook **EX-57**

3 Select column C and then press CTRL while you select column F, row 8, and the range from cell H6 through cell I9.

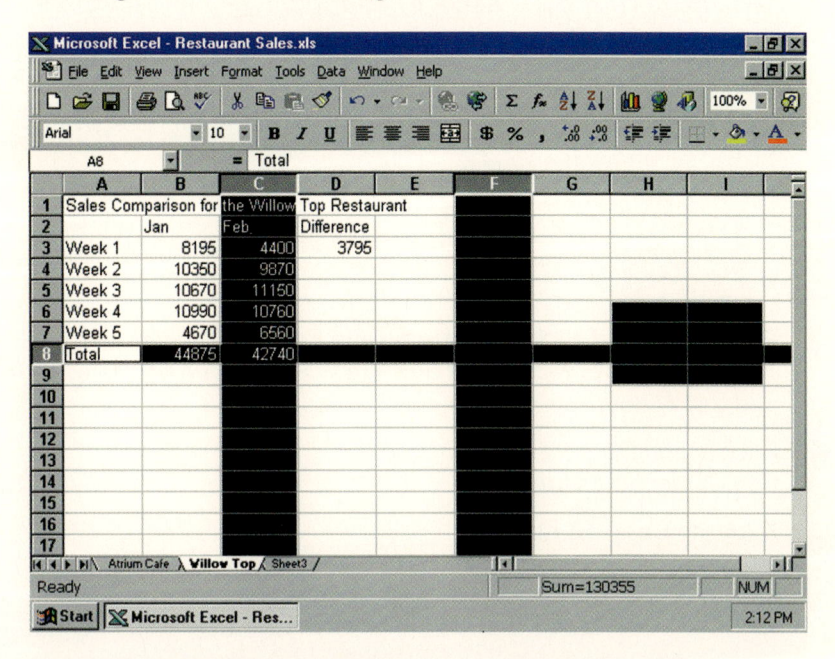

4 Select cell B3 through cell B7.

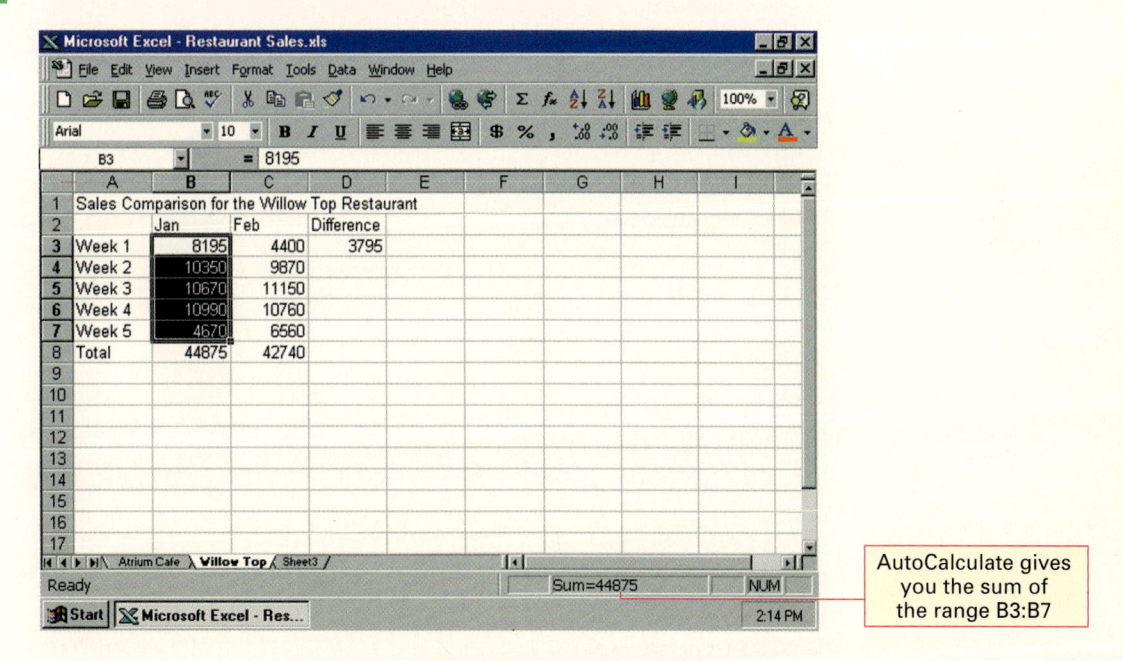

AutoCalculate gives you the sum of the range B3:B7

Tip When you select a range with values, the *AutoCalculate* feature displays a calculation in the status bar. To change the type of calculation, right-click the calculation and choose a different one.

EX-58

Copying Data

When you copy data, Excel 97 stores the data in a memory area called the ***Clipboard.*** Data in the Clipboard can be pasted in any cell, or range of cells in any worksheet or any workbook. If you copy or cut additional data, the new data replaces the existing data in the Clipboard. Pasting data from the Clipboard does not remove data from the Clipboard; therefore, you can paste it repeatedly.

TASK 5: TO COPY DATA:

1 Press CTRL and click the Atrium Cafe tab.
The Atrium Cafe worksheet and the Willow Top worksheet are both selected, and the Willow Top worksheet still displays.

2 Click in cell D3.
Cell D3 becomes the active cell.

3 Click the Copy button.

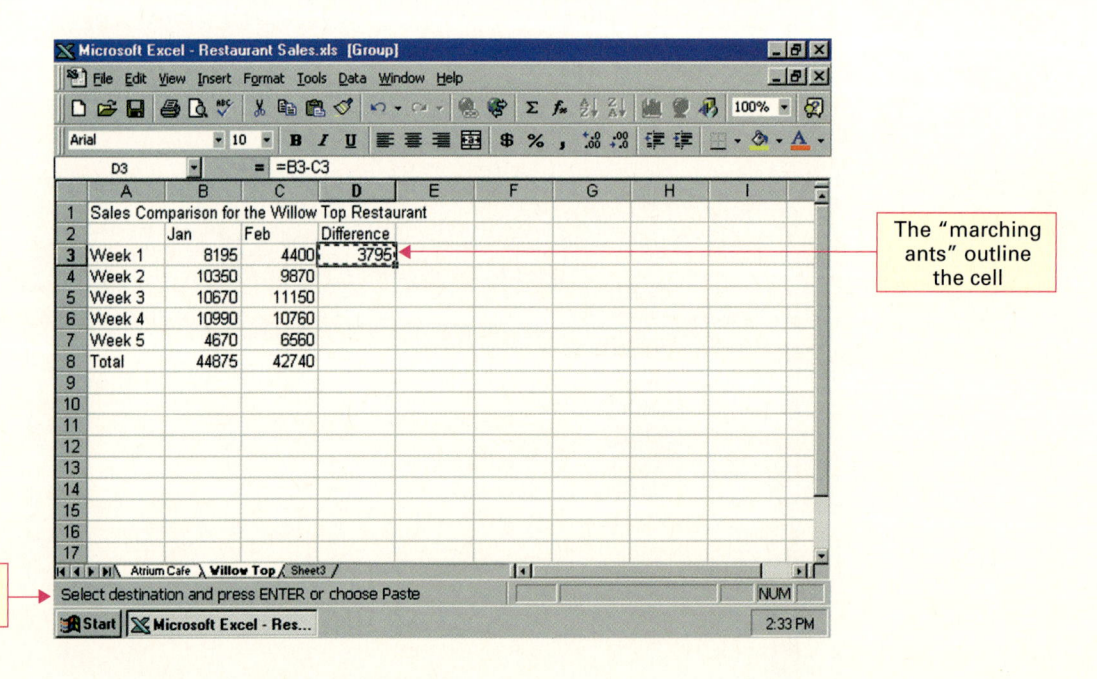

The "marching ants" outline the cell

The status bar tells you what to do next

Project 2: Editing a Workbook EX-59

4 Select the range from cell D4 through cell D7.

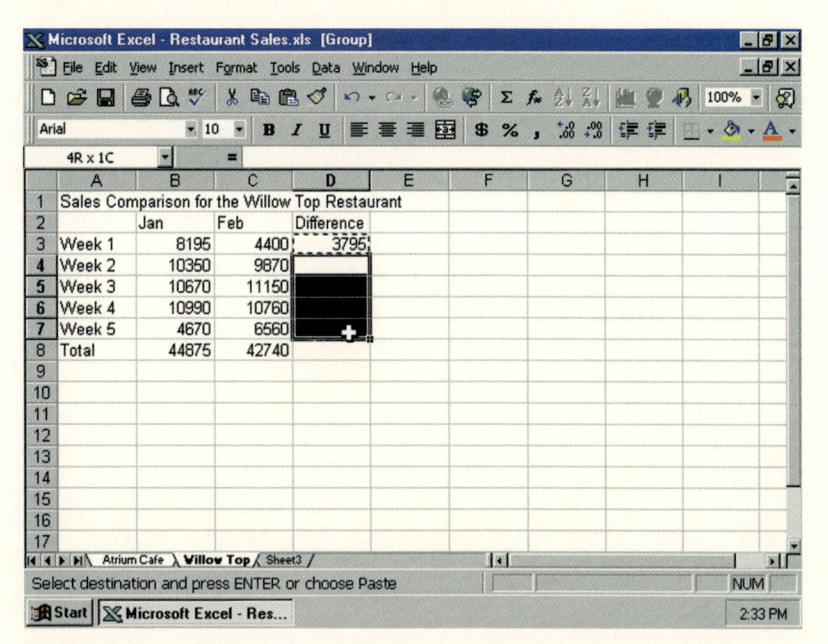

5 Click the Paste button.

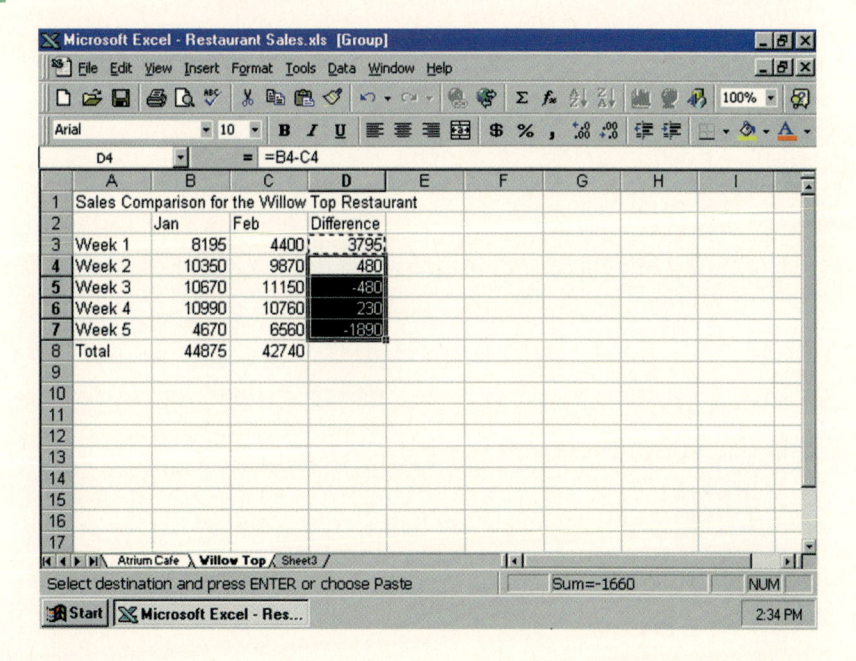

6 Click the Atrium Cafe tab.
The Copy command has been executed on this worksheet, too.

7 Press CTRL and click the Willow Top tab.
The Willow Top worksheet is deselected.

EX-60

8 Select the range from cell B2 through cell B8.

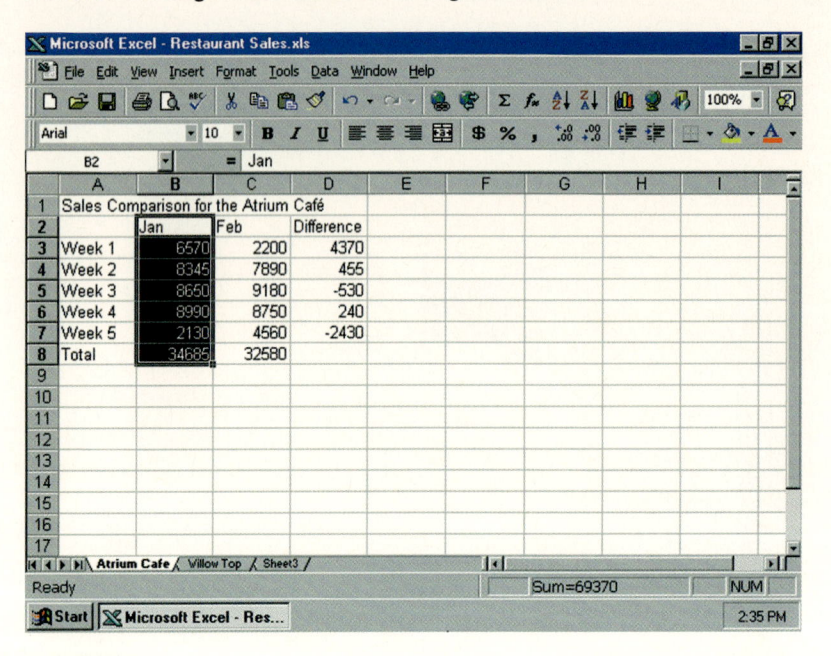

9 Click 📋.
The cells are copied to the Clipboard.

10 Click the Sheet3 tab.
The Sheet3 worksheet displays.

11 Click in cell A3.
Cell A3 becomes the active cell.

12 Click 📋.

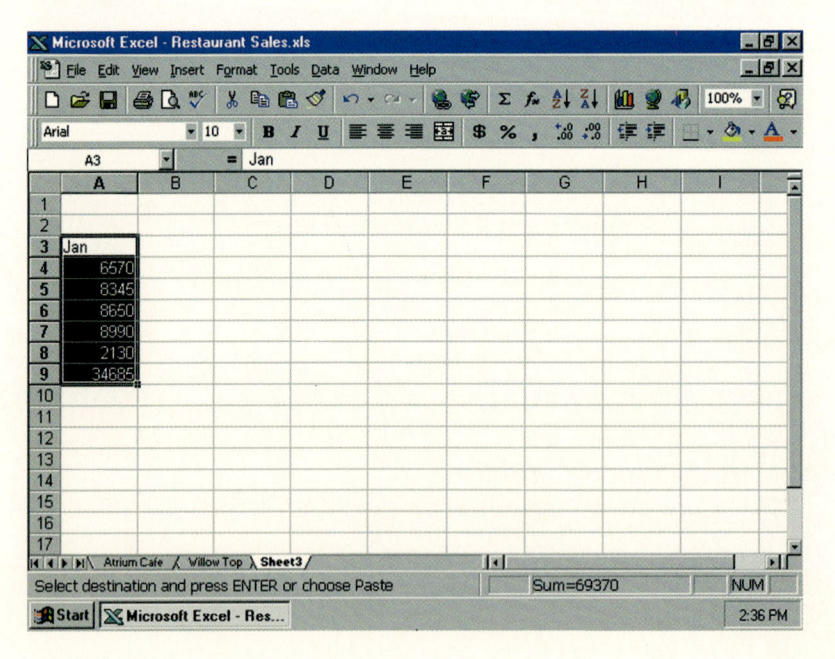

> **Caution** Pasting data into cells automatically replaces data already contained in the cells — without notice. Use the Undo feature to restore data, if necessary.

13 Copy and paste the same range from the Willow Top worksheet to cell B3 in Sheet3.

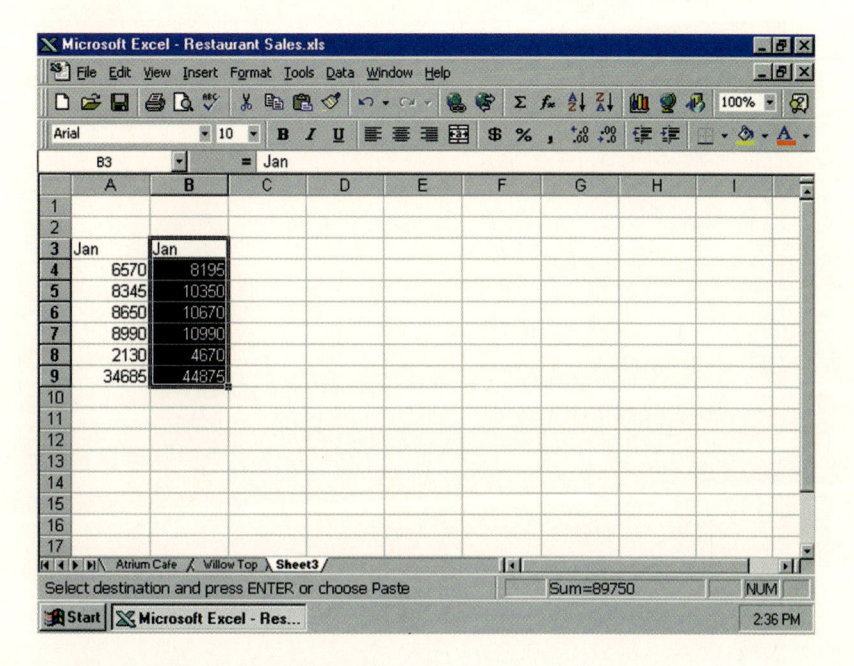

14 Rename Sheet3 to "January."
The name January appears on the tab.

Deleting Data

To erase the data in a cell or a range of cells, simply select the cells and press the Delete key. If you change your mind, click the Undo button.

> **Warning** Some users try to erase cells by passing the space bar. Although the cell looks blank, it really isn't; it contains the character for a space. You should never use this method to erase a cell; you could get arrested by the SSP (Special Spreadsheet Police).

> **Note** The Edit, Clear command accomplishes the same as pressing the ⌈DEL⌋ key.

EX-62

TASK 6: TO DELETE DATA:

1 Select cell A8 through cell B8 on the January worksheet.

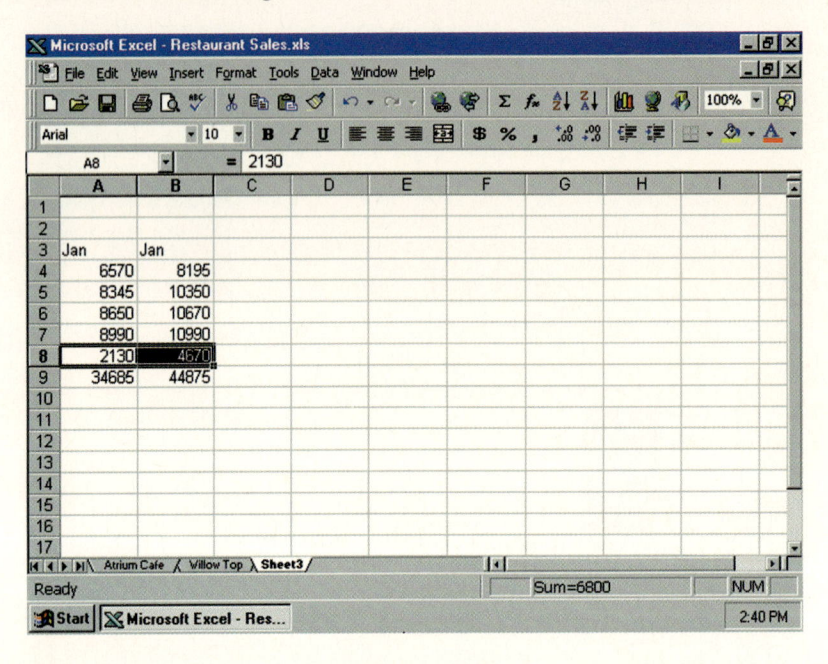

2 Press DEL.

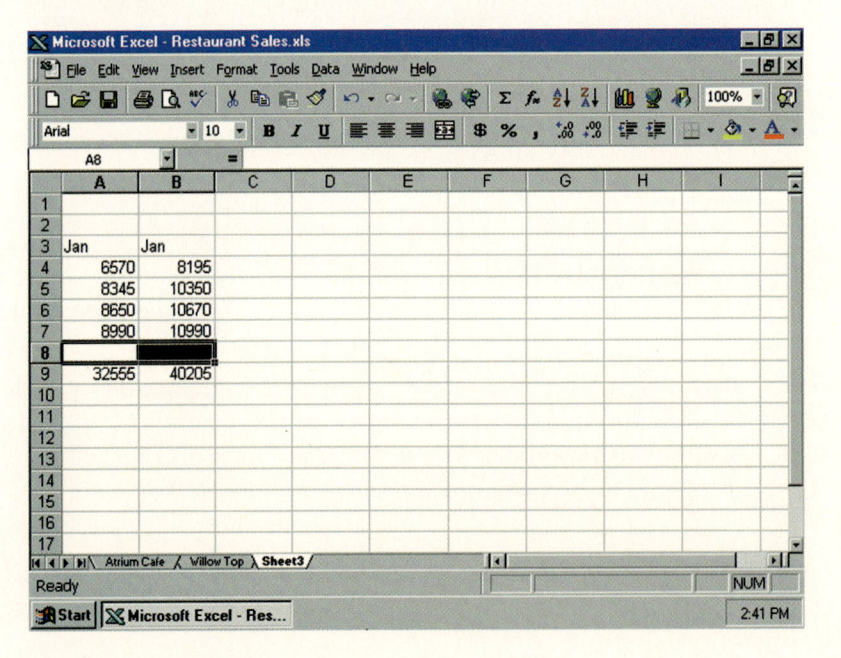

3 Click the Undo button.
The data appears again.

Project 2: Editing a Workbook EX-**63**

> **Tip** When you delete text with the DEL key, the text isn't stored in the Clipboard and therefore it can't be pasted in another location. You can press SHIFT+DEL if you want deleted text placed in the Clipboard.

Moving Data

You can move data to a different location in the same worksheet or to a location in a different worksheet.

TASK 7: TO MOVE DATA:

1. Click on the Atrium Cafe tab.
   The Atrium Cafe worksheet displays.

2. Select cell D2 through cell D7.

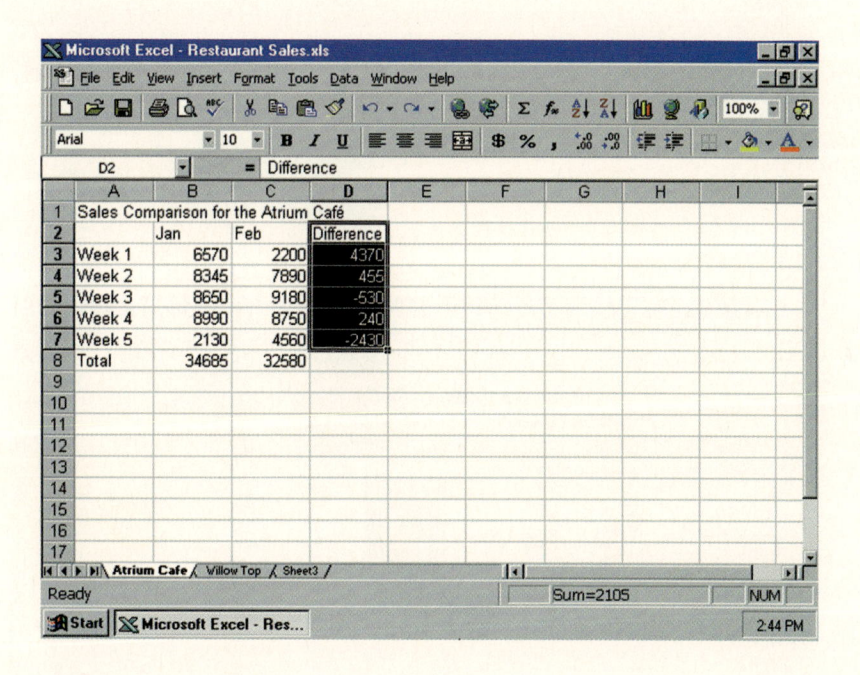

EX-64

3 Click the Cut ✂ button.

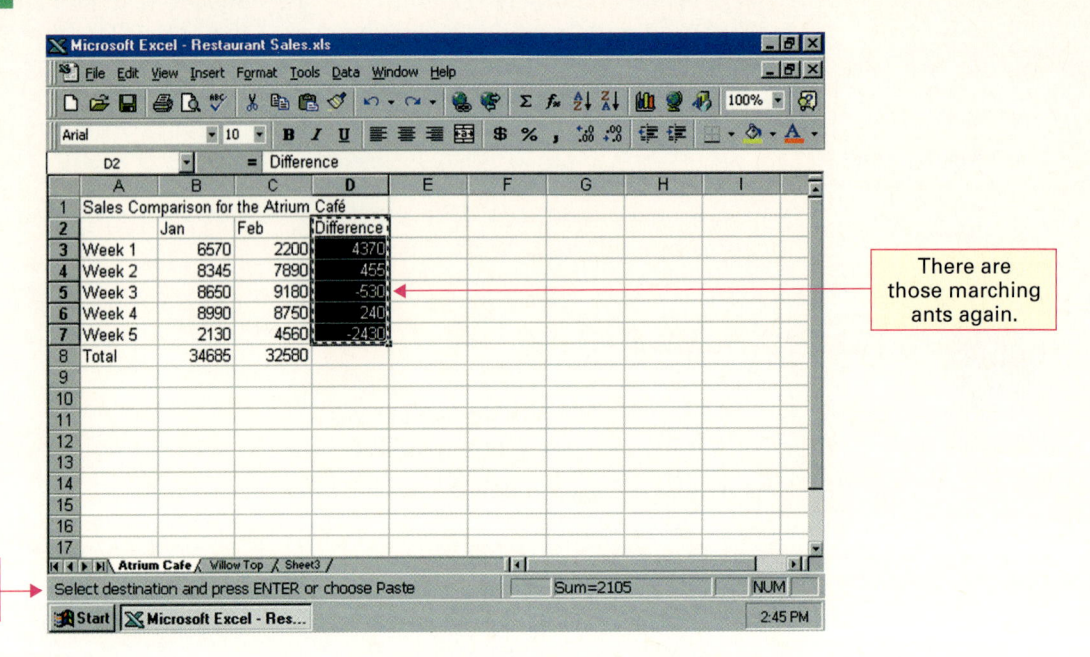

There are those marching ants again.

The status bar tells you what to do next

4 Click in cell E2.
Cell E2 becomes the active cell.

5 Click 📋.

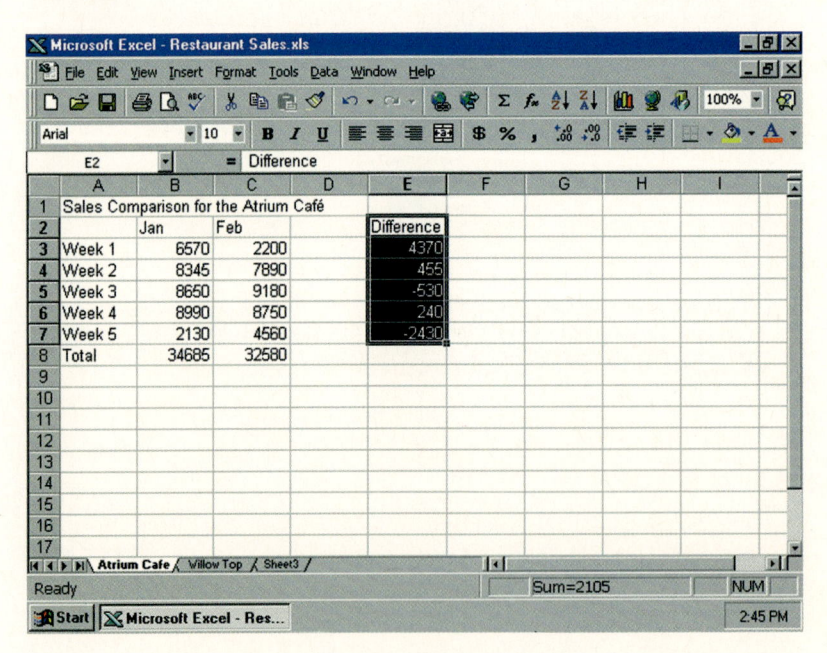

Warning Pasting anything that has been cut (or copied) to a new location that contains data overwrites the data.

Project 2: Editing a Workbook   EX-65

6 Display the Willow Top worksheet and move the range D2 through D7 to cell E2.

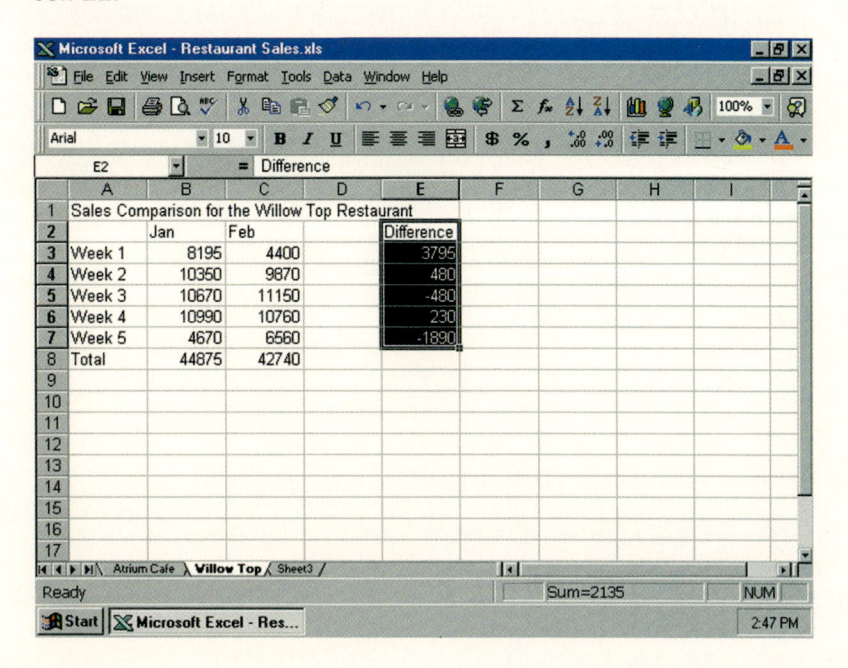

Adding Comments

You can attach **comments** to cells in a worksheet to provide additional information. The comment will contain the user name that is specified on the General page of the Options dialog box accessed from the Tools menu. The text in a comment displays on the screen and it can be made to print as well.

TASK 8: TO ADD COMMENTS:

1 Click in cell A1 on the Willow Top worksheet. Cell A1 becomes the active cell.

2 Choose Insert from the Menu bar.

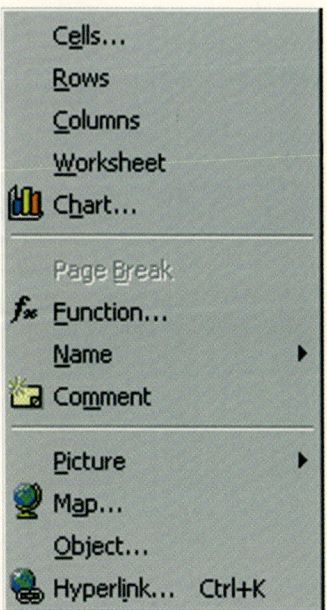

3 Choose Comment.

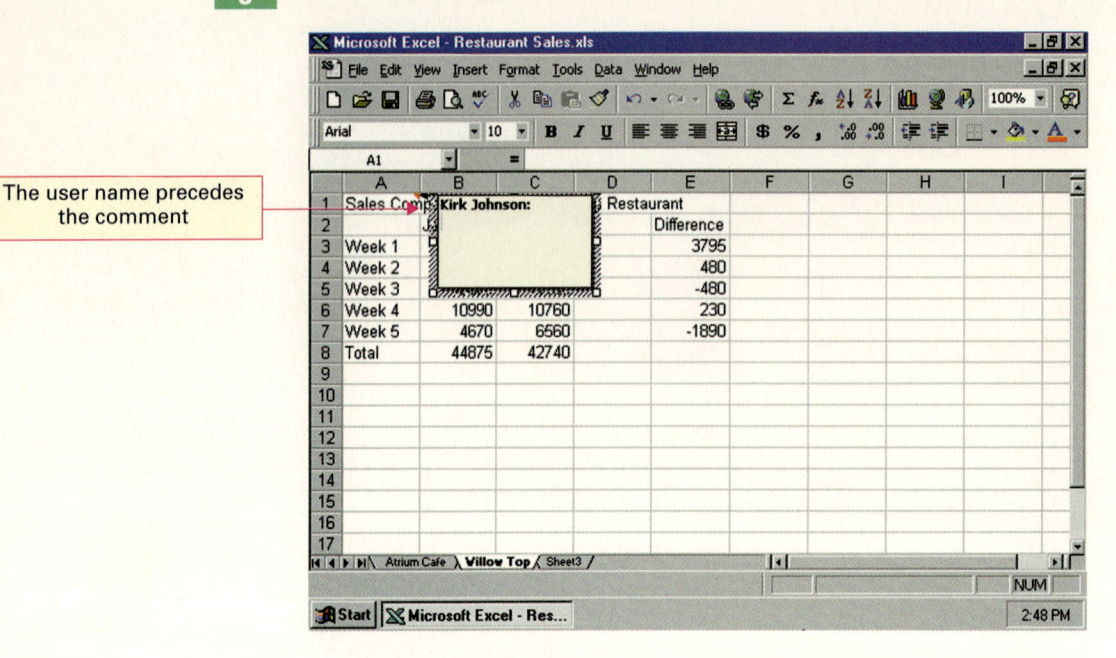

The user name precedes the comment

4 Type **Open for dinner only.**

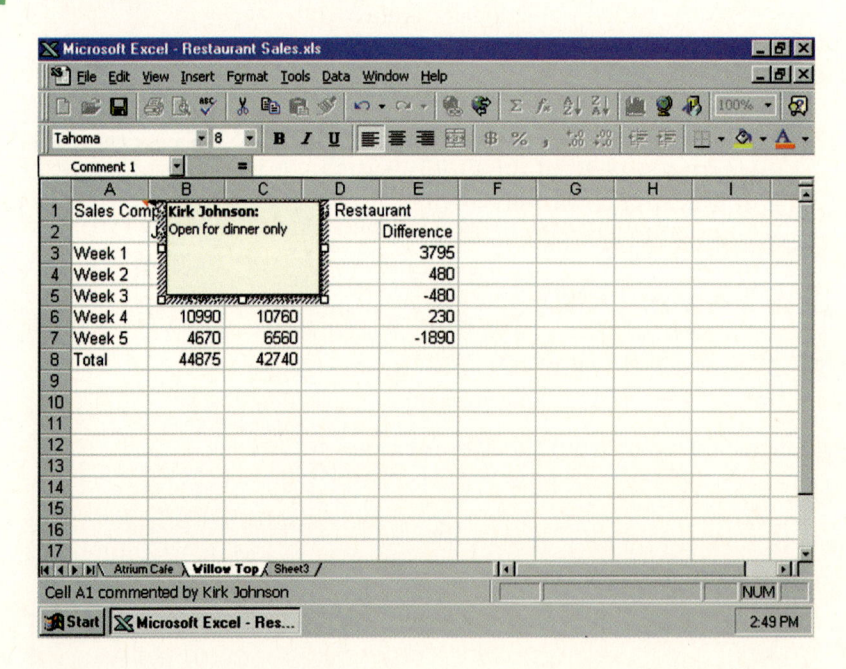

5 Click anywhere outside the comment box.

The red mark denotes a comment

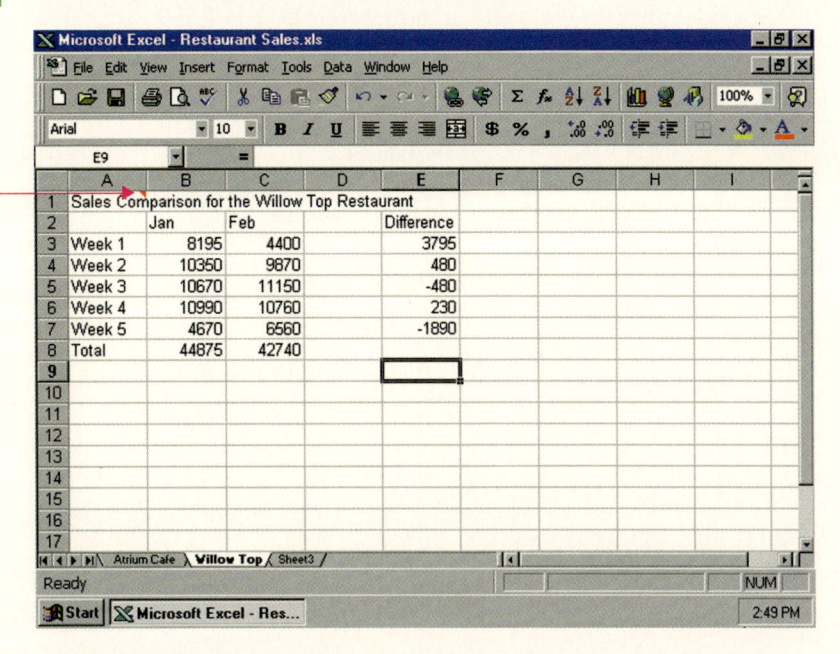

6 Click the Atrium Cafe tab.
The Atrium Cafe worksheet displays.

7 Click in cell A1.
Cell A1 becomes the active cell.

8 Choose Insert, Comment, and type **Open for breakfast, lunch, and dinner.**
Do not correct the spelling of "breakfast."

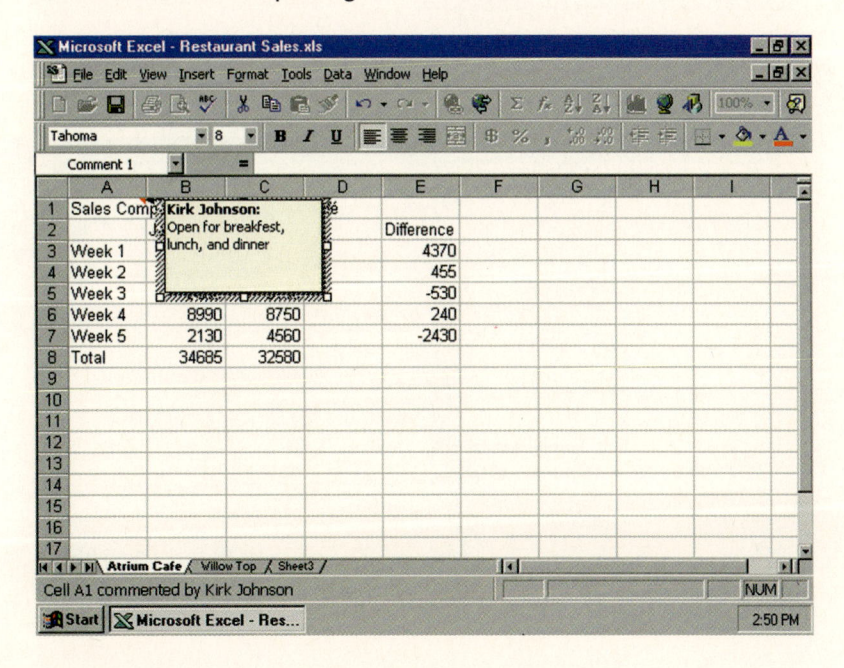

9 Click anywhere outside the comment box.
A red mark appears in cell A1.

EX-68

If you want to see the comments on a worksheet, you can point to the cell that has a red mark and the comment box will pop up, or you can turn on the Comment view and all the comments will be visible.

TASK 9: TO TURN ON THE COMMENT VIEW AND TURN IT OFF AGAIN:

1 Choose View.

2 Choose Comments.

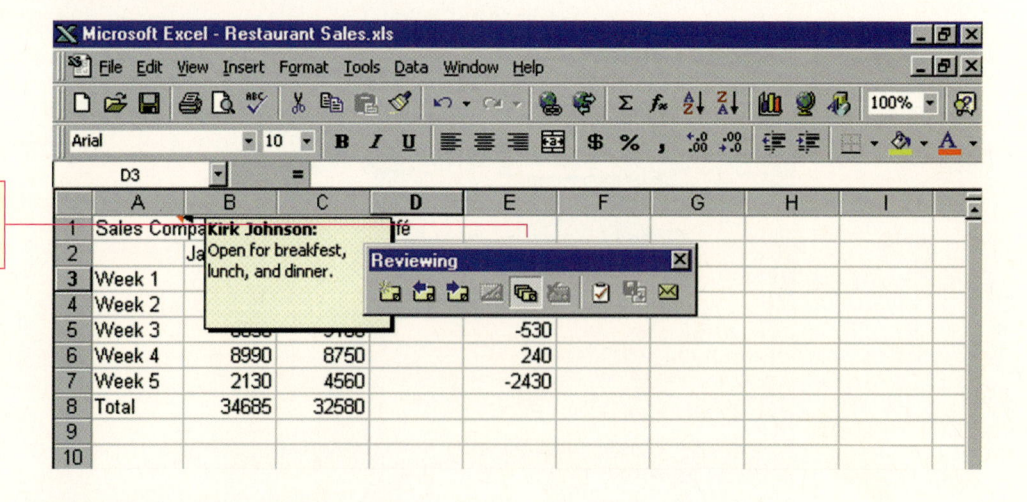

The Reviewing toolbar displays when you turn on the Comments view

Project 2: Editing a Workbook EX-**69**

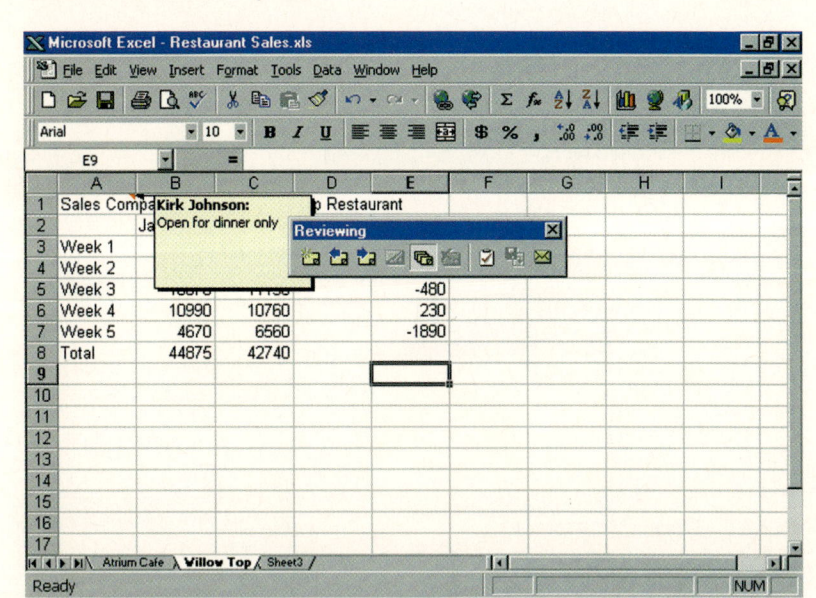

3 Click the Willow Top tab.

4 Click ✕ on the Reviewing toolbar.
The toolbar closes.

5 Choose View, Comments.
The comments are hidden.

> **Tip** Use the Find command to find text or values in comments by selecting Comments from the Look in drop-down list.

Checking Spelling

When you have made all the revisions in a worksheet, it is a good idea to check the spelling, especially since Excel 97 doesn't underline spelling errors as you make them (as Word 97 does).

> **Note** Even though Excel 97 doesn't check your spelling as you go, it does make automatic corrections for many typing errors.

TASK 10: TO CHECK THE SPELLING:

1 Click the Atrium Cafe tab.
The Atrium Cafe worksheet displays.

EX-70

2 Click in cell A1 so that Excel 97 will begin its check of the spelling with cell A1.

3 Click the Spelling button.

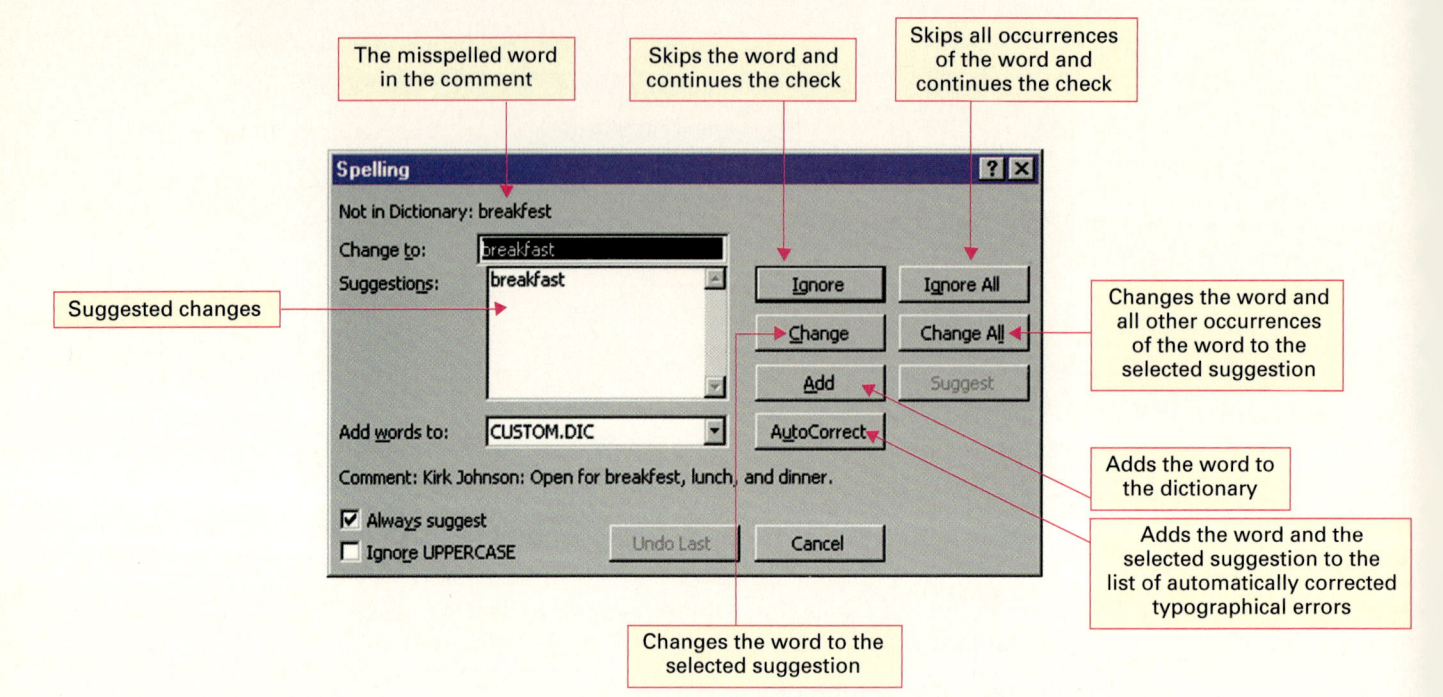

The misspelled word in the comment

Skips the word and continues the check

Skips all occurrences of the word and continues the check

Suggested changes

Changes the word and all other occurrences of the word to the selected suggestion

Adds the word to the dictionary

Adds the word and the selected suggestion to the list of automatically corrected typographical errors

Changes the word to the selected suggestion

4 Choose Change.
If there is another word not found in the dictionary, Excel 97 lists it, but if there are no more words, a message displays telling you that the spell check is complete.

5 Click OK.
The worksheet redisplays.

> **Note** If you have used multiple worksheets, you must spell check each sheet individually. Sorry!

Conclusion

If you have time, you may want to spell check the other worksheets. Then save the file and close it.

Summary and Exercises

Summary

- The Find command finds specific text or values in a worksheet.
- You can edit the data in a cell or simply reenter the data.
- Excel 97 automatically recalculates formulas if the numbers in the cells change.
- When you copy data it is stored in the Clipboard.
- Comments provide additional information in a workbook.
- You can check the spelling of worksheets in a workbook.

Key Terms and Operations

Key Terms
AutoCalculate
Clipboard
comment

Operations
add comments
copy data
delete data
edit data
find data
move data
open a workbook
paste data
select cells
spell check a worksheet

Study Questions

Multiple Choice

1. A workbook's name may appear at the bottom of the File menu,
   a. if it is in the current path.
   b. if the workbook has multiple worksheets.
   c. unless it is on a floppy disk.
   d. if it has been opened recently.

2. To edit a cell, first
   a. select the cell.
   b. click in the formula bar.
   c. activate the edit mode.
   d. press F4.

3. The easiest way to select the entire worksheet is to
   a. triple-click in any cell.
   b. click the button above the row numbers and to the left of the column letters.
   c. drag the pointer through all the cells in the worksheet.
   d. select all the rows in the worksheet.

4. The Find command can find
   a. only text.
   b. only numbers.
   c. only cell addresses.
   d. text in comments.

5. The Spell Checker will
    a. not check all worksheets at once.
    b. not check comments.
    c. only start in the first cell of a worksheet.
    d. not add words to the dictionary.

6. When you press DEL, the
    a. contents of the selected cells are erased.
    b. selected cells are removed from the worksheet.
    c. contents of the selected cells are stored in the Clipboard.
    d. same result is achieved as when you choose Edit, Delete.

7. The Find command
    a. searches only the current worksheet.
    b. searches all worksheets in the workbook.
    c. searches only formulas.
    d. is useful only in large worksheets.

8. Which of the following do not require pressing the CTRL key?
    a. non-adjacent columns
    b. non-adjacent rows
    c. adjacent columns
    d. selecting non-adjacent ranges.

9. To move data, use the
    a. Cut and Paste buttons.
    b. Copy and Paste buttons.
    c. Move and Paste buttons.
    d. Cut and Insert buttons.

10. A comment
    a. is attached to the worksheet.
    b. is attached to a cell.
    c. is only visible when you point to the cell.
    d. displays when you click a cell.

Short Answer

1. When you open a workbook, what is the location of the active cell?
2. How do you use the AutoCalculate feature?
3. What happens if you copy data to a range that already contains data?
4. What toolbar displays when you turn on the Comments view?
5. How would you select both Column C and the range A1 through A10?
6. How do you move data?
7. What happens to the data in the Clipboard when you copy new data?
8. What happens to the data in the Clipboard when you exit Excel 97?
9. How do you select several consecutive rows?
10. How do you insert a comment?

For Discussion

1. What do you do if you need to find all the formulas that reference cell B3?
2. Discuss the two methods of changing data in a cell and when you use each method.
3. Describe several scenarios in which comments are useful.
4. Describe several scenarios in which the AutoCalculate feature could be used.

Review Exercises

1. Revising the restaurant sales worksheet

In this exercise, you will revise the Restaurant Sales worksheet, revising data and adding a comment.

1. Open the workbook named *Restaurant Sales.xls*, unless it is already open.
2. Make the revisions (highlighted in yellow) shown in Figure 2.2.
3. Add a comment to cell A7 in the Atrium Cafe worksheet that says "This

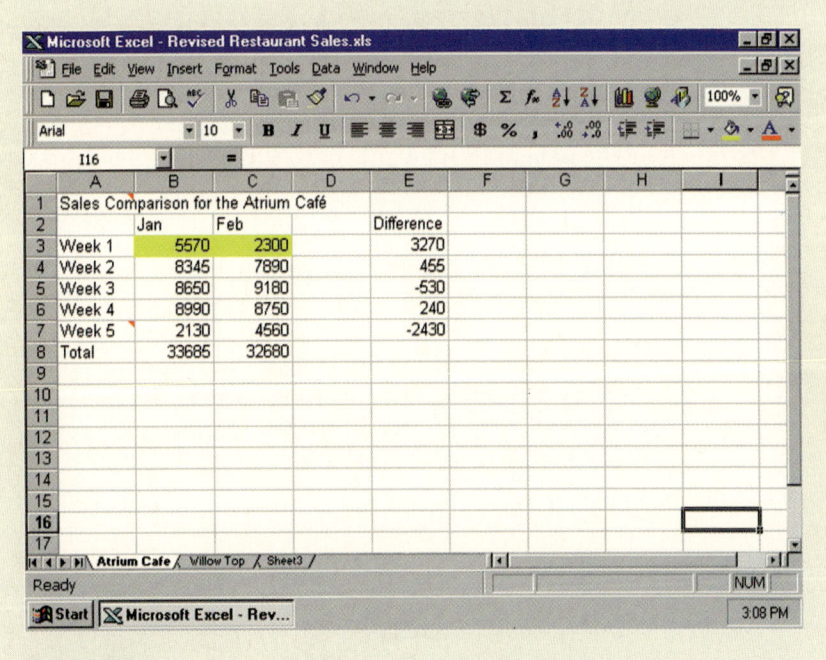

Figure 2.2

week had 4 days in January and 3 days in February."

4. Make sure the numbers on the January worksheet match the numbers on the Atrium Cafe and Willow Top worksheets.
5. Save the file as *Revised Restaurant Sales.xls* and close it.

2. Revising a timesheet

In this exercise, you will revise a timesheet workbook.

1. Ask your instructor how to obtain the file *Tmsheet.xls*. (If you have Internet access, you can download this file from the Addison Wesley Longman website at http://hepg.awl.com/select and follow the appropriate links).

2. Open the file and find the word "sum" in a formula in the Smith worksheet. Copy the formula to the next six cells on the right.

3. Delete the text in row 4.

4. Move the data in cell B1 to cell D1.

5. Copy A1:H9 to the same location in the Jones worksheet.

6. Save the file as *Times.xls* and close it.

3. Moving and copying data in a worksheet

1. Launch Excel and open *Container Corporation Sales xxx.xls* (where *xxx* represents your initials).

> **Note** If you do not have a workbook named *Container Corporation Sales xxx.xls*, ask your instructor for a copy of the file you should use to complete this exercise.

2. Make the following changes to the workbook:
   - Delete *Multi-Size* from the name of the container company in Cell A1.
   - Move the data in Columns C, D, and E and place the data in Columns D, E, and F.
   - Copy the data in Columns A, B and F to the second and third worksheets in the workbook.
   - Copy the data in Rows 4 and 10 to the second and third worksheets.
   - Rename Sheet2 *<Last Year> Sales*, substituting last year's date as indicated.
   - Rename Sheet3 *Sales Increase*.

3. Add a comment note that contains your name and the current date to Cell A1.

4. Spell check the workbook and make appropriate corrections.

5. Save the workbook using the filename *2 Container Corporation Sales xxx*.

6. Print a copy of each worksheet in the workbook and then close the workbook and exit Excel.

Assignments

1. Creating and revising a budget

Create a worksheet that lists expenses for your personal budget. List expense items in column A starting in row 4. List the projected amounts for the next three months in columns B through D. Total each month at the bottom of the column. Save the worksheet as *My Budget.xls*. Revise the amounts so they are more conservative. Move the totals to row 3. Add comments for expenses that need further explanation. Save the revised worksheet as *Lower Budget.xls*.

2. Tracking the American Stock Exchange (Optional Exercise)

Go to the web site http://www.amex.com and explore the site. Create a worksheet to track individual stocks or the market summary. Save the worksheet as *Amex.xls*. Check the site on several different days and add the information to the worksheet.

PROJECT 3

Enhancing the Appearance of a Workbook

Now that you can create and edit a worksheet, it's time for you to add a little pizzazz to the worksheet with various formatting techniques. In this project you will use borders and colors to give the worksheet a classy look.

Objectives

After completing this project, you will be able to:

- ➤ **Format text**
- ➤ **Change cell alignment**
- ➤ **Format numbers**
- ➤ **Format dates**
- ➤ **Format numbers as text**
- ➤ **Add borders and fill**
- ➤ **View and change a page break**
- ➤ **Use AutoFormat**

The Challenge

Mr. Williams, the manager of the golf and tennis property at The Willows, has created a worksheet named *Income.xls* that estimates the income for the upcoming Pro-Celebrity Tournament. He has entered all the data and formulas, but he wants you to format the worksheet so it looks better and is easier to read.

The Solution

You will open the workbook, format the numbers and dates, add a border to the important information and emphasize the totals with shading. Additionally, you will format and align the data in some of the cells and use AutoFormat to format a group of cells automatically. The formatted worksheet will look like Figure 3.1 when you are finished. (The Full Screen view is used in Figure 3.1.)

Before you can begin you must download *Income.xls* from the Addison Wesley Longman web site. The file can be found at http://hepg.awl.com/select. (Follow the appropriate links.). If you are unable to download, obtain the file from your instructor.

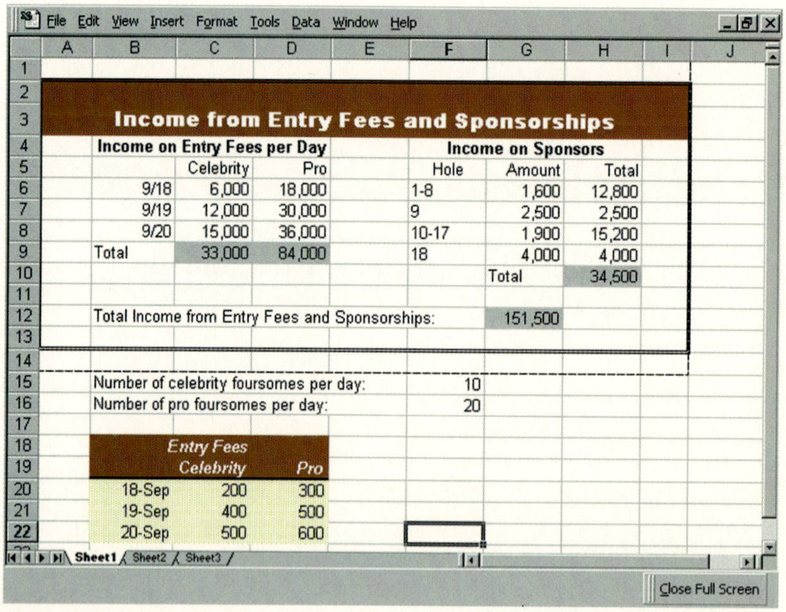

Figure 3.1

The Setup

So that your screen will match the illustrations in this chapter and to ensure that all the tasks in this project will function as described, you should set up Excel as described in Table 3.1. Because these are the default settings for the toolbars and view, you may not need to make any changes to your setup.

Project 3: Enhancing the Appearance of a Workbook   EX-77

Table 3.1 Excel Settings

Location	Make these settings:
View, Toolbars	Deselect all toolbars except Standard and Formatting.
View	Use the Normal view and display the Formula Bar and Status Bar.

Formatting Text

You can format text in a number of ways. You can make it bold, italic, or underlined, or change the font, the font size, and the font color. The Formatting toolbar includes buttons for many of the text formatting options. Before you begin formatting the worksheet, you will save it as *Income2.xls* so you can use the original again later.

TASK 1: TO FORMAT TEXT:

1. Open *Income.xls* and choose File, Save As. Select the drive or folder, type *Income2.xls* in the filename text box and click Save.

2. Select cells D3, B4, and F4.

Click the first cell to select it and then press Ctrl when you click the other cells

3. Click the Bold **B** button.
   The text in all three cells changes to bold.

4. Select cell D3. Click the drop-down arrow for Font Size and choose 12.
   The text in the cell changes from 10 point to 12 point.

EX-78

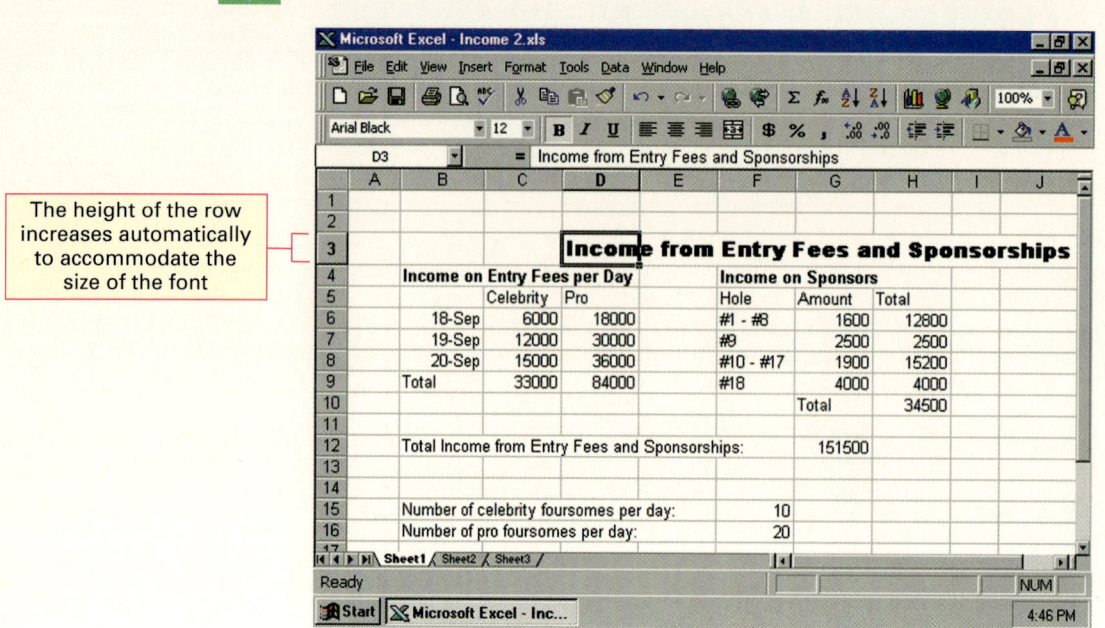

5 Click the drop-down arrow bar Font and choose Arial Black.

The height of the row increases automatically to accommodate the size of the font

Changing Cell Alignment

Data in a cell can be aligned on the left, in the center, or on the right. Each type of data that you enter uses a default alignment—text is left aligned and numbers and dates are right aligned.

You can change the alignment of data in a selected cell by clicking on one of the alignment buttons in the Formatting toolbar. Sometimes you may want to align data across several cells; for example, you might want to center a title in the first row so that the title spans the columns used in the worksheet. In this case, you can merge the cells into one wide cell, and then center the data in the wide cell.

TASK 2: TO CHANGE THE CELL ALIGNMENT:

1 Select A3:I3.
The cells are highlighted.

2 Choose Format.

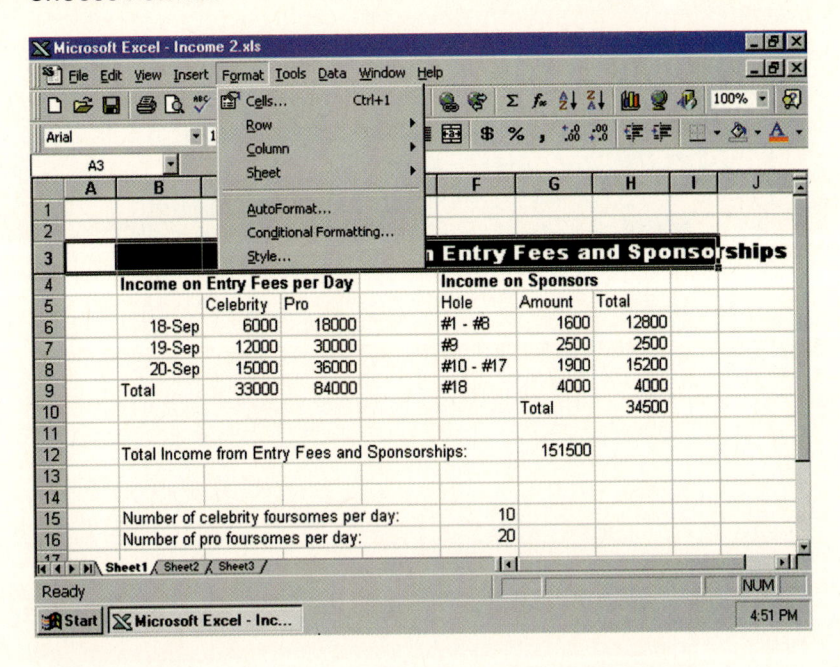

3 Choose Cells.

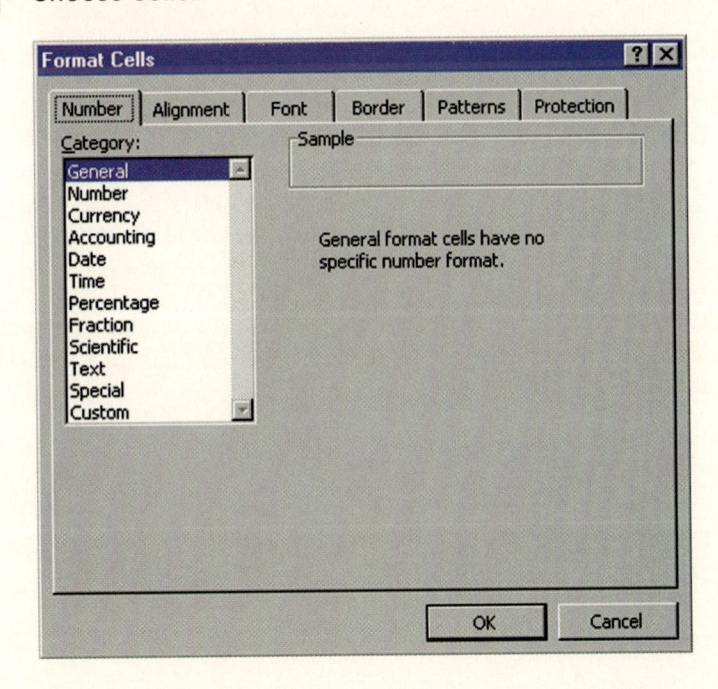

4 Click the Alignment tab.

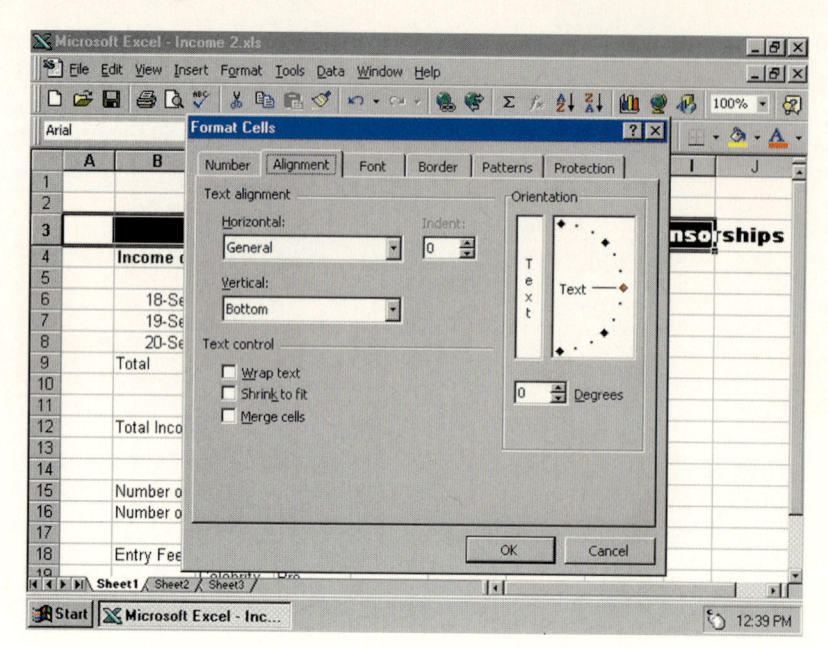

5 Choose Merge cells and click OK.
The cells become one cell.

6 Click the Center button on the Formatting toolbar.

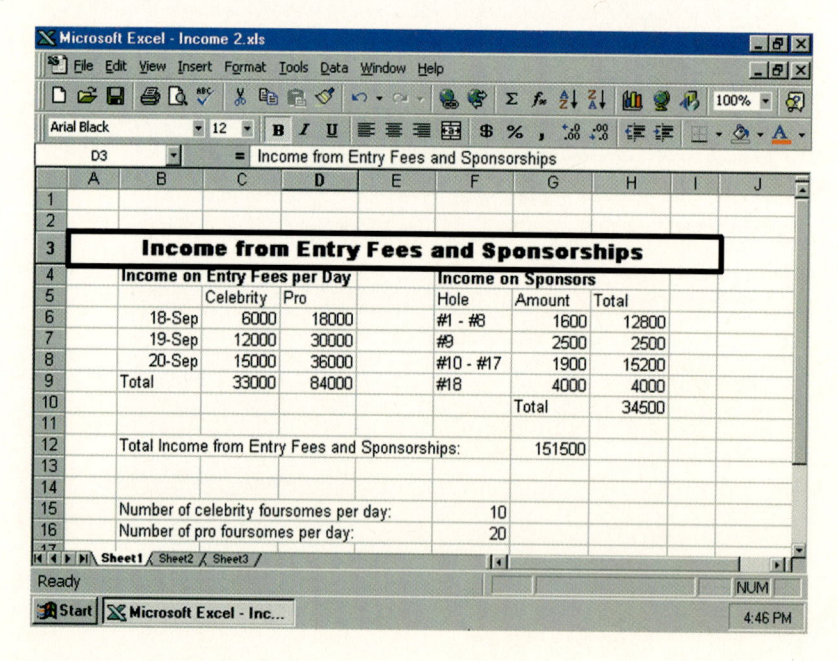

Project 3: Enhancing the Appearance of a Workbook EX-81

> **Tip** To merge and center at the same time, select the cells and click the Merge and Center button.

7 Merge and align the remaining cells:
Merge the cells B4:D4 into one cell and center the text in the cell. Merge the cells F4:H4 into one cell and center the text in the cell. Center the text in cell F5. Select cells C5, D5, G5, and H5 and click the Align Right button.

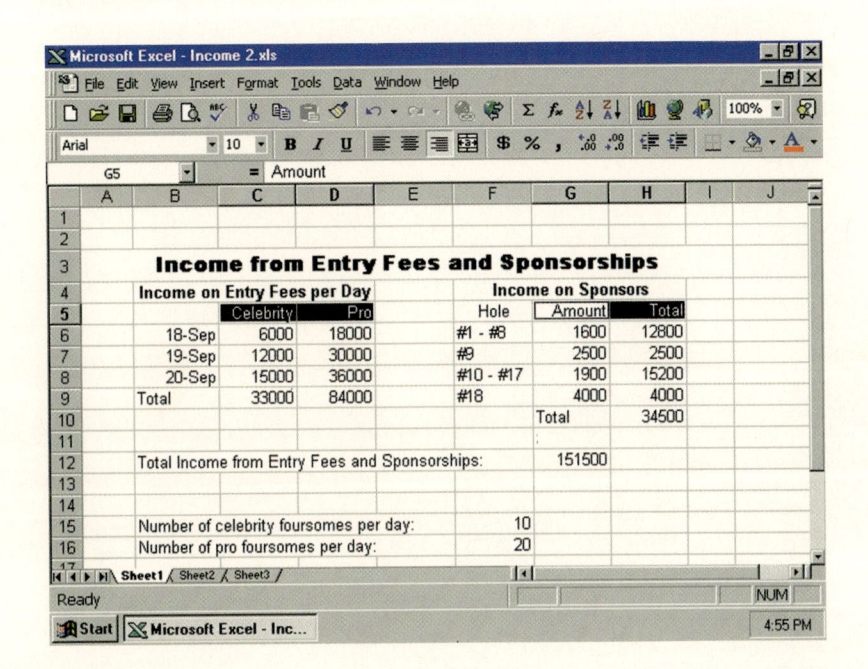

Formatting Numbers

The numbers you enter in a workbook can be "dressed up" with several different formats. As with text, you can make numbers bold, italic, change the font size, and font color. But there are other formatting options available for numbers. Table 3.2 describes the formats that are available in Excel and Figure 3.2 shows some examples.

Table 3.2 Number Formats

Format	Description
General	Numbers appear as entered except for fractions in the form of 1/2 which must be entered as 0 1/2. Commas and decimal points can be entered with the numbers. If commas are not entered, they will not display automatically as in other formats. You can enter a minus or parentheses for negative numbers.
Number	Numbers have a fixed number of decimal places, comma separators can be displayed automatically, and negative numbers can be displayed with a minus, in red, with parentheses, or in red with parentheses.
Currency	Numbers have thousands separators and can have a fixed number of decimal places, a currency symbol, and negative numbers can be displayed with a minus, in red, with parentheses, or in red with parentheses.
Accounting	Numbers have thousands separators, a fixed number of decimal places, and can display a currency symbol. Currency symbols and decimal points line up in a column.
Date	Dates can display with numbers, such as 3/4/97 or 03/04/97, or with numbers and text, such as March 4, 1997 or March-97. Some date formats also display the time.
Time	Times can display as AM or PM or use the 24-hour clock, as in 13:15 for 1:15 PM. Some Time formats also display dates.
Percentage	Numbers are multiplied by 100 and display a percent sign.
Fraction	Numbers display as one, two, or three digit fractions.
Scientific	Numbers display as a number times a power of 10 (represented by E).
Text	Numbers display exactly as entered but are treated as text; therefore, the number would not be used in a calculation.
Special	These formats are used for zip codes, phone numbers, and social security numbers.
Custom	Numbers display in a format created by the user.

	A	B	C	D	E
1	This column is formatted with the **General** Format which is the default.	This column is formatted with the **Number** format with two decimal places.	This column is formatted with the **Currency** format, two decimal places, a dollar sign, and negative numbers in red.	This column is formatted with the **Accounting** format and two decimal places.	This column is formatted with the **Scientific** format with two decimal places.
2					
3	1.37512349	1.38	$1.38	$ 1.38	1.38E+00
4	1000000000	1000000000.00	$1,000,000,000.00	$ 1,000,000,000.00	1.00E+09
5	-98	-98.00	$98.00	$ (98.00)	-9.80E+01
6	12345.6	12345.60	$12,345.60	$ 12,345.60	1.23E+04
7	10	10.00	$10.00	$ 10.00	1.00E+01
8					

Figure 3.2

Project 3: Enhancing the Appearance of a Workbook   EX-83

TASK 3: TO FORMAT NUMBERS:

1. Select cells C6:D9, G6:H9, H10, and G12.
   The cells are highlighted.

2. Choose Format, Cells, click the Number tab, and select Currency from the Category list.

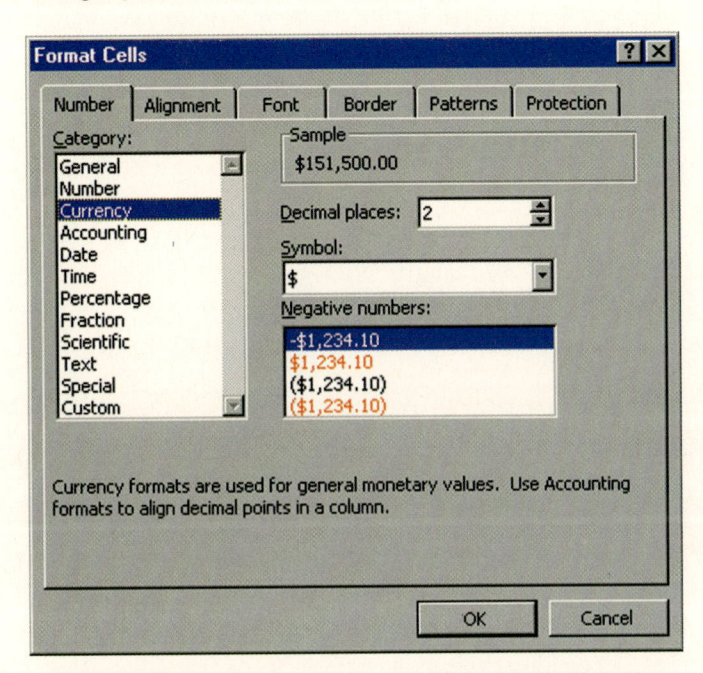

3. Select 0 for Decimal places and None for Symbol.

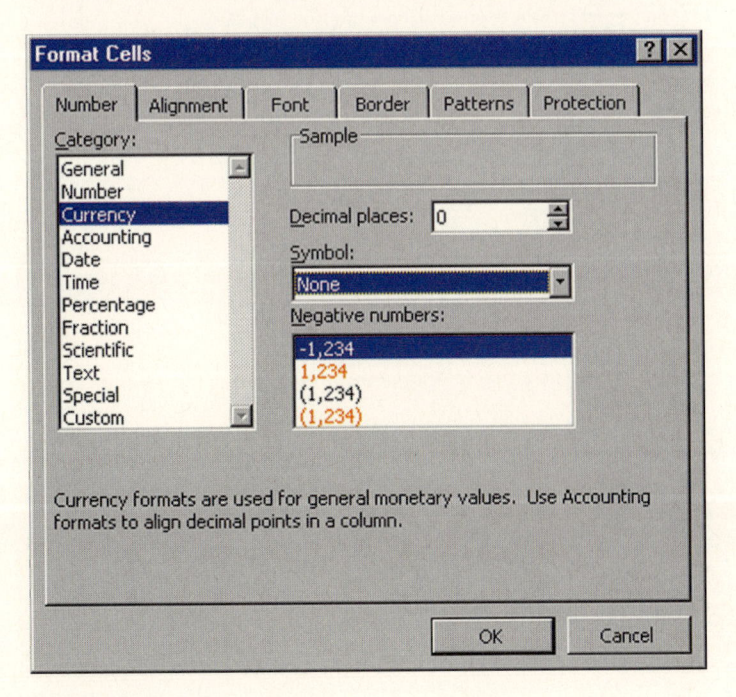

4. Click OK.
   The format is applied.

Formatting Dates

The date format is included in the number formats because Excel stores dates as numbers. You can format dates in several ways. For example, if you enter the date 3/4/98, you can format it to look like any of the following:

3/4	Mar-98
3/4/98	March-98
03/04/98	March 4, 1998
4-Mar	M
4-Mar-98	M-98
04-Mar-98	

Some numbers that you enter are really text. For example, in Figure 3.1, shown on page 77 and again below, the range of 1–8 refers to holes 1 through 8 on the golf course. If you do not format "1–8" as text, Excel will interpret the entry as a date. You will learn how to format dates in Tasks 4 and 5.

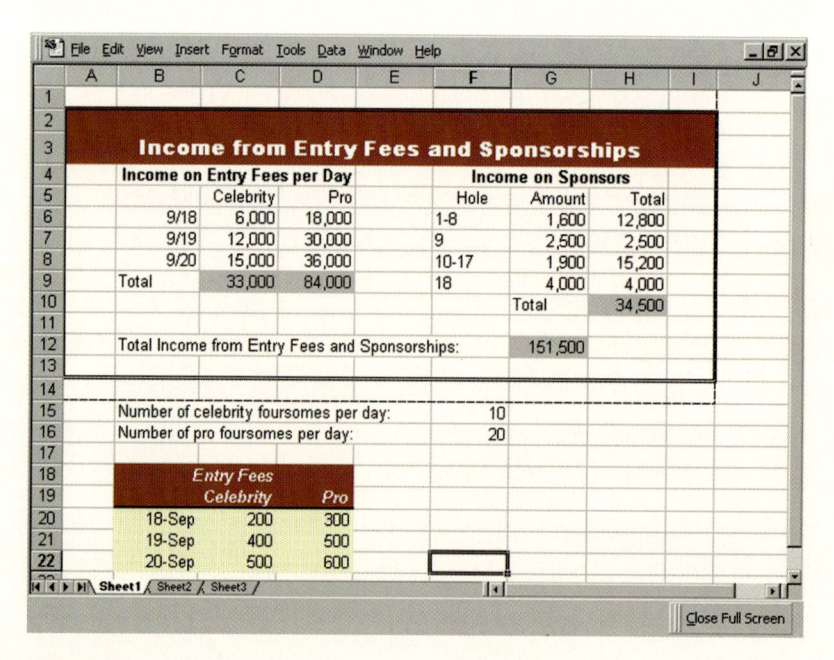

Figure 3.1

TASK 4: TO FORMAT DATES:

1 Select B6:B8.
The cells are highlighted.

2 Choose Format, Cells, and click on the Number tab (if necessary).
The default Date format is selected.

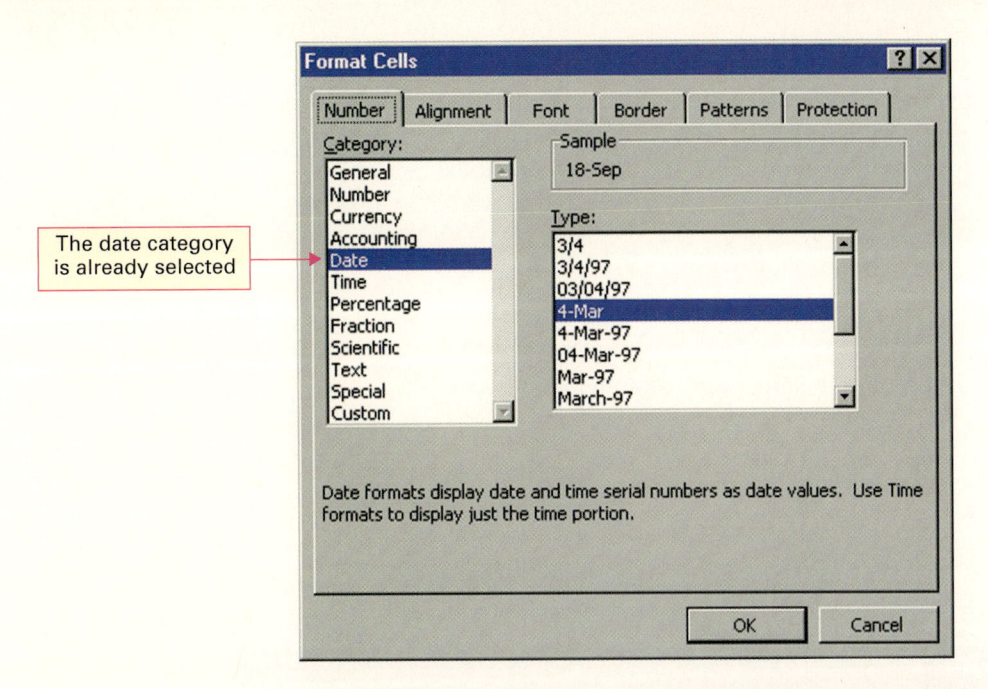

Project 3: Enhancing the Appearance of a Workbook **EX-85**

The date category is already selected

3 Select the first option from the Type list (3/4) and click OK.

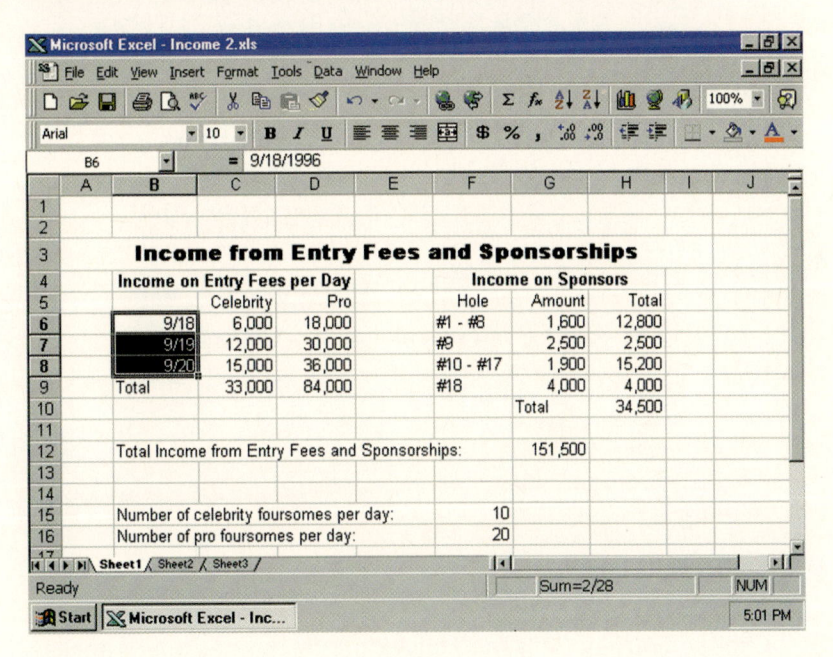

EX-86

Formatting Numbers as Text

When you enter numbers with dashes or slashes in a worksheet, as we did in golf course holes 1–8 and 10–17 shown below, Excel interprets the entry as a date. To avoid this, you must format the numbers as text.

TASK 5: TO FORMAT NUMBERS AS TEXT:

1 Reenter the data in cells F6:F9 exactly as shown:
F6: **1 - 8**
F7: **9**
F8: **10 - 17**
F9: **18**

Excel has interpreted the text in these two cells as dates

2 Select cells F6:F9.
The cells are highlighted.

3 Choose Format, Cells, and click on the Number tab (if necessary). Select Text for the Category and click OK.

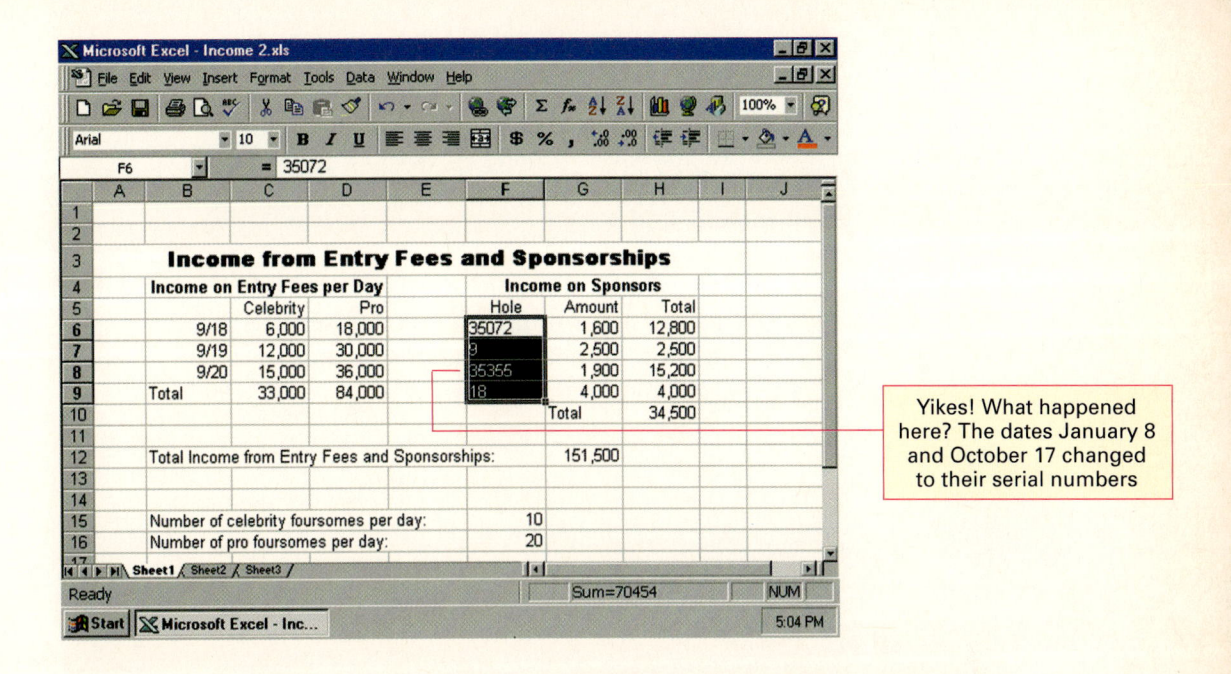

Project 3: Enhancing the Appearance of a Workbook   EX-87

[Screenshot of Microsoft Excel - Income 2.xls showing cell F6 = 35072, with cells F6 containing 35072, F7 containing 9, F8 containing 35355, F9 containing 18]

Yikes! What happened here? The dates January 8 and October 17 changed to their serial numbers

Note A serial number is a sequential number given to every day of every year since the turn of the century. So the number 35072 means that January 8, 1997 is the 35,072nd day of the 20th century.

4 Type **1 - 8** in cell F6. Type **10 - 17** in cell F8.

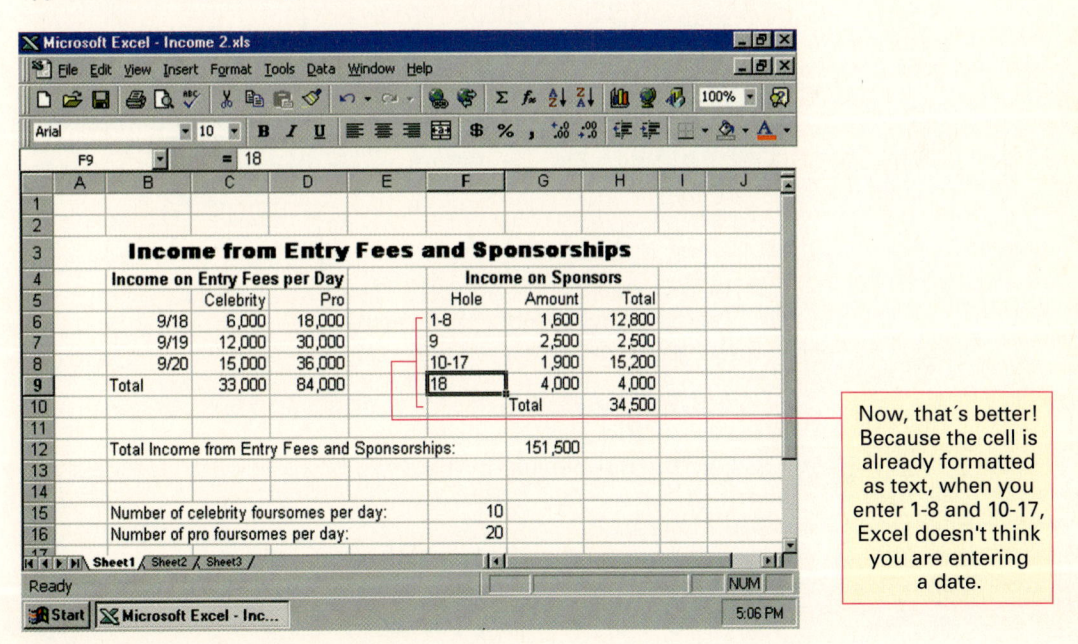

[Screenshot of Microsoft Excel - Income 2.xls showing cell F9 = 18, with F6 containing 1-8, F7 containing 9, F8 containing 10-17, F9 containing 18]

Now, that's better! Because the cell is already formatted as text, when you enter 1-8 and 10-17, Excel doesn't think you are entering a date.

Adding Borders and Fill

A *border* is a line that displays on any side of a cell or group of cells. You can use borders in a variety of ways: to draw rectangles around cells, to create dividers between columns, to create a total line under a column of numbers, and so on.

Fill, also called *shading* or *patterns*, is a color or a shade of gray that you apply to the background of a cell. Use fill carefully if you do not have a color printer. Sometimes it doesn't look as good when it prints in black and white as it does on screen.

TASK 6: TO ADD A BORDER AND FILL:

1 Select cells A2:I13.
The cells are highlighted.

2 Choose Format, Cells, and click the Border tab.

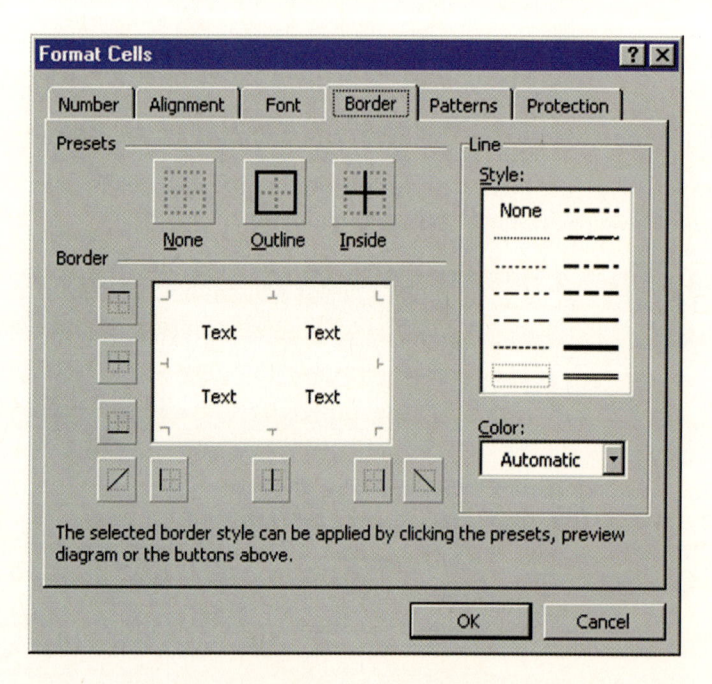

3 Select the double line in the Style box, click the Outline button, and click OK.

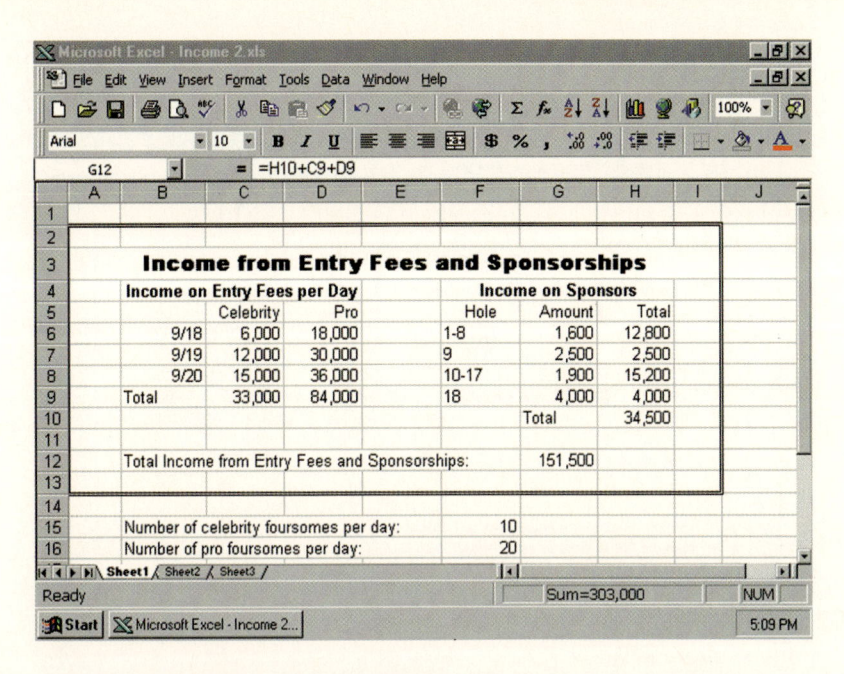

Project 3: Enhancing the Appearance of a Workbook **EX-89**

4 Select cells C9:D9, H10, and G12.
The cells are highlighted.

5 Choose Format, Cells, and click the Patterns tab.

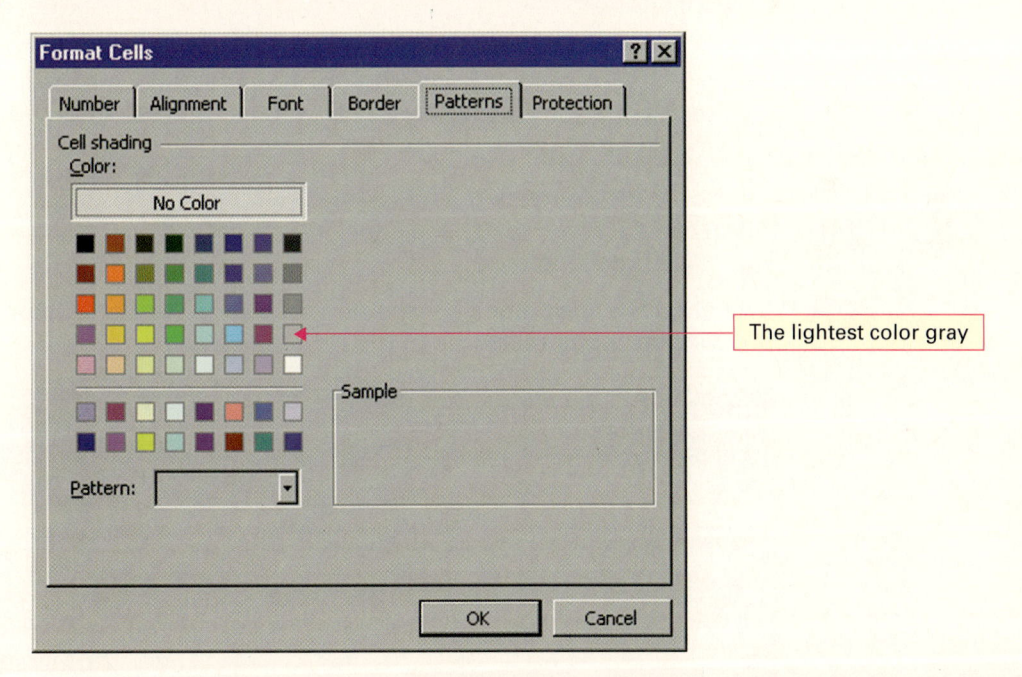

The lightest color gray

6 Select the lightest color gray and click OK.

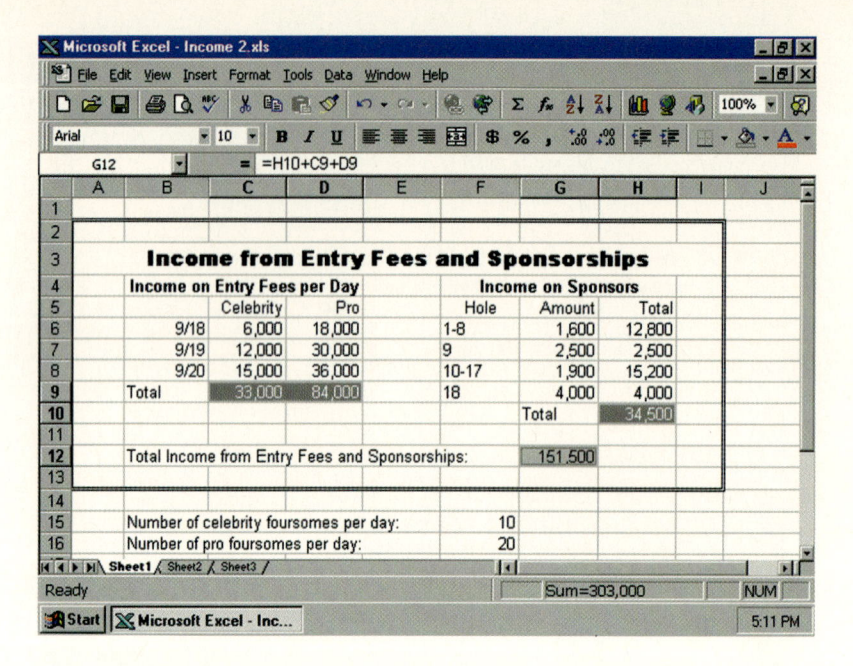

7 Select cells A2:I3 and format them with the first color on the second row of the color chart on the Patterns page.
The cells are shaded with the selected color, but you cannot tell because the cells are still selected.

> **Tip** You also can apply color by clicking the down arrow on the Fill Color button on the Formatting toolbar and selecting a color from a smaller palette.

8 Select cell A3.
The cell is highlighted.

9 To change the text color, click the down arrow in the Font Color button and click the white rectangle in the color palette.

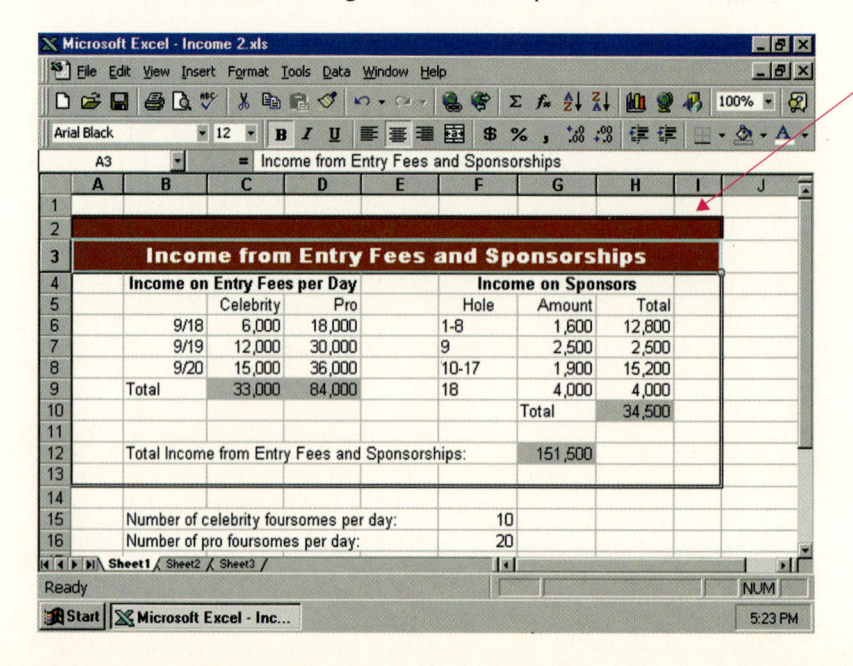

The border is in the same place, but it is hard to see because of the selected cells

Project 3: Enhancing the Appearance of a Workbook EX-91

Viewing and Changing a Page Break

Unlike word processing documents, worksheets are not represented on the screen by pages. The complete worksheet, all 16,777,216 cells of it, is one big page on the screen. So that you can see where the pages will break when the worksheet prints, Excel provides a *Page Break view*. You can adjust the location of the *page breaks* in this view.

TASK 7: TO VIEW THE PAGE BREAK IN THE INCOME WORKSHEET AND CHANGE IT:

1. Click the Print Preview button.

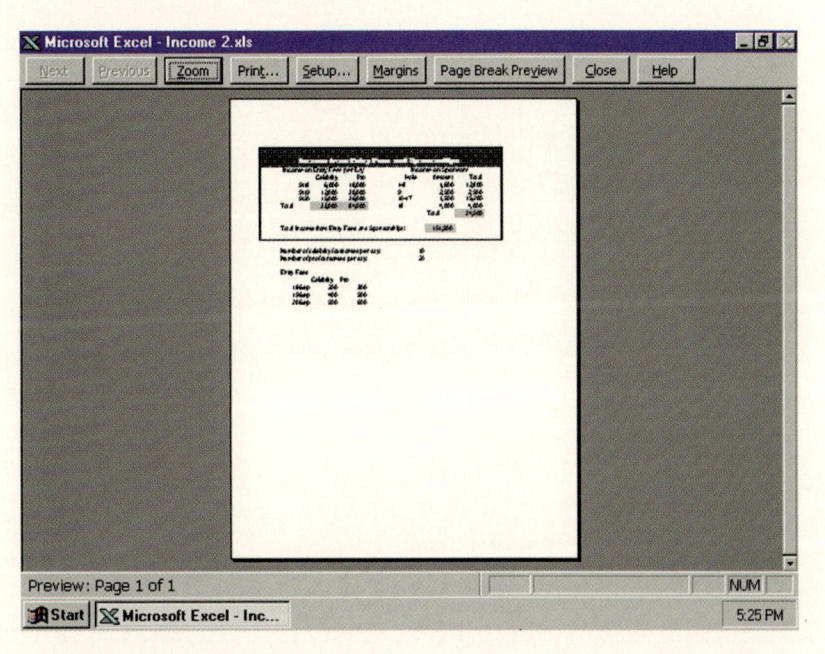

2. Click the Page Break Preview button. (Click OK if a message displays.)

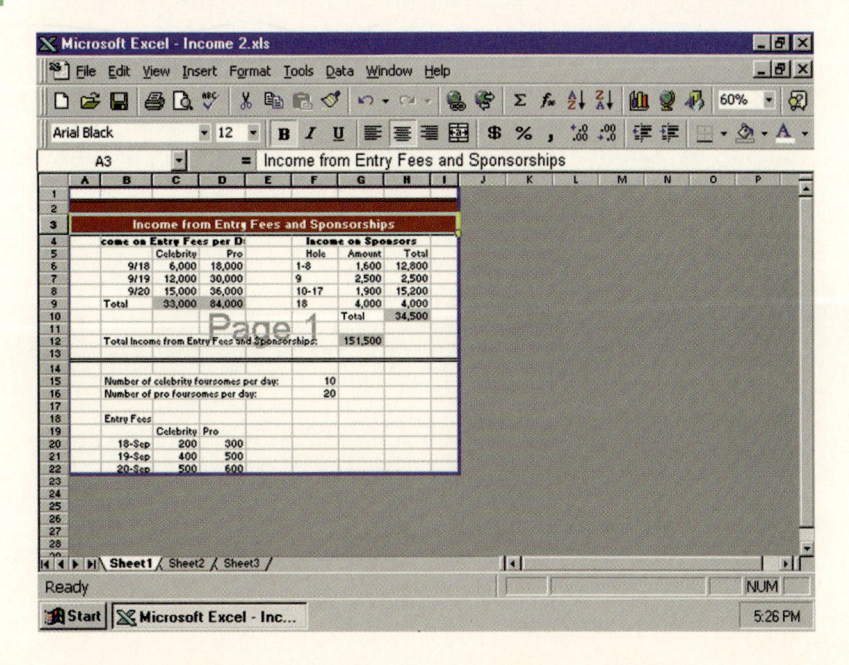

EX-92

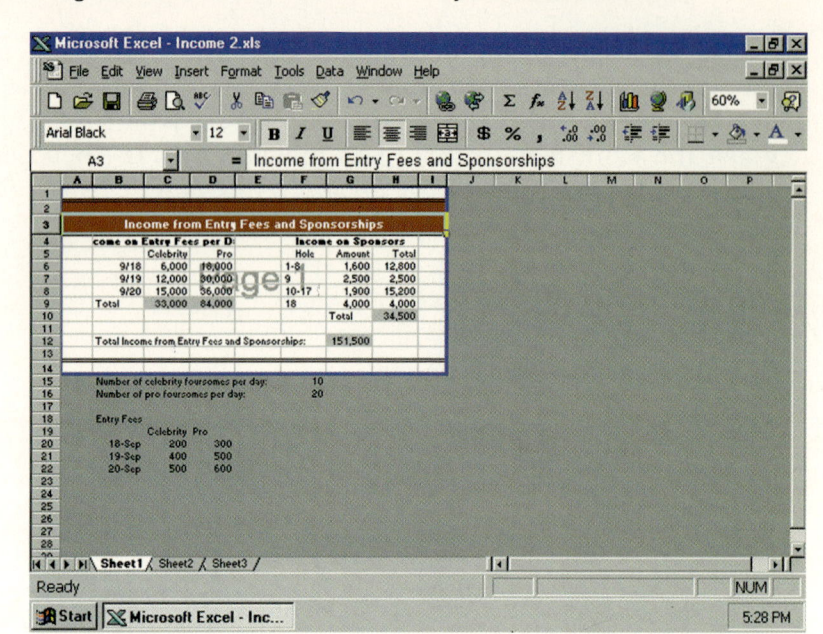

3 Drag the blue line at the bottom to just below row 14.

4 Click 🔍.
Now, only the bordered text displays in the print preview for page 1.

5 Click the Normal View button.
The worksheet displays in Normal view. Notice that the page break location is indicated with a dotted line.

Using AutoFormat

Excel provides several formats that you can apply to a complete worksheet or to a single range. The **AutoFormat** feature enables you to apply many formatting features automatically, creating very professional looking worksheets without much effort on your part. (Excel works hard so you don't have to.)

> **Note** AutoFormats are designed for worksheets or ranges that have row headings in the first column and column headings in the first row.

TASK 8: TO APPLY AN AUTOFORMAT:

1 Select B18:D22.
The cells are highlighted.

Project 3: Enhancing the Appearance of a Workbook   EX-93

2 Choose Format, AutoFormat.

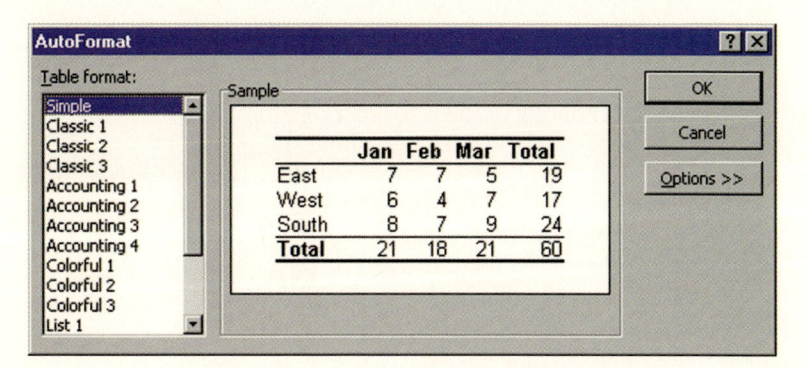

3 Select Colorful 2. Click Options, deselect Width/Height, and click OK. Click in a cell outside the selected range to see the true colors.

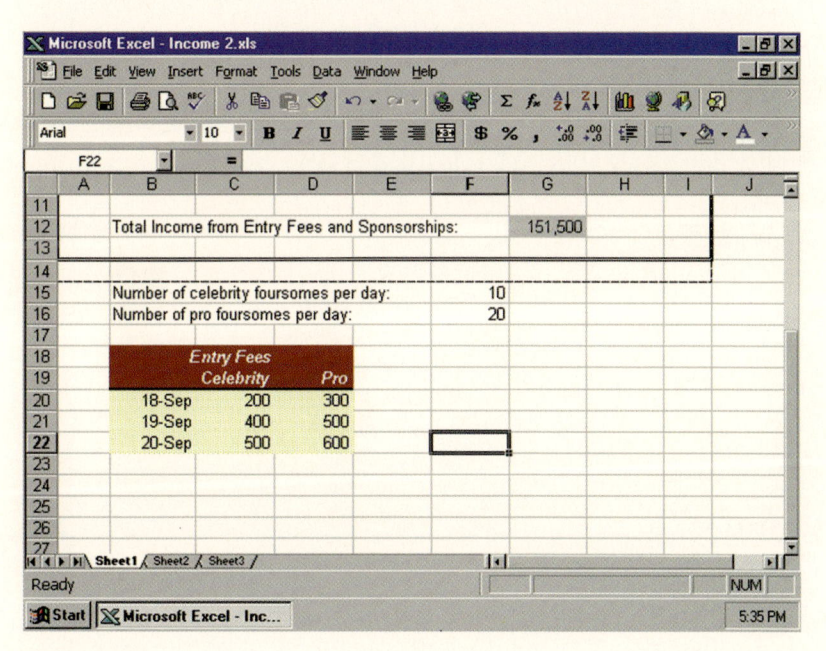

The Conclusion

If you have access to a printer, print page 1 of the worksheet. Save the workbook and close it.

Summary and Exercises

Summary

- You can format text with bold, italic, underline, different fonts and font sizes, and so on.
- Data in a cell can be left, right, or center aligned.
- Excel provides many formats for displaying numbers.
- You can apply a border to any side of a cell.
- You can apply a background color to a cell.
- You can apply a color to text.
- The Page Break view shows where page breaks are located.
- You can rearrange page breaks in the Page Break view.
- An AutoFormat can be applied to a worksheet or a range.

Key Terms and Operations

Key Terms	Operations
border	add a border
fill	add fill
page break	align cells
Page Break view	AutoFormat
pattern	change a page break
shading	format dates
	format numbers
	format text
	view a page break

Study Questions

Multiple Choice

1. If you type text in cell A1 and you want to center the text across cells A1 through A5,
   a. merge the cells and click the Center button.
   b. select A1:A5 and click the Center button.
   c. select A1:A5 and choose Format, Cells, Alignment, Center, and click OK.
   d. merge the cells, and choose Format, Align, Center.

2. You can apply an AutoFormat
   a. to a cell.
   b. only to a complete worksheet.
   c. to a single range.
   d. to noncontiguous ranges.

3. To make text bold,
   a. click in the cell, type the text, click the Bold button, and press Enter.
   b. select the cell and click the Bold button.
   c. select the cell and choose Format, Bold.
   d. All of the above.

4. Borders can be applied to
   a. any side of a range.
   b. all sides of a range.
   c. the top and bottom sides of a range.
   d. All of the above.

5. To add shading to a cell, select the cell and
   a. click the drop-down arrow on the Shading button and choose the color.
   b. choose Format, Cells, Shading, select the color, and click OK.
   c. choose Format, Cells, Patterns, select the color, and click OK.
   d. choose Format, Shading, select the color, and click OK.

6. A page break is marked with
   a. a dotted line in the worksheet.
   b. a blue line in the Print Preview.
   c. a dotted line in the Page Break Preview.
   d. a blue line in the worksheet.

7. Which of the following format(s) (if any) would be used to achieve this format: $ 1,200.00?
   a. general format with a dollar sign symbol and two decimal places
   b. accounting format with a dollar sign symbol and two decimal places
   c. currency format with a dollar sign symbol and two decimal places
   d. number format with a dollar sign symbol and two decimal places

8. When you increase the point size of text,
   a. you must first increase the height of the row.
   b. the text may wrap in the cell if the cell is not wide enough to accommodate the new size.
   c. the row height increases automatically to accommodate the size of the text.
   d. the cell width increases automatically to accommodate the size of the text.

9. The option to rotate text in a cell is found
   a. on the Orientation page of the Format Cells dialog box.
   b. on the Format menu.
   c. on the Rotate button in the Formatting Toolbar.
   d. on the Alignment page of the Format Cells dialog box.

10. Excel stores a date as
    a. a number.
    b. a date.
    c. text.
    d. a mixture of text and numbers.

Short Answer

1. How are numbers aligned in a cell?

2. How can you enter 1–2–97 and make it appear as January 2, 1997?

3. How do you change the font of the text entered in a cell?

4. How do you change the color of the text entered in a cell?

5. Under what circumstances do you have to format a cell as text?

6. How do you merge cells?

7. How are dates aligned in a cell?

8. The entry 1.2E103 is an example of what number format?

9. What is a serial number?

10. What is the default alignment for text in a cell?

For Discussion

1. Describe the AutoFormat feature and discuss the advantages of using it.

2. How can you designate where the pages will break when the worksheet prints?

3. Compare the Page Break Preview with the Print Preview view.

4. Give examples of ways you could use borders.

Review Exercises

1. Enhancing the restaurant sales worksheet

In this exercise, you will enhance the worksheet with border, shading, and number formats.

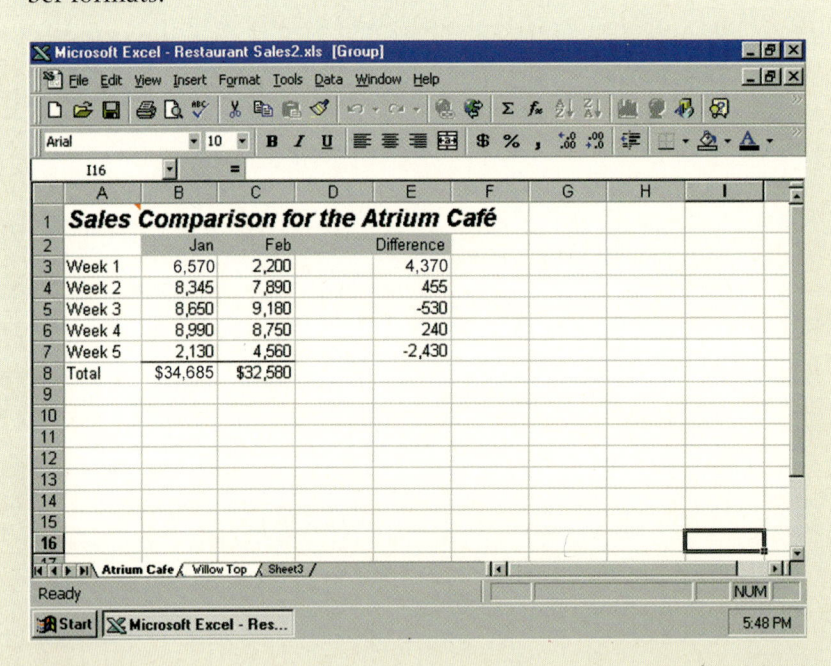

Figure 3.3

1. Open *Restaurant Sales.xls*, the file you saved at the end of Project 2.

2. Right align cells B2 and C2 on both worksheets.

3. Format all numbers on both worksheets (except for cells B8 and C8) with the Currency format, using no decimal places and no dollar sign. Format B8 and C8 on both worksheets with Currency, no decimal places, and a dollar sign.

4. Format cell A1 on both worksheets with bold, italic, 14 point.

5. Add a border to the bottom of cells B7 and C7 on both worksheets.

6. Add light gray fill to cells B2:E2 on both worksheets.

7. Save the file as *Restaurant Sales2.xls* and close it.

2. Creating a concert list

In this exercise, you will create a workbook for a list of concerts and enhance the worksheet with formatting.

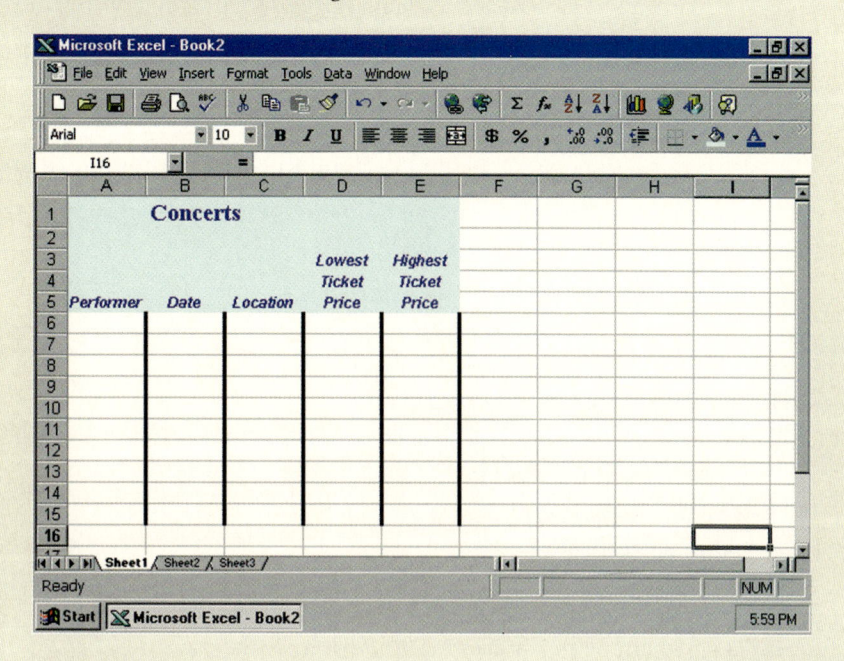

Figure 3.4

1. Go to http://www.ticketmaster.com and follow the link to the Box Office.

2. Search for at least 10 concerts by groups or performers that you like. Obtain information about when and where the concert will be and how much the tickets cost.

3. Create a worksheet based on Figure 3.4, with these column headings: Performer, Date, Location, Lowest Ticket Price, Highest Ticket Price.

4. Format the title with 14 point Times New Roman.

5. Format the column headings in bold, italic, 9 point and center them.

6. Use a thick border between each column.

7. Fill the range A1:E5 with light blue and change the color of the text in the range to dark blue.

8. Save the file as *Concerts.xls* and close it.

3. Enhancing the Container Corporation sales worksheet

1. Launch Excel and open *2 Container Corporation Sales xxx.xls* (where *xxx* represents your initials).

Note If you do not have a workbook named *2 Container Corporation Sales xxx.xls*, ask your instructor for a copy of the file you should use to complete this exercise.

2. Make the following changes to all three worksheets in the workbook:
   - Center the data contained in Cells A1 and A2 across Columns A through F.
   - Change the color of text in Cells A1 and A2.
   - Format the text in Cell A1 to 26-point bold.
   - Format the text in Cell A2 to 16-point italics.
   - Format cells containing dollar values as Currency with 0 decimal points.
   - Center the column headings in Row 4 and add a fill color to cells containing data in Row 4.
   - Center the Produce #s in Column A and add a different fill color to cells containing product numbers.
   - Center the data contained in Column B across Columns B and C.

3. Save the workbook using the filename *3 Container Corporation Sales xxx* and print a copy of each worksheet.

Assignments

1. Reformatting the *Income.xls* File

Open the Income.xls file. Move the data in cells B15:F22 to cell A1 Sheet2. Format the data on Sheet1 using your own ideas for borders, shading, fonts, and so on. When finished, save the file as *Income 3.xls*.

2. Using AutoFormat

If you have Internet access, download *Revenues.xls* from http://hepg.awl.com/select. If you are unable to download this file, ask your instructor how to obtain it. Experiment with different AutoFormats. Choose one of the formats you like and save the file as *Revenues2.xls*. Open *Revenues.xls* again and save it with another format that you like as *Revenues3.xls*. Open *Revenues.xls* and save it with another format that you like as *Revenues4.xls*.

PROJECT 4

Editing the Structure of a Worksheet and a Workbook

Think of yourself as an Excel architect. You design workbooks using the Excel "materials" — cells, columns, rows, and worksheets. When you want to edit the structure of a worksheet or a workbook, you have to request that materials be added to or removed from the file. Sometimes the design you want calls for different-sized materials or special materials — such as headers and footers. This project introduces you to the tools you'll need to modify the structure of a worksheet.

Objectives

After completing this project, you will be able to:

- ▶ Insert, delete, and arrange worksheets
- ▶ Change the size of columns and rows
- ▶ Insert columns, rows, and cells
- ▶ Delete columns, rows, and cells
- ▶ Create headers and footers

The Challenge

You have a workbook that contains March and April restaurant sales information that you have been preparing for the hotel manager, Mr. Gilmore.

You need to delete some information, add some information, make some adjustments in the columns and rows, and add a header and footer.

The Solution

You will begin your edits by deleting one of the worksheets, inserting a new worksheet, and rearranging worksheets. Then you will adjust the width of columns and the height of rows as needed. Next, you will insert and delete columns, rows, and cells, and, finally, you will add the headers and footers. Figure 4.1 shows the first worksheet in the workbook.

To obtain the files you need for this project, download them from the Addison Wesley Longman web site (http://hepg.awl.com/select or obtain them from your instructor.

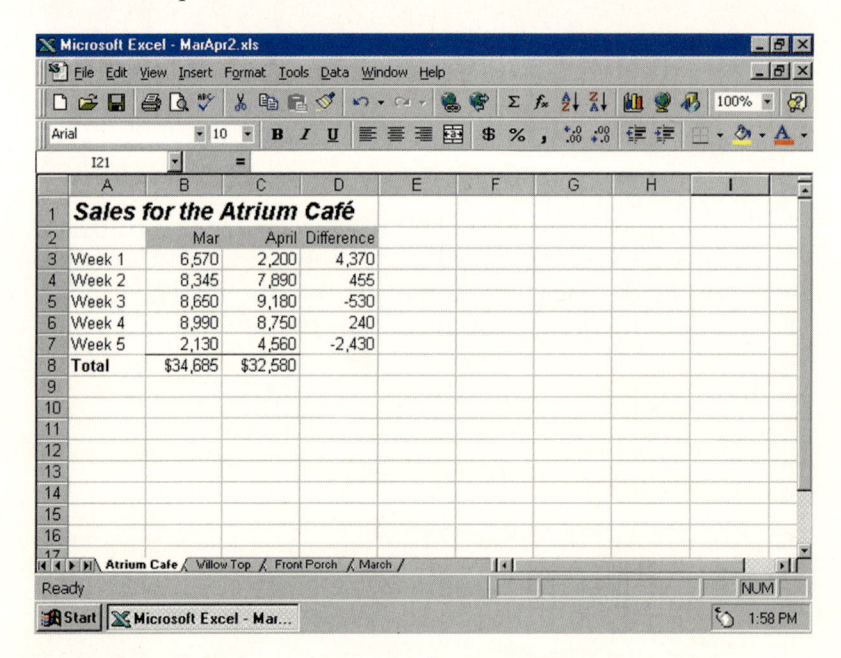

Figure 4.1

The Setup

So that your screen will match the illustrations and the tasks in this project will function as described, make sure that the Excel settings listed in Table 4.1 are selected on your computer. Because these are the default settings for the toolbars and view, you may not need to make any changes to your setup.

Table 4.1: Excel Settings

Location	Make these settings:
View, Toolbars	Deselect all toolbars except Standard and Formatting.
View	Use the Normal view and display the Formula Bar and Status Bar.

Project 4: Editing the Structure of a Worksheet and a Workbook   EX-101

Inserting, Deleting, and Arranging Worksheets

As you remember (if you don't remember, just keep it to yourself and no one will be the wiser), a workbook starts out with three worksheets. You can add more worksheets or delete up to two of the three. You also can re-arrange the order of worksheets.

TASK 1: TO INSERT AND DELETE PAGES:

1. Open *MarApr.xls*.

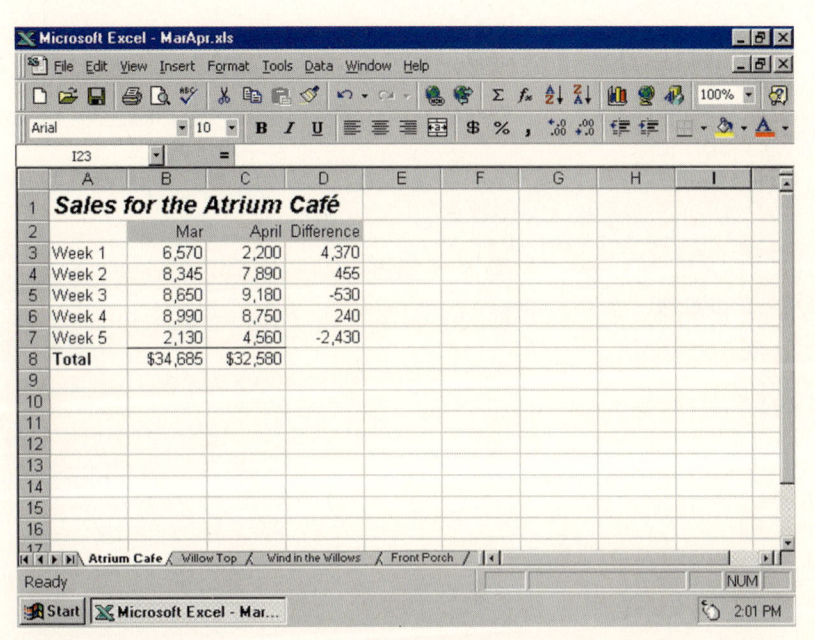

	A	B	C	D
1	Sales for the Atrium Café			
2		Mar	April	Difference
3	Week 1	6,570	2,200	4,370
4	Week 2	8,345	7,890	455
5	Week 3	8,650	9,180	-530
6	Week 4	8,990	8,750	240
7	Week 5	2,130	4,560	-2,430
8	Total	$34,685	$32,580	

2. Click each worksheet tab to see each page of the workbook.

3. Right-click the tab for Wind in the Willows.

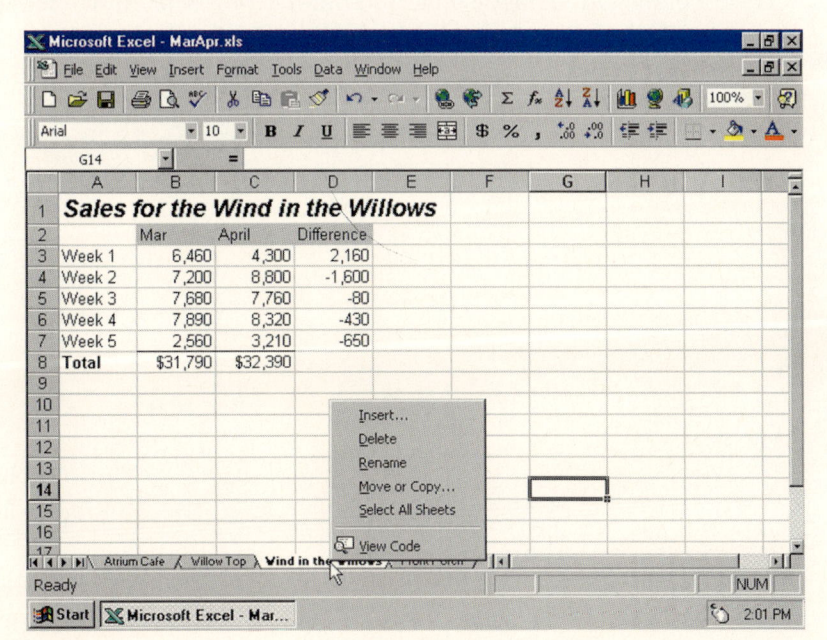

	A	B	C	D
1	Sales for the Wind in the Willows			
2		Mar	April	Difference
3	Week 1	6,460	4,300	2,160
4	Week 2	7,200	8,800	-1,600
5	Week 3	7,680	7,760	-80
6	Week 4	7,890	8,320	-430
7	Week 5	2,560	3,210	-650
8	Total	$31,790	$32,390	

   Context menu:
   - Insert...
   - Delete
   - Rename
   - Move or Copy...
   - Select All Sheets
   - View Code

4 Choose Delete from the shortcut menu.

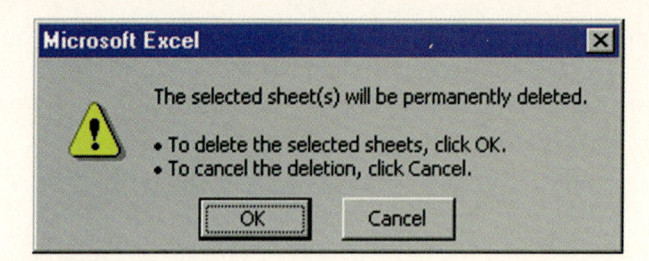

5 Click OK.
The worksheet is permanently deleted from the workbook, and no amount of clicking the Undo button will bring it back.

6 Right-click the Atrium Café tab and choose Insert from the shortcut menu.

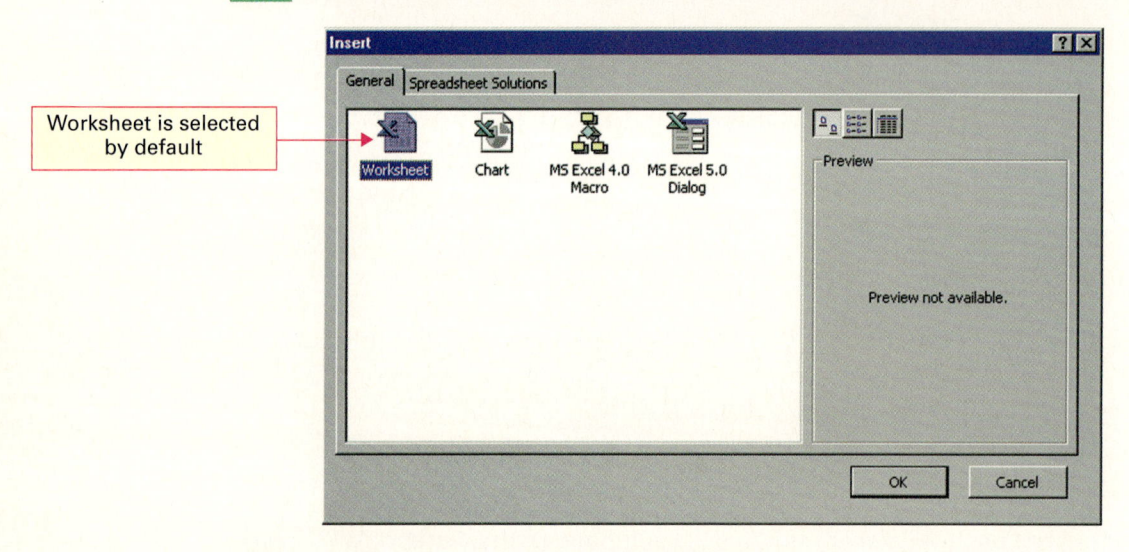

Worksheet is selected by default

7 Click OK.
A new blank worksheet is inserted before the selected worksheet.

8 Rename the new worksheet **March**.

Project 4: Editing the Structure of a Worksheet and a Workbook EX-103

New worksheet

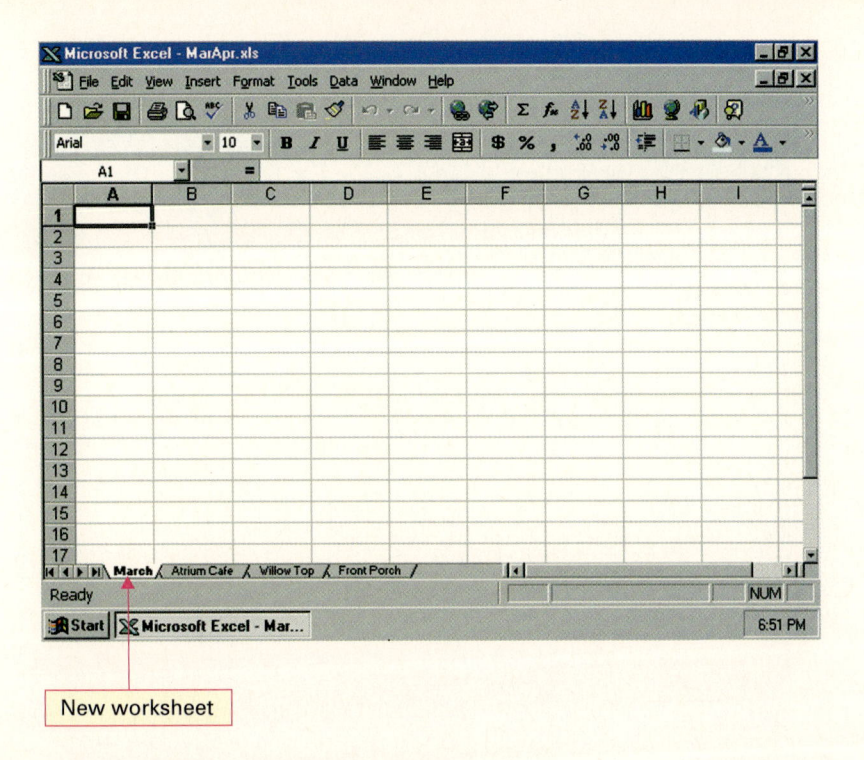

9 Drag the March tab between the Atrium Café tab and the Willow Top tab, but don't release the mouse button yet.

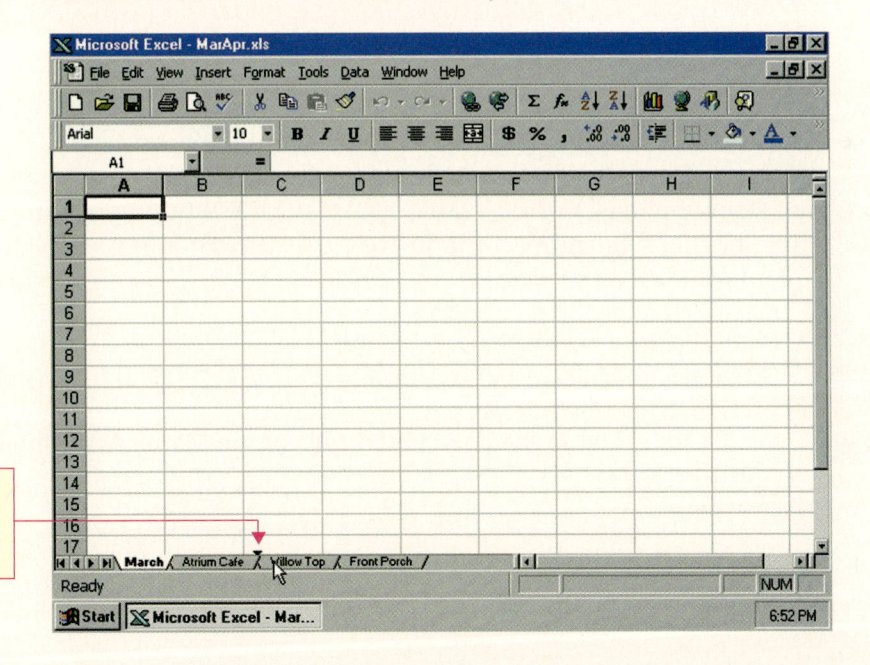

The black triangle marks the location where the new worksheet will be positioned

EX-104

10 Continue dragging to the end of the tabs and then release the mouse button.

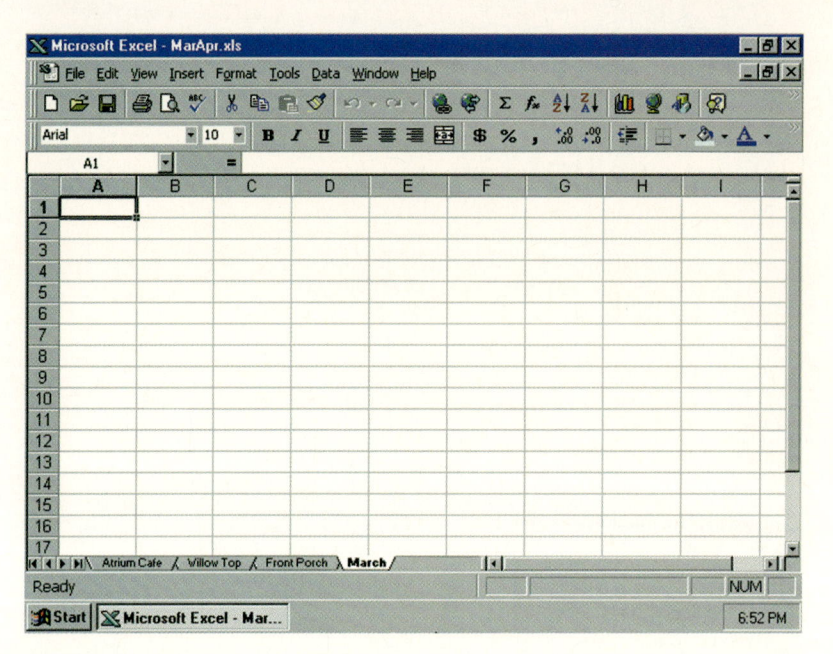

Changing the Size of Columns and Rows

When you create a new workbook, all the columns are the same width, and all the rows are the same height. When you add data to a worksheet, you often must change the row heights and column widths to accommodate the data. As you have already seen in a previous project, the height of a row increases or decreases automatically when you change the point size of the data; however, you may want to change the height of a row just to improve the spacing.

TASK 2: TO CHANGE THE WIDTH OF COLUMNS BY DRAGGING:

1 Type the following in the designated cells of the March worksheet:
A1: **March Sales**
A2: **Atrium Café**

> **Note** Excel will add the accent to the "e" in "café" automatically.

A3: **Willow Top Restaurant**
A4: **Front Porch Restaurant**

2 Point to the line that divides column letters A and B in the Column heading row.

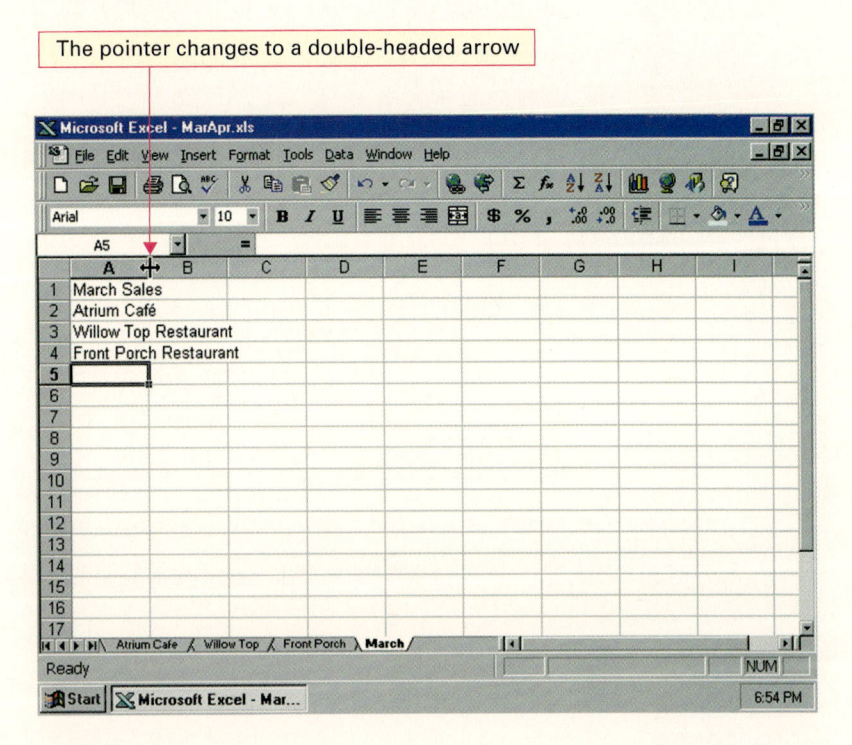

The pointer changes to a double-headed arrow

3 Drag the line to the right until the column is wide enough to hold the text.

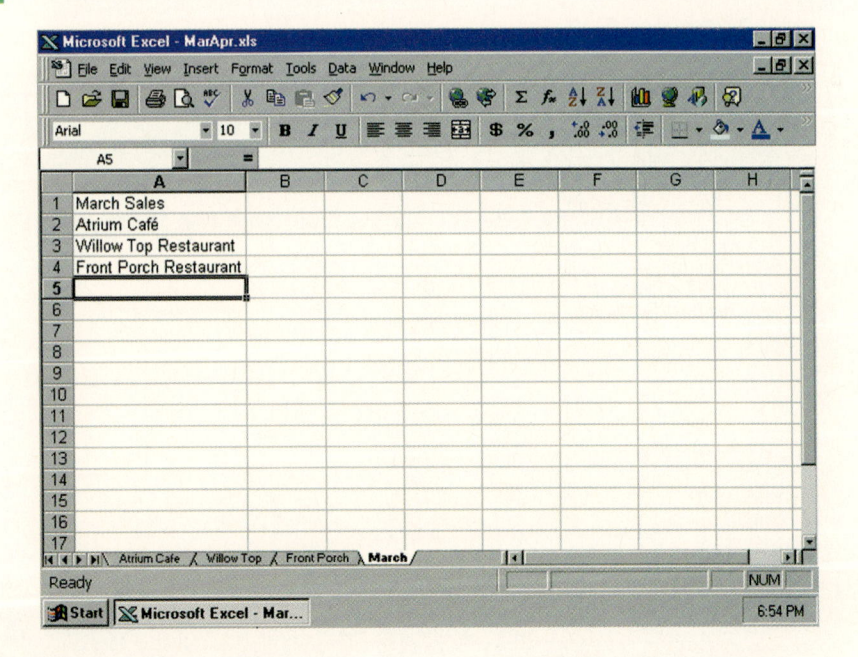

4 Drag the column until it is too wide as shown:

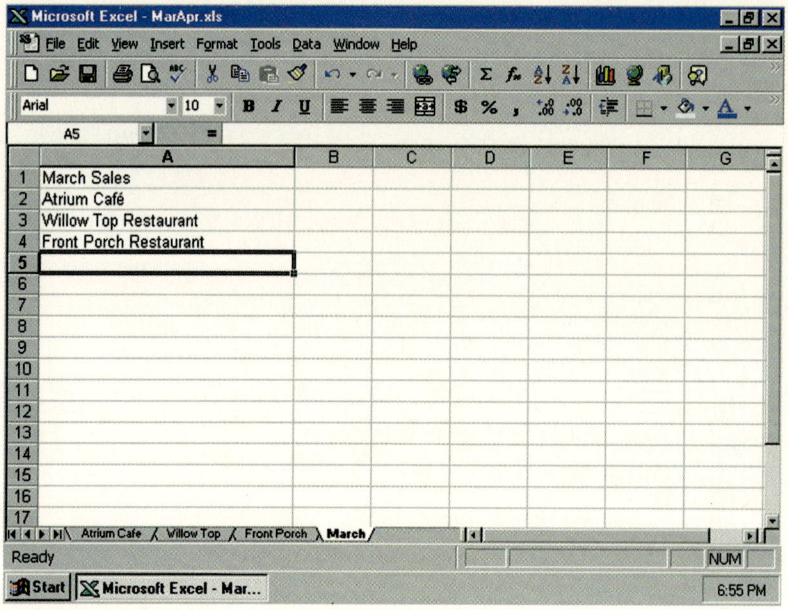
Microsoft Excel - MarApr.xls
File Edit View Insert Format Tools Data Window Help
Arial
10
A5
March Sales
Atrium Café
Willow Top Restaurant
Front Porch Restaurant
Atrium Cafe
Willow Top
Front Porch
March
Ready
NUM
Start
Microsoft Excel - Mar...
6:55 PM

5 Type the following in the designated cells:
B2: **34685**
B3: **45240**
B4: **30835**

6 Drag the line between column letters B and C until column B is too wide as shown:

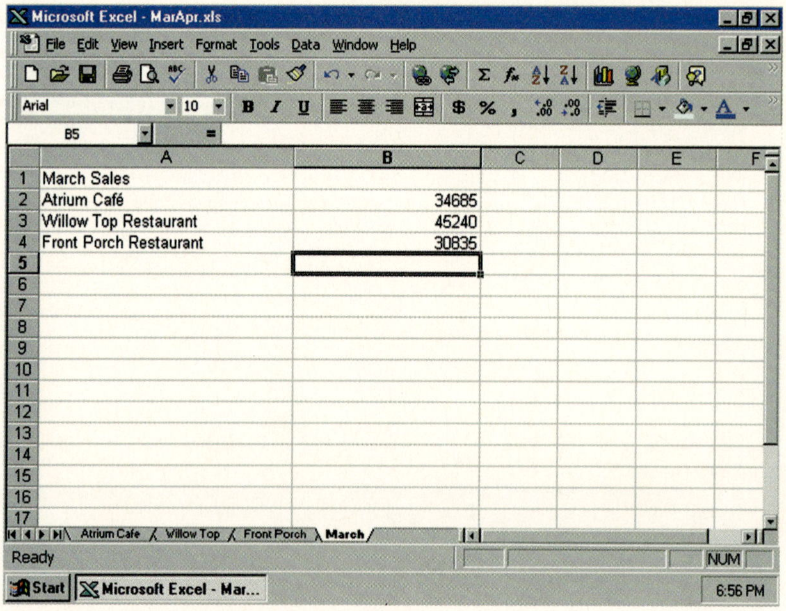
Microsoft Excel - MarApr.xls
File Edit View Insert Format Tools Data Window Help
Arial
10
B5
March Sales
Atrium Café
34685
Willow Top Restaurant
45240
Front Porch Restaurant
30835
Atrium Cafe
Willow Top
Front Porch
March
Ready
NUM
Start
Microsoft Excel - Mar...
6:56 PM

Using AutoFit

Another way to change the width of a column is to use AutoFit. ***AutoFit*** automatically adjusts columns to be just wide enough to accommodate the widest entry and can adjust the widths of several columns at once.

Project 4: Editing the Structure of a Worksheet and a Workbook   EX-107

TASK 3: TO CHANGE THE WIDTH OF COLUMNS BY USING AUTOFIT:

1 Select columns A and B by dragging the mouse pointer through A and B at the top of the columns.
The columns are highlighted.

2 Choose Format, Column.

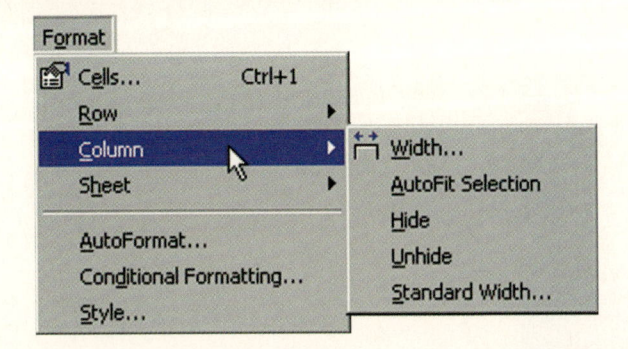

3 Choose AutoFit Selection.

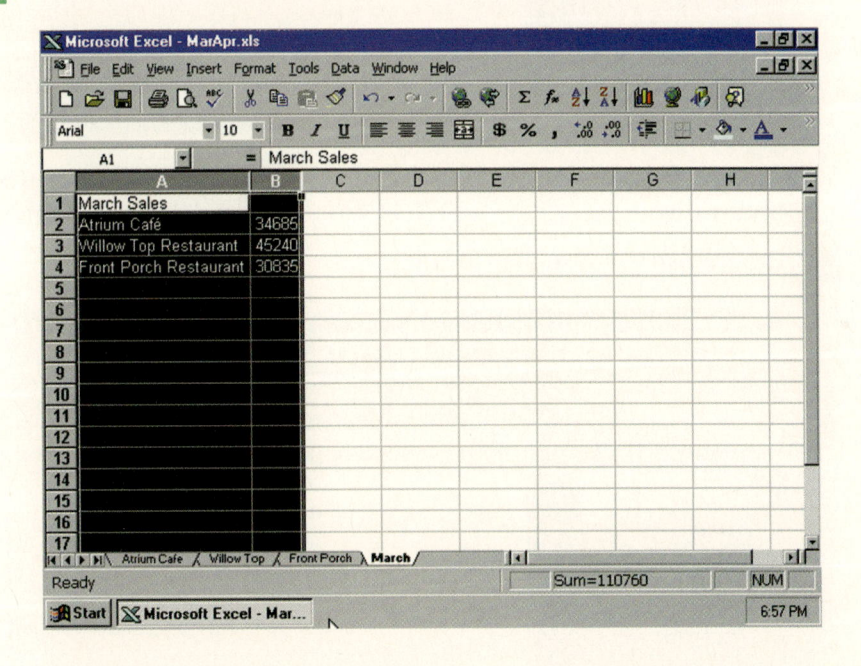

> **Tip** You can select multiple columns and double-click the line between the column letters to AutoFit the selections.

Adjusting Row Height

If you want to control the spacing in a worksheet, you can make rows taller or shorter by dragging them to the desired height.

EX-108

TASK 4: TO CHANGE THE HEIGHT OF ROWS:

1 Point to the line that divides row numbers 1 and 2 in the row indicators column.

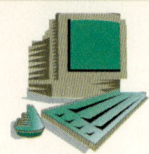

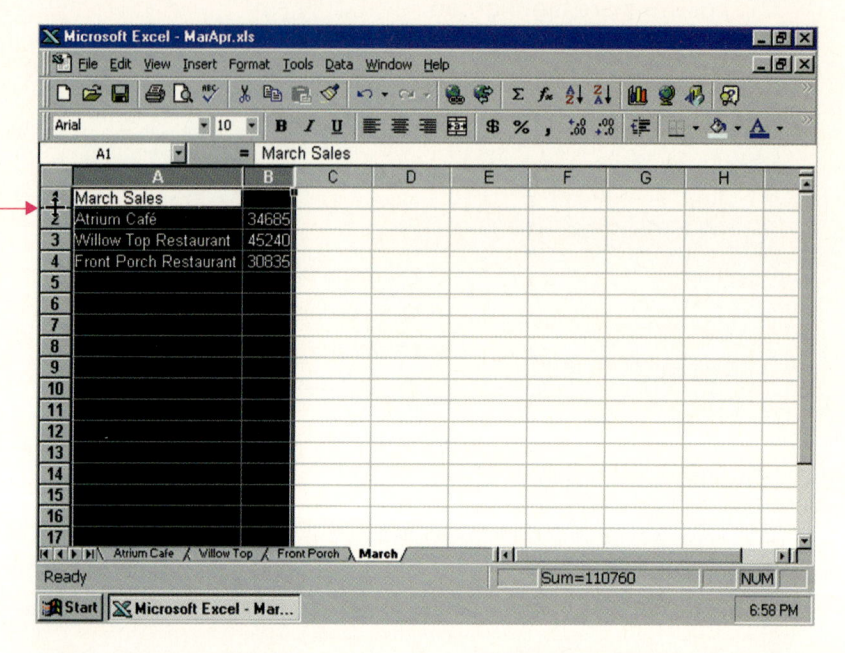

The pointer changes to a double-headed arrow

It doesn't matter if columns are selected when you change the row height because you don't have to select anything to change the height.

2 Drag down to make the row taller.

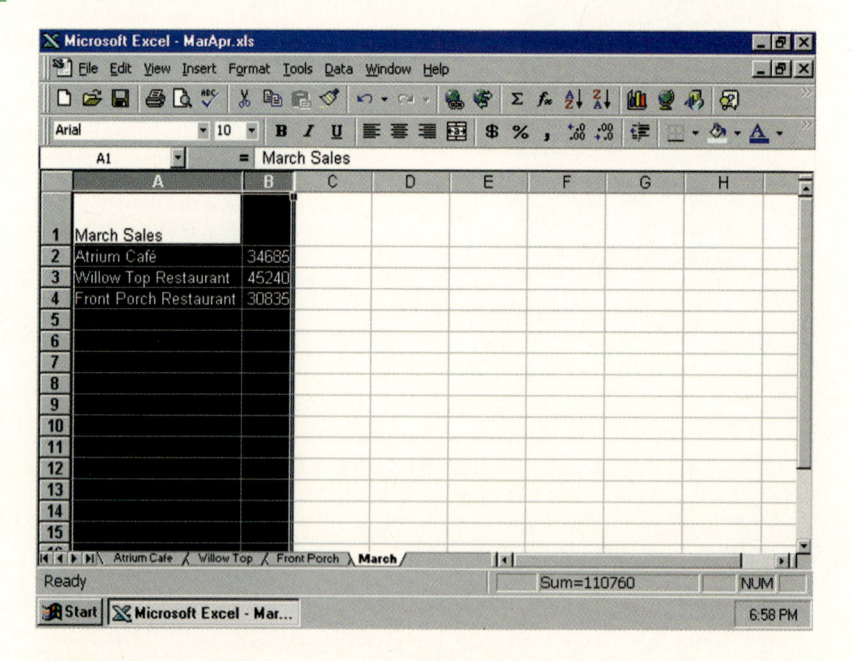

Tip You also can size rows with AutoFit. As you probably can guess, the command is under Format, Row or you can select the rows and double-click the line between the row numbers.

Project 4: Editing the Structure of a Worksheet and a Workbook   EX-109

Inserting Columns, Rows, and Cells

When you insert a column, all the other columns move to the right to give the new column room. When you insert rows, all the other rows move down, and when you insert cells, the other cells move to the right or move down. Excel is so polite!

TASK 5: TO INSERT A COLUMN, A ROW, AND A CELL:

1. Click anywhere in column A.
   The cell is selected.

2. Choose Insert.

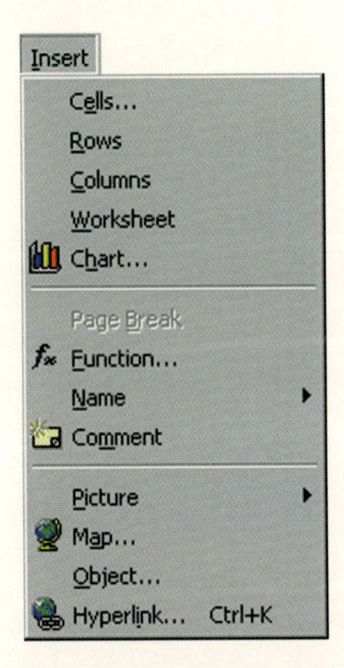

3. Choose Columns.

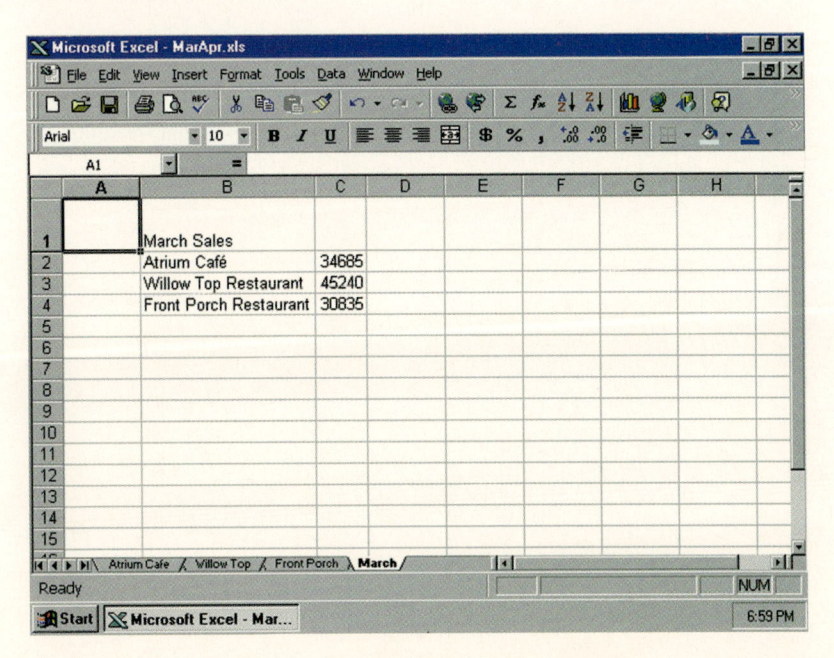

EX-110

Tip To insert multiple columns, select the number of columns you want to insert in the location where you want to insert them, and then choose Insert, Columns.

4 Click anywhere in row 2. The cell is selected.

5 Choose Insert, Rows. (The new rows take on the dimensions of the row above.)

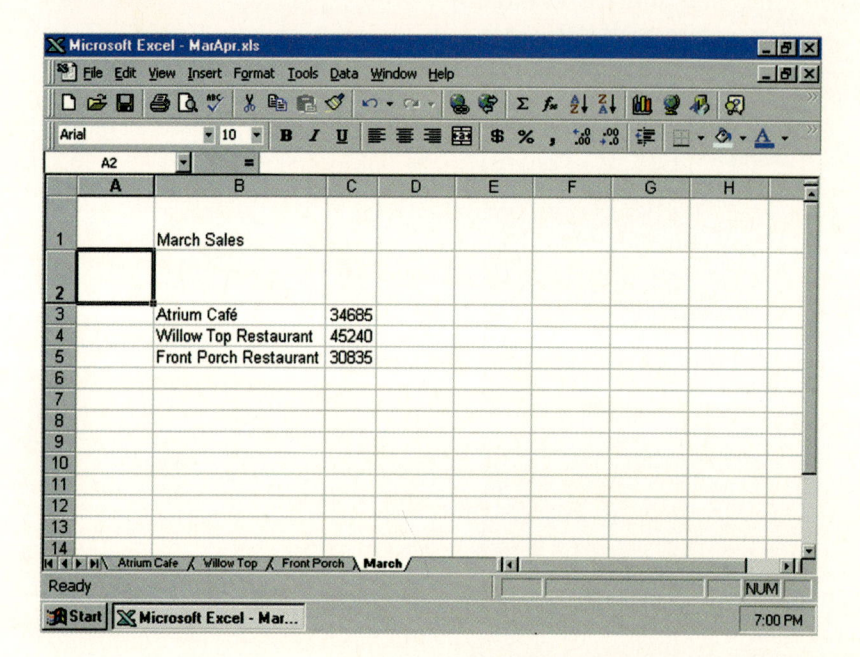

Tip To insert multiple rows, select the number of rows you want to insert in the location where you want to insert them, and then choose Insert, Rows.

6 Type the following in the designated cells:
D1: **March Banquets**
D3: **D.A.R.**
D4: **L.W.V.**
D5: **B.S.A**
E3: **2560**
E4: **1500**
E5: **900**

7 Select cells D4 and E4.

8 Choose Insert, Cells.

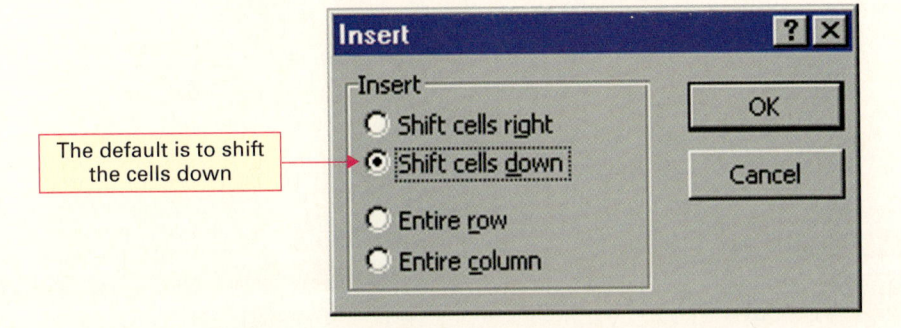

The default is to shift the cells down

9 Click OK.

If you had inserted a row instead of a cell, cells B4 and C4 would be blank

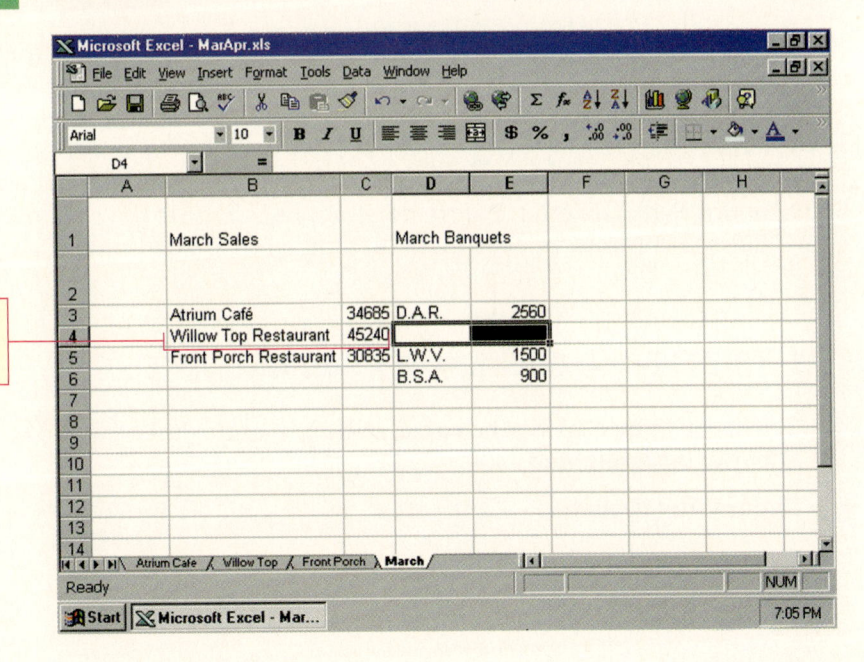

10 Type **G.S.A.** in cell D4, press →, type **950**, and press ENTER.

Deleting Columns, Rows, and Cells

When you delete columns, rows, or cells, you actually cut the space they occupy out of the worksheet. You don't just delete the data they contain.

Caution When you delete a column or row, the entire column or the entire row is deleted. Before deleting, be sure that the column or row doesn't contain data in a location that is off screen.

TASK 6: TO DELETE A COLUMN, A ROW, AND A CELL:

1 Select row 2 by clicking the row 2 button — at the left of the row. The row is highlighted.

2 Choose Edit, Delete.

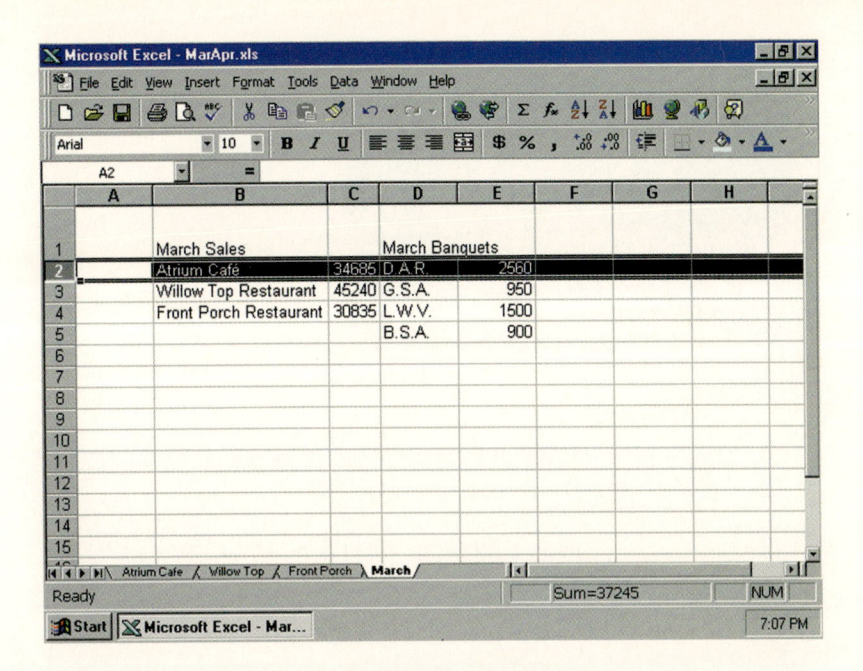

Project 4: Editing the Structure of a Worksheet and a Workbook EX-113

3 Select column A by clicking the column button A above the column. The column is highlighted.

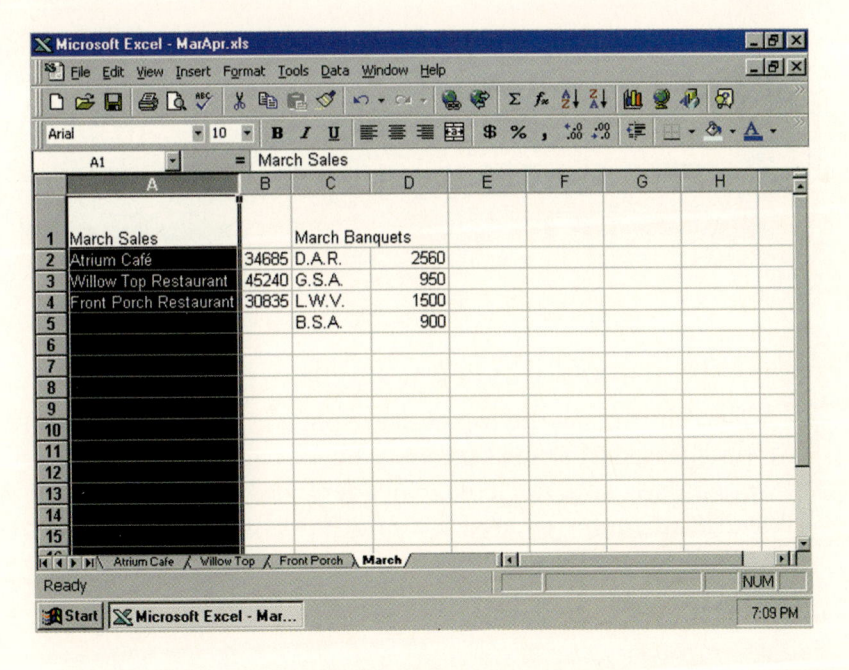

4 Choose Edit, Delete.

EX-114

5 Select cells C2 and D2 and choose Edit, Delete.

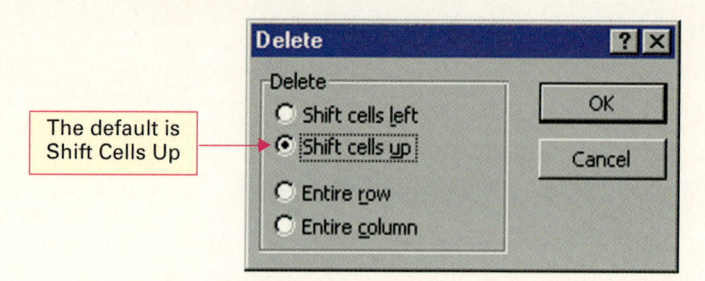

The default is Shift Cells Up

6 Click OK.

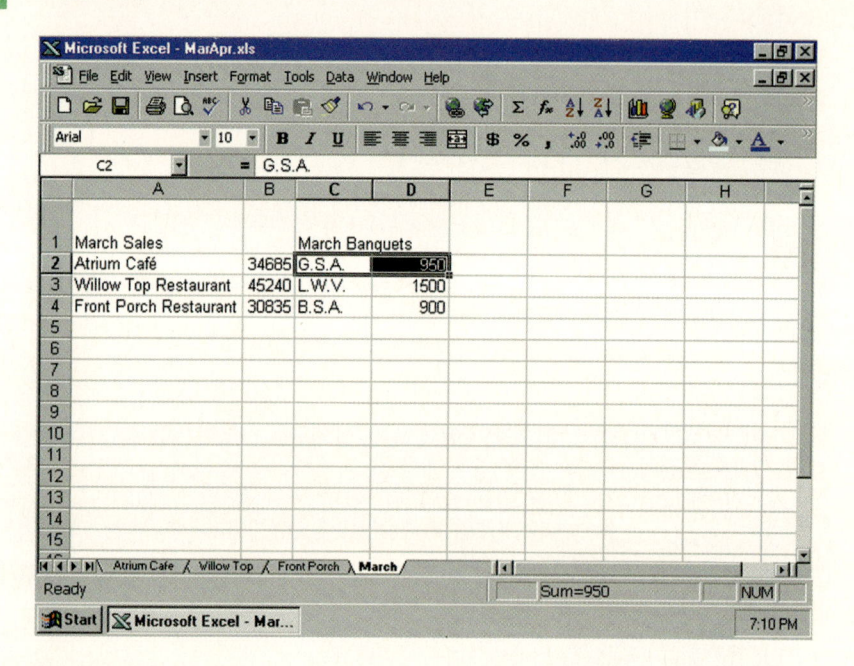

Creating Headers and Footers

A *header* prints at the top of every page of a worksheet, and a *footer* prints (you guessed it) at the bottom of every page. If the workbook has multiple worksheets, you can create headers and footers for each worksheet. A header or footer created for one worksheet doesn't print on any other worksheets in the same workbook.

Project 4: Editing the Structure of a Worksheet and a Workbook   EX-115

TASK 7: TO CREATE A SIMPLE HEADER AND A FOOTER:

1 Choose View.

2 Choose Header and Footer.

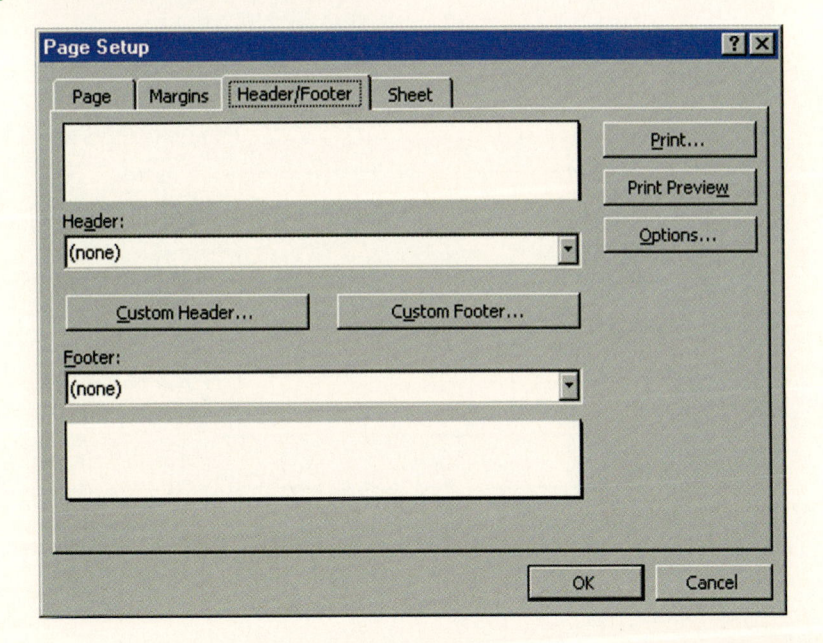

EX-116

3 Click the down arrow for the Header list and choose Page 1.

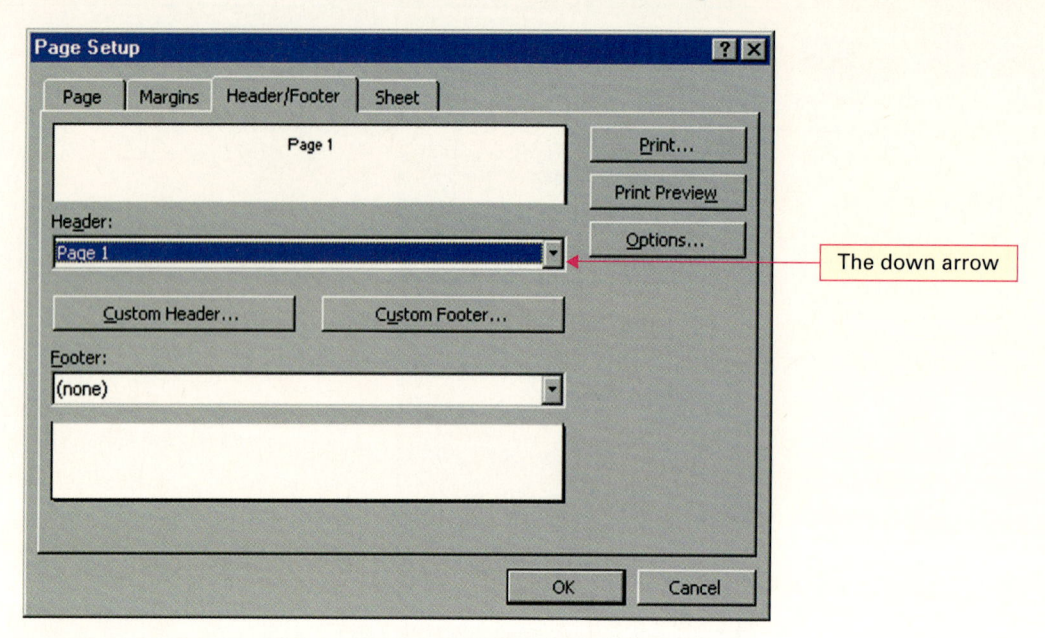

The down arrow

4 Click the down arrow for the Footer list and choose MarApr.xls.

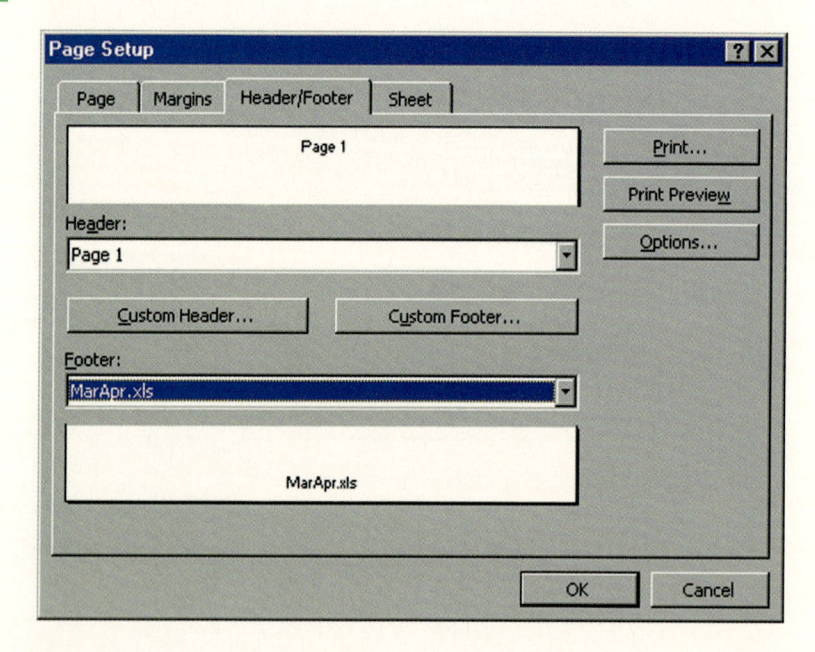

Project 4: Editing the Structure of a Worksheet and a Workbook   EX-117

5 Click Print Preview.

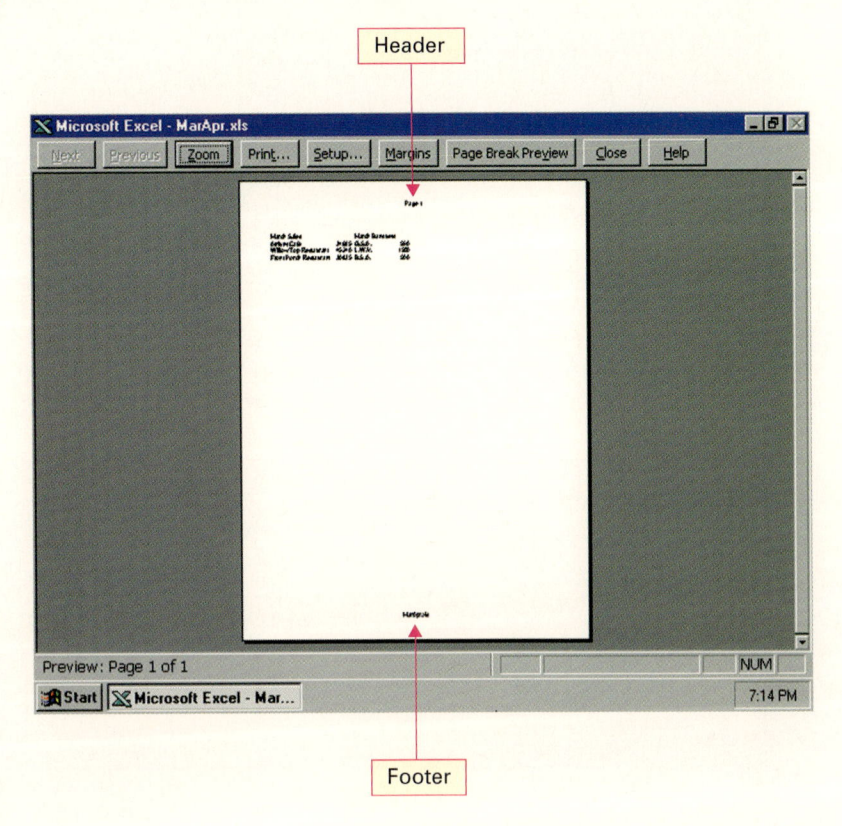

Header

Footer

6 Click Close.
The preview closes, and the worksheet displays in Normal view.

Creating a Custom Header and Footer

If you don't want to use the text supplied for a simple header or footer, you can create a custom header or footer and type the text that you want. Custom headers and footers are divided into three typing areas. The area on the left is left-justified, the area in the middle is centered, and the area on the right is right-justified.

TASK 8: TO CREATE A CUSTOM HEADER AND FOOTER:

1 Click the Atrium Café tab.
The Atrium Café worksheet displays.

2 Choose View, Headers and Footers. The Page Setup dialog box displays.

3 Click Custom Header.

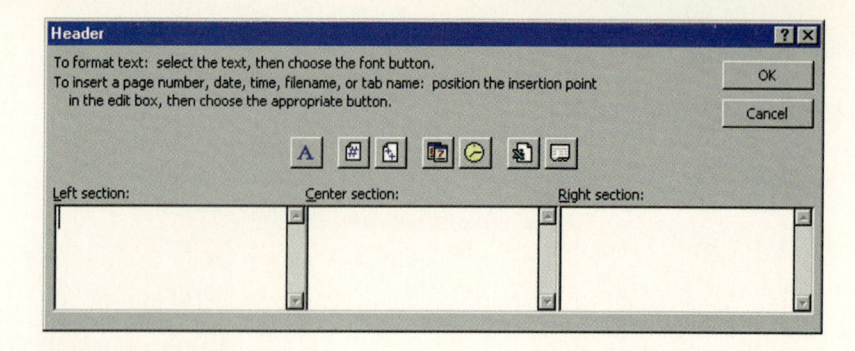

EX-118

4 Type **Sales Report** in the left section, press TAB twice, and click the Date button. (When you click the Date button instead of typing the date, Excel adjusts the date to the current date each time the workbook is used.)

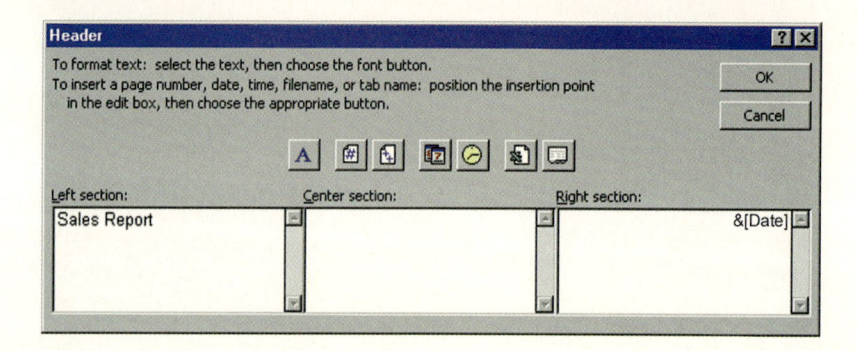

5 Click OK.
The Header dialog box closes and the Page Setup dialog box reappears.

6 Click Custom Footer.

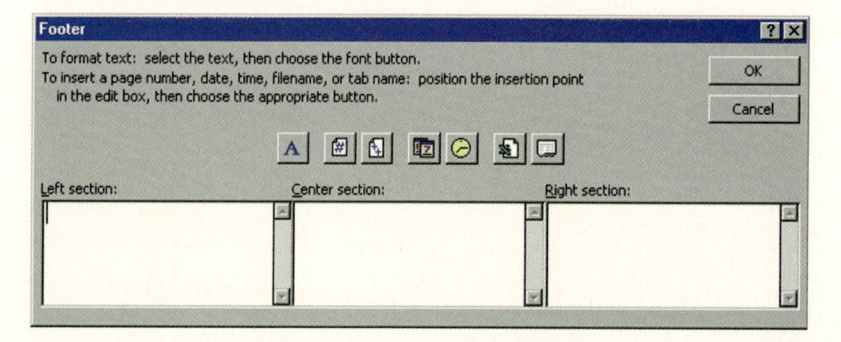

7 Press TAB and type **Prepared by Accounting** in the center section.

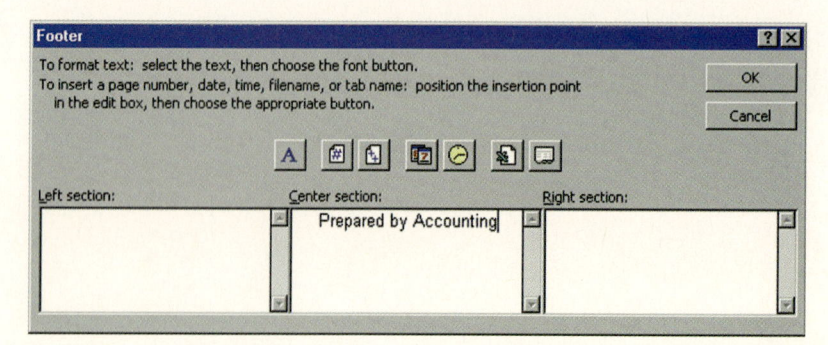

8 Click OK.
The Footer dialog box closes.

9 Click Print Preview.

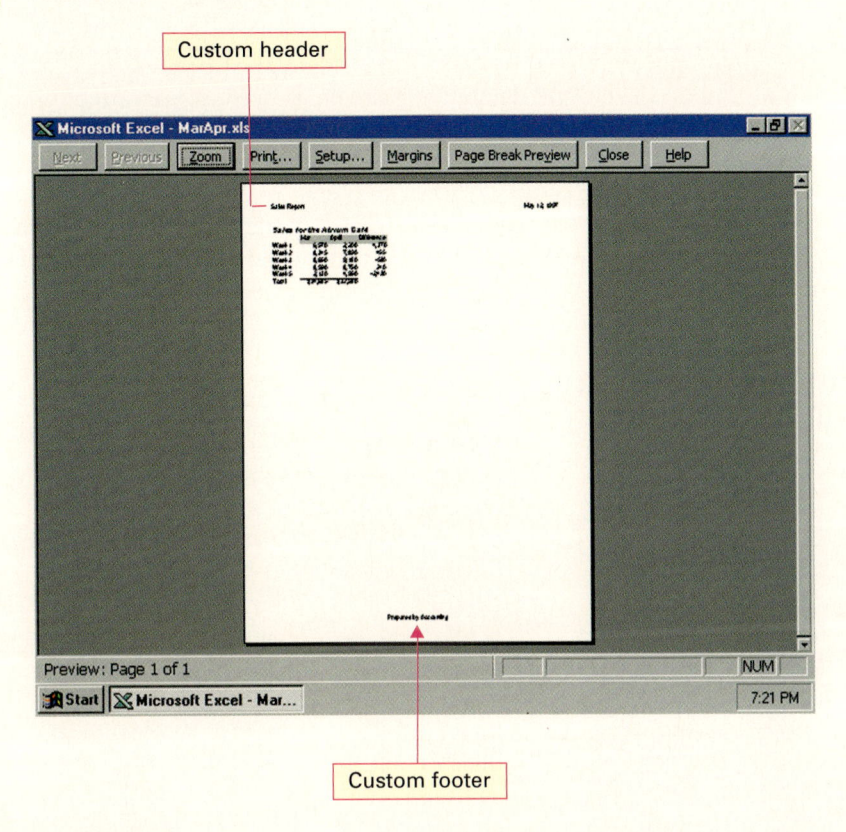

Custom header

Custom footer

10 Click Close.
The Print Preview closes, and the worksheet displays in Normal view.

The Conclusion

Save the worksheet as *MarApr2.xls* and close the file.

Summary and Exercises

Summary

- You can insert and delete worksheets, as well as rearrange them.
- You can change the width of columns and the height of rows.
- You can insert columns, rows, and cells.
- You can delete columns, rows, and cells.
- You can create a header that prints at the top of the page and a footer that prints at the bottom of a page. Headers and footers do not appear on screen in Normal view.

Key Terms and Operations

Key Terms
AutoFit
footer
header

Operations
change the height of a row
change the width of a column
create a footer
create a header
delete a cell
delete a column
delete a row
delete a worksheet
insert a cell
insert a column
insert a row
insert a worksheet
move a worksheet

Study Questions

Multiple Choice

1. A header prints at the
   a. top of every page in a workbook.
   b. bottom of every page in a workbook.
   c. top of every page in a worksheet.
   d. bottom of every page in a worksheet.

2. When you delete a column,
   a. the data in the column is deleted but the cells remain in the worksheet.
   b. the data in the column is deleted and so are the cells.
   c. the column is really just hidden.
   d. the column is moved to the end of the worksheet.

3. When you insert a cell, the other cells move
   a. down.
   b. to the left.
   c. to the right.
   d. down or to the right, as specified by the user.

4. A footer prints at the
   a. top of every page in a workbook.
   b. bottom of every page in a workbook.
   c. top of every page in a worksheet.
   d. bottom of every page in a worksheet.

5. AutoFit can adjust the width of
   a. only one column at a time.
   b. only a row.
   c. columns or rows.
   d. the page.

6. A custom header
   a. is divided into three typing areas.
   b. is created by choosing Format, Header and Footer.
   c. isn't visible in Print Preview mode.
   d. only uses default data, such as the page number or the name of the file.

7. If you delete a cell,
   a. the data is deleted.
   b. the cell is deleted and the data displays in the next cell.
   c. the data and the cell are deleted.
   d. None of the above.

8. When you delete a cell, the other cells move
   a. up.
   b. down.
   c. to the left.
   d. up or to the left, as specified by the user.

9. When you drag to change the column width, the pointer displays as
   a. a four-headed arrow.
   b. an arrow.
   c. a two-headed arrow.
   d. a hand.

10. To insert a column, first
    a. select the column where you want the new column to go.
    b. click in the column where you want the new column to go.
    c. A or B
    d. None of the above.

Short Answer

1. How do you insert multiple rows?
2. How do you insert multiple columns?
3. What is a custom header?
4. How do you delete a worksheet?
5. How do you delete a row?
6. How do you delete a cell?
7. How do you create a header with the filename in the center?
8. If the row height adjusts automatically, why would you need to change the height of a row?

9. How do you move a worksheet?
10. How do you see a header or footer without actually printing the worksheet?

For Discussion

1. When would it be an advantage to use AutoFit instead of dragging columns to change the width?
2. Discuss the advantages of using a custom header or footer.
3. Describe a circumstance in which it would be preferable to insert a cell instead of a row.
4. What precautions should you take before deleting a column or a row?

Review Exercises

1. Editing the *MarApr2* workbook

In this exercise you will enhance the worksheet and create a footer.

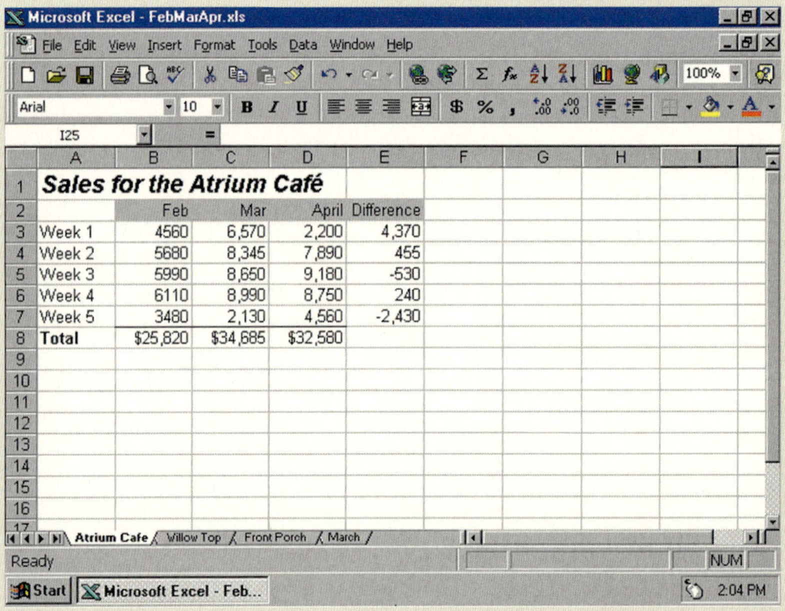

	A	B	C	D	E
1	Sales for the Atrium Café				
2		Feb	Mar	April	Difference
3	Week 1	4560	6,570	2,200	4,370
4	Week 2	5680	8,345	7,890	455
5	Week 3	5990	8,650	9,180	-530
6	Week 4	6110	8,990	8,750	240
7	Week 5	3480	2,130	4,560	-2,430
8	Total	$25,820	$34,685	$32,580	

Figure 4.2

1. Open *MarApr2.xls* and click the Atrium Café tab, if necessary.
2. Insert a column before column B and type this information:

   B2: **Feb**

   B3: **4560**

   B4: **5680**

   B5: **5990**

   B6: **6110**

   B7: **3480**

   B8: **=SUM(B3:B7)**

3. Apply a gray fill to cell B2, apply a border to the bottom of cell B7, and format cell B8 with a Currency format (no decimal places) and remove the bold.

4. Create a footer for the Willow Top worksheet that says "Located in The Grande Hotel" and center the footer.

5. Save the file as *FebMarApr.xls* and close it.

2. Creating a sales workbook for the sandwich shops and snack bars

In this exercise, you will create a workbook that can be used to track the sales of all the sandwich shops and snack bars at The Willows Resort.

1. Download the file *Willows.doc* from the Addison Wesley Longman web site (http://hepg.awl.com/select), or ask your instructor for this file. Open the file and find the list of sandwich shops and snack bars.

2. Create a workbook with a worksheet for each of the nine shops and name each worksheet with the name of the shop.

3. Type a title on each worksheet that says "Sales for *xxx*," where *xxx* is the name of the sandwich shop or snack bar. In column A, starting in cell A3, list the weeks in the month (Week 1, Week 2, and so on) and the word "Total" (as in Figure 4.2). In cells B2, C2, and D2, list the first three months of the year (Jan, Feb, and Mar).

4. Create a footer with a centered page number for each worksheet.

5. Save the file as *ShopSales.xls*.

3. Editing and enhancing the Container Corporation sales worksheet

1. Launch Excel and open the workbook *3 Container Corporation Sales xxx.xls*.

> **Note** If you do not have a workbook named *3 Container Corporation Sales xxx.xls*, ask your instructor for a copy of the file you should use to complete this exercise.

2. Make the following changes to the Sales Increase worksheet:
   - Move the *Sales Increase* worksheet so that it appears as the first worksheet in the workbook.
   - Search for the word Actual and replace it with the current year.
   - Search for the word Expected and replace it with the last year.

3. Copy the *<Last Year> Sales* worksheet to create a new worksheet at the end of the workbook.

4. Rename the worksheet *Projected <Next Year> Sales*.

5. Delete the *Sales Increase* worksheet.

6. Make the following changes to all worksheets in the workbook:
   - Change the data in Cell B4 to *Product Description*.
   - Change the width of Column C to accommodate the new column heading.
   - Change the height of Row 5 and Row 10 so that there is more room between Row 4 and Row 5 and between Row 9 and 10.

- Add a bottom border to Cells D9, E9, and F9 and center the word *Total* in bold in Cell A10.

- Change the fill color for cells in Row 10 to the same color added to Cells A5–A9.

7. Save the workbook using the filename *4 Container Corporation Sales xxx*.

8. Add a header that contains your name right aligned to the workbook and print a copy of each worksheet in the workbook.

Assignments

1. Creating a banquet workbook

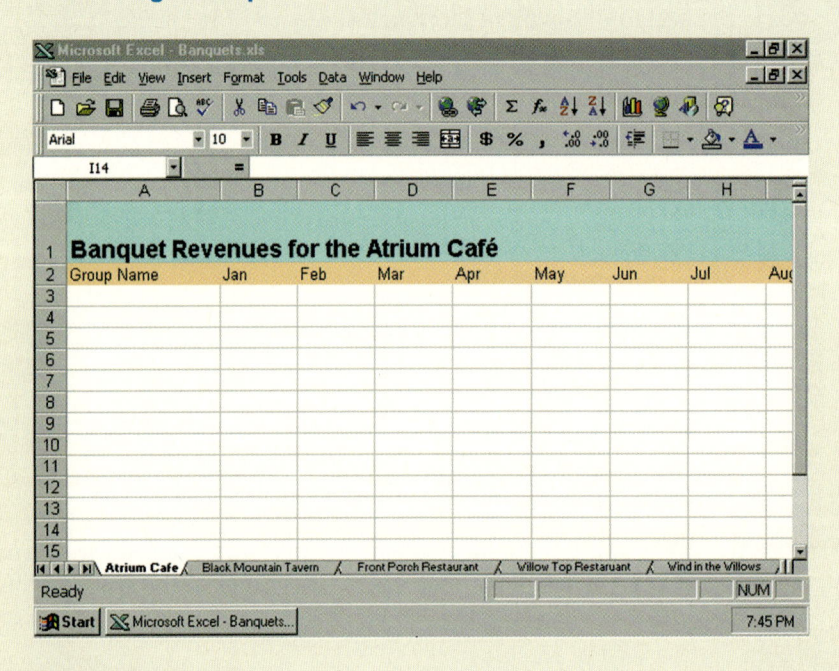

Figure 4.3

Create a workbook with five worksheets and name each worksheet as follows: Atrium Café, Willow Top Restaurant, Wind in the Willows, Front Porch Restaurant, and Black Mountain Tavern. Arrange the worksheets in alphabetical order. Add the text and formatting shown in Figure 4.3 to all the worksheets. (Remember, you can enter the same data on multiple worksheets at the same time.) Save the file as *Banquets.xls* and close it.

2. Creating a shopping list (Optional Exercise)

Take an international shopping trip via the Planet Shopping Network (http://www.planetshopping.com). Create a workbook that lists the items you would like to buy, their prices (including any shipping, handling, taxes, and duties), and their Web addresses. Use the SUM formula to total the prices and other costs. Create a worksheet for each shopping category (apparel, books, music, jewelry, automobiles, and so on). Save the workbook as *ShopTilYouDrop.xls*.

PROJECT 5

Creating a More Complex Workbook

Well, you're getting pretty good at this, so you're probably ready for something more challenging. This project provides both challenge and fun.

Objectives

After completing this project, you will be able to:

- ➤ Copy data from another workbook
- ➤ Sort data
- ➤ Enter formulas with relative references
- ➤ Use headings in formulas
- ➤ Enter formulas with absolute references
- ➤ Create and modify a chart

The Challenge

Ruth Lindsey, the manager of most of the gift shops at The Willows Resort, would like for you to work on an inventory of the ten top selling items and create some charts for the first quarter sales.

The Solution

You will copy data from an existing workbook into the inventory workbook, enter new data, and create formulas to calculate the number of items that you need to order and the wholesale prices of the items. Additionally, you will create a chart for the first quarter sales and a chart for the January sales. Figure 5.1 shows the results.

You can download the files needed for this project from the Addison Wesley Longman web site (http://hepg.awl.com/select) or you can obtain them from your instructor.

The Setup

So that your screen will match the illustrations in this chapter and to ensure that all the tasks in this project will function as described, you should set up Excel as described in Table 5.1. Because these are the default settings for the toolbars and view, you may not need to make any changes to your setup.

Table 5.1: Excel Settings

Location	Make these settings:
View, Toolbars	Deselect all toolbars except Standard and Formatting.
View	Use the Normal view and display the Formula Bar and Status Bar.

Copying Data from Another Workbook

You have copied data from one range to another on the same worksheet, and you have copied data from one worksheet to another in the same workbook. Now you will copy data from one workbook to another. The procedure is very similar to what you have already learned.

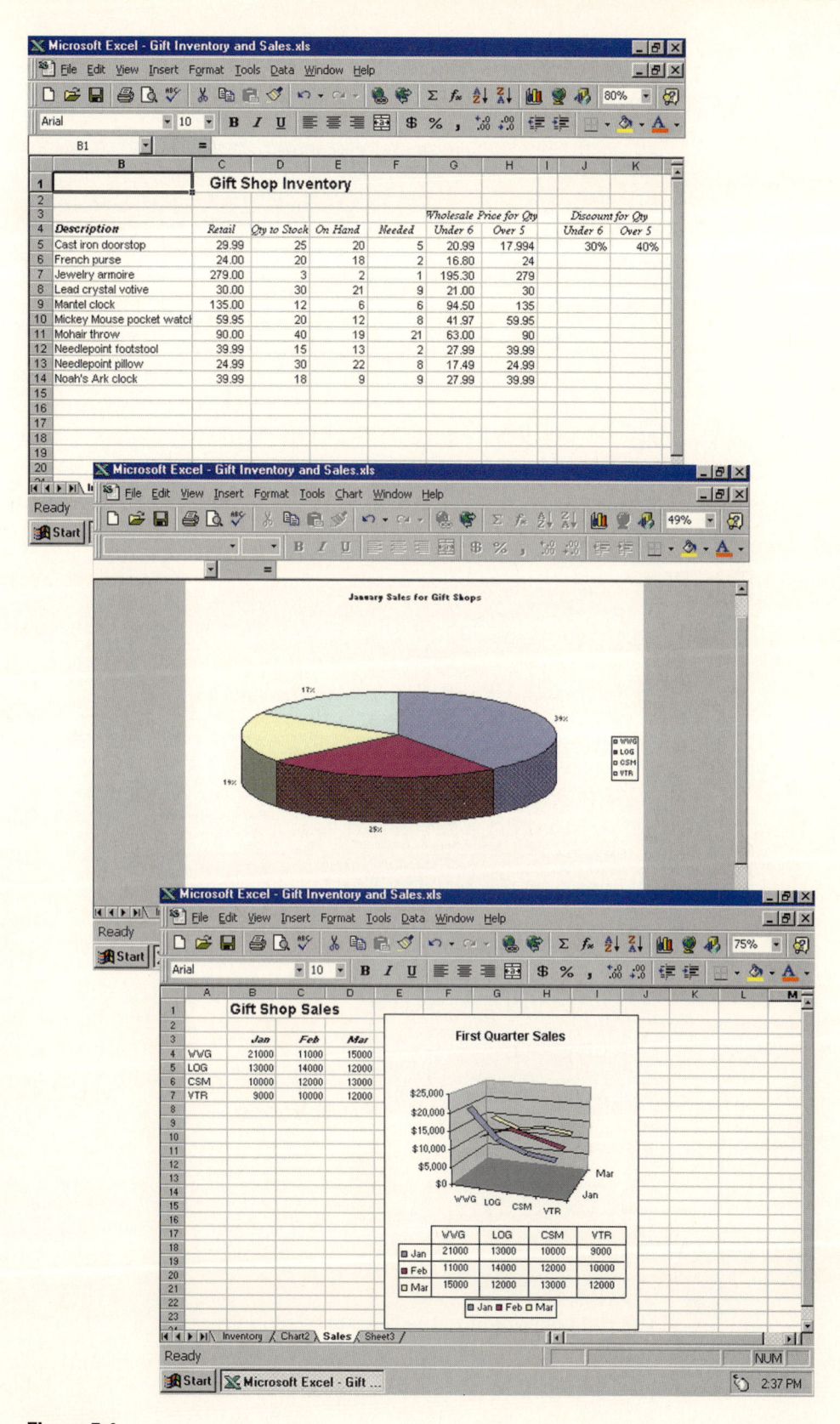

Project 5: Creating a More Complex Workbook   EX-127

Figure 5.1

EX-128

TASK 1: TO COPY DATA FROM ANOTHER WORKBOOK:

1 Open *Giftinv.xls*.

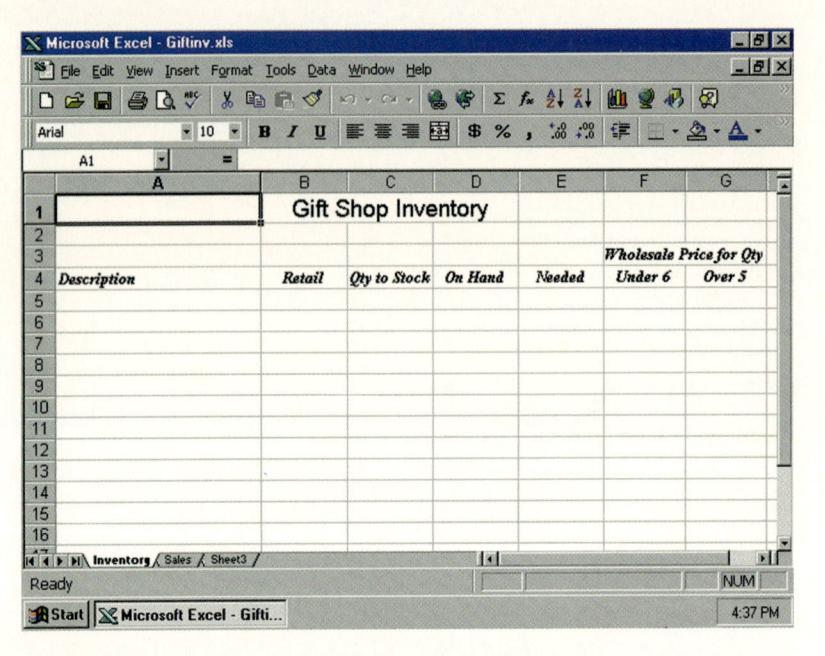

2 Open *TopTen.xls* and select the range A4:B13.

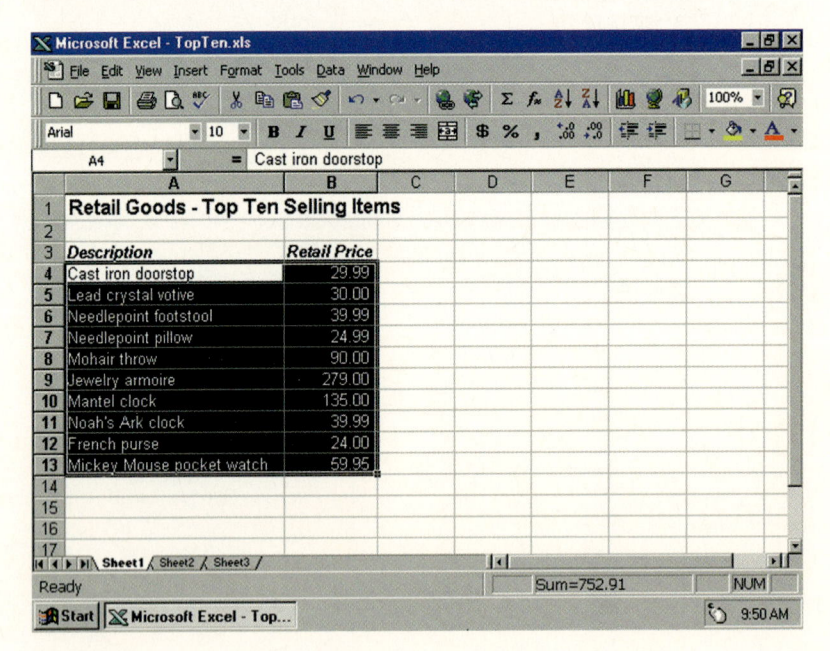

3 Click 📋.
The data is copied to the Clipboard.

4 Choose Window from the menu bar and then choose Giftinv.xls.
The *Giftinv.xls* workbook displays.

Project 5: Creating a More Complex Workbook   EX-129

5 Click in cell A5 and click 📋.

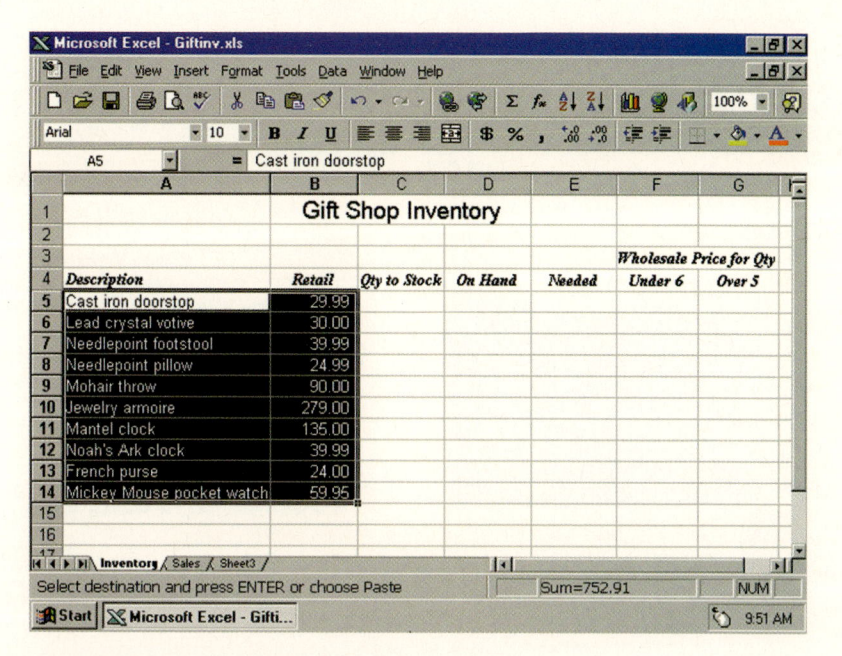

[Screenshot of Microsoft Excel - Giftinv.xls showing the Gift Shop Inventory worksheet with columns: Description, Retail, Qty to Stock, On Hand, Needed, Wholesale Price for Qty Under 6, Over 5. Rows 5-14 contain:
- Cast iron doorstop — 29.99
- Lead crystal votive — 30.00
- Needlepoint footstool — 39.99
- Needlepoint pillow — 24.99
- Mohair throw — 90.00
- Jewelry armoire — 279.00
- Mantel clock — 135.00
- Noah's Ark clock — 39.99
- French purse — 24.00
- Mickey Mouse pocket watch — 59.95

Status bar shows "Select destination and press ENTER or choose Paste" and "Sum=752.91".]

6 Choose Window, TopTen.xls.
The *TopTen.xls* workbook displays.

7 Click ❌ in the menu bar.
The *TopTen.xls* workbook closes, and the Giftinv.xls workbook displays.

Sorting Data

You can sort columns of data in an Excel worksheet in ascending order or descending order. The Standard toolbar has a button for each function.

TASK 2: TO SORT DATA:

1 Make sure that the range A5:B14 is still selected.
When you sort data, you must be careful to select all the columns that should be included in the sort. When selecting the rows to include, don't include the row with the column headings.

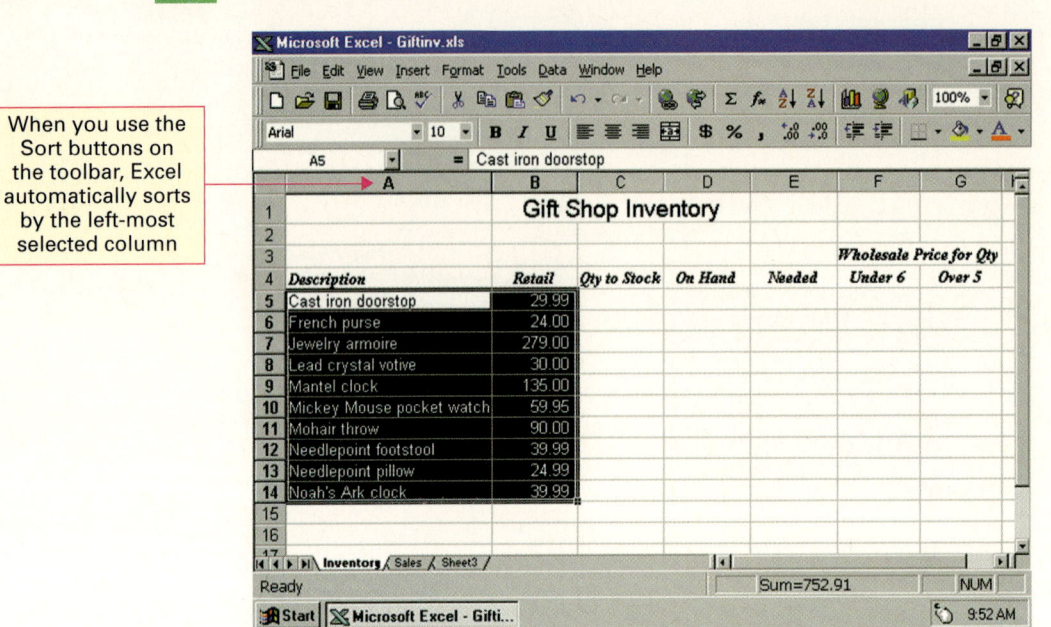

2 Click the Sort Ascending button.

When you use the Sort buttons on the toolbar, Excel automatically sorts by the left-most selected column

> **Tip** If you want to sort a range by any column other than the first column, you must use the Sort command on the Data menu. This command displays a dialog box that allows you to specify the column you want to sort on and the order of the sort. You also can specify two other columns to sort on after the first column is sorted. Check it out. Choose Data, Sort to see the dialog box.

Entering Formulas with Relative References

All the formulas you have used so far have included cell addresses that are relative references. A *relative reference* is an address that Excel automatically changes when the formula is copied to another location to make it true for its new location. For example, if the formula =A1+A2 is in cell A3 and you copy it to cell B3, Excel changes the formula in column B to refer to the corresponding cells in column B, and the formula becomes =B1+B2. Generally, this is precisely what you want, and you are happy that Excel can make such intelligent decisions on its own.

Perhaps you are wondering how this works. Here's the scoop: Excel doesn't interpret a relative cell address in a formula as the actual cell address but rather as a location relative to the location of the formula. For example, Excel interprets the formula =A1+A2 in cell A3 as "Add the cell that is two rows above the formula in the same column to the cell that is one row above the formula in the same column." Therefore, when you copy the formula to any other column, the formula will add the cells that are two rows and one row above the location of the formula.

Project 5: Creating a More Complex Workbook   EX-131

TASK 3: TO ENTER AND COPY A FORMULA WITH RELATIVE ADDRESSES:

1 Enter the following data in the *Qty to Stock* column and the *On Hand* column so that you can write a formula to calculate the value for the *Needed* column.

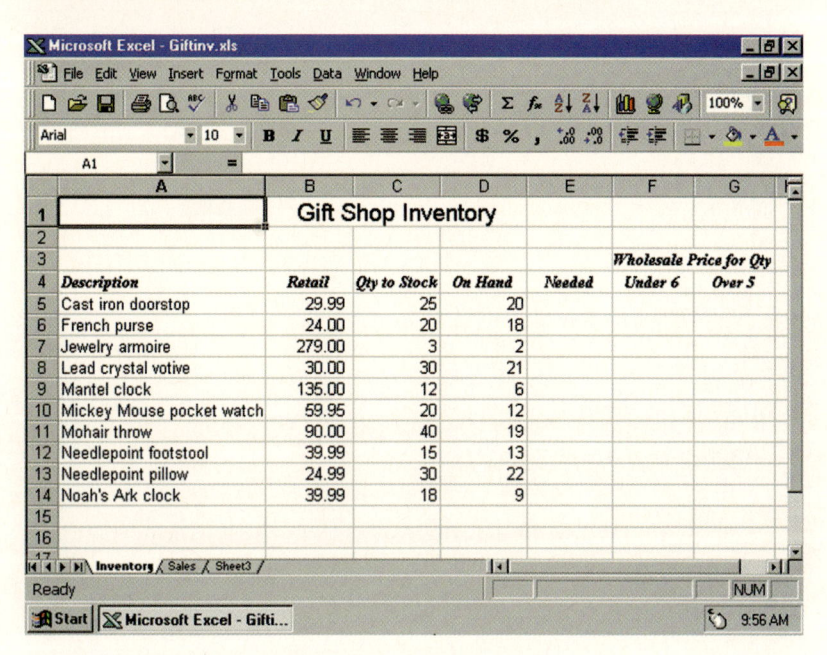

	A	B	C	D	E	F	G
1			Gift Shop Inventory				
2							
3						Wholesale Price for Qty	
4	Description	Retail	Qty to Stock	On Hand	Needed	Under 6	Over 5
5	Cast iron doorstop	29.99	25	20			
6	French purse	24.00	20	18			
7	Jewelry armoire	279.00	3	2			
8	Lead crystal votive	30.00	30	21			
9	Mantel clock	135.00	12	6			
10	Mickey Mouse pocket watch	59.95	20	12			
11	Mohair throw	90.00	40	19			
12	Needlepoint footstool	39.99	15	13			
13	Needlepoint pillow	24.99	30	22			
14	Noah's Ark clock	39.99	18	9			

2 Click in cell E5, type **=C5−D5**, and press ENTER.

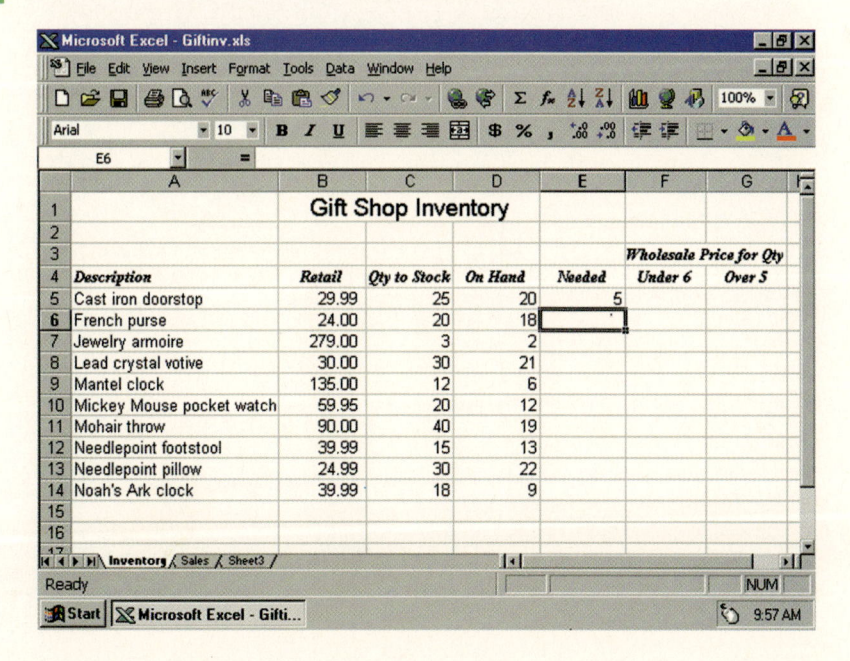

	A	B	C	D	E	F	G
1			Gift Shop Inventory				
2							
3						Wholesale Price for Qty	
4	Description	Retail	Qty to Stock	On Hand	Needed	Under 6	Over 5
5	Cast iron doorstop	29.99	25	20	5		
6	French purse	24.00	20	18			
7	Jewelry armoire	279.00	3	2			
8	Lead crystal votive	30.00	30	21			
9	Mantel clock	135.00	12	6			
10	Mickey Mouse pocket watch	59.95	20	12			
11	Mohair throw	90.00	40	19			
12	Needlepoint footstool	39.99	15	13			
13	Needlepoint pillow	24.99	30	22			
14	Noah's Ark clock	39.99	18	9			

3 Copy cell E5 to the range E6:E8.

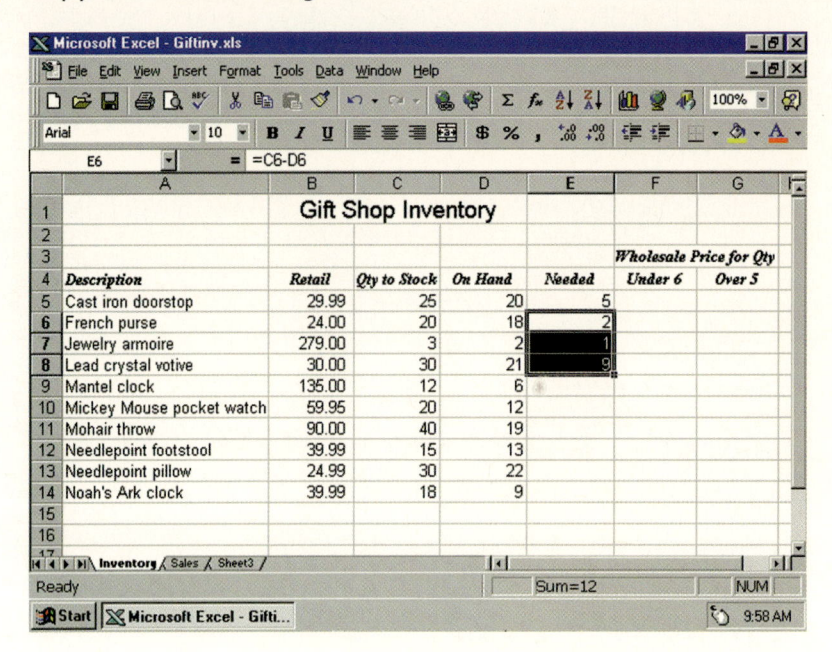

4 Click in cell E6 and notice the formula in the formula bar.

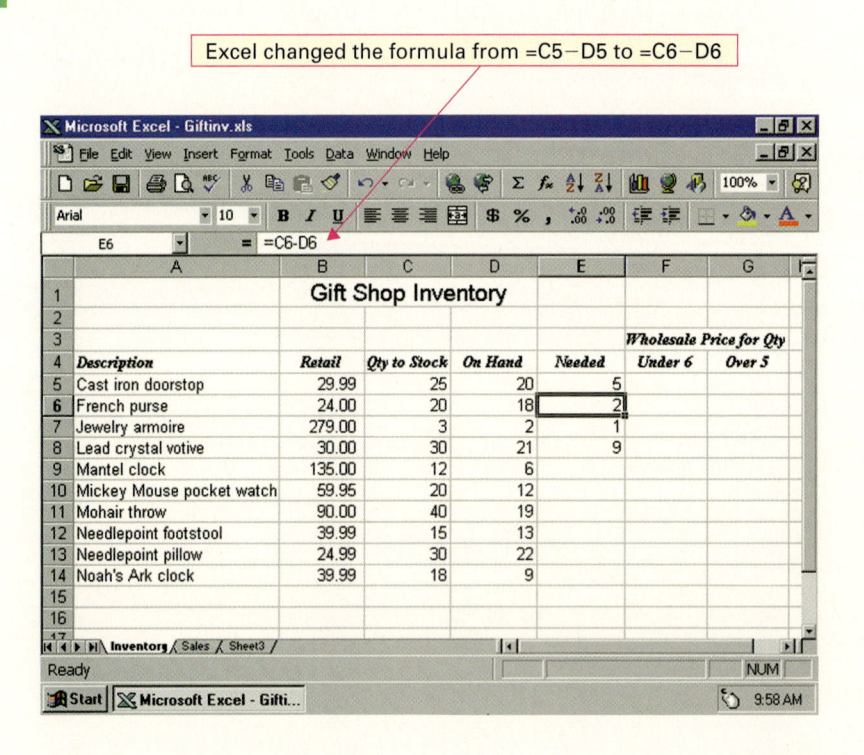

Excel changed the formula from =C5−D5 to =C6−D6

Using Headings in Formulas

Using headings in formulas instead of cell addresses is a new feature in Excel 97. The *headings* feature is helpful in two ways: when you create a formula, you can think in logical terms (such as "quantity times cost") and you can easily recognize the purpose of the formula. When you see the formula "Quantity*Cost," you know immediately what it does, but the formula A1*B1 gives you very little information.

TASK 4: TO ENTER A FORMULA THAT USES HEADINGS:

1. Click in cell E9, type **=qty to stock−on hand**, and press (ENTER).
   The cell displays the correct calculation.

   > **Tip** You do not have to capitalize the headings in formulas, but spelling and spaces must be exact.

2. Copy cell E9 to the range E10:E14.
   The range also displays the correct calculations relative to the rows.

3. Click in cell E10 and look at the formula in the formula bar.
   The formula in cell E10 is the same as in E9.

Entering Formulas with Absolute References

As you have already seen, when formulas with relative references are copied, the cell addresses change appropriately; however, sometimes formulas refer to a cell or range that should never be changed when the formula is copied. To prevent the cell or range address from changing, you must make the address an *absolute reference*. An absolute reference is denoted with the dollar sign symbol, as in $A$1.

TASK 5: TO ENTER AND COPY A FORMULA WITH AN ABSOLUTE REFERENCE:

1. Scroll the worksheet so that columns B through J are visible.

2. Click in cell F5, type **=B5−(B5*I5)**, and press (ENTER).
   This formula calculates the wholesale price of the item using the discount that applies if you are ordering a quantity of less than six. The wholesale price is the retail price minus the discount (which is determined by multiplying the retail price by 30%).

3. Copy cell F5 to F6.
   The answer is obviously not correct.

4 Click in cell F6 and look at the formula in the formula bar.

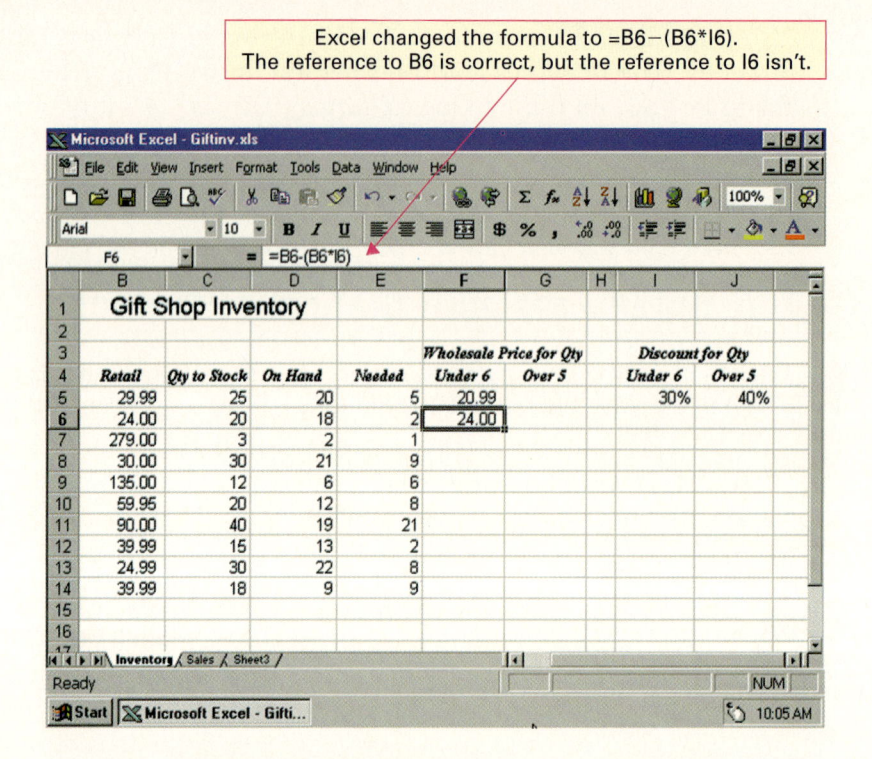

> Excel changed the formula to =B6−(B6*I6). The reference to B6 is correct, but the reference to I6 isn't.

5 Edit the contents of cell F5 and insert dollar signs before and after "I" so the formula looks like **=B5−(B5*$I$5)** and press (ENTER).
The result in cell F5 is the same as before, but watch what happens when you copy it.

6 Copy cell F5 to the range F6:F13.

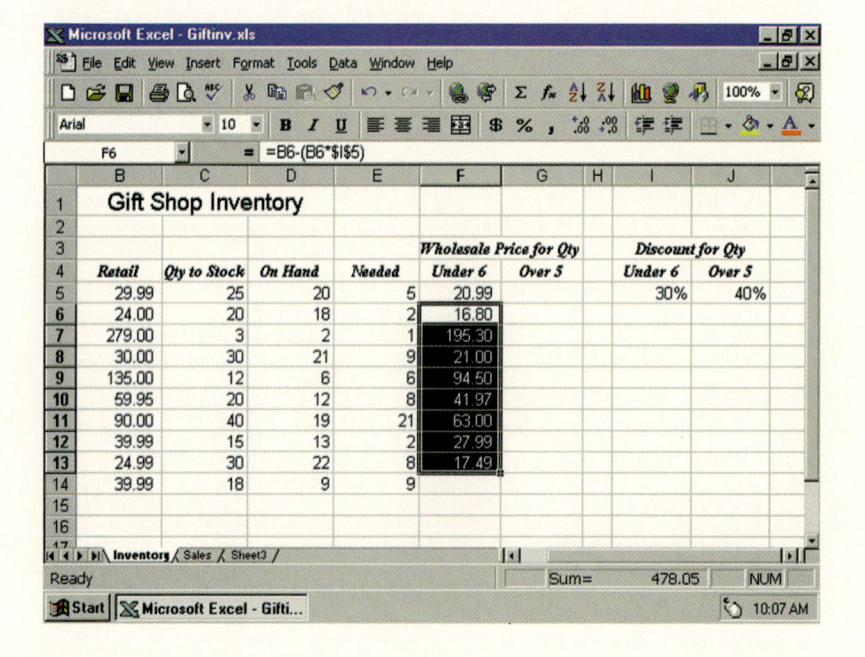

Project 5: Creating a More Complex Workbook EX-135

Pointing to Enter Absolute References

In the previous task, you typed the complete formula in the cell, but, as you have seen in other projects, you can enter a formula with the pointing method. When you use this method, you can designate an absolute reference with the F4 key.

TASK 6: TO ENTER A FORMULA WITH AN ABSOLUTE REFERENCE USING THE POINTING METHOD:

1. Click in cell F14, type an equal sign (=), move to cell B14 using ←, and then type a minus sign followed by an open parenthesis.

2. Move to cell B14 again, type an asterisk (*), move to cell I5, and then press F4.

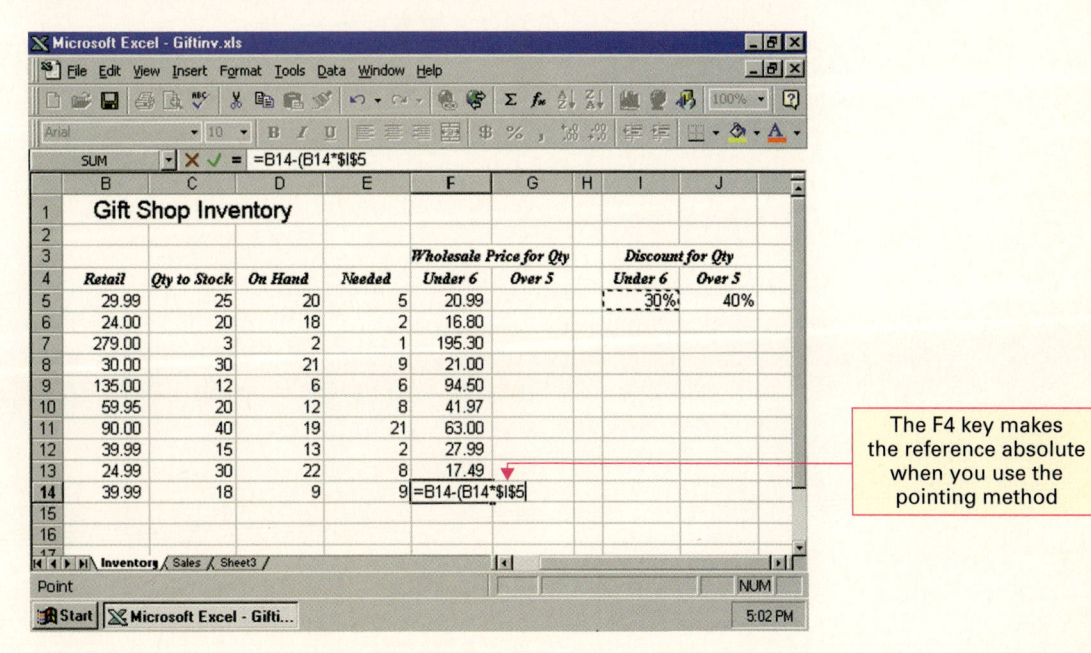

> The F4 key makes the reference absolute when you use the pointing method

EX-136

3 Type a closing parenthesis and press ENTER.
The correct calculation (27.99) displays in the cell.

Using Headings with Absolute References

The heading feature in Excel 97 also works with absolute references. When designating an absolute reference for a heading, only one dollar sign is used, and it precedes the heading.

TASK 7: TO ENTER AND COPY A FORMULA WITH AN ABSOLUTE REFERENCE USING HEADINGS:

1 Copy cell J5 to the range J6:J14.

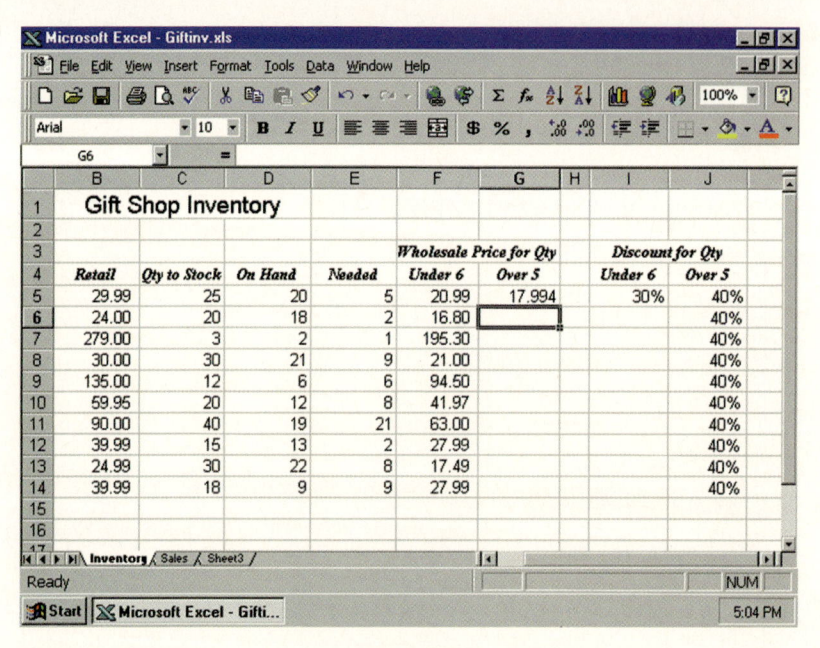

2 Click in cell G5, type **=retail−(retail*$over 5)**, and press ENTER.

3 Copy cell G5 to the range G6:G14.
The cells display the correct computations.

Creating and Modifying a Chart

Charts present data in a worksheet in a way that numbers never can — visually. Seeing trends and data relationships is so much easier when you look at a chart than when you read numbers. To put a new spin on a tired, old saying, you might say, "A chart is worth 16,777,216 cells." The *Chart Wizard* helps you create charts in Excel.

Project 5: Creating a More Complex Workbook   EX-137

TASK 8: TO CREATE A COLUMN CHART:

1 Click the Sales tab.

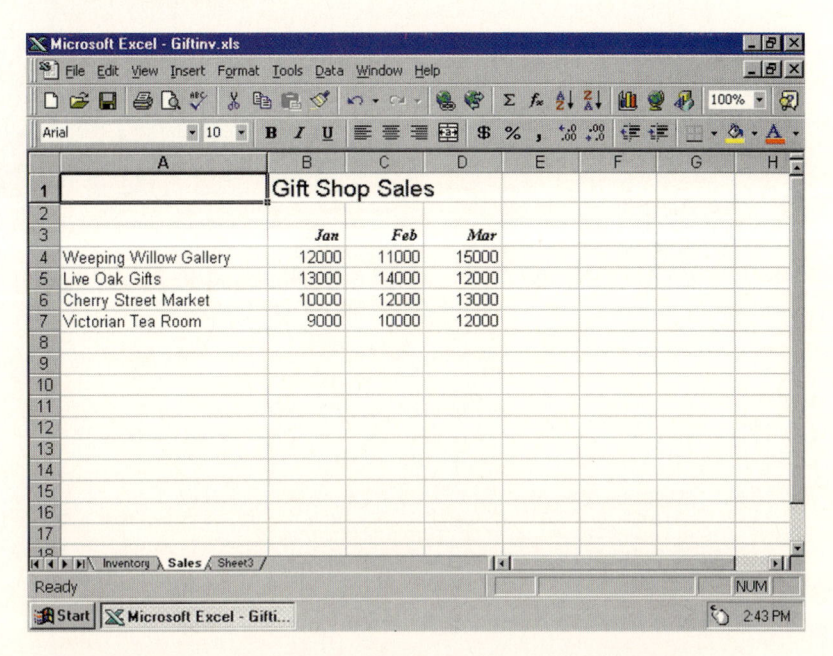

2 Select the range A3:D7 and click the Chart Wizard button.

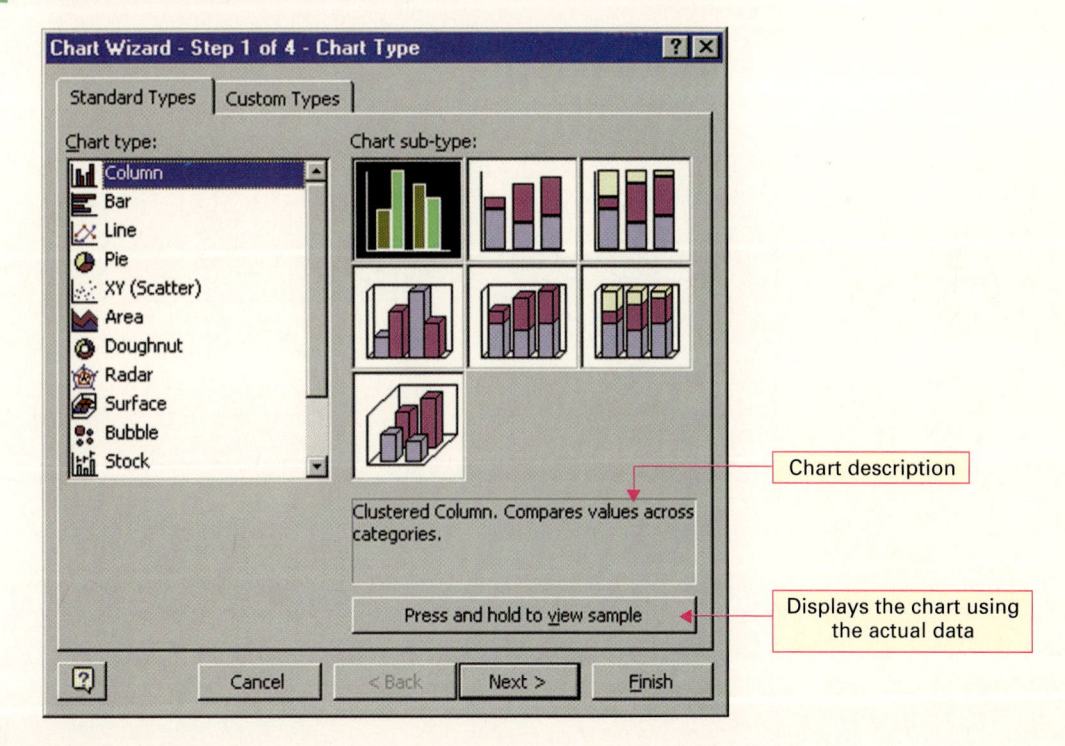

Chart description

Displays the chart using the actual data

3 Click Next to accept the chart type.

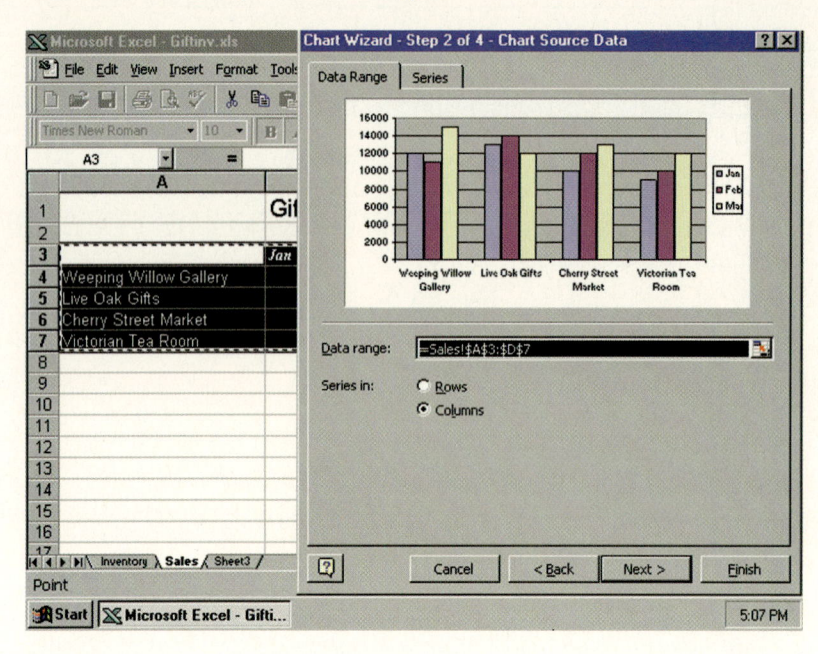

4 Click Next to accept the data range.

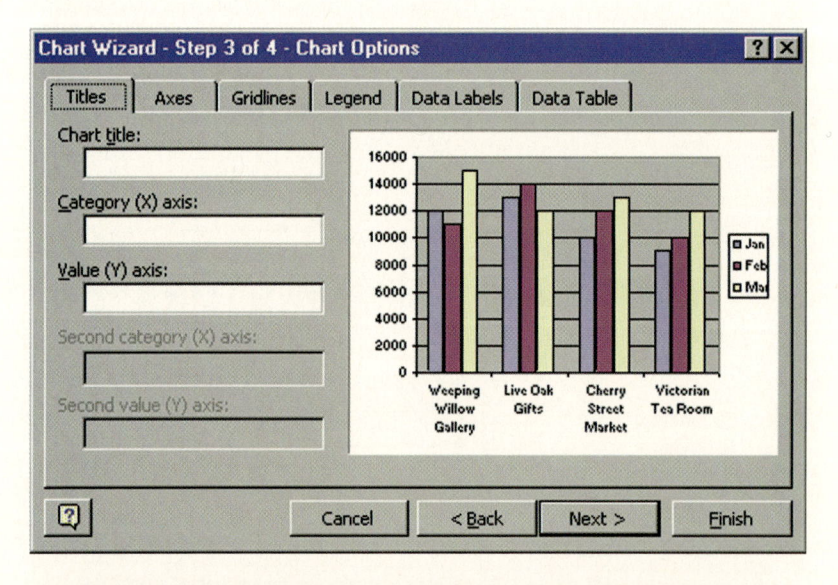

5 Type **First Quarter Sales** for the Chart title and click Next.

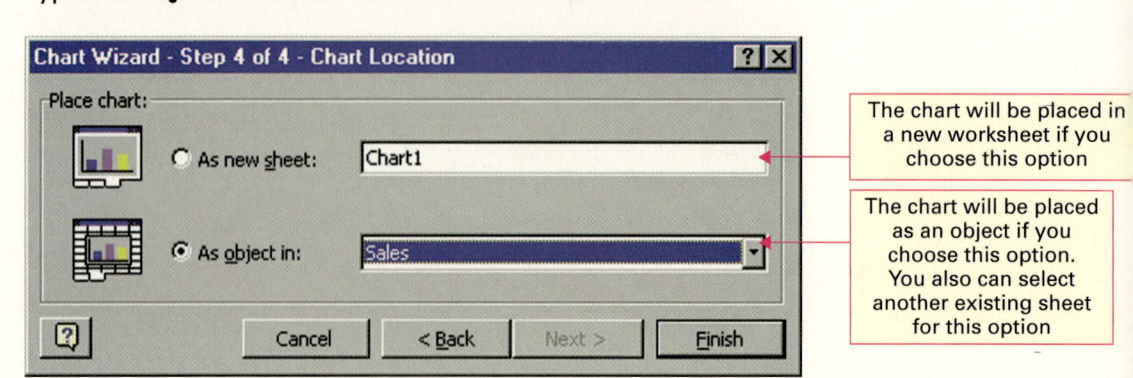

The chart will be placed in a new worksheet if you choose this option

The chart will be placed as an object if you choose this option. You also can select another existing sheet for this option

6 Click Finish.

The chart displays in the current worksheet with **selection handles**. You may want to close the Chart toolbar to see the complete chart.

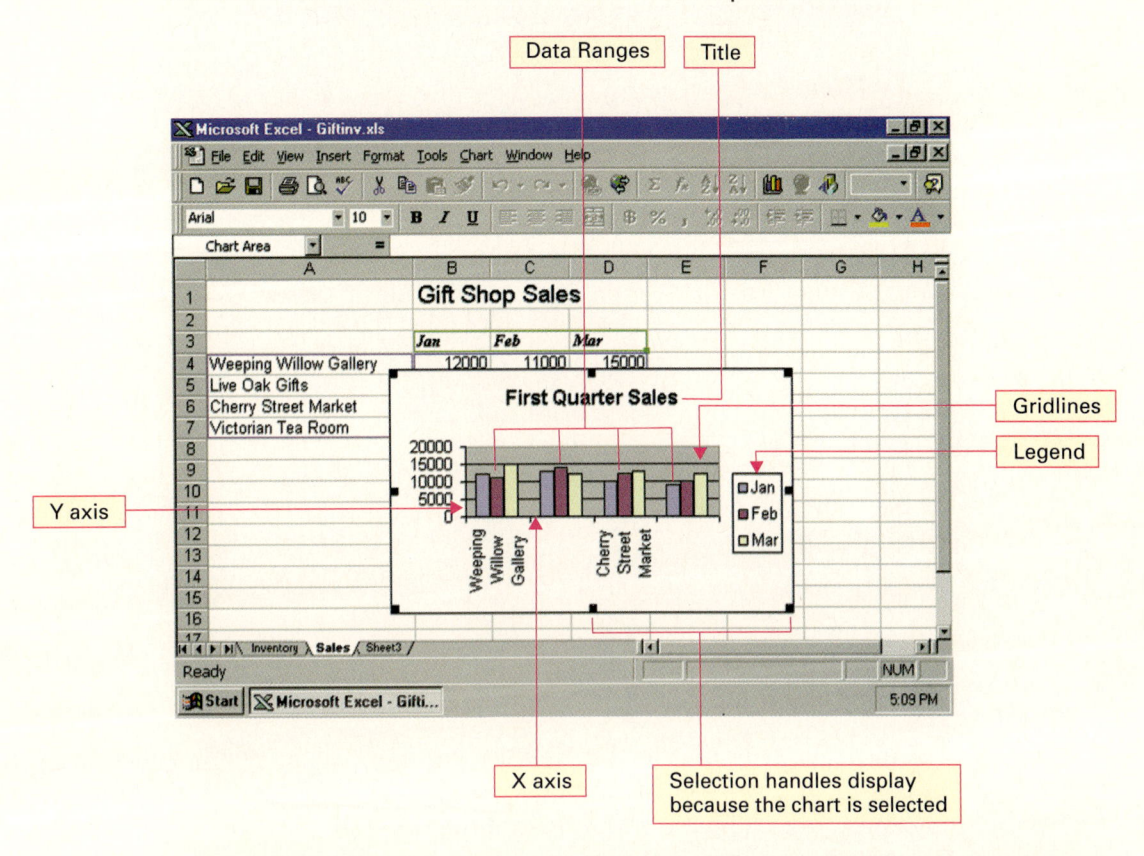

[Screenshot of Excel worksheet showing a chart with callouts pointing to: Data Ranges, Title, Gridlines, Legend, Y axis, X axis, and "Selection handles display because the chart is selected"]

> **Note** The Chart Wizard arbitrarily displays every other data label (in this example, Weeping Willow Gallery and Cherry Street Market), because there is too much text to show all the labels.

Moving and Sizing a Chart

When you place a chart on the same page as the worksheet, the Chart Wizard may place the chart in a location that obscures the data in the worksheet, and it may make the chart too small. Because the chart is an object, you can move it and size it however you want.

TASK 9: TO MOVE AND SIZE THE CHART:

1 Point to a blank area of the chart and drag the chart to the right of the data that created the chart.

The chart moves to the new location.

EX-140

2 Point to a handle at the bottom of the chart and drag the handle down to make the chart about three rows taller.

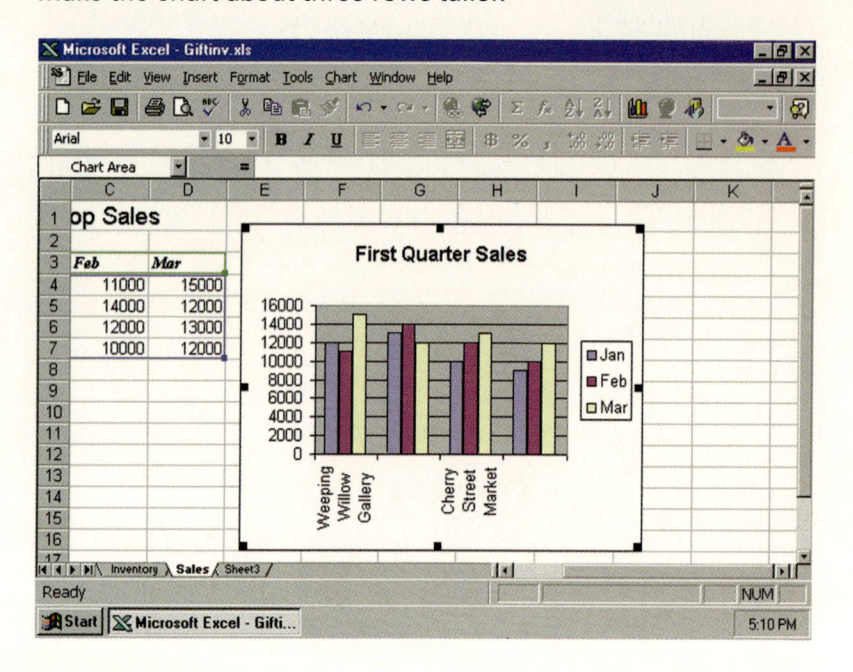

Changing Chart Data

The chart is linked to the data in the worksheet; when you change the data in the worksheet, the chart reflects the change. By the same token, when you change a value in a **data range** in the chart, the data in the worksheet reflects the change.

TASK 10: TO CHANGE CHART DATA:

1 In the worksheet, change the names of the gift shops to abbreviations as follows:
Weeping Willow Gallery: **WWG**;
Live Oak Gifts: **LOG**;
Cherry Street Market: **CSM**;
Victorian Tea Room: **VTR**.
After changing the names, make column A narrower.

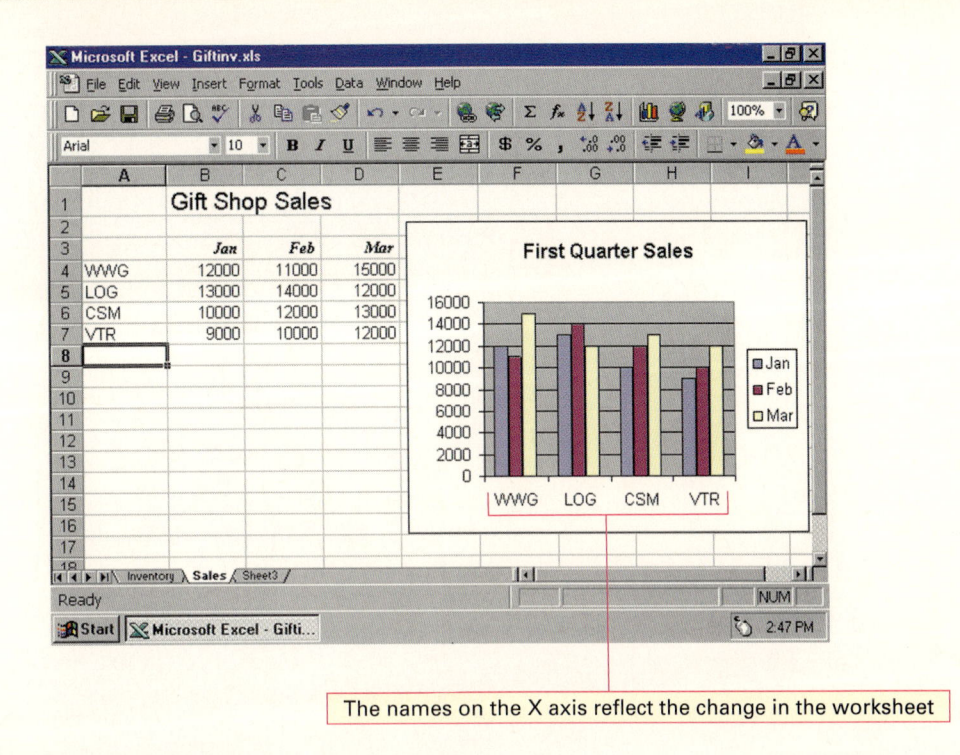

Project 5: Creating a More Complex Workbook **EX-141**

The names on the X axis reflect the change in the worksheet

2 Change the value in cell B4 to 18000 and notice the change in the chart as you press ENTER.
The height of the first column increases when you change the value.

3 Click the first column in the chart to select the data range for January.

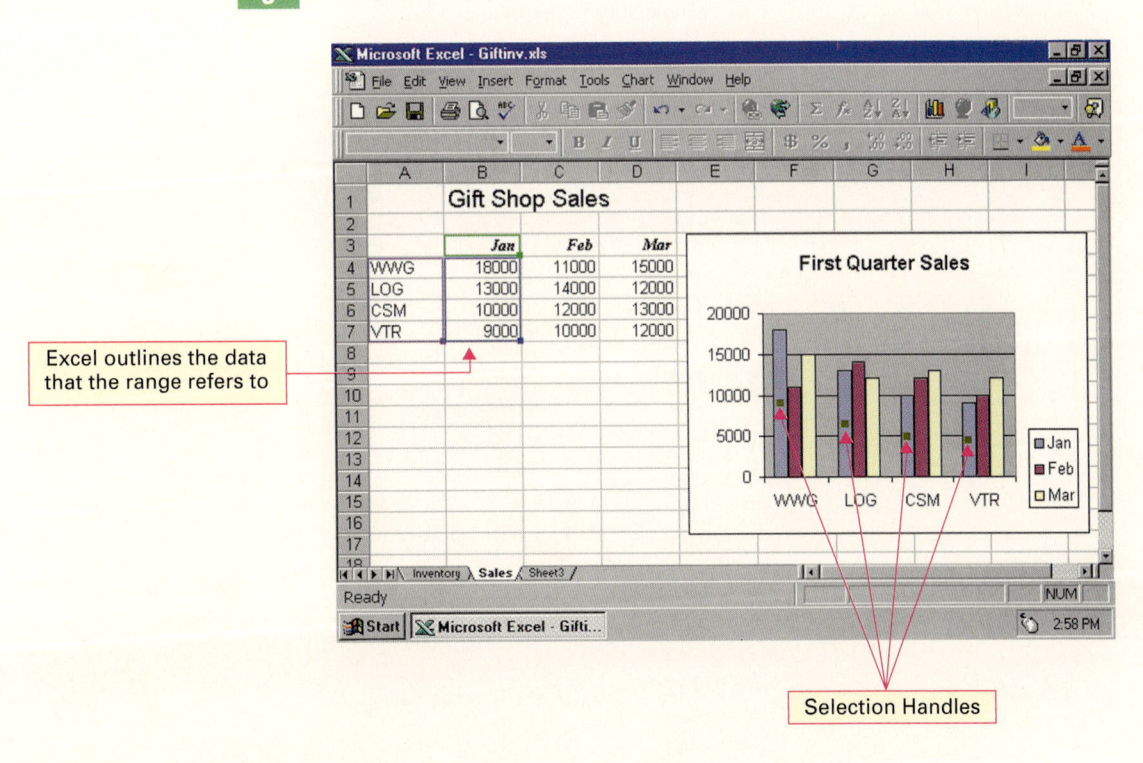

Excel outlines the data that the range refers to

Selection Handles

4 Click the first column again.

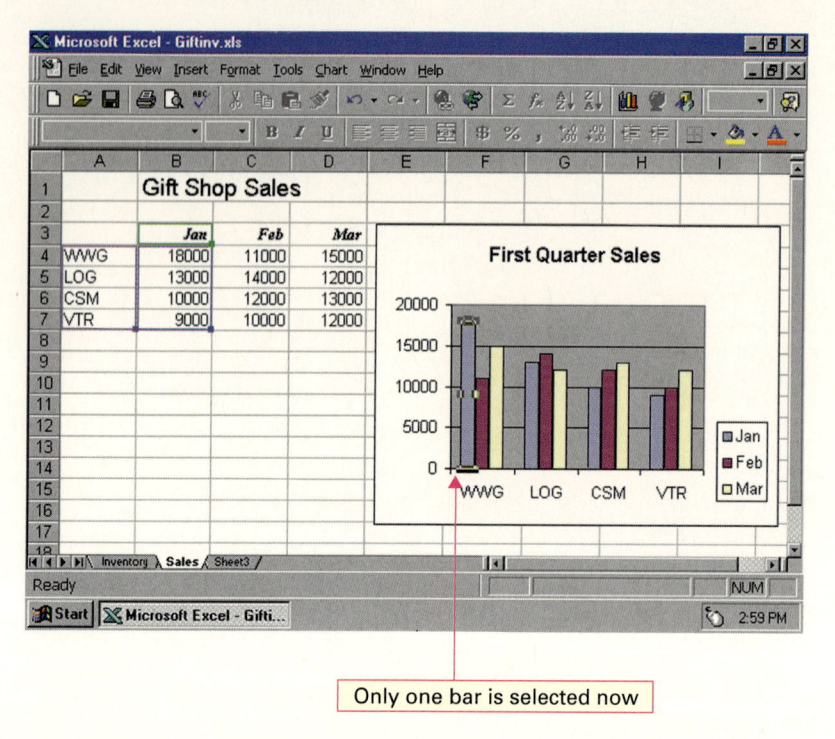

Only one bar is selected now

5 Drag the top of the column up until the value is 21000.

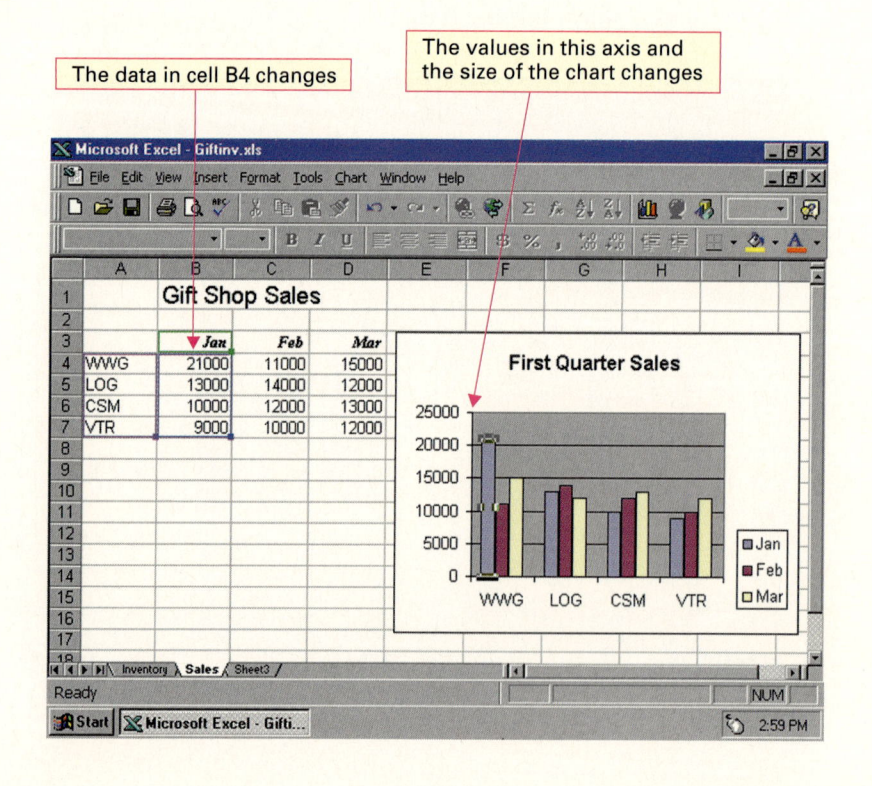

The data in cell B4 changes

The values in this axis and the size of the chart changes

Project 5: Creating a More Complex Workbook   EX-143

Formatting Chart Elements

When you create a chart with the Chart Wizard, the Chart Wizard decides how the chart elements will look. For example, the Chart Wizard uses the General number format for the scale on the Y axis. After the chart is created, you can format each element of a chart and use the settings that you want.

TASK 11: TO FORMAT CHART ELEMENTS:

1 Right-click the legend, choose Format Legend from the Shortcut menu, and click the Placement tab.

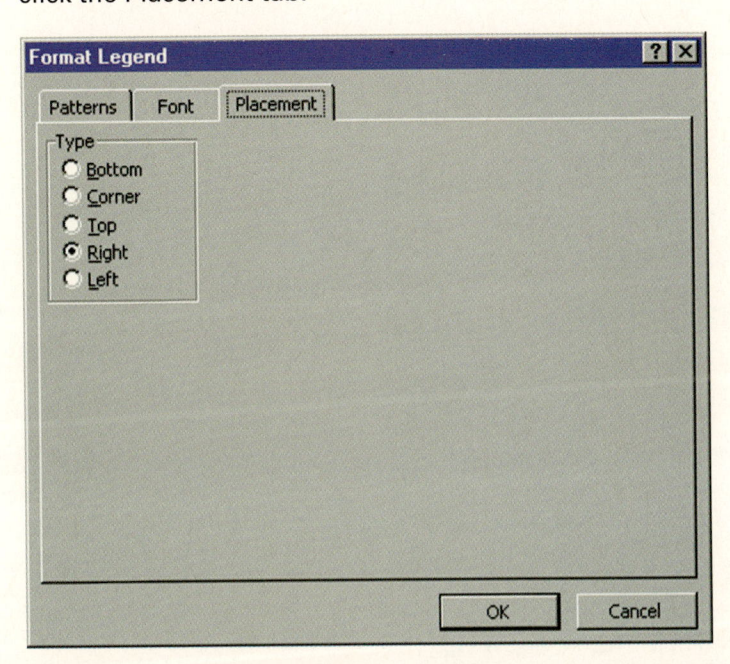

2 Select Bottom and click OK.

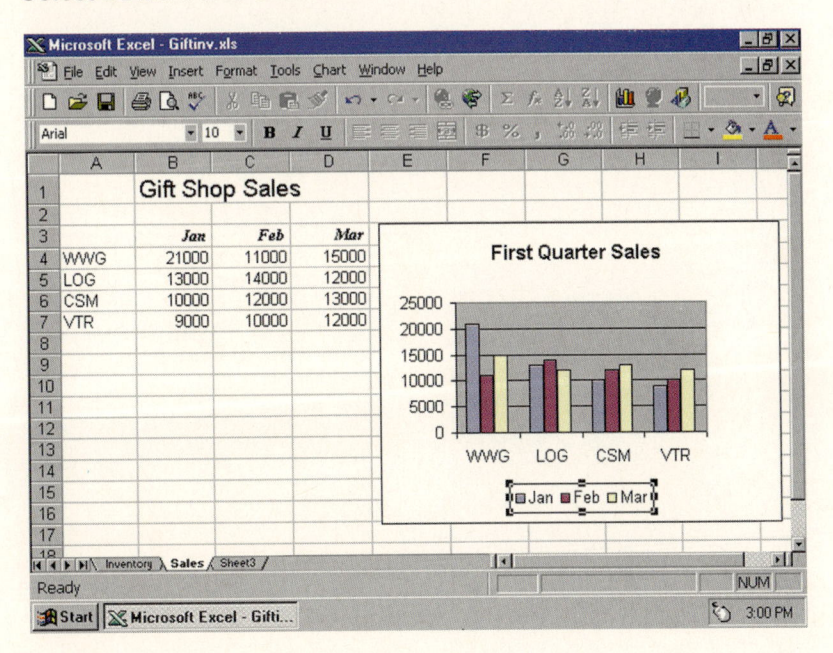

EX-144

3 Right-click the numbers on the Value axis (Y axis), choose Format Axis from the Shortcut menu, and click the Number tab.

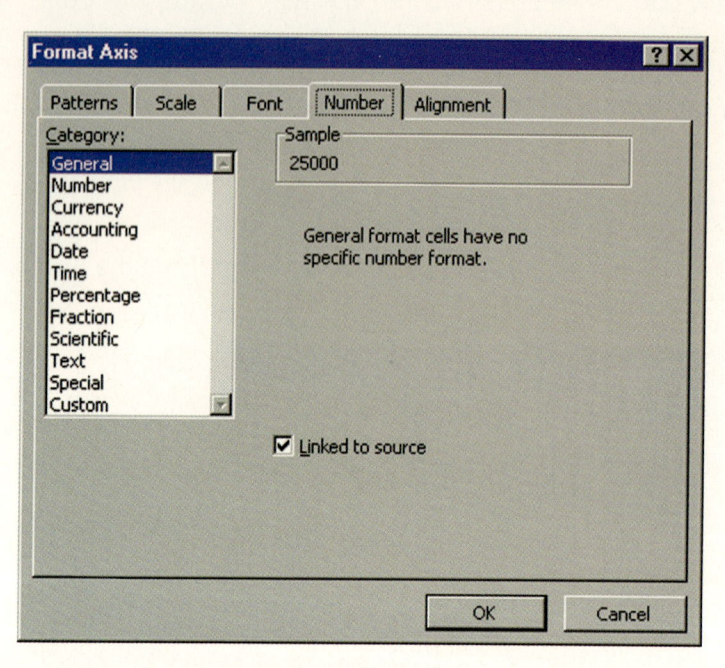

4 Select Currency, 0 decimal places, and click OK.

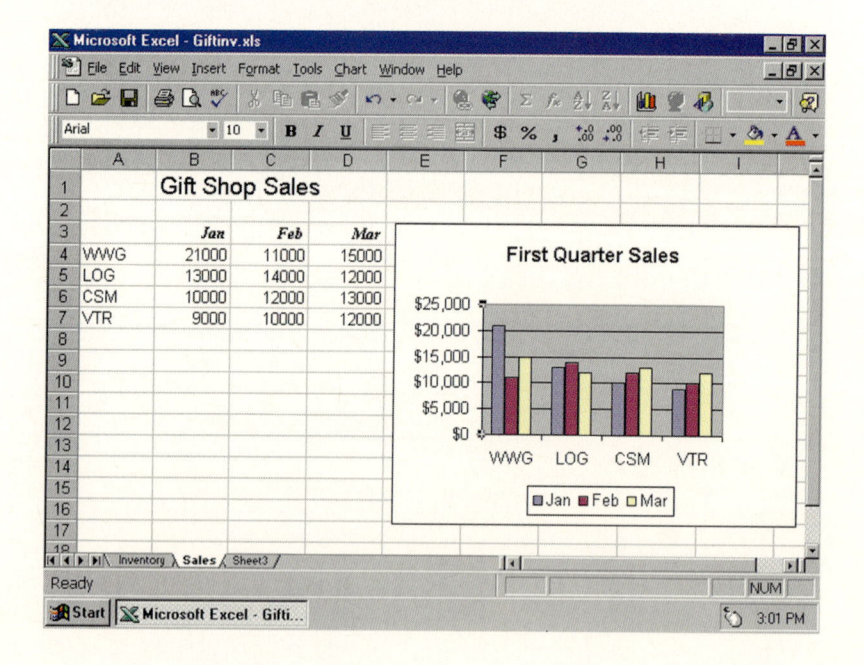

5 Right-click the text on the Category axis (X axis), choose Format Axis, and click the Font tab.

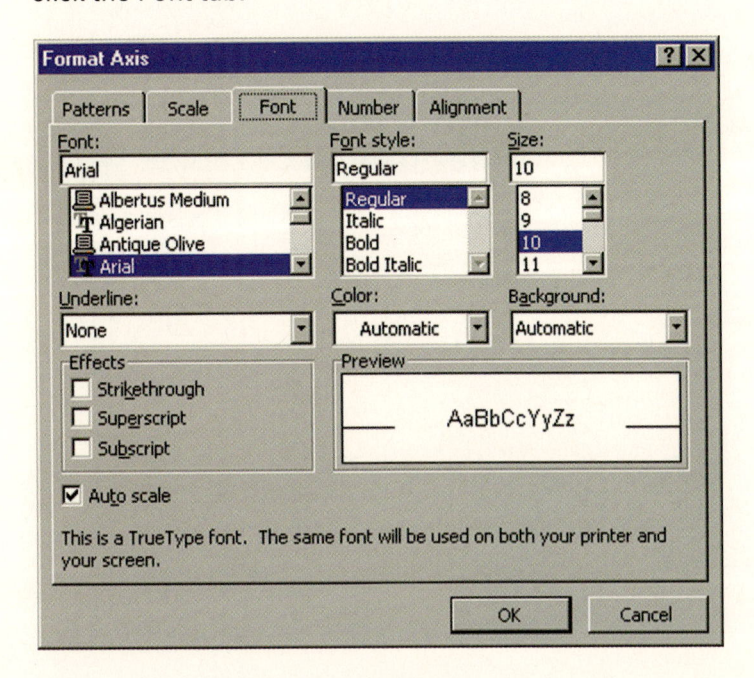

6 Select 8 for the Size and click OK.
The font size of the text is decreased.

Changing the Chart Type

Excel 97 provides many *chart types* and *chart sub-types*. Not all chart types are appropriate for the data in a workbook. Some charts are designed especially for certain types of data. For example, the Stock chart requires three series of data which must be arranged in a specific order: high, low, and close (a stock's high and low values for the day and the closing price of the stock).

TASK 12: TO CHANGE THE CHART TYPE:

1 Right-click a blank area of the chart and choose Chart type from the Shortcut menu.

EX-146

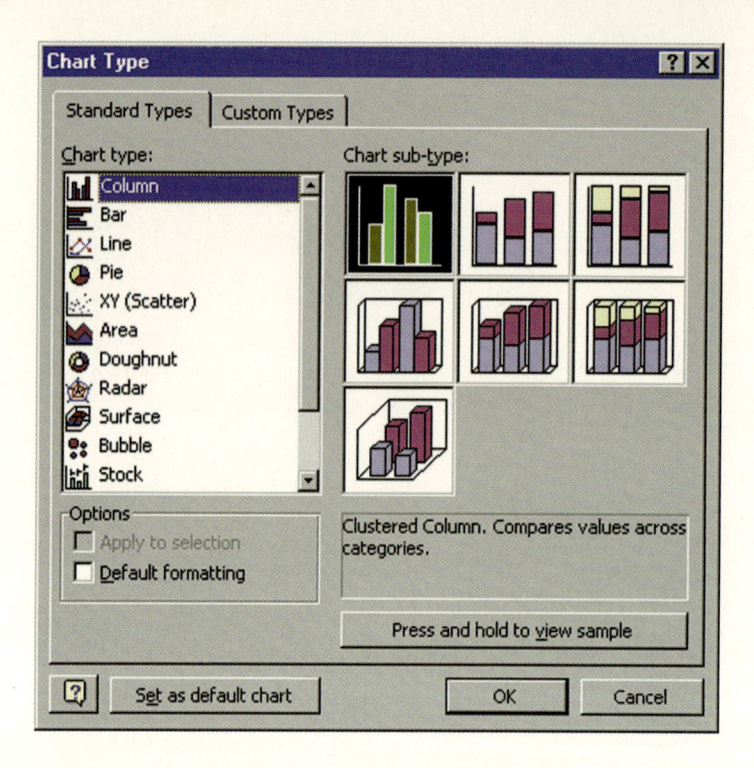

2 Select Line for Chart Type, select the 3-D line sub-type, and click OK.

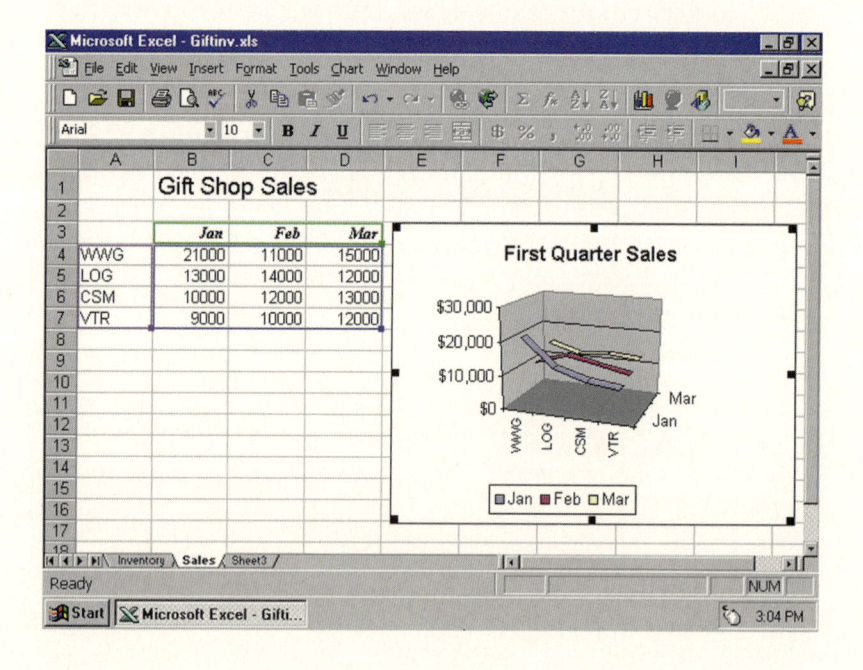

Changing the Chart Options

Settings for the chart *titles*, *X axis*, *Y axis*, *gridlines*, *legend*, *data labels*, and *data table* are all contained in the Chart Options dialog box. After you have created a chart, you can select the options that you want.

Project 5: Creating a More Complex Workbook   EX-147

TASK 13: TO CHANGE THE CHART OPTIONS:

1 Right-click a blank area of the chart, choose Chart Options from the Shortcut menu, and click the Data Table tab.

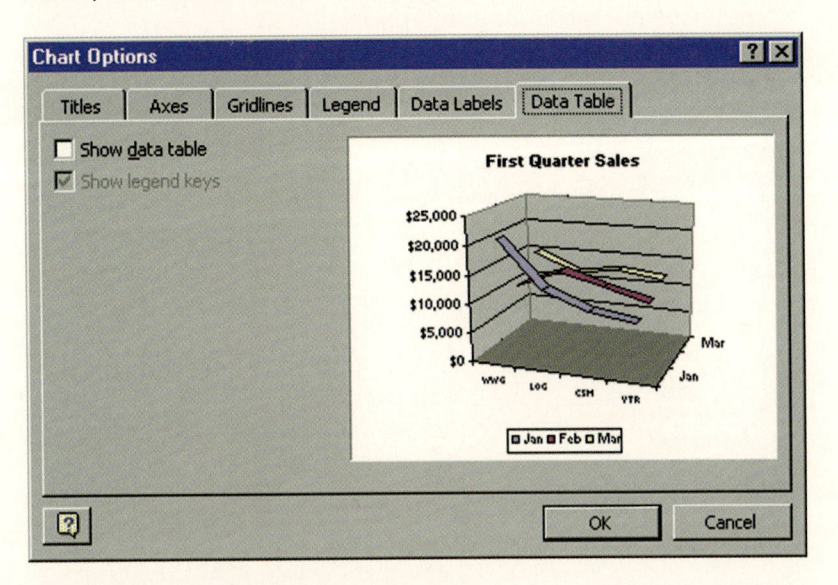

2 Select Show data table and click OK.

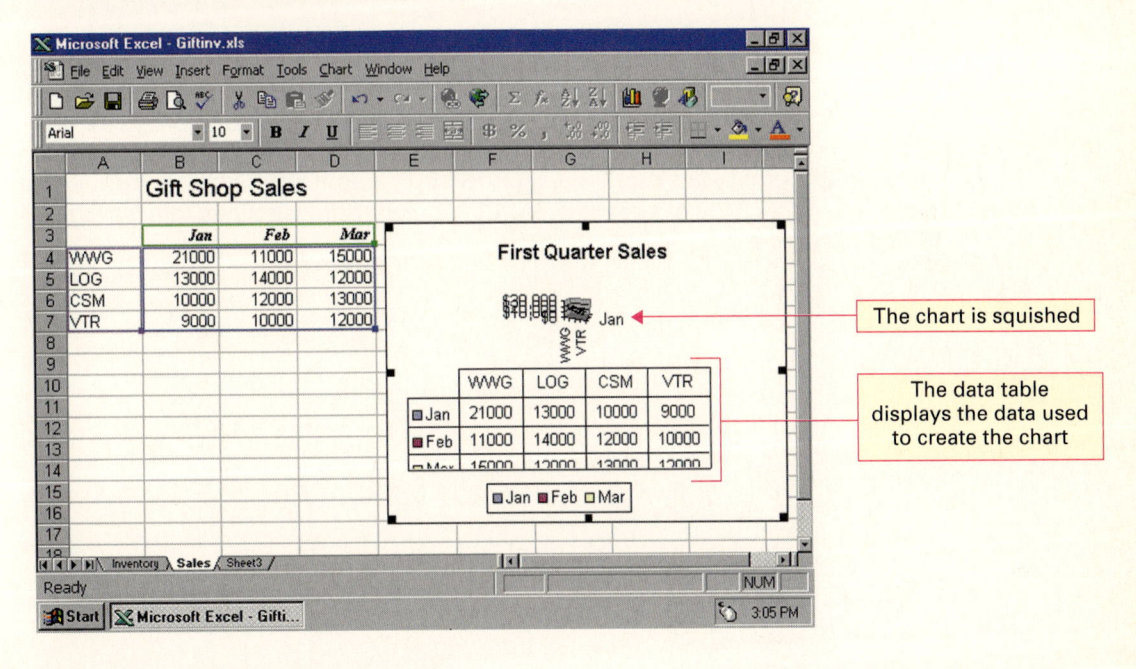

The chart is squished

The data table displays the data used to create the chart

3 Make the chart about 9 rows taller.
The graph returns to its former size.

Creating a Pie Chart

A pie chart is a popular type of chart that shows the relationship of parts to the whole. When selecting data for a pie chart, you will select only one data range.

TASK 14: TO CREATE A PIE CHART:

1 Select the range A4:B7, click 📊, and select Pie as the Chart type and Exploded pie as the sub-type. (A description of the selected chart sub-type shows below the chart sub-type pictures.)

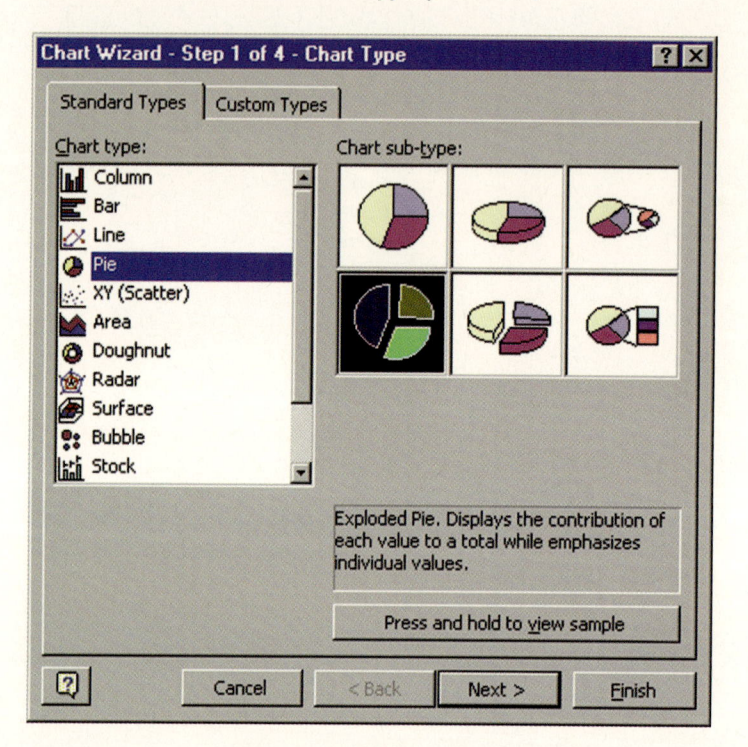

2 Click but don't release the button named Press and hold to view sample. A preview of the chart using your data displays in a Sample box.

Project 5: Creating a More Complex Workbook EX-149

3 Release the mouse button and click Next.

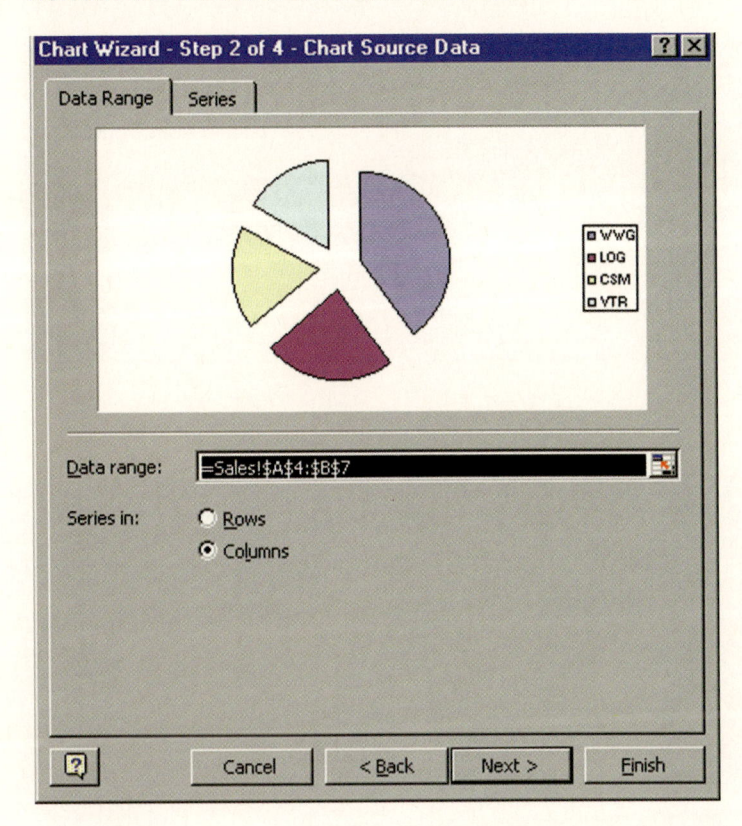

4 Click Next.

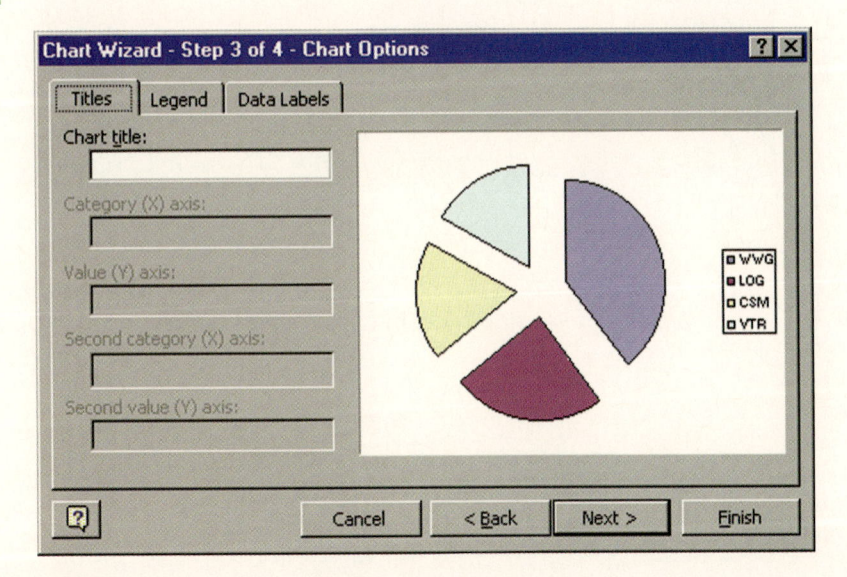

EX-150

5 Type **January Sales for Gift Shops** for Chart title and click Next.

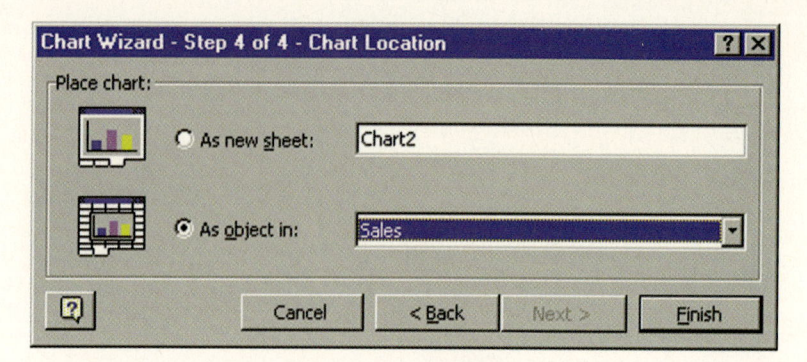

6 Select As new sheet and click Finish.

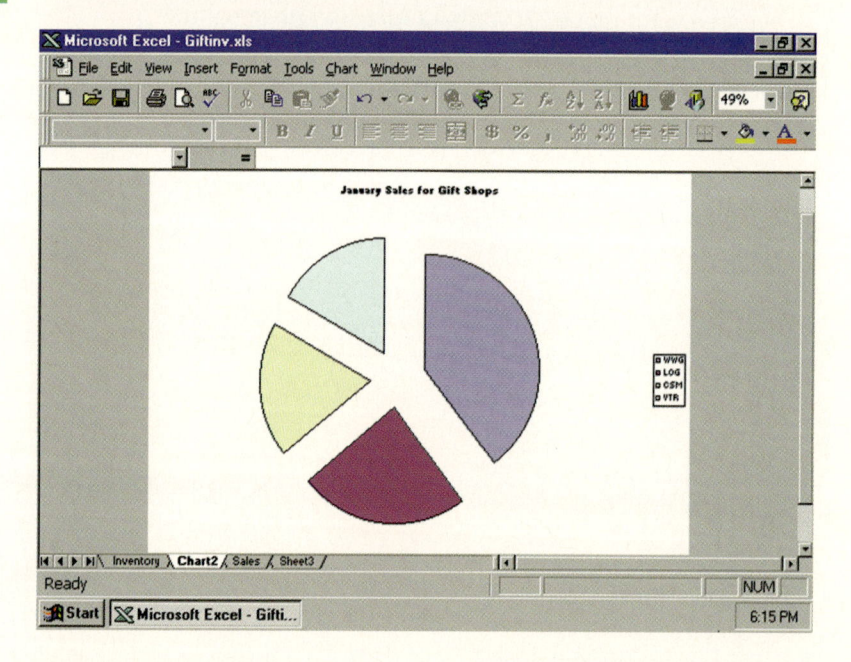

Tip You can change the name of the worksheet that the chart appears on just as you would any other worksheet name.

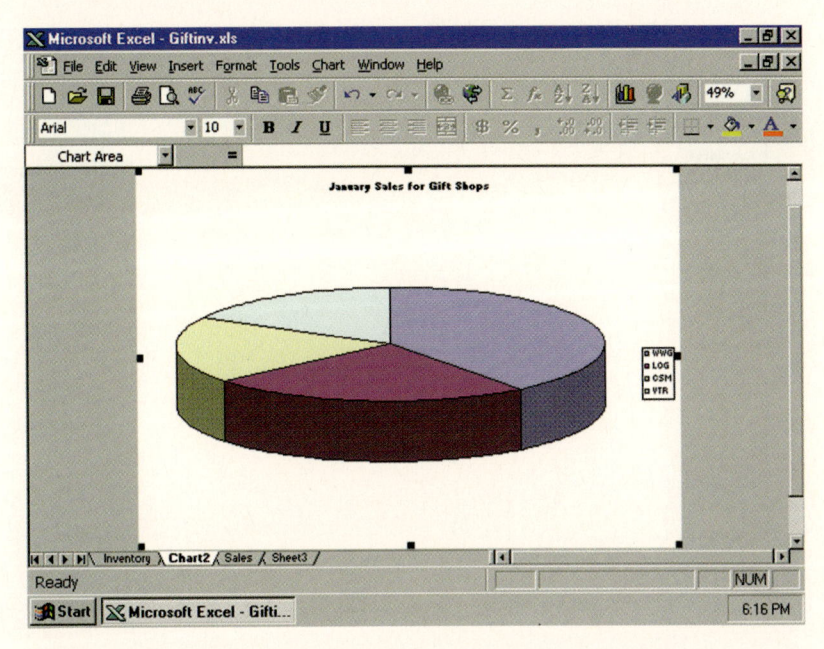

Project 5: Creating a More Complex Workbook EX-151

7 Change the chart sub-type to Pie with a 3-D visual effect.

8 Right-click the pie, choose Format Data Series, and click the Data Labels tab.

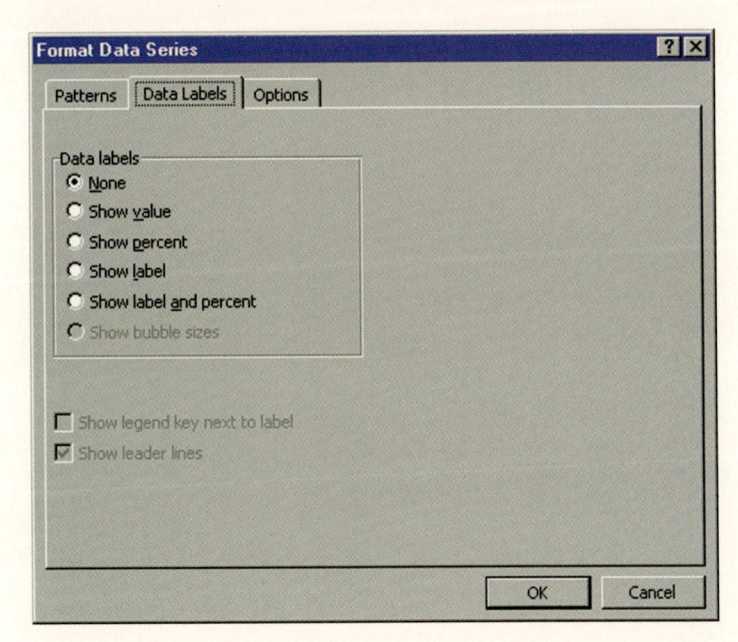

9 Select Show percent and click OK.

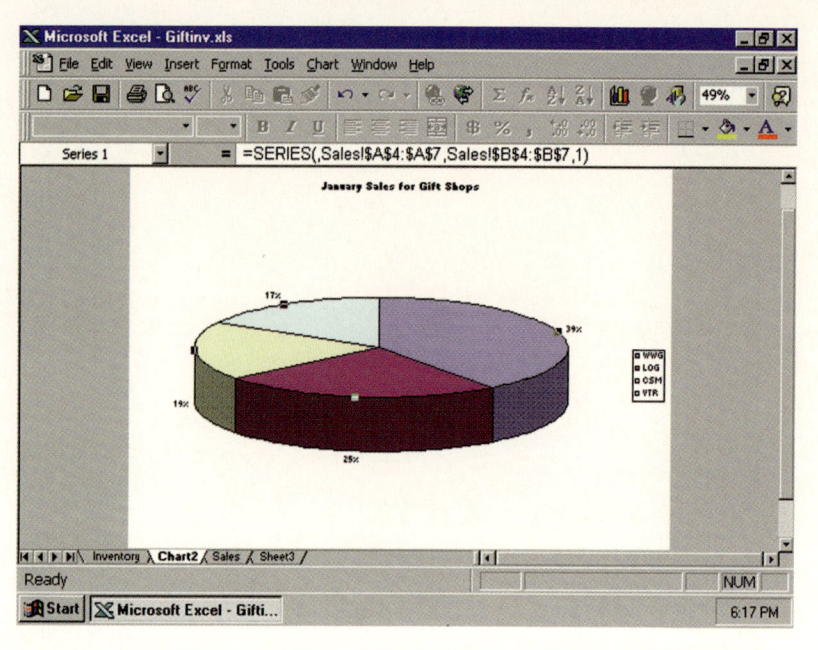

The Conclusion

Save the file as *Gift Inventory and Sales.xls*. Preview each page of the workbook and print each page if you have access to a printer. Close the file.

Summary and Exercises

Summary

- You can copy data from one workbook to another.
- You can sort data in ascending or descending order.
- Formulas use relative references, headings, and absolute references to refer to particular cells on the worksheet.
- Excel can change the address of relative references when a formula is copied, but it cannot change the address of an absolute reference.
- Charts represent the data in a worksheet visually.
- Charts can be displayed on any worksheet in a workbook.
- Once a chart has been created you can change the type, format the elements, or choose different chart options.

Key Terms and Operations

Key Terms	Operations
absolute reference	change the chart type
chart	copy data from another workbook
chart sub-type	create a chart
chart type	enter formulas with relative or absolute addresses
Chart Wizard	format a chart
data labels	move a chart
data range	size a chart
data table	sort data
gridlines	
heading	
legend	
relative reference	
selection handles	
title	
X axis	
Y axis	

Study Questions

Multiple Choice

1. Which of the following categories isn't included in the Chart Options dialog box?
   a. Data Labels
   b. Data Table
   c. Axes
   d. Pattern

2. When you sort by using the Sort Ascending button on the Standard toolbar,
   a. columns are sorted individually.
   b. you can sort on only one row.
   c. the first column must be the key column.
   d. you can sort by as many as three columns.

EX-153

3. Which of the following statements about the Chart Wizard is false?
   a. The Chart Wizard creates charts by guiding you through a step-by-step process.
   b. The Chart Wizard can create only a limited number of charts that are available in Excel 97.
   c. The Chart Wizard is launched by a button on the Standard toolbar.
   d. The Chart Wizard doesn't give you an opportunity to format the chart before it is created.

4. Which of the following formulas is written in incorrect form?
   a. =A1/A10
   b. =A1/$A$1
   c. =quantity*retail
   d. =quantity*$retail$

5. A relative reference
   a. is the actual address of a cell.
   b. is the range that contains the data labels for a chart.
   c. can be changed by Excel when the formula that contains it is copied to another location.
   d. is denoted by a dollar sign.

6. When a chart is selected,
   a. it has selection handles.
   b. the outline of the chart is blue.
   c. it opens in a separate window.
   d. None of the above.

7. An exploded pie chart is a chart
   a. type.
   b. sub-type.
   c. option.
   d. element.

8. To designate a cell address as an absolute reference when entering a formula using the pointing method, press
   a. F2.
   b. F3.
   c. F4.
   d. F5.

9. If you want to show the relationship of individual values to a total, which chart type would you use?
   a. column
   b. stock
   c. line
   d. pie

10. To prevent a cell address from changing when the formula that contains it is copied to a new location,
    a. use a relative address for the cell.
    b. use an absolute address for the cell.
    c. use the value of the cell instead of the address.
    d. copy the formula with the Edit, Copy command.

Short Answer

1. When you create a chart, where are the two locations that you can place the chart?

2. What is a data table?

3. Where can a legend be placed on a chart?

4. What command do you use if you want to sort on more than one column?

5. How do you move a chart?

6. How do you size a chart?

7. What is the difference between a relative and an absolute reference?

8. Can you use an absolute reference in a formula that uses headings instead of cell addresses?

9. What happens if you change the data in a worksheet after you have created a chart that uses the data?

10. What happens in the worksheet when you select the data ranges in a chart?

For Discussion

1. Discuss the advantages of using headings in formulas.

2. Discuss the advantages of presenting information in charts as opposed to numbers.

3. Name and describe the elements of a chart.

4. Explain how Excel interprets the following formula if it were located in cell H10: =I5+I6*$A$1.

Review Exercises

1. Revising the gift inventory and sales workbook

In this exercise, you will make changes to an existing chart.

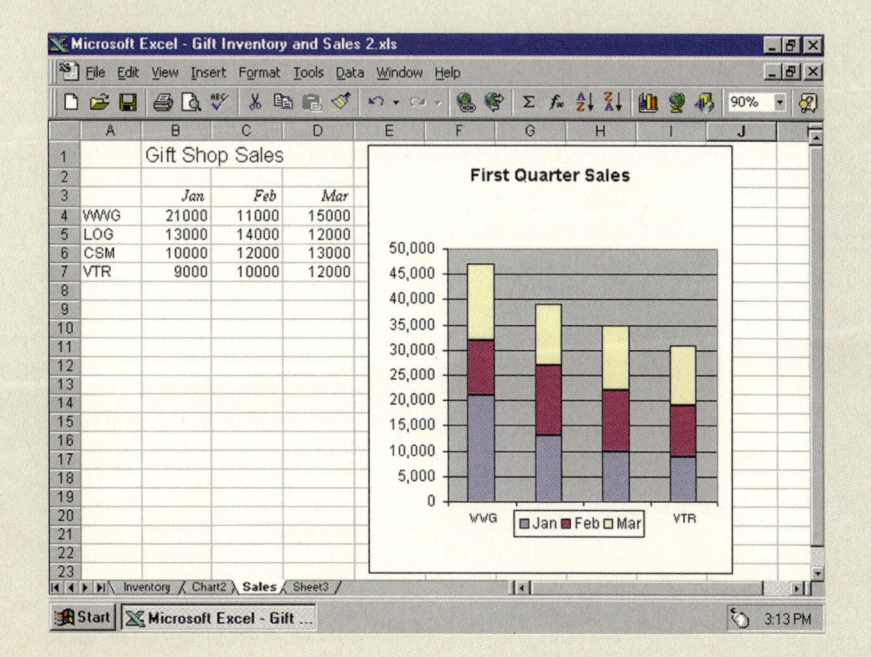

1. Open *Gift Inventory and Sales.xls*.
2. Click the Sales tab if necessary.
3. Change the chart type to a stacked column.
4. Remove the data table.
5. Remove the dollar sign from the numbers on the Y axis.
6. Save the file as Gift Inventory and Sales 2.xls and close the file.

2. Creating a new items workbook

In this exercise, you will create a workbook that lists five possible new items and computes the discount on the items.

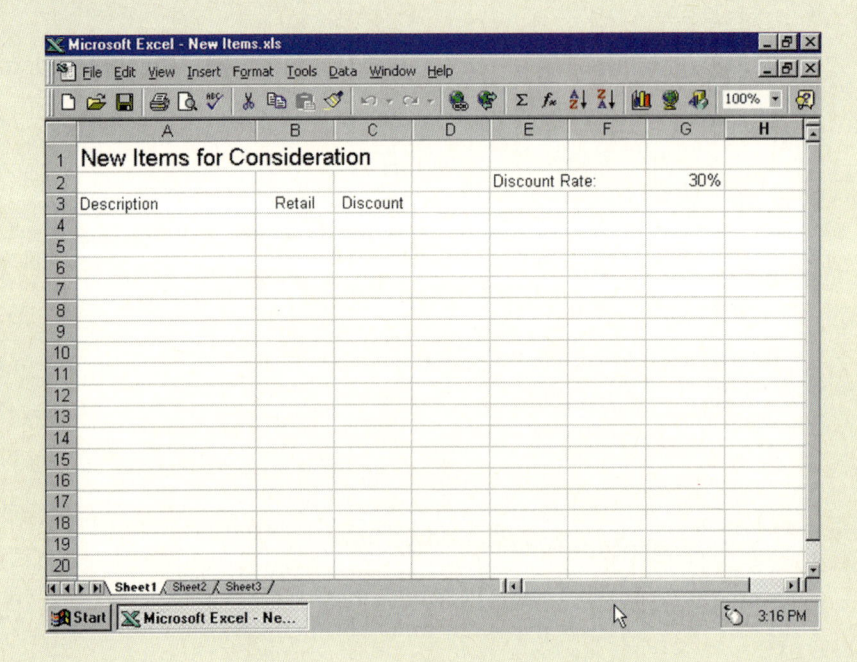

1. Create the workbook shown above.
2. Find five items on the Web that you can suggest as new items for the gift shops to carry. Enter the descriptions of the items and their retail prices in the worksheet in the appropriate columns.
3. In cell C4, enter the formula that multiplies the discount rate in cell G2 times the retail price in cell B4. Copy the formula to the range C5:C8.
4. Save the file as *New Items.xls* and close the file.

3. Sorting data and creating a sales chart in a worksheet

1. Launch Excel and open the workbook *Container Corporation Regional Sales.xls*.
2. Sort the data so that it appears in order by total sales per region with the region with the highest sales at the top.
3. Print a copy of the worksheet after sorting.

4. Create a column chart which displays a comparison of sales by quarter according to region and format the chart as follows:

- Add a chart title *Regional Sales by Quarter*.

- Place the chart in the workbook as a new sheet.

5. Save the workbook using the filename *Container Corporation Regional Sales xxx*.

6. Print a copy of the chart.

Assignments

1. Creating a chart of expenditures

Create a workbook that lists your expenditures for the past month. Create a pie chart for the data. Are you spending too much on pizza?

2. Completing a vacation package workbook

Download the workbook *Vacation.xls* from the Addison Wesley Longman web site (http://hepg.awl.com/select) or ask your instructor for this workbook file. Sort the data in ascending order in the range A4:C8. Enter a formula in cell D4 that multiplies the Price/Person times the appropriate discount rate (cell H4). Copy the formula to the other cells in the column. Enter appropriate formulas for the Travel Agency discounts and the Resort Club discounts. Use headings in the formulas for the Resort Club discounts.

PROJECT 6

Using Financial Functions

One of the advantages of electronic spreadsheets is that the user has the capability of performing "What if" analyses. The computer can easily store and retrieve data and perform calculations, so Microsoft Excel can be used to develop sophisticated models to assist in decision making.

One decision that individuals and managers often undertake involves assessing the terms under which they will borrow money. Loan payments are amortized; *amortization* is the process of distributing monthly payments over the life of a loan. The factors determining a loan's repayment include the amount of the loan, the percent interest charged by the bank or lending organization, and the length of time over which the loan will be repaid. Each of these factors has a technical name:

- The amount borrowed is the *principal*.
- The percent interest is the *rate*.
- The time period over which payments are made is the *term*.

Depending on the values associated with each factor, varying portions of each loan payment apply to the principal and the interest payment. In general, borrowers aim to pay off the principal in as short an amount of time as financially possible.

An *amortization schedule* lists the outstanding balance, monthly payment, amount of each payment that applies to the principal, and the amount of each payment that applies to the outstanding principal for the life of a loan. In this project, you will learn to use financial functions to create an amortization schedule.

Objectives

After completing this project, you will be able to:

- ▶ Define the structure of the amortization schedule
- ▶ Enter the numeric data for the loan
- ▶ Calculate the monthly payment using the PMT function
- ▶ Calculate the remaining balance using the PV function
- ▶ Calculate the principal and interest paid in each loan payment using the PPMT and IPMT functions
- ▶ Construct formulas to calculate the cumulative principal, cumulative interest, total payments, and ending balance
- ▶ Use the Fill Handle to complete the amortization schedule
- ▶ Freeze worksheet panes to assist in viewing the amortization schedule
- ▶ Create and apply a macro

The Challenge

The Atrium Café will expand next year, so Mr. Gilmore has asked you to construct an amortization schedule so he can compare different loan scenarios. After you complete the workbook, Mr. Gilmore will determine the optimum loan scenario before contacting specific lending institutions for funding.

The Solution

Excel has a number of financial functions that will make creating this workbook a simple task! By entering four numeric constants and using the PMT, PPMT, IPMT, and PV financial functions, you can create the workbook Mr. Gilmore needs. Your completed amortization schedule will look like the one shown in Figure 6.1.

EX-160

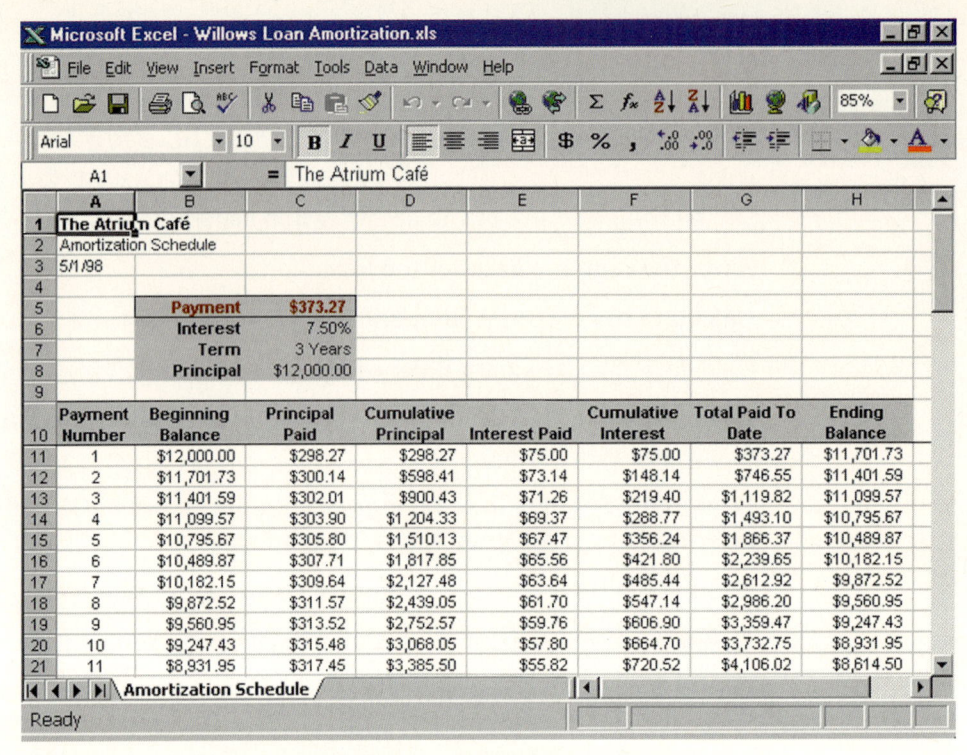

Figure 6.1: Mr. Gilmore's Amortization Schedule

The Setup

Make sure that the Excel settings listed in Table 6.1 are selected on your computer. This will ensure that your screen matches the illustrations and that the tasks in this project function as described.

Table 6.1   Excel Settings

Location	Make these settings
Office Assistant	Close the Office Assistant
View, Toolbars	Display the Standard and Formatting toolbars
View, Formula bar	Display the Formula bar
View, Status bar	Display the Status bar
Maximize	Maximize the Application and Workbook windows
Tools, Options	In the General tab, set the default worksheet font to Arial, 10 point
File, Page Setup	Click the Page tab and set the orientation to landscape
Worksheet Tab for Sheet1	Double-click and rename this tab as Amortization Schedule, and delete the remaining worksheets

Project 6: Using Financial Functions   EX-161

Defining the Structure of the Amortization Schedule

The amortization schedule's structure is defined by entering constants to specify where the payment, interest, term, and loan repayment data appear in the worksheet. Excel uses two categories of constants: *text constants* define the structure of the worksheet and *numeric constants* comprise the data upon which the *loan scenario* is based.

When you enter the constants, you format them to enhance the appearance of the worksheet.

TASK 1: DEFINE THE STRUCTURE OF THE AMORTIZATION SCHEDULE:

1. Type **The Atrium Cafe** in cell A1, and change the format to bold.

2. Type **Amortization Schedule** in cell A2.

3. Type **=NOW()** as a formula in cell A3 and click the Enter button ✓ on the Formula Bar.

   > **Comment** The =NOW() function is a Date & Time function that displays the date and time according to the computer's system clock. This date is dynamic; as the system clock changes, the date is updated.

4. Select Cells from the Format menu. Select the Number tab in the Format Cells dialog box, select Date as the category, and select the date type shown in the figure below.

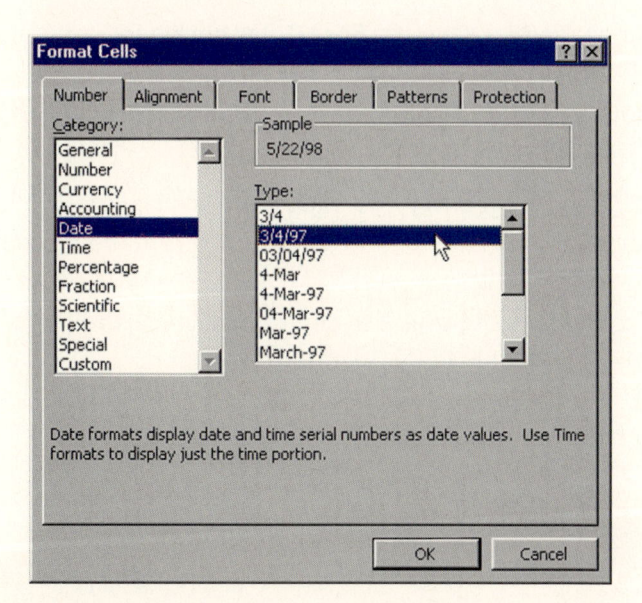

5. Set the alignment of the cell to left.

6. Click OK.

7. Type **Payment** in cell B5, **Interest** in cell B6, **Term** in cell B7, and **Principal** in cell B8. Set the alignment of these cells to right aligned.

8 Type **Payment Number** in cell A10, **Beginning Balance** in cell B10, **Principal Paid** in cell C10, **Cumulative Principal** in cell D10, **Interest Paid** in cell E10, **Cumulative Interest** in cell F10, **Total Paid To Date** in cell G10, and **Ending Balance** in cell H10.

TASK 2: APPLY ADDITIONAL FORMATS TO THE TEXT CONSTANTS:

1 Select the range A10:H10, and set the font style to bold. Using the Fill Color button on the Formatting toolbar, set the fill color of the selection to 25% Gray.

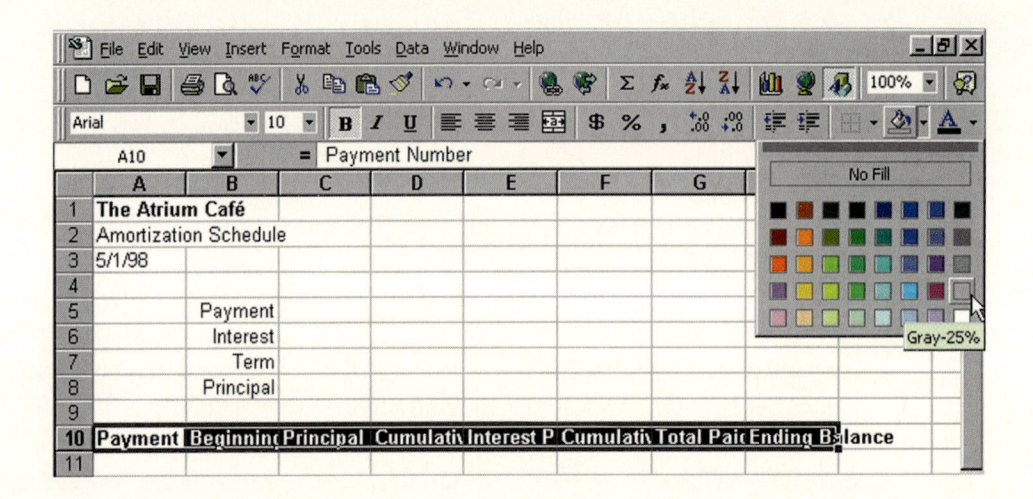

2 Select the range B5:C8. Set the fill color of the selection to 25% gray.

3 Select the range B5:C5. Using the Font Color button on the Formatting toolbar, set the font color of this selection to dark red.

4 Select the Borders button on the Formatting toolbar. Insert a thin border around the selection.

5 Select the range B5:B8. Set the font style of the selection to Bold.

6 Highlight the range A10 to H10, and select Cells from the Format menu. Select the Alignment tab.

7 Set the Horizontal text alignment to center, and check the option to wrap text, as shown on the next page. Click OK.

Project 6: Using Financial Functions   EX-163

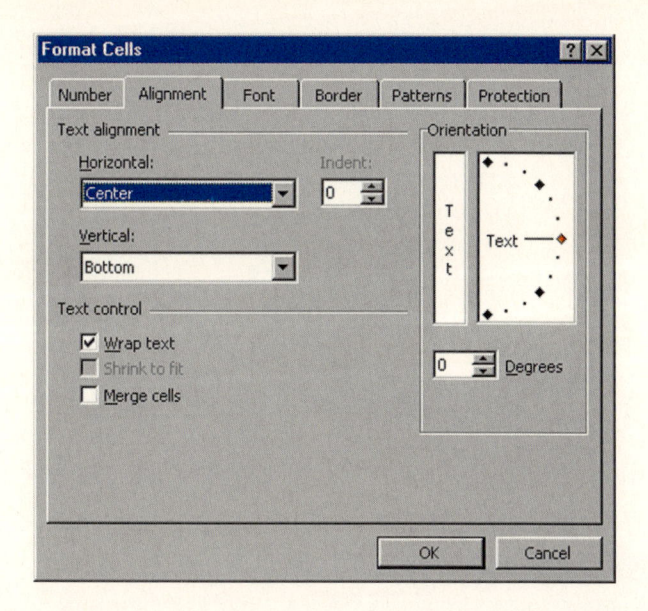

8 Select the Borders tool on the Standard toolbar. Select the option to add a thin border to the top and bottom of the selection.

9 Use the column headings to select columns B through H. Set the width of the selected columns to 12.00. Save your workbook to your floppy disk as *Willows Loan Amortization.xls*.

10 Change the Zoom control 85% on the Standard toolbar to 85%. Your workbook should look like the one shown below.

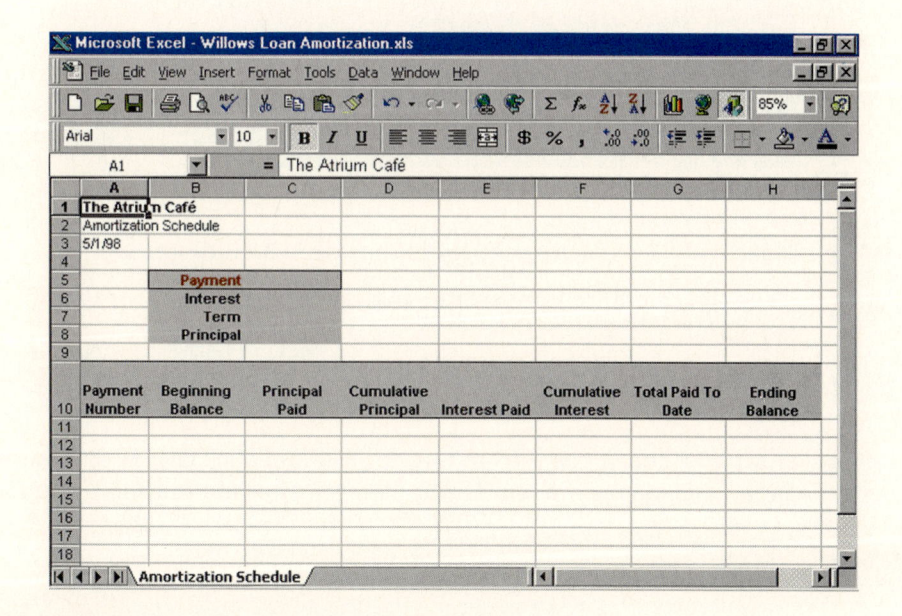

Entering Numeric Constants

A loan payment is calculated using three factors: the loan principal, the interest rate, and the term. These values are entered in the range C6:C8 of your worksheet. All loan repayment data is calculated using these values.

TASK 3: ENTERING NUMERIC CONSTANTS:

1. Place the cell pointer in cell C6, type **.075**, and press (ENTER).

2. Click cell C6 again to make it the active cell, select Cells from the Format menu, and click the Number tab.

3. Select Percentage as the category, and specify two decimal places. Click OK.

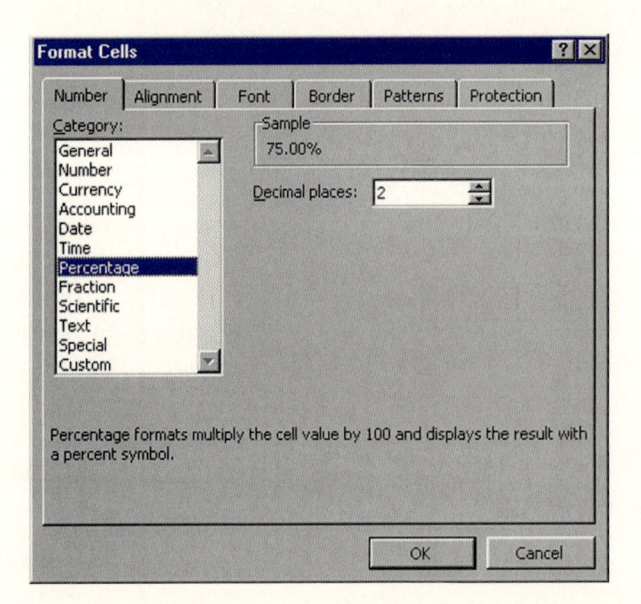

4. Make cell C7 the active cell, type the value **3**, and press (ENTER).

5. Place the cell pointer in cell C7, select Cells from the Format menu, and click the Number tab.

6. Select Custom as the category, and place the insertion point in the Type: text box.

7. Enter **## "Years"** as the custom format and click OK, as shown on the next page. This places the text string "Years" after the numeric value in the cell.

Project 6: Using Financial Functions   EX-165

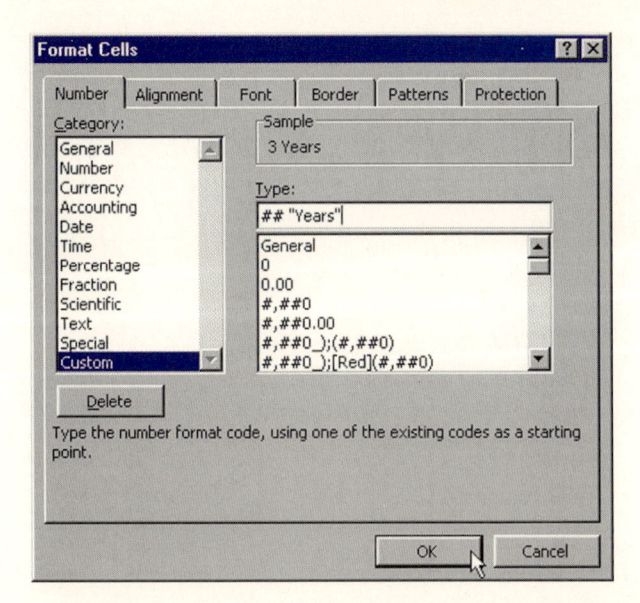

> **Tip** When specifying a custom format, the dialog box displays a sample of the current cell with the custom format applied.

8 Place the cell pointer in cell C8, type **12000** and press ENTER.

9 Make cell C8 the active cell and select Cells from the Format menu. Click the Number tab, and select Currency as the category. Make sure two decimal places are specified. Click OK.

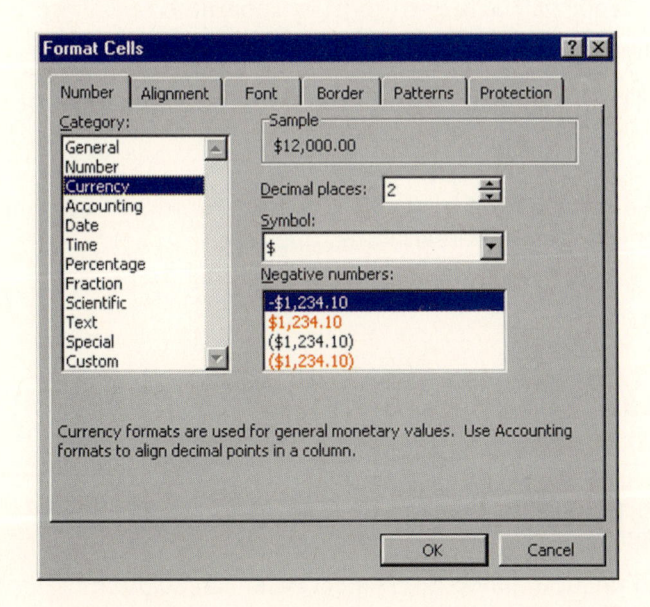

10 After entering and formatting the three numeric constants, the worksheet should look like the one on the next page.

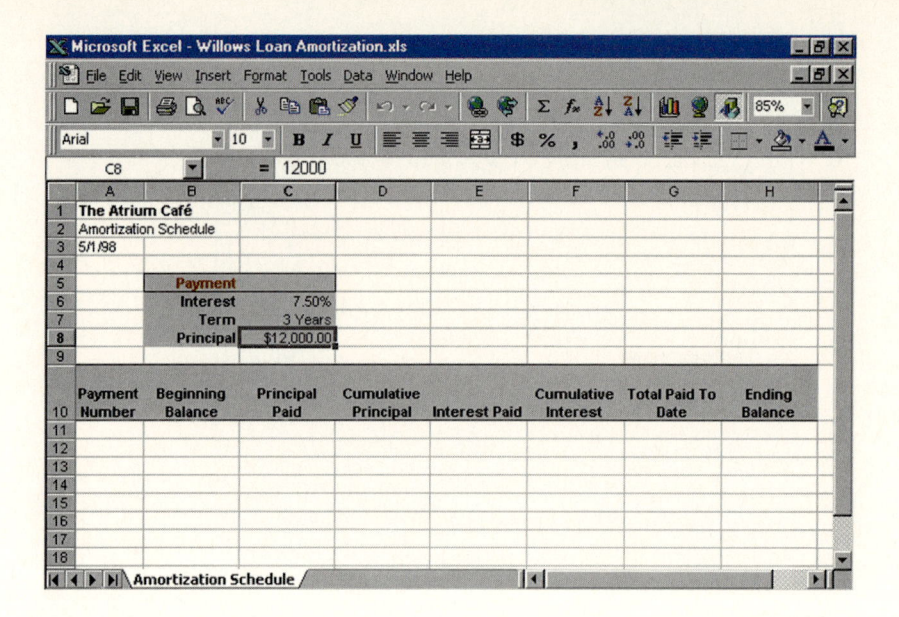

Calculating the Loan Payment

After you specify the rate, term, and principal, you can calculate the loan payment. The PMT (payment) function is a financial function used to calculate the periodic payment of a loan, assuming a constant interest rate and constant payments over the life of the loan. Functions perform calculations by using specific values, called *arguments*, in a particular order, called the syntax. The PMT function uses five arguments, three of which are required. A function's *syntax* specifies the order in which the arguments must appear. Each argument is separated from the others with a comma. The general syntax for the PMT function is:

=PMT(interest rate, number of payments, present value)

> **Note** Search for PMT in the Help system for more information about the arguments accompanying this function.

TASK 4: CALCULATE THE LOAN PAYMENT USING THE PMT FUNCTION:

1. Place the cell pointer in cell C5 to make it the active cell. Select Function from the Insert menu.

2. In the Paste Function dialog box, select Financial as the function category and select PMT as the function name, as shown on the next page. Note that the Paste Function dialog box also displays the arguments used by the function.

Project 6: Using Financial Functions   EX-167

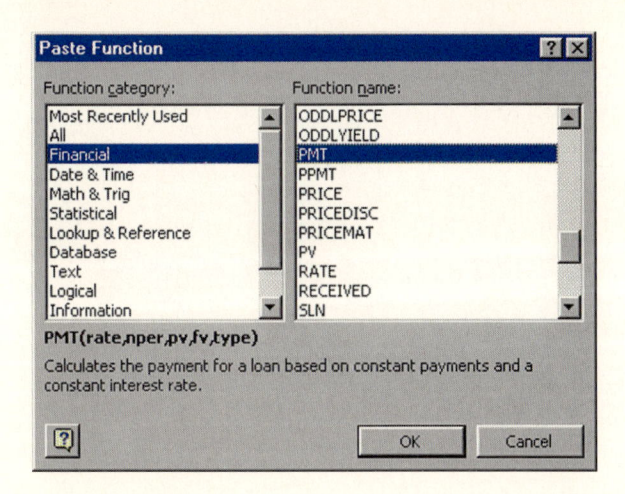

3 Click OK. The function's arguments can be entered in the box that appears.

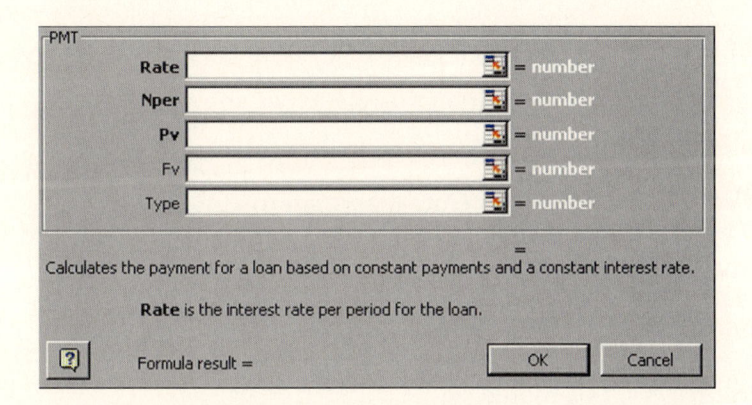

4 Click the button ￼ = number immediately to the right of the text box for specifying the rate.

5 Point to cell C6 and click the left mouse button, as shown in the figure below. Notice that the reference C6 appears both in the Formula bar and the text box below the Formula bar.

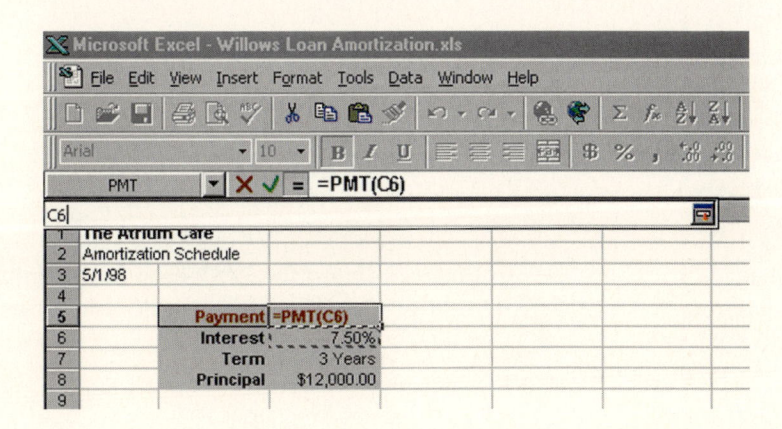

6 The interest rate specified in the worksheet is an annual interest rate. Therefore, it must be divided by 12 (the number of interest periods in one year) for the function to calculate the correct payment.

7 Place the insertion point in the text box that appears under the Formula bar, and type **/12**.

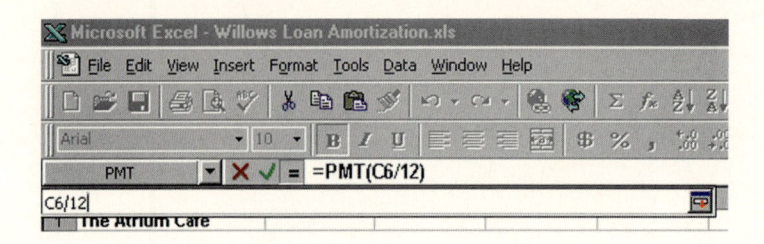

8 Press (ENTER).

The pointing method is one way of entering the arguments the PMT function needs. Because you know the term appears in cell C7 and the payment appears in cell C8, you can enter these values directly.

9 Enter the remaining required arguments, as shown below.

> **Troubleshooting** Note that the term "numeric constant" specifies years. The PMT function requires monthly payments, so you must multiply the value by 12. The PV is the present value of the loan, which is the same as the loan principal. In **annuity functions** (functions that involve payments that are constant), the cash you pay out is represented as a negative value. Therefore, you must precede the reference to cell C8 with a minus sign.

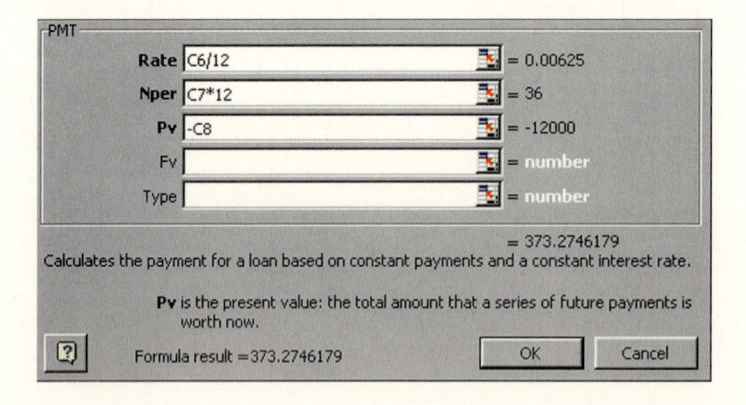

10 Click OK to enter the formula containing the PMT function in cell C5, and save your workbook. The results of the formula should appear as shown on the next page.

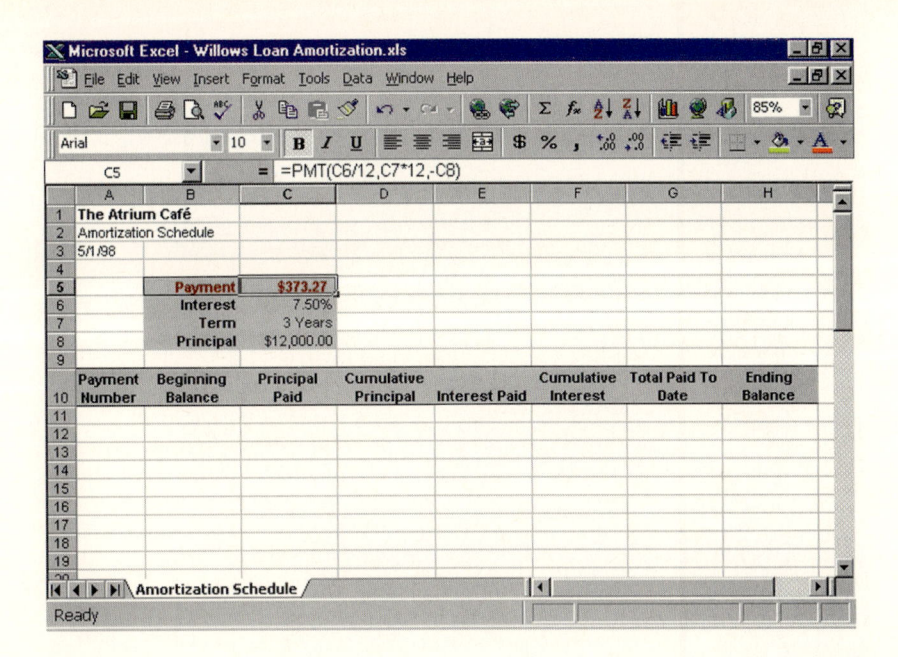

Calculating the Beginning Balance Using the PV Function

Although the beginning balance of the loan that appears in cell B11 is the same as the principal displayed in cell C8, the PV function can be used to enter a "check" into the worksheet. By using the PV function in cell B12 rather than merely including a reference to cell C5, you verify the accuracy of the worksheet.

As with the PMT function, the PV (present value of an annuity) function requires three arguments: rate, term, and payment. The general syntax for the PV function is:

=PV(interest rate, number of payments, periodic payment)

TASK 5: CALCULATE THE BEGINNING BALANCE USING THE PV FUNCTION:

1. Place the cell pointer in cell B11.
2. Type **=PV(C6/12,C7*12,–C5)** and press ENTER.

Tip As with the PMT function, the annual interest rate must be divided by the number of annual periods (12) per year. In addition, the term (in years) must be multiplied by the number of payments made each year (12), and the payment must be preceded by a minus sign.

The value displayed in cell B11 should appear as shown below.

[Screenshot of Microsoft Excel - Willows Loan Amortization.xls showing cell B11 selected with formula =PV(C6/12,C7*12,-C5) and value $12,000.00. The spreadsheet shows The Atrium Café Amortization Schedule dated 5/1/98 with Payment $373.27, Interest 7.50%, Term 3 Years, Principal $12,000.00, and column headers: Payment Number, Beginning Balance, Principal Paid, Cumulative Principal, Interest Paid, Cumulative Interest.]

3 Save your workbook.

Calculating the Principal Paid in Each Payment

The amount of each loan payment that applies to the loan principal (rather than the accrued interest) varies throughout the term of the loan. As with most annuity functions, the actual variance depends upon the loan's rate, term, and principal. The PPMT (periodic principal payment) returns the payment on the principal for a given period. The PPMT function requires four arguments: the rate, the specific period, the number of payments, and the present value of the annuity for the period.

In this function, the *present value* refers to the total amount that a series of future payments is worth now—this is the loan principal. The general syntax is:

=PPMT(interest rate, payment period, number of payments, present value)

This function, which is copied to other cells in the amortization schedule, includes both absolute cell references and one mixed cell reference. A *mixed reference* means that the column reference remains constant, but the row reference varies. The function also will need to reference the specific payment (by payment number) within the period. This data is supplied to the function from column A of the amortization schedule.

Project 6: Using Financial Functions EX-171

> **Tip** The term *mixed reference* is a carryover from Lotus 1-2-3 and is not used in Microsoft Excel. Therefore, this term will not be found in the Help System. It is a useful term, however, because it conveys the idea that part of the reference is relative and part is absolute. In Excel, mixed references are also referred to as absolute references.

TASK 6: CALCULATE THE PERIODIC PRINCIPAL PAYMENT USING THE PPMT FUNCTION:

1 Click cell A11 to make it the active cell.

2 Type **1** as a numeric constant representing the first periodic payment.

3 Place the insertion point in cell C11, making it the active cell.
Type **=-PPMT($C$6/12,$A11,$C$7*12,$C$8)** and press ENTER.

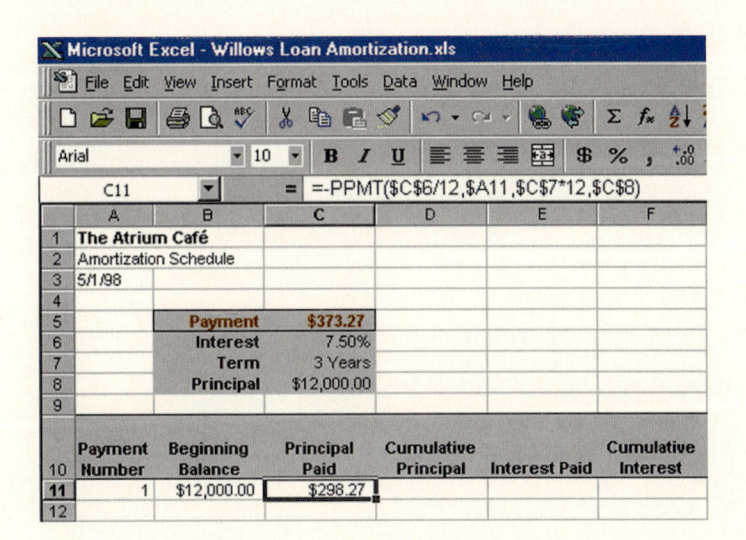

Now let's analyze this formula. The entire payment is preceded by a minus sign, because annuity payments must be specified as a negative value. The references to the rate (cell C6), term (cell C7), and present value (cell C8) are absolute, because the formula must always reference the same cells, regardless of where the formula is copied in the worksheet. Cell C11 contains a mixed reference: The row reference must change to reflect the periodic payment as the formula is copied down the amortization schedule, but column A must be referenced when the formula is copied to cell E11 to construct the IPMT function.

Tip It is not mandatory that cells C6, C7, and C8 contain absolute references. Technically, these could contain mixed references to specify which part of the reference should remain constant (C$6, for example); only the row designation must remain constant as the formulas are copied. The worksheet also uses the IPMT function, which shares the same arguments as the PPMT function, so absolute references are used to assist in creating these formulas. In general, it is a good practice to use absolute references unless the column reference must change if the formula is copied to another column in the worksheet.

Calculating the Interest Paid in Each Payment

The method for calculating the portion of a loan payment that applies to the interest payment is almost identical to the method for calculating a periodic principal payment. The only difference is that the IPMT (periodic interest payment) function is used. The general syntax for the IPMT function is:

=IPMT(interest rate, payment period, number of payments, present value)

TASK 7: CALCULATE THE PERIODIC INTEREST PAYMENT:

1. Select cell C11.
2. Copy the contents of the cell.
3. Place the insertion point in cell E11.
4. Select Paste using either the Edit menu or the Standard toolbar.
5. Edit the formula in the Formula bar by changing the function from PPMT to IPMT.

Your worksheet should now look like the one shown below.

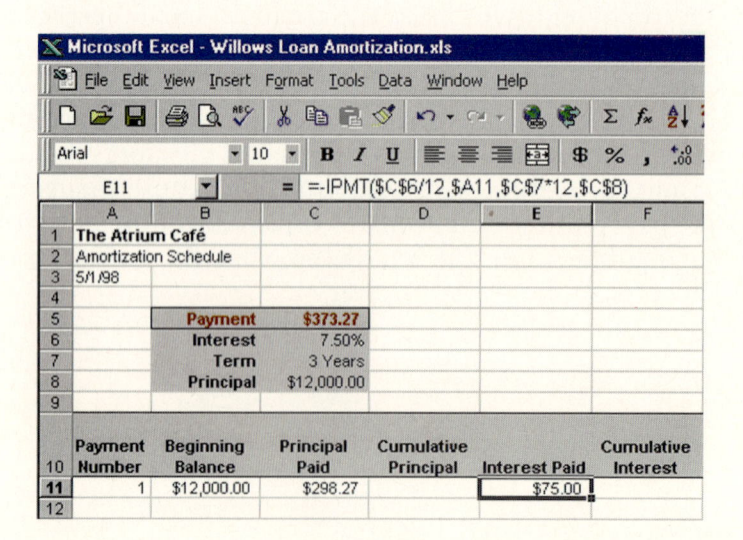

Constructing Formulas to Calculate the Cumulative Principal, Cumulative Interest, Total Payments, and Ending Balance

When building an amortization schedule, it is helpful to display not only the current principal and interest payments, but the cumulative payments as well. For the first payment, the periodic principal and interest payment equal the cumulative payments. In subsequent rows, however, the cumulative payment figures increase. The total payments to date can be calculated by adding the cumulative principal and the cumulative interest payments.

TASK 8: CONSTRUCT FORMULAS TO DETERMINE THE CUMULATIVE INTEREST, CUMULATIVE PRINCIPAL, TOTAL PAYMENTS, AND ENDING BALANCE:

1. Select cell D11 as the active cell.
2. Type **=C11**.
3. Place the insertion point in cell F11, and type **=E11**.
4. Place the insertion point in cell G11, and type **=D11+F11**.

> **Reminder** The value displayed in cell G11 should be identical to the value in cell C5. This provides another "check" to verify the accuracy of your worksheet.

5. Place the insertion point in cell H11.
6. Type **=B11–C11**. The ending balance is the principal that must be paid to fulfill the repayment obligation. This is equal to the beginning balance minus the principal payment. Your worksheet should now look like the one shown on the next page.

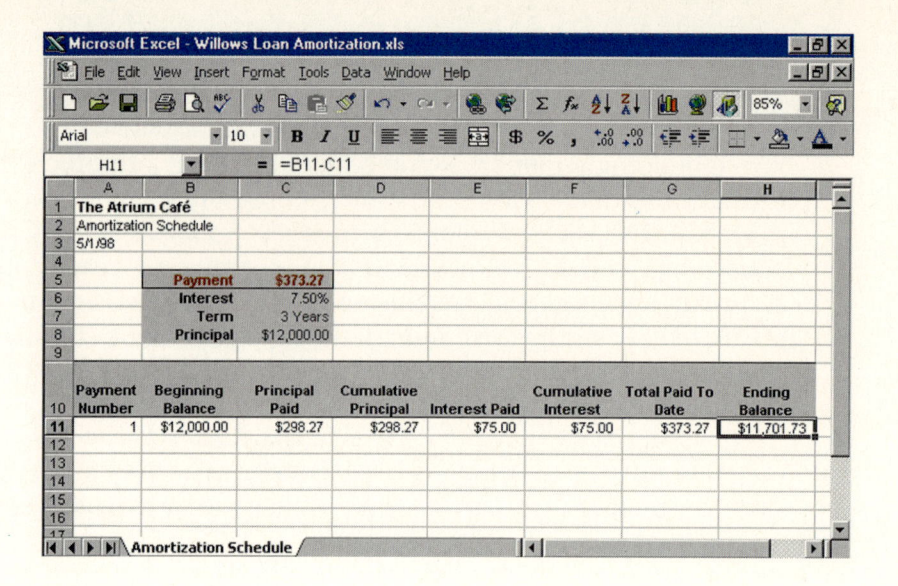

EX-174

[Screenshot of Microsoft Excel - Willows Loan Amortization.xls showing the amortization schedule with Payment $373.27, Interest 7.50%, Term 3 Years, Principal $12,000.00, and row 11 data: Payment 1, Beginning Balance $12,000.00, Principal Paid $298.27, Cumulative Principal $298.27, Interest Paid $75.00, Cumulative Interest $75.00, Total Paid To Date $373.27, Ending Balance $11,701.73. Cell H11 formula =B11-C11.]

7 Save your worksheet.

Using the Fill Handle to Complete the Amortization Schedule

After you enter formulas in row 12 of the amortization schedule, you can use the Fill Handle to copy the formula to other portions of the worksheet. The default amortization schedule covers a loan with a term of three years, a principal of $12,000, and an annual interest rate of 7.50%.

TASK 9: USE THE FILL HANDLE TO COMPLETE THE AMORTIZATION SCHEDULE:

1 Place the insertion point in cell A12 to make it the active cell.

2 Type **=A11+1**.

3 Type **=H11** in cell B12. The beginning balance for this payment equals the ending balance after the last payment was made.

4 Highlight the range C11:H11. Using the Fill Handle, copy the range down to row 12, as shown on the next page.

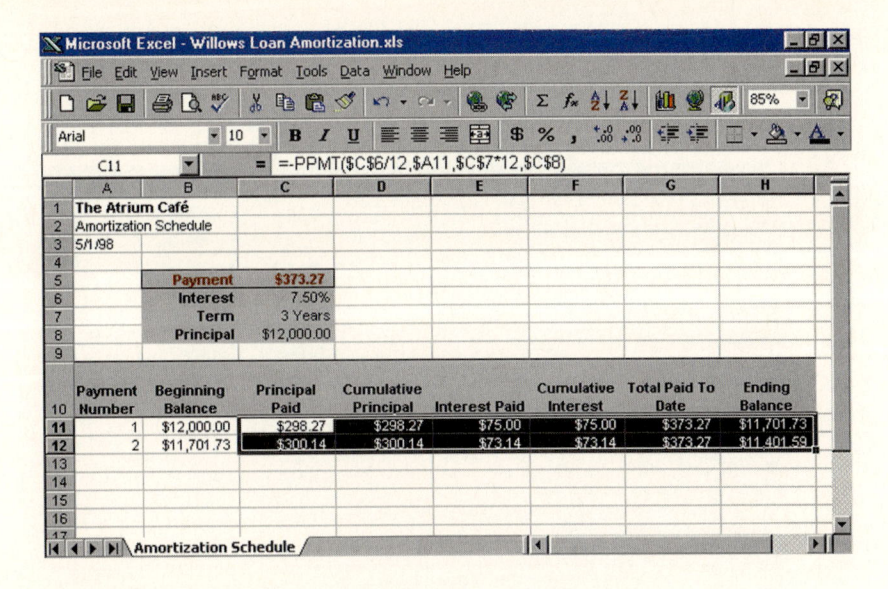

5 Highlight cell D12, and change the formula to **=D11+C12**.

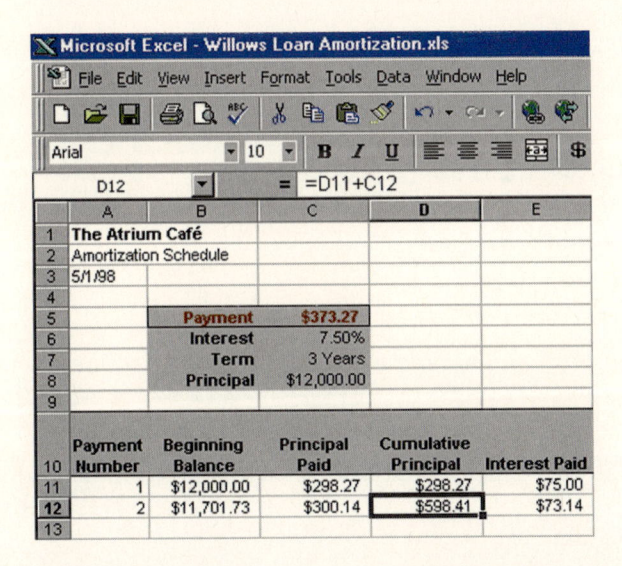

6 Highlight cell F12, and change the formula to **=F11+E12**.

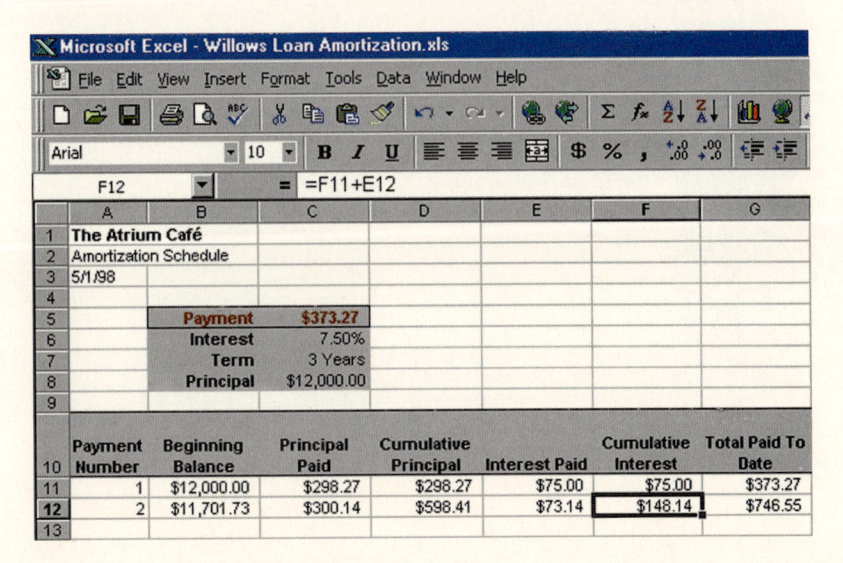

EX-176

7 Highlight the range A12:H12. Using the Fill Handle, copy this row of formulas through row 46, as shown below.

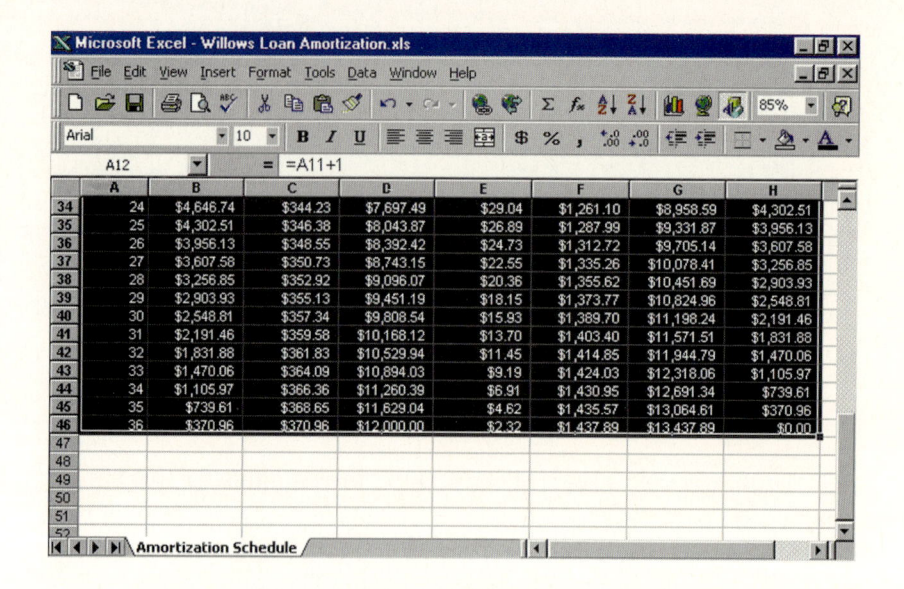

Tip Notice that the Ending Balance equals zero at payment 36. This verifies that the amortization schedule is calculating the loan repayment figures correctly.

8 Highlight Column A and set the alignment of the selection to center.

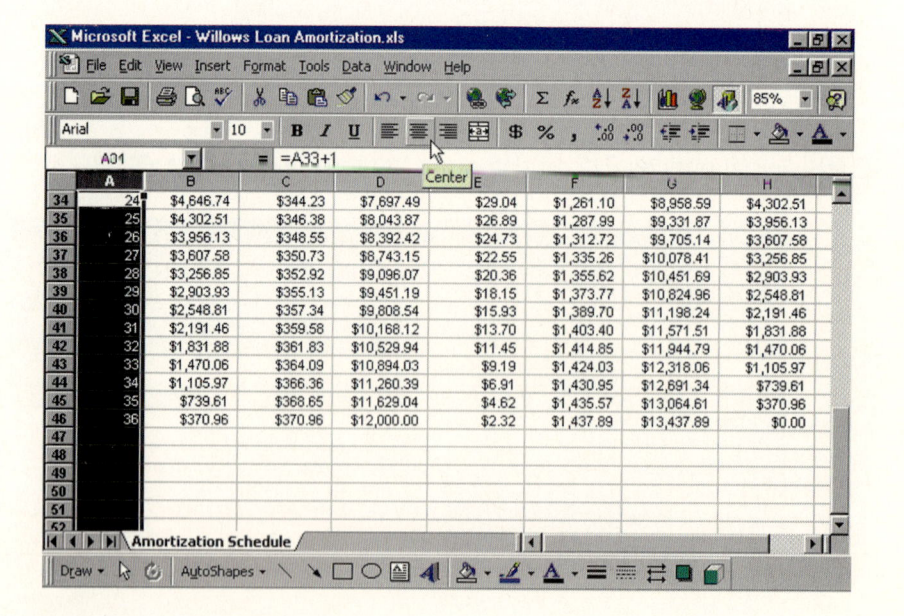

9 Highlight the range A1:A3. Set the alignment to left.

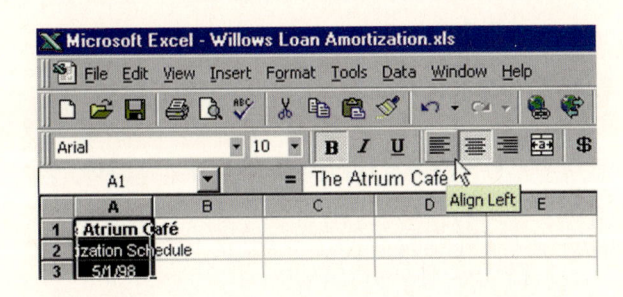

10 Save your changes. Your workbook should now look like the one shown in the figure below.

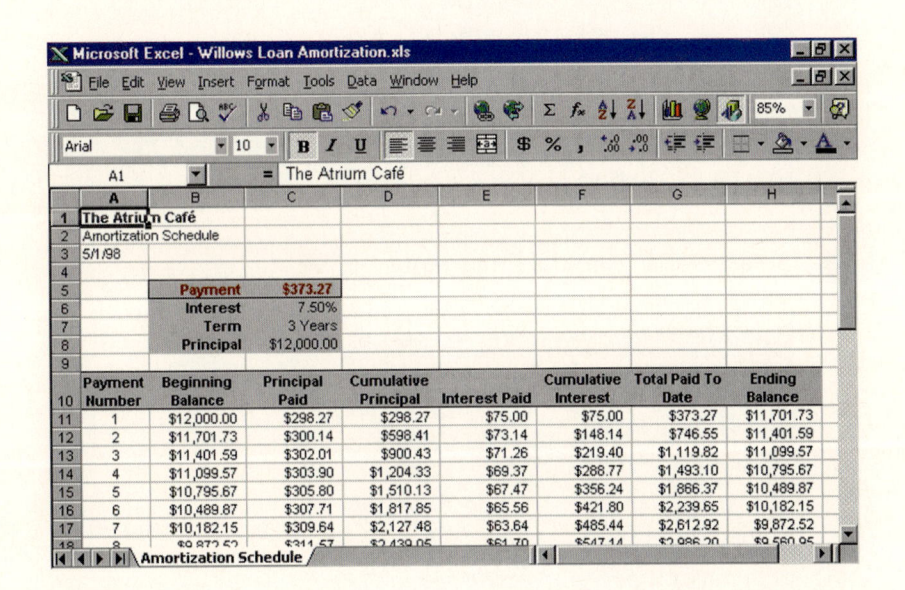

Freezing Worksheet Panes to Assist in Viewing Large Worksheets

Your amortization schedule is now fully functional. Take a moment to note the power of Microsoft Excel. By using financial functions and copying these formulas down the worksheet, the entire loan repayment table is based upon four numeric constants—even though your worksheet presently contains almost 300 formulas.

Viewing large worksheets can be problematic because the heading rows scroll out of view as you move down the worksheet. To alleviate this problem, certain rows can be "frozen" so they always appear on the screen. In the next task, you will freeze the worksheet headings so the entire amortization schedule can be viewed with the headings visible on the screen.

EX-178

TASK 10: FREEZE WORKSHEET PANES TO ASSIST VIEWING:

1 Place the insertion point in cell A11.

2 Select Freeze Panes from the Window menu.

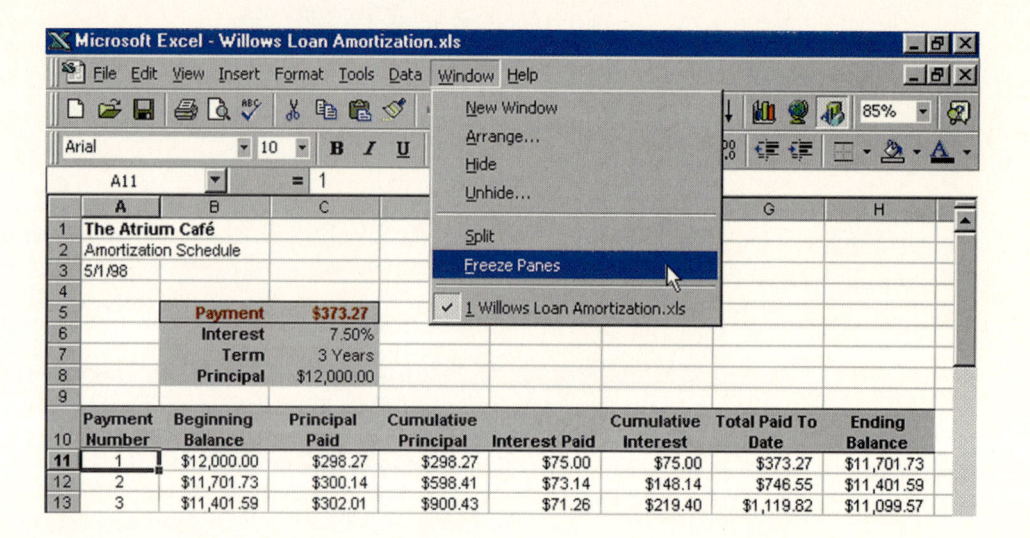

3 Select Go To from the Edit menu.

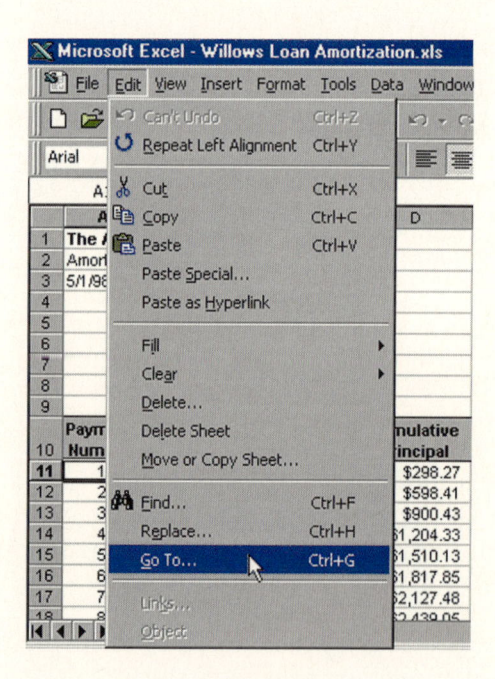

4 Type **A46** in the Reference text box of the Go To dialog box.

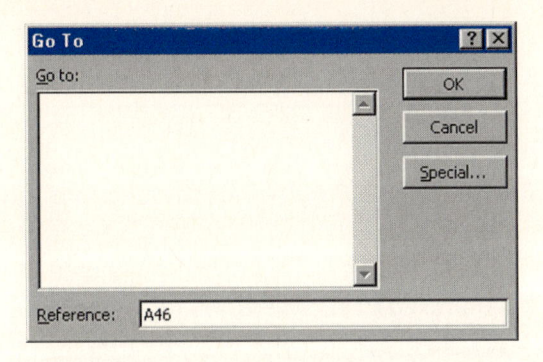

5 Click OK. Cell A46 becomes the active cell, and rows 1 through 10 and additional rows up to row 46 become visible.

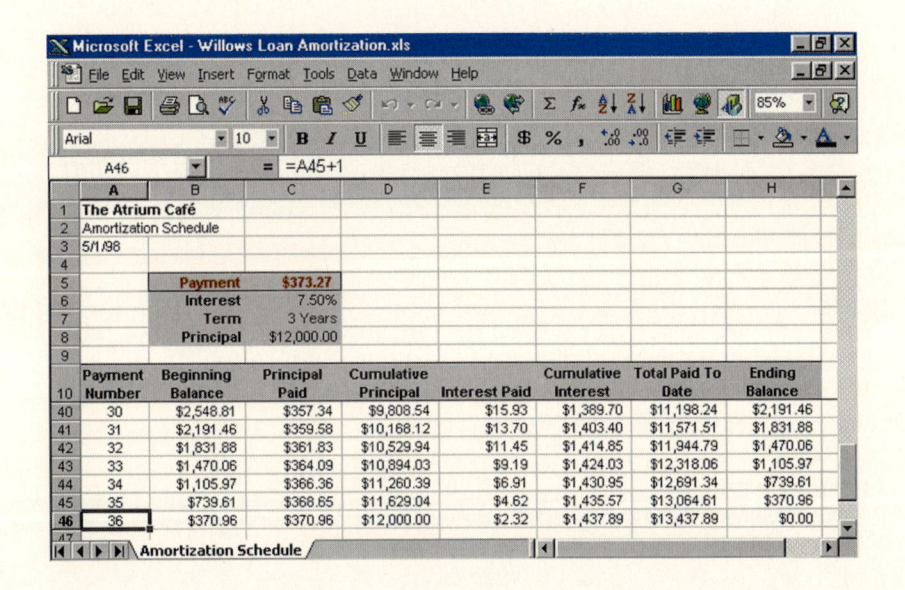

As you scroll through the worksheet, rows 1 through 10 always remain visible.

> **Tip** To unfreeze the panes, select Unfreeze Panes from the Window menu.

Changing the Loan Scenario

Using this workbook, Mr. Gilmore can easily compare alternative loan scenarios. To see how easy it is to view another loan scenario, simply change the principal and term values, and then add additional rows to the worksheet.

EX-180

TASK 11: TO CHANGE THE LOAN SCENARIO:

1. Enter **4** in cell C7 and press ENTER.

2. Type **10000** in cell C8 and press ENTER. Notice that the monthly payment changes to $241.79.

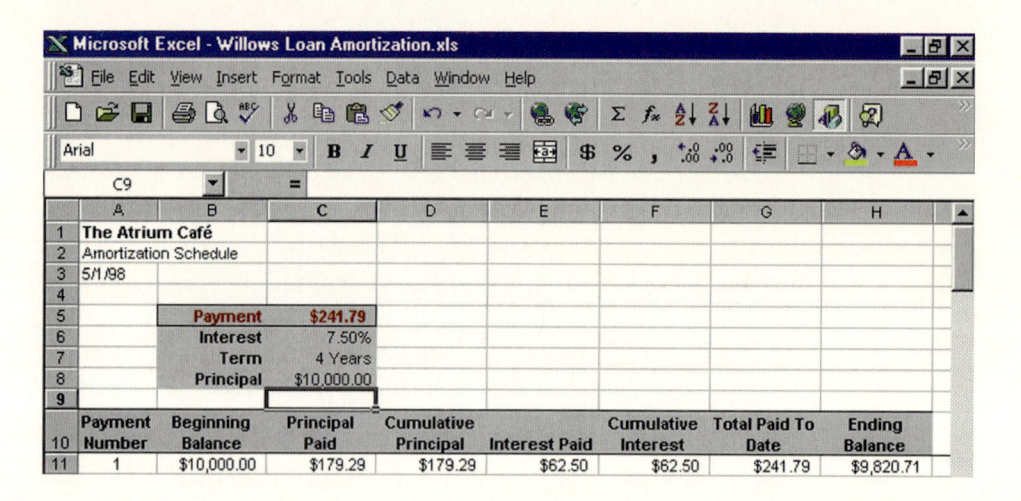

3. Scroll to the bottom of the worksheet, and highlight the range A46:H46.

4. Using the Fill Handle, drag the selection through row 58 and release the left mouse button. Your amortization schedule should now resemble the one shown in the figure below.

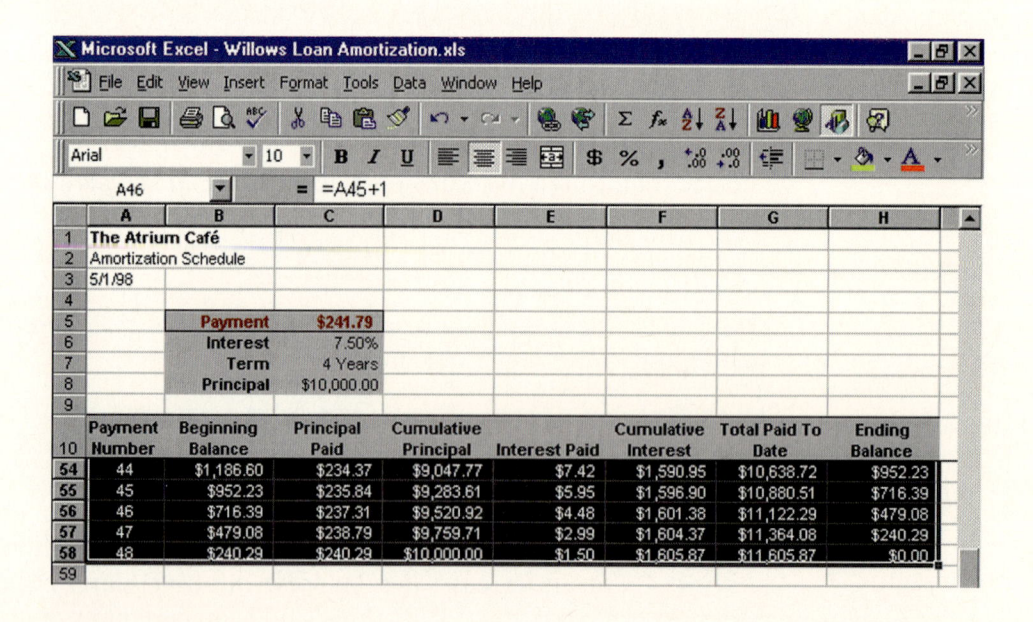

5. Using the vertical scroll bar, move to the top of the worksheet, and make cell A1 the active cell.

6. Save your workbook.

Creating Excel Macros

When using Excel you often may need to complete a series of tasks more than once. By recording a macro, you can easily apply these procedures again by simply playing the macro. A *macro* is a series of commands and functions stored in a Visual Basic module that can be run whenever you need to perform the task again. (*Visual Basic* is the programming language used throughout the Office environment for recording macros. If you know Visual Basic, you can easily edit a macro you have created.)

It would be nice if your amortization worksheet could easily be returned to a predictable state after the loan's term is changed, because the worksheet will either display errors or not display the entire repayment schedule. You can create a macro to set the default values and create the appropriate number of loan repayment formulas.

TASK 12: TO RECORD A MACRO:

1. Select Macros from the Tools menu, and choose Record New Macro.

2. Type **SetDefaults** as the name of the macro, and make sure the macro is stored in the current workbook, as shown in the figure below. Click OK.

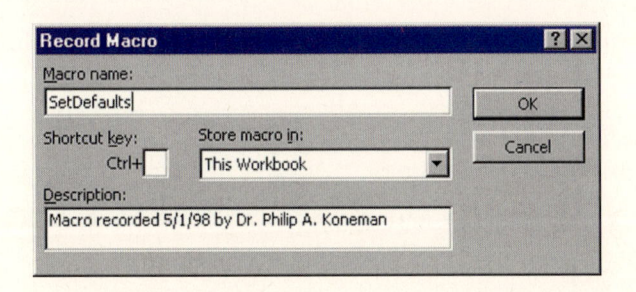

Tip Every procedure you now apply will become a part of the macro. You will also notice that the Stop Recording toolbar is now visible on the screen.

3. Click cell A13 to make it the active cell.

4. While simultaneously holding down the (SHIFT) and (CTRL) keys, press the (END) key. The range A13:H56 is now selected.

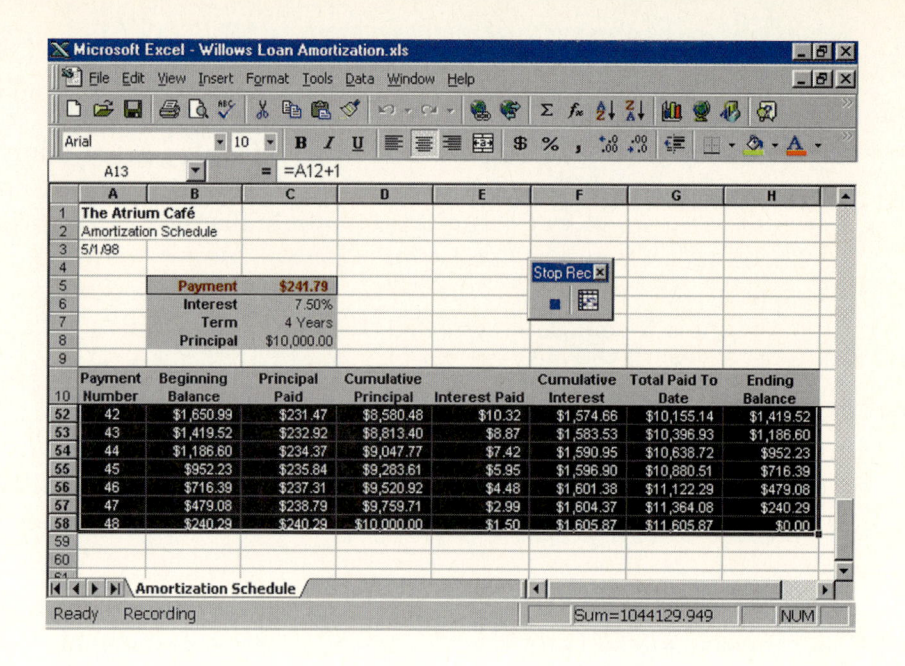

5 Press the DELETE key to delete the selected portion of the amortization schedule.

6 Type **3** in cell C7 as the term, and type **12000** in cell C8 as the principal.

7 Select the range A12:H12 and use the Fill Handle to copy the formulas through row 46.

8 Scroll to the top of the worksheet and make cell A1 the active cell.

9 Click the Stop Recording button.

10 You have now successfully recorded a macro. Save your workbook.

Running a Macro

After you have recorded a macro, it can be run. When you *run* a macro, each step included in the macro is applied to the workbook. Before running the macro, you will change the loan scenario to see the results of applying the macro.

TASK 13: TO RUN A MACRO:

1 Type **10** in cell C7 and **50000** in cell C8.

2 Scroll to the bottom of the worksheet and select the range A46:H46.

3 Using the Fill Handle, copy the selection through row 130, as shown on the next page.

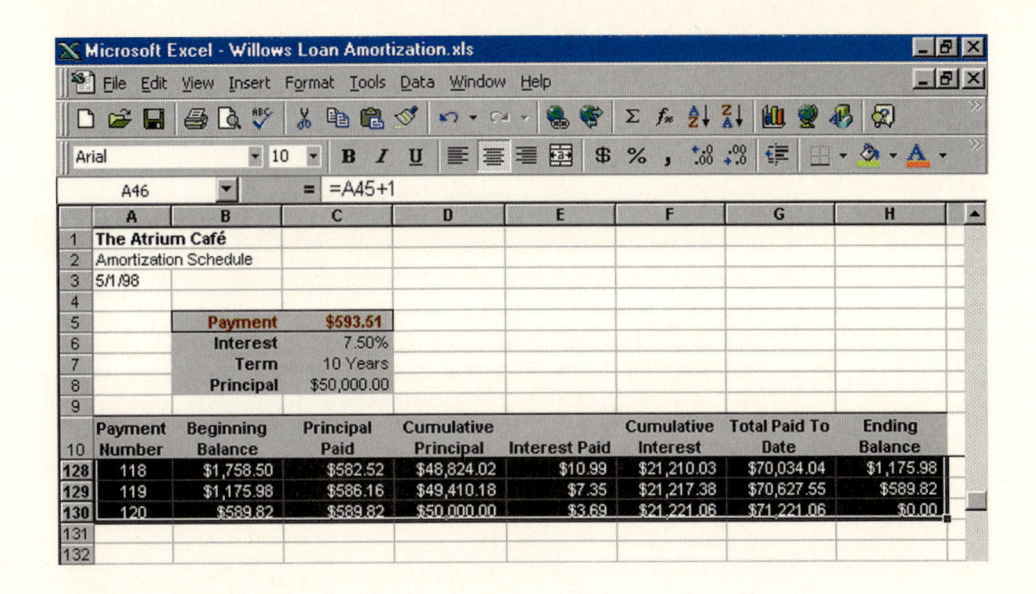

4 Select Macro from the Tools menu, and then choose Macros.

5 Select the SetDefaults macro and click the Run command button.

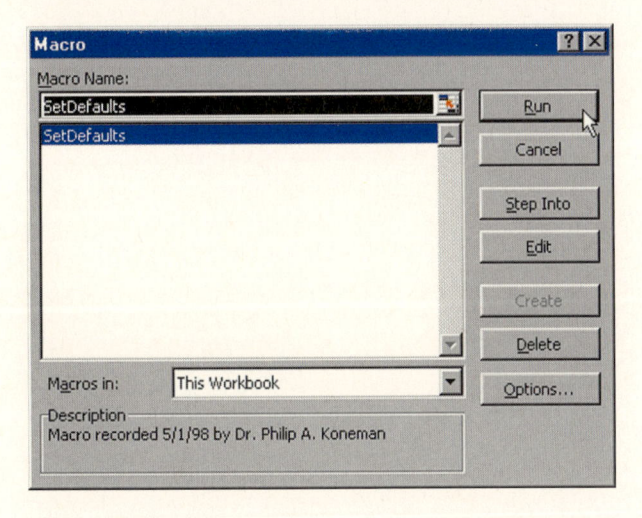

The macro will change the term and principal of the loan, and modify the amortization schedule accordingly. You can easily change the loan scenario to a predictable state at any time by simply running the SetDefaults macro.

The Conclusion

The worksheet you have created in this project serves as a powerful tool for analyzing different loan scenarios. The numeric constants in the upper portion of the Amortization Schedule worksheet can easily be changed to compare alternate loan scenarios.

Summary and Exercises

Summary

- Text constants are used to define a workbook's structure.
- Excel contains many financial functions.
- In an amortization schedule workbook, numeric constants for the principal, rate, and term are used to calculate the loan payment.
- The PMT function is used to calculate a loan payment.
- The PV function is used to calculate the present value of an annuity.
- The PPMT function is used to calculate the portion of a loan payment that applies toward the loan principal.
- The IPMT is used to calculate the portion of a loan payment that applies toward the accrued interest.
- A complex workbook such as an amortization schedule will often contain hundreds of formulas.
- Once created, formulas are easily copied using the Fill Handle.
- Worksheet panes can be frozen to assist in viewing large worksheets.
- A macro is used to record redundant tasks that can be applied again and again.

Key Terms and Operations

Key Terms

amortization	present value
amortization schedule	principal
annuity functions	rate
argument	run
loan scenario	syntax
macro	term
mixed reference	text constants
numeric constants	Visual Basic

Operations

construct a formula using the IPMT (interest payment) function
construct a formula using the PMT (payment) function
construct a formula using the PPMT (periodic payment) function
construct a formula using the PV (present value of an annuity) function
create an amortization schedule
create formulas to calculate the cumulative interest and cumulative principal
determine the ending balance
freeze worksheet panes
record a macro
run a macro
use AutoFill to copy formulas

Study Questions

Multiple Choice

1. A worksheet is being constructed to determine the monthly payment required to return $250,000 in the year 2025. Which financial function should be used to perform this calculation?
   a. PMT
   b. IPMT
   c. PV
   d. FV
   e. PPMT

2. A worksheet includes a formula for calculating the payment on a loan. To see the amount of the monthly payment that applies to the interest payment, you will use which function?
   a. PMT
   b. PV
   c. NOW()
   d. PPMT
   e. IPMT

3. Which statement concerning the use of the PV annuity function is false?
   a. An annuity payment should be entered as a negative value.
   b. The present value of the investment is required.
   c. The total number of payment periods in the annuity is required.
   d. Parentheses are not used when constructing this function.
   e. The interest rate cannot change over the life of the annuity.

4. Which of the following most likely refers to the principal of a loan in a financial function?
   a. H6/12
   b. I7*12
   c. −J7
   d. g3/12
   e. −a1*24

5. Which of the following formulas includes an absolute reference to an annuity payment?
   a. =PMT(a1/12,c7*12,d7)
   b. =PPMT(a1/12,c7*12,e7)
   c. =PMT(h6/12,I$7*12,−j7)
   d. =IPMT(a1/12,c7*12,−e7)
   e. =PMT(a1/12,$b7*12,−$r$5)

6. Which of the following is true about macros?
   a. After a macro is created, it cannot be edited.
   b. Macros aren't very useful in worksheets containing financial functions.
   c. Macros are used to record a series of redundant tasks.
   d. Macros cannot perform copy and paste operations.
   e. Macros are rarely used in Excel workbooks.

7. The Principal Payment (PPMT) function is similar to which function?
   a. PMT
   b. PV
   c. IPMT
   d. PPMT
   e. NOW()

8. Which function calculates the portion of a loan payment applied toward the principal?
   a. PMT
   b. PV
   c. IPMT
   d. PPMT
   e. FV

9. You can freeze worksheet panes using which menu?
   a. Format
   b. Edit
   c. Data
   d. View
   e. Window

10. The =NOW() function is in which category of functions?
    a. Financial
    b. Statistical
    c. Date/Time
    d. Logical
    e. String

Short Answer

1. Examine the function =PMT(H6/12,I7*12,–J7). Which element refers to the present value of the loan? How is it identified?

2. Explain how the term of a loan impacts the total amount paid.

3. What does the PMT function calculate?

4. What is a mixed cell reference?

5. Why should the formulas in an amortization schedule contain absolute references?

6. What is the maximum number of arguments that can be included with the PMT function?

7. What value does the PPMT function return?

8. If you are having difficulty viewing the headings in a large worksheet, what should you do?

9. What happens when you record a macro?

10. How should annuity payments be entered in a formula?

For Discussion

1. What is the FV function? How does the data it returns differ from the PV function?

2. What is a macro? How is a macro recorded and applied?

3. How can worksheets, such as the amortization schedule you created in this project, be protected from changes?

4. What arguments are required by the PMT function? Is the order in which these appear in a formula significant?

Review Exercises

1. Protecting cells in a workbook

In many settings, portions of a worksheet should be protected to prohibit users from inadvertently making destructive changes to the workbook. By unlocking the cells to which users need access and protecting the worksheet, this objective can easily be achieved. Open the *Willows Loan Amortization* workbook and do the following:

1. Select the following nonadjacent ranges: C6:C8 and A13:H370.
2. Select Cells from the Format menu.
3. Click the Protection tab.
4. Deselect the Locked check box in the Format Cells dialog box.
5. Click the OK button.
6. Select Protection from the Tools menu.
7. Select Protect Sheet from the cascading menu.
8. Do not enter a protection password in the Protect Sheet dialog box.
9. Click OK.
10. Save the updated workbook as *Protected Loan Analysis.xls*.

2. Creating a worksheet to predict the future value of an investment

The FV function is similar to the PV function, except that it returns the future value of an investment, assuming a constant interest rate. Create the workbook shown below as follows:

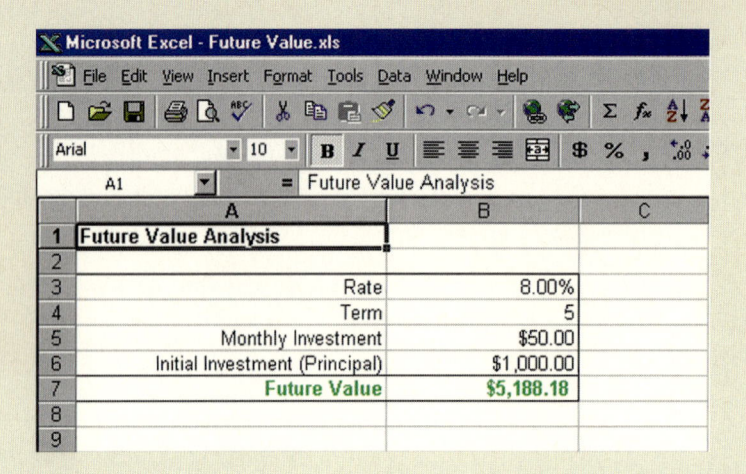

	A	B
1	Future Value Analysis	
2		
3	Rate	8.00%
4	Term	5
5	Monthly Investment	$50.00
6	Initial Investment (Principal)	$1,000.00
7	Future Value	$5,188.18
8		
9		

1. Launch Excel if isn't already running.

2. Create a new workbook.

3. Save the workbook as *Future value.xls*.

4. Enter the text and numeric constants shown in the figure on the previous page into the worksheet.

5. Type **=FV(B3/12,B4*12,–B5,–B6,1)** as the formula in cell B7. Look up FV in the Excel Help System for information about the arguments.

Assignments

1. Creating macros to enable and disable protection for a worksheet

Open the *Protected loan analysis.xls* workbook. Create two macros: one that sets the protection for the worksheet, and one that removes the worksheet protection. Save the workbook as *Protected Loan Y-N.xls*.

2. Repaying a loan early

Visit Microsoft's New Spreadsheet Solutions site, which contains spreadsheet solutions created by Village Software. (http://www.microsoft.com/excel/freestuff/templates/villagesoftware/). Download the Loan Manager file self-extracting file(*Loan.exe*), and install the *Loan.xlt* template to your floppy diskette. Open the *Loan.xlt* file, and enter the loan data from this project. Make three additional payments of $100.00 each. Save the workbook as *Prepaid.xls*.

More Excel 97

This section contains additional topics that are necessary for you to know if you plan to take the Microsoft Proficient exam for Excel. The topics are listed in the same order as the Skill Sets outlined in the *Microsoft Excel 97 Exam Preparation Guide*, which you can download from Microsoft's Web site (www.microsoft.com/office/train_cert). All other topics necessary for successful completion of the exam are covered in projects one through six of this book.

Modifying Workbooks

Rotating and Indenting Text

Sometimes, for the sake of format, it is better to rotate the text in a cell. For example, if a column heading is much wider than the data in the column, you can rotate the heading to make the column narrower. To rotate the text in cell(s), select the cell(s), choose Format, Cells, and click the Alignment tab. Using the mouse, drag the Text line in the Orientation box to the desired angle or specify the angle in the Degrees spin box. Then click OK.

To indent text in a cell, select the cell(s), choose Format, Cells, and click the Alignment tab. Specify the number of characters the text should be indented in the Indent spin box and click OK.

Revise Formulas

You can edit a formula with the same technique described in Project 2, Task 3. Basically, you edit a formula with these steps: select the cell that contains the formula, click in the Formula bar, make the desired changes, and press (ENTER).

Print Workbooks

Printing the Screen and Ranges

Although you can use the PrintScreen key to print what you see on the screen (including the column and row headings), you generally will want to print a range, especially if the worksheet is too large to print on one page. To print a range, first select the range and then choose File, Print. For Print What, choose Selection and click OK.

Creating and Applying Ranges

Creating and Naming Ranges

In Project 1, you learned how to use ranges in formulas. In doing so, however, you either pointed to the range or typed the address of the range. The third way to refer to a range in a formula is to use the name of the range.

To name a range, select the cells and choose Insert, Name, Define. Type the desired name for the range and click OK. To use a range name in a formula, simply type the name where you would normally specify the range address. For example, if the range A1 through A10 is named "January," you would use the formula =sum(january) instead of =sum(a1:a10).

> **Note** Range names are not case-sensitive.

Using Draw

Creating and Modifying Lines and Objects

Excel provides several drawing tools in the Drawing toolbar, which can be displayed by clicking the Drawing button in the Standard toolbar. Drawing tools include the Line tool, Arrow tool, Rectangle tool, and Oval tool. To draw a shape with any of these tools, click the tool in the toolbar and drag the shape in the desired location. Additional drawing tools are available on the AutoShapes menu. The AutoShape tools include additional line styles, basic shapes, block arrows, flowchart symbols, stars, banners, and call outs. To draw with one of these tools, click the arrow in the AutoShapes button, point to a category, and click the desired tool. Then drag to draw the shape.

Creating and Modifying 3D Shapes

With the 3-D tool, you can add a three-dimensional look to shapes that you have drawn. First draw the shape; then click the 3-D button and select the desired shape.

You can modify a 3-D shape with the 3-D Settings toolbar, which contains buttons for changing tilt, depth, direction, lighting, surface, and color of the 3-D object. To display the 3-D Settings toolbar, click the 3-D button in the Drawing toolbar and choose 3-D Settings. Then select the drawing object and use the buttons in the toolbar to modify the object. For example, to change the direction of the light on the object (and thus the shading of the object), click the Lighting button and select a lighting direction and intensity.

Using Charts

Previewing and Printing Charts

If a chart is an object on a worksheet page, the chart will print when you print the page. If the chart is a completely separate page, you can print just that page. Before printing a chart, however, you can preview it to make sure the format and information is correct.

To preview and print a chart that is an object on a worksheet, choose File, Print. Select the page that contains the chart in the print range. Then click Preview. After viewing, click Close or click Print. To preview and print a chart located on a Chart page, select the page and choose File, Print. Select Active Sheet(s) for Print What and then click Preview. After viewing, click Close or click Print.

Saving Spreadsheets as HTML

Saving Spreadsheets as HTML Documents

Excel can save a worksheet as an HTML file that can be used either as an independent Web page or as a table that can be inserted into an existing Web page. To create an HTML file, select the range you want to convert to HTML and choose File, Save As HTML. The Internet Assistant Wizard opens. Click Add to add an additional range; then specify the range and click OK. Click the Next button. Select either the option to create an independent Web page or the option to create a file that can be inserted as a table. Click the Next button. The next steps in the wizard depend on whether you are creating an independent Web page or a table.

If you are creating an independent Web page, specify the title text, the header text, and the description text, if desired; select horizontal lines, if desired; and specify the update and e-mail information, if desired. Click Next. Type the path and name for the file and click Finish.

> **Note** By default, the wizard uses the extension "htm" instead of "html," but you can change the extension, if desired.

If you are creating a file to be inserted as a table, specify how you want the file to open, and specify the path and name of the existing file that will contain the Excel table. (The existing file must already contain the code described at the top of the dialog box.) Click Next. Specify the name of the path and the name of the new HTML file that will be created by the wizard. (The new file will combine the existing Web page and the Excel table.) Click Finish.

Formatting Worksheets

The following topic, Applying Outlines, has not been clearly defined in the Microsoft guidelines. It may refer to one of two features—a border or collapsible data. If the topic refers to applying a border, the topic is covered in Project 3. If the topic refers to collapsible data, the following topic explains the procedure.

Applying Outlines

You can apply outline groupings to data in worksheets that contain summary rows arranged consistently above or below related detail data or summary columns arranged consistently to the left or right of related detail data. By applying outline groupings, you can collapse or expand the detail data.

To outline a worksheet automatically, choose Data, Group and Outline, Auto Outline. To apply an outline level to a range of cells manually, select the range and choose Data, Group and Outline, Group. Choose Rows or Columns (whichever is appropriate) and click OK. The outline symbols appear beside the data.

To collapse an outline level, click the minus sign. The detail (denoted by the period symbols) is hidden, and the minus sign changes to a plus sign. To expand a level, click the plus sign. To expand or collapse all the levels, click an appropriate number button. The previous figure, shows only two number buttons above the outline symbols: 1 and 2. When you click the 2 button, all the data displays. When you click the 1 button, the data collapses.

To turn off the outlining, choose Data, Group and Outline, Clear Outline.

Excel 97 Function Reference Guide

Function	Mouse Action or Button	Menu	Keyboard Shortcut
AutoFormat		Select the cells and choose Format, AutoFormat	
Border, add	Select the cells(s), click the down arrow on ▦▾, and click on the desired border	Select the cell(s) and choose Format, Cells, Border	
Cell, align	Select the cell(s) and click ≡, ≡, or ≡	Select the cells(s) and choose Format, Cells, Alignment	
Cell, delete		Select the cells(s) and choose Edit, Delete	
Cell, delete data in		Select the cells(s) and choose Edit, Clear	Select the cells(s) and press (DEL)
Cell, copy	Select the cells(s) and click 📋	Select the cells(s) and choose Edit, Copy	Select the cells(s) and press (CTRL)+C
Cell, cut	Select the cells(s) and click ✂	Select the cells(s) and choose Edit, Cut	Select the cells(s) and press (CTRL)+X
Cell, format	Select the cells(s) and click appropriate formatting button (**B**, *I*, and so on)	Select the cells(s) and choose Format, Cells, and choose the desired tab	(CTRL)+1 - (one)
Cell, insert		Select the cells(s) and choose Insert, Cells	
Cell, paste	Select the cells(s) and click 📋	Select the cells(s) and choose Edit, Paste	Select the cells(s) and press (CTRL)+V
Cell, select	Drag mouse pointer through desired cells		Press (SHIFT)+any navigation key
Chart, create		Choose Insert, Object, Microsoft Graph 97 Chart	
Chart, move	Select the graph and drag	Select the chart, choose Format, Object, click on the Position tab	
Chart, size	Select a handle and drag	Select the chart, choose Format, Object, click on the Size tab	

Guide-1

Guide-2

Function	Mouse Action or Button	Menu	Keyboard Shortcut
Column, change the width	Drag the vertical border of the column in the column indicator row	Select the column and choose Format, Column, Width	
Column, delete		Select the column(s) and choose Edit, Delete	
Column, insert		Select the column(s) and choose Insert, Columns	
Comments, add		Select the cell and choose Insert, Comment	
Data, edit	Select the cell, click in the Formula bar, and edit as desired		Select the cell, press F2, and edit as desired
Data, enter			Select cell, type data, and press ENTER or any navigational key
Data, find		Choose Edit, Find	Press CTRL+F
Data, sort	Select the cells(s) and click A↓ or Z↓	Select the cells(s) and choose Data, Sort	
Exit Excel 97	Click X in the application window	Choose File, Exit	Press ALT+F4
Fill, add	Select the cells(s), click the down arrow on the ⬧, and select a color	Select the cells(s) and choose Format, Cells, Patterns	
Footer, create		Choose View, Header and Footer	
Format dates		Select the cells(s) and choose Format, Cells, Number	
Format numbers	Select the cells(s) and click $, %, ,, .0, or .00	Select the cells(s) and choose Format, Cells, Number	
Header, create		Choose View, Header and Footer	
Help	Click ?	Choose Help, Microsoft Help	Press F1
Page break, change		Choose View, Page Break Preview, and drag the page break line	

Function	Mouse Action or Button	Menu	Keyboard Shortcut
Page break, view		Choose View, Page Break Preview	
Preview	Click	Choose File, Print Preview	
Print	Click	Choose File, Print	Press CTRL+P
Row, change the height	Drag the horizontal border of the row indicator	Select the row(s) and choose Format, Row, Height	
Row, delete		Select the row(s) and choose Edit, Delete	
Row, insert		Select the number of rows you want to insert and choose Insert, Rows	
Spell check	Click	Choose Tools, Spelling	Press F7
Start Excel 97		Choose Start, Programs, Microsoft Excel 97	
Workbook, close	Click ✕ in the workbook window	Choose File, Close	
Workbook, create	Click	Choose File, New	Press CTRL+END
Workbook, open	Click	Choose File, Open	Press CTRL+O
Workbook, save	Click	Choose File, Save	Press CTRL+S
Worksheet, delete		Click the worksheet tab and choose Insert, Worksheet	
Worksheet, insert		Click the worksheet tab that should follow the new worksheet and choose Edit, Delete Sheet	
Worksheet, move	Drag the worksheet tab to new location	Select the worksheet tab and choose Edit, Move or Copy sheet	
Worksheet, name		Right-click the worksheet tab and choose Rename	

Glossary

Absolute reference An address you use to reference a specific cell or range of cells in a worksheet; this reference, which doesn't change, is denoted with the dollar sign symbol, as in $A$1.

Active cell The cell in which you can enter data or perform calculations. You make the cell active by clicking in the cell or by moving to the cell with keystrokes. This cell is outlined with a black border.

Amortization The process of paying a debt over time by making periodic payments.

Amortization schedule A schedule of loan payments that includes a breakdown of the principal and interest portions of each periodic payment.

Annuity functions A class of financial functions in Excel that involves payments or investments at regular intervals.

Argument The values an Excel function uses to perform operations or calculations.

Arithmetic operators The operators you use to perform calculations in formulas and functions: + (addition), − (subtraction), * (multiplication), / (division), % (percent), and ^ (exponentiation).

AutoCalculate A feature that displays a calculation in the status bar when you select a range with values.

AutoFit A feature that automatically adjusts the column or row to be just wide enough to accommodate the widest or tallest entry.

Border A line that displays on any side of a cell or group of cells. You can use borders to draw rectangles around cells, to create dividers between columns, to create a total line under a column of numbers, and so on.

Cell The intersection of a column and a row in a worksheet.

Chart A visual representation of data in a worksheet.

Chart sub-type A variation on a Chart type. For example, the column type chart has these sub-types in both 2-D and 3-D: Clustered Column, Stacked Column, and 100% Stacked Column.

Chart type A chart that represents data in a specific format, such as columns, a pie, scatter points, etc.

Chart Wizard An Excel feature you use to create charts. When you create a chart with the Chart Wizard, the Chart Wizard decides how the chart elements will look.

Clipboard A memory area in which data that has been cut or copied is stored.

Column A vertical block of cells in a worksheet that extends from row 1 to row 65,536.

Column indicators The letters associated with the columns on a worksheet.

Comment Text that you can attach to cells in a worksheet to provide additional information.

Constant A value that remains unchanged.

Data labels The names you attach to different types of data in a chart. You define this setting in the Chart Options dialog box.

Data range A block of cells used to create an element in a chart.

Data table A table showing the data that is used to create a chart.

Edit mode The mode in which you edit the contents of a cell.

Enter mode The mode in which you enter data in a worksheet.

Error mode The mode Excel switches to if you make an error when entering data in a cell.

Fill A color or a shade of gray that you apply to the background of a cell. Also called *shading* or *patterns*.

Footer Text that prints at the bottom of every page of a worksheet.

Formatting toolbar Contains buttons and controls for formatting. To use the toolbar, click a button to perform a command or view a dialog box.

Formula A mathematical statement that performs calculations. You create and enter formulas to perform the specific calculations needed.

Formula bar The area at the top of the window that displays the cell address and the contents of the active cell. You can use it to enter and edit data and formulas.

Function A mathematical statement that performs calculations. Functions are formulas that have already been created by Excel. They perform calculations that are commonly used such as calculating a sum or an average.

Gridlines The vertical and horizontal lines in a chart that mark the values.

Header Text that prints at the top of every page of a worksheet.

Information Data that is meaningful within a specific context.

IPMT function An Excel function that returns the interest payment for a given period for an investment based on periodic, constant payments and a continuous interest rate.

Gloss-1

Legend The description of elements in a chart. You define this setting in the Chart Options dialog box.

Loan scenario The principal, interest, and term values used to calculate a loan payment.

Menu bar The bar at the top of the window that contains menu options. To use the menu, click an option to display a drop-down menu, and then click an option on the drop-down menu to perform a command, view another menu, or view a dialog box.

Mode indicator A feature displayed on the far left side of the status bar. It shows a word that describes the current working condition of the program. For example, the word *Ready* means that the worksheet is ready to receive data or execute a command. Other modes include *Edit, Enter, Point, Error,* and *Wait*.

Numeric constant Numeric data that is entered into a cell of an electronic spreadsheet.

Office Assistant The new Help feature that offers help on the task you're performing, often referred to as context-sensitive help.

Order of precedence The sequence in which each operation should be performed when a formula has more than one operation. The Excel order of precedence is as follows: exponentiation, then multiplication or division (from left to right), and finally addition or subtraction (from left to right). If the formula has parentheses, the operation(s) in the parentheses are performed first.

Page break A mark that indicates where one page ends and another one begins.

Page Break Preview The view in which you can see where the pages will break when the worksheet prints.

Pattern A color or a shade of gray that you apply to the background of a cell. Also called *fill* or *shading*.

PMT function An Excel function that returns the payment on the principal for a given period for an investment based on periodic, constant payments and a constant interest rate.

Point mode The mode in which you're pointing to cells to build a formula or function in a worksheet.

Present value The total amount that a series of future payments is worth now, calculated using the PV function.

Principal The amount of money borrowed through a loan.

Print Preview mode The mode that shows the full page view of the current page of the current worksheet. In this mode you can view additional pages of the worksheet, or you can zoom in on the page so that you can actually read the data, if necessary.

PV function An Excel function that returns the present value of an investment. The present value is the total amount that a series of future payments is worth now.

Range A block of cells selected as a group.

Rate The periodic interest rate used to calculate a loan payment.

Ready mode The mode in which the worksheet is ready to receive data or execute a command.

Relative reference A worksheet address that Excel automatically changes when a formula is copied to another location.

Row A horizontal block of cells in a worksheet that extends from column A to column IV.

Row indicators The numbers associated with the rows on a worksheet.

Run The procedure used to play back a macro that has been recorded.

Scientific notation A number format used for very large numbers and very small decimal numbers. For example, the scientific notation for 1,000,000,000 is 1E+09 which means 1 times 10 to the ninth power. If you enter a number that won't fit in a cell, Excel either converts the number to scientific notation or displays pound signs (#) in the cell.

Scroll bars The bars on the side or the bottom of the window that enable you to scroll the screen vertically and horizontally.

Selection handles The black squares that appear when a chart is selected. You use them to size the chart.

Shading A color or a shade of gray that you apply to the background of a cell. Also called *fill* or *pattern*.

Standard toolbar Contains buttons and controls used to the most common perform commands. To use the toolbar, click a button to perform a command or view a dialog box.

Status bar The bar at the bottom of the window that displays information about the current workbook.

Syntax A set of rules, like grammar rules, that dictate the structure or order of the elements in a formula.

Term The amount of time over which a loan is repaid.

Title The name of the chart. You define this setting in the Chart Options dialog box.

Title bar The bar at the top of a window that displays the Minimize, Maximize/Restore, and Close buttons.

Toolbar A bar that contains buttons for performing commands. To use the toolbar, click a button to perform a command or view a dialog box.

Variable A symbol, such as the letter *x*, that represents an item of data. A variable may change its value within a function or formula.

Visual Basic Visual Basic is the programming language, by Microsoft, that is used in Excel and throughout the Office environment for recording and editing macros.

Wait mode The mode in effect when the worksheet is busy and cannot accept data or commands.

Web toolbar The toolbar containing buttons for Internet use. To display the Web toolbar, click the Web Toolbar button in the Standard toolbar. To hide the Web toolbar, click the Web Toolbar button again.

Workbook A file that contains Excel worksheets. By default, a new workbook file has three worksheets.

Worksheet A page in a workbook file.

Worksheet scroll buttons The buttons you use on the scroll bar to scroll the tabs for the worksheets.

Worksheet tab A part of the window that displays the names of worksheets in the current workbook. Clicking a tab displays the worksheet.

X axis The horizontal axis in a chart. You define this setting in the Chart Options dialog box.

Y axis The vertical axis in a chart. You define this setting in the Chart Options dialog box.

Index

Windows 95 (WIN)

Applications, 1
Articles, printing help, 16

Buttons, description of, 7

Commands, selecting menu, 7
Context-sensitive help, 10
Customizing desktop, 2

Desktop
   customizing, 2
   defined, 2
   identifying elements, 2
Dialog boxes
   defined, 8
   using, 8–9

Elements, identifying desktop, 2
Exiting Windows 95, 16

Graphics, 1
GUI (Graphical User Interface), 1

Hardware defined, 1
Help, 10–16
   context-sensitive, 10
   using Contents, 10–16
   using Find, 10–16
   using Index, 10–16
   What's This?, 10
Help articles, printing, 16

Icons, 1
Identifying desktop elements, 2

Keyboard, 1

Menu bars, using, 7–8
Menu commands, selecting, 7
Menus defined, 4
Minimizing Windows, 6
Mouse, 1
   actions, 3
   using, 3–4
My Computer, 2

Operating system, Windows 95, 1–16
Overview of Windows 95, 1–16

Pictures, 1
Printing help articles, 16
Print Topic, 16

Programs, launching, 5

Recycle Bin, 2

Selecting menu commands, 7
Starting
   programs, 5
   Windows 95, 2
Start Menu, using, 4–5

Taskbar, 2
Toolbars, using, 7–8

What's This?, 10
Windows
   minimizing, 6
Windows 95
   exiting, 16
   launching, 2
   operating system, 1–16
   overview of, 1–16
   using basic features, 4–9
   using, 5–6
   working with, 5–6
Working with Windows, 5–6

Active Desktop (WIN98)

Active Desktop
   customizing, 10–13
      identifying elements of Windows 95, 3–5
      wallpaper, 5
      and Windows 98 Preview, 1–16
Adding items to Start menu, 14–15

Channel bar
   displaying, 4–5
   Internet Explorer, 4–5
Creating shortcuts from Start menu, 13–14
Customizing
   desktop, 3
   Taskbar toolbars, 11–12
   Windows 95 Active Desktop, 10–13
Customizing Active Desktop, 10–13

Desktop
   customizing, 3
   restoring, 15–16
Desktop ToolTips, using, 6–7
Displaying
   Channel bar, 4–5
   Desktop ToolTips, 6–7
   toolbars on Taskbar, 11
   wallpaper, 5
Displaying ToolTips, 6–7

Editing Start menu, 13–14

Floating toolbars, 12–13

Identifying elements of Windows 95
   Active Desktop, 3–5
Internet Explorer Channel bar, 4–5

Launching programs, 7–9

Mouse button, releasing, 14
Mouse pointers, 12
Moving
   Taskbar, 10
   toolbars, 12–13

Pointers, mouse, 12
Programs, launching, 7–9

Releasing mouse button, 14
Repositioning Taskbar, 10
Restoring desktop, 15–16
Restoring toolbars, 12–13

Shortcuts, creating from Start menu, 13–14
Sizing Taskbar, 10
Start menu
   adding items to, 14–15

   creating shortcuts from, 13–14
   editing, 13–14

Taskbar
   displaying toolbars on, 11
   moving, 10
   repositioning, 10
   sizing, 10
   toolbars, 11–12
Toolbars
   customizing Taskbar, 11–12
   displaying on Taskbar, 11
   floating, 12–13
   moving, 12–13
   restoring, 12–13
ToolTips
   appearances of, 6
   displaying, 6–7
   using desktop, 6–7

Wallpaper
   Active Desktop, 5
   displaying, 5
Windows 95 Active Desktop
   customizing, 10–13
   identifying elements of, 3–5
Windows 98 preview, and Active Desktop, 1–16

Excel 97 (EX)

=NOW() function, 161

Absolute references, 171–172
   defined, 133
   entering formulas with, 133–136
   pointing to enter, 135–136
   using headings with, 136
Active, cells, 18
Active worksheets defined, 21
Adding
   borders and fill, 88–90
   comments, 65–69
Adjusting row height, 107–108
Amortization
   defined, 158
   schedule, 176
      completing, 174–177
      defined, 158
      structure, 161–163
Annuity functions, 168
Answers to frequently asked Web
      questions, 10
Application title bar, button in, 5
Applying
   AutoFormat, 92–93
   color, 90
   formats to text constants, 162–163
   outlines, 192
   ranges, 190
Arguments defined, 32, 166
Arithmetic operators, 32
Arranging worksheets, 101–104
AutoCalculate feature, 57
AutoComplete feature, 25
AutoFit
   sizing rows with, 108
   using, 106–107
AutoFormat, using, 92–93

Balance
   calculating ending, 173–174
   Ending, 176
Beginning balances, calculating, 169–170
Beta testing program of Microsoft, 10
Borders, defined, 88
Borders and fill, adding, 88–90
Buttons
   in Application title bars, 5
   Center, 81
   Close, 5
   in document title bars, 5
   Fill Color, 90
   Merge, 81
   New, 18

Calculating
   beginning balances, 169–170
   cumulative interest, 173–174
   cumulative principal, 173–174
   ending balance, 173–174
   interest paid in each payment, 172
   loan payments, 166–169
   principal paid in each payment,
      170–172
   total payments, 173–174
Calculations, changing, 57
Capitalizing headings in formulas, 133

Cells
   active, 18
   changing alignment, 78–81
   changing numbers in, 36
   data that doesn't fit in, 24
   defined, 2
   deleting, 112–114
   editing data in, 52–55
   entering data in, 21
   erasing, 61
   inserting, 109–112
   pasting data into, 61
   selecting, 55–57
   values in, 173
Center button, 81
Changes, saving, 11
Changing
   calculations, 57
   cell alignment, 78–81
   chart
      data, 140–142
      options, 146–147
      types, 145–146
   loan scenarios, 179–180
   numbers in cells, 36
   page breaks, 91–92
   sizes of
      columns, 104–108
      rows, 104–108
   widths of columns, 104–107
Chart data, changing, 140–142
Chart elements, formatting, 143–145
Chart options, changing, 146–147
Charts
   creating, 136–152
      column, 137–139
      pie, 147–152
   modifying, 136–152
   moving, 139–140
   previewing, 191
   printing, 191
   sizing, 139–140
   using, 191
Chart sub-types, 145–146
Chart types, changing, 145–146
Chart Wizard, 136, 139, 143
Checking spelling, 69–70
Clipboard
   defined, 58
   and deleted text, 63
Close buttons, 5
Closed sites, 10
Closing
   files, 40
   workbooks, 11, 40
Color, applying, 90
Column charts, creating, 137–139
Column letters, line between, 107
Columns
   changing sizes of, 104–108
   changing width of, 104–107
   deleting, 112–114
   inserting, 109–112
   inserting multiple, 110
   selecting multiple, 107
Commands, Find, 52, 69
Comments

   adding, 65–69
   finding text or values in, 69
Comment view, 68
Completing amortization schedule,
      174–177
Complex workbooks, creating,
      125–127
Constants
   applying formats to text, 162–163
   entering numeric, 164–166
   numeric, 161
   text, 161
Constructing formulas, 173–174
Context-sensitive help, 8
Copying
   data, 58–61
   from other workbooks, 126–129
   formulas with relative addresses,
      131–132
Corrections, typing error, 69
Creating
   3D shapes, 190
   charts, 136–152
   column charts, 137–139
   complex workbooks, 125–157
   custom headers and footers,
      117–119
   headers and footers, 114–119
   lines and objects, 190
   macros, 181–182
   new workbooks, 18
   pie charts, 147–152
   ranges, 190
   workbooks, 16–46
Cumulative interest, calculating,
      173–174
Cumulative principal, calculating,
      173–174
Custom formats, specifying, 165
Custom headers and footers, creating,
      117–119

Data
   changing chart, 140–142
   contained off screen, 112
   copying, 58–61
   copying from other, 126–129
   copying from other workbooks,
      126–129
   deleting, 61–63
   editing, 52–55
   editing in cells, 52–55
   entering, 24–31
   entering across rows, 21
   entering in cells, 21
   entering on multiple worksheets,
      25–30
   finding, 50–52
   moving, 63–65
   pasting into cells, 61
   ranges, 140
   sorting, 129–130
   that doesn't fit in cells, 24
   working with, 55–65
Date & Time function, 161
Dates, formatting, 84–85

Defining structures of amortization schedules, 161–163
Deleted text and Clipboard, 63
Deleting
　cells, 112–114
　columns, 112–114
　data, 61–63
　pages, 101–104
　rows, 112–114
　text, 63
　worksheets, 101–104
Deselecting worksheets, 37
Displays, Group indicator, 26
Documents
　saving periodically, 38
　saving spreadsheets as HTML, 191–192
Document title bar, button in, 5
Dragging
　changing width of columns by, 104
　technique, 29
Draw, using, 190

Editing
　data, 52–55
　data in cells, 52–55
　structures of workbooks, 99–124
　structures of worksheets, 99–124
　workbooks, 47–74
Ending Balance, 176
　calculating, 173–174
Enhancing workbook appearance, 75–98
Enter absolute references, pointing to, 135–136
Entering
　data, 24–31
　　across rows, 21
　　in cells, 21
　　on multiple worksheets, 25–30
　formulas
　　with absolute references, 133–136
　　and functions, 31–36
　　with relative addresses, 131–132
　　with relative references, 130–132
　fractions, 24
　functions, 31–36
　numbers, 30–31
　numeric constants, 164–166
　text, 24–25
Erasing cells, 61
Excel 97
　exiting, 11
　identifying features, 2–3
　launching, 3–4
　screen displays two Close buttons, 5
Exiting Excel 97, 11

Filenames, long, 36
Files
　closing, 40
　opening existing, 49
　workbook, 3
File Save As, 38
Fill Color button, 90
Fill defined, 88
Fill Handle, using, 174–177
Financial functions, using, 158–192
Find command, 52, 69
Finding
　data, 50–52
　text or values in comments, 69

Footers, defined, 114; See also Headers and footers
Formats, specifying custom, 165
Formatting
　chart elements, 143–145
　dates, 84–85
　numbers, 81–87
　numbers as text, 86–87
　text, 77–78
　toolbar, 90
　worksheets, 192
Formulas
　constructing, 173–174
　entering, 31–36
　entering with absolute references, 133–136
　entering with relative references, 130–132
　and order of precedence, 36
　revising, 189
　using headings in, 133
Formulas or functions, recalculation of, 36
Formulas with relative addresses
　copying, 131–132
　entering, 131–132
Fractions, entering, 24
Freezing worksheet panes 177–179; See also Unfreezing worksheet panes
Functions
　annuity, 168
　Date & Time, 161
　entering, 31–36
　=NOW(), 161
　payment (PMT), 166–169
　periodic interest payment (IPMT), 172
　PPMT, 172
　present value of an annuity (PV), 169–170
　recalculation of, 36

Group indicator displays, 26

Handles
　pointer appears as plus when pointed to, 28
　selection, 139
Headers and footers, creating, 114–119
Headers defined, 114
Headings
　with absolute references, using, 136
　features, 133
　using in formulas, 133
Help, 8–10
　context-sensitive, 8
　using Office Assistant, 8–10
　from World Wide Web, 10
Horizontal scroll bars, 19
HTML documents, saving spreadsheets as, 191–192

Identifying Excel 97 features, 2–3
Identifying screen elements, 4–7
Indenting text, 189
Inserting
　cells, 109–112
　columns, 109–112
　multiple columns, 110
　multiple rows, 110
　pages, 101–104

rows, 109–112
worksheets, 101–104

Interest, calculating cumulative, 173–174
IPMT (periodic interest payment) function, 172

Launching Excel 97, 3–4
Line between column letters, 107
Lines and objects
　creating, 190
　modifying, 190
Loan payments, calculating, 166–169
Loan scenarios, changing, 179–180
Long filenames, 36

Macros
　creating, 181–182
　defined, 181
　recording, 181–182
　running, 182–183
Merge button, 81
Microsoft, beta testing program of, 10
Microsoft Excel 97, overview, 2–15
Mistakes made while typing, 25
Mixed references, 171–172
Modifying
　3D shapes, 190
　charts, 136–152
　lines and objects, 190
　workbooks, 189
Moving
　around in workbooks, 18–22
　around in worksheets, 18–22
　charts, 139–140
　data, 63–65
Multiple columns
　changing, 107
　inserting, 110
Multiple rows, inserting, 110
Multiple worksheets
　entering data on, 25–30
　and Group indicator display, 26
　and spell-checking, 70

Naming worksheets, 22–23
New button, 18
New workbooks, creating, 18
Notation, scientific, 30
Numbers
　changing in cells, 36
　entering, 30–31
　formatting, 81–87
　formatting as text, 86–87
　serial, 87
Numeric constants
　defined, 161
　entering, 164–166

Objects
　creating, 190
　modifying, 190
Office Assistant, using, 8–10
Opening workbooks, 49–50
Operators, arithmetic, 32
Order of precedence, 36
Outlines, applying, 192

Page breaks
　changing, 91–92
　viewing, 91–92

Page Break view, 91
Pages
    deleting, 101–104
    inserting, 101–104
Panes
    freezing worksheet, 177–179
    unfreezing worksheet, 179
Pasting data into cells, 61
Patterns defined, 88
Payments
    calculating interest paid in each, 172
    calculating loan, 166–169
    calculating principal paid in each, 170–172
    calculating total, 173–174
Pie charts, creating, 147–152
PMT (payment) function, 166–169
Pointer appears as plus when pointed to handles, 28
Pointing to enter absolute references, 135–136
Pound signs, 30
PPMT (periodic principal payment), 170–172
Precedence, order of, 36
Present value defined, 170
Previewing
    charts, 191
    worksheets, 38–40
Principal
    calculating cumulative, 173–174
    defined, 158
Printing
    charts, 191
    ranges, 189
    screens, 189
    workbooks, 189
    worksheets, 38–40
Print Preview, 38
Programming language, Visual Basic, 181
PV (present value of an annuity) function, 169–170

Questions, answers to frequently asked Web, 10

Ranges
    applying, 190
    creating, 190
    data, 140
    defined, 32
    printing, 189
    selecting, 56–57
Ranges of columns, sorting, 130
Rate defined, 158
Recording macros, 181–182
References
    absolute, 171–172
    mixed, 171–172
Relative addresses
    copying formulas with, 131–132
    entering formulas with, 131–132
Relative references
    defined, 130
    entering formulas with, 130–132
Revising formulas, 189
Rotating text, 189
Row height, adjusting, 107–108
Rows, 2
    changing sizes of, 104–108
    deleting, 112–114

entering data across, 21
inserting, 109–112
inserting multiple, 110
sizing with AutoFit, 108
Running macros, 182–183

Save As file, 38
Saving
    changes, 11
    documents periodically, 38
    spreadsheets as HTML documents, 191–192
    workbooks, 36–38
Schedules
    amortization, 158, 176
    completing amortization, 174–177
Scientific notation, 30
Screen elements, 5–6
    identifying, 4–7
Screens
    data contained off, 112
    printing, 189
Scroll bars
    horizontal, 19
    vertical, 19
Selecting; See also Deselecting
    cells, 55–57
    handles, 139
    multiple columns, 107
    ranges, 56–57
Serial numbers defined, 87
Shading defined, 88
Shapes
    creating 3D, 190
    modifying 3D, 190
Signs, pound, 30
Sites, closed, 10
Sizing
    charts, 139–140
    rows with AutoFit, 108
Sorting
    data, 129–130
    ranges of columns, 130
Spaces and headings in formulas, 133
Specifying custom formats, 165
Spell-checking, and multiple worksheets, 70
Spelling
    checking, 69–70
    and headings in formulas, 133
Spreadsheets, saving as HTML documents, 191–192
Starting Excel 97, 3–4
Syntax defined, 166

Tabs, worksheets, 19
Technique, dragging, 29
Term defined, 158
Text
    deleting, 63
    entering, 24–25
    formatting, 77–78
    formatting numbers as, 86–87
    indenting, 189
    rotating, 189
Text constants
    applying formats to, 162–163
    defined, 161
3D shapes
    creating, 190
    modifying, 190

Title bar
    button in Application, 5
    button in document, 5
Toolbars
    Formatting, 90
    Web, 6
    working with, 6–7
Total payments, calculating, 173–174
Typing
    error corrections, 69
    mistakes made while, 25

Unfreezing worksheet panes, 179

Values
    in cells, 173
    present, 170
Vertical scroll bars, 19
View
    Comment, 68
    Page Break, 91
Viewing; See also Previewing
    large worksheets, 177–179
    page breaks, 91–92
Visual Basic programming language, 181

Web
    answers to frequently asked questions, 10
    toolbar, 6
Wizard, Chart, 136, 139, 143
Workbooks
    appearance of, 75–98
    closing, 11, 40
    copying data from other, 126–129
    creating, 16–46
    creating complex, 125–157
    creating new, 18
    editing, 47–74
    editing structures of, 99–124
    files, 3
    modifying, 189
    moving around in, 18–22
    opening, 49–50
    printing, 189
    saving, 36–38
Working
    with data, 55–65
    with toolbars, 6–7
Worksheet panes
    freezing, 177–179
    unfreezing, 179
Worksheets
    active, 22
    arranging, 101–104
    defined, 2
    deleting, 101–104
    deselecting, 37
    editing structures of, 99–124
    entering data on multiple, 25–30
    formatting, 192
    inserting, 101–104
    moving around in, 18–22
    naming, 22–23
    previewing, 38–40
    printing, 38–40
    tabs, 19
    viewing large, 177–179
World Wide Web
    getting help from, 10
    See also Web

Notes

Notes

Notes